Visual Media in Indonesia

In the age of digital communication and global capitalism, people's mental, social and natural environments are interconnected in complex and often unpredictable ways.

This book focuses on the visual media, one of the key factors in shaping the contemporary ecology of colliding environments. Case studies include video artists, community media activists, television programme makers and literary authors in the fourth most populous country in the world, Indonesia. The author demonstrates that these actors are part of an international creative and social vanguard that reflect on, criticise and rework the multidimensional impact of the visual media in imaginative and innovative ways. Their work explores alternative and more sustainable presents and futures for Indonesia and the world. This research is urgent and timely, as Indonesia has emerged in recent years as one of the world's most vibrant hubs for contemporary art and media experimentation.

Using an innovative interdisciplinary framework of visual culture analysis that derives from a wide range of academic fields, the book will be of interest to academics in the fields of Southeast Asian Studies, Media Studies, Cultural Studies, Art History, Anthropology and Sociology.

Edwin Jurriëns is a Lecturer in Indonesian Studies at the Asia Institute, Faculty of Arts, the University of Melbourne, Australia. He is also Adjunct Lecturer with the School of Humanities and Social Sciences at the University of New South Wales (UNSW) in Canberra, Australia. His most recent publication is *Disaster Relief in the Asia-Pacific: Agency and Resilience* (co-edited, 2014), also published by Routledge.

Routledge Contemporary Southeast Asia Series

71 **Philippine Politics**
Progress and Problems in a Localist Democracy
Lynn T. White III

72 **Human Trafficking in Colonial Vietnam**
Micheline Lessard

73 **Conflict Resolution and Peacebuilding in Laos**
Perspective for Today's World
Stephanie Stobbe

74 **Urbanization in Vietnam**
Gisele Bousquet

75 **Social Democracy in East Timor**
Rebecca Strating

76 **The Politics of Aid to Myanmar**
A Humanitarian Struggle on the Thai-Burmese Border
Anne Décobert

77 **Animism in Southeast Asia**
Edited by Kaj Århem and Guido Sprenger

78 **Brunei – History, Islam, Society and Contemporary Issues**
Edited by Ooi Keat Gin

79 **Political Institutions in East Timor**
Semi-Presidentialism and Democratisation
Lydia M. Beuman

80 **Religious Violence and Conciliation in Indonesia**
Christians and Muslims in the Moluccas
Sumanto Al Qurtuby

81 **Identity Politics and Elections in Malaysia and Indonesia**
Ethnic Engineering in Borneo
Karolina Prasad

82 **Rethinking Power Relations in Indonesia**
Transforming the Margins
Edited by Michaela Haug, Martin Rössler and Anna-Teresa Grumblies

83 **Indonesia and the Politics of Disaster**
Power and Representation in Indonesia's Mud Volcano
Phillip Drake

84 **Nation-Building and National Identity in Timor-Leste**
Michael Leach

85 **Visual Media in Indonesia**
Video Vanguard
Edwin Jurriëns

86 **Maritime Security and Indonesia**
Cooperation, Interests and Strategies
Senia Febrica

Visual Media in Indonesia

Video Vanguard

Edwin Jurriëns

Routledge
Taylor & Francis Group
LONDON AND NEW YORK

First published 2017
by Routledge
2 Park Square, Milton Park, Abingdon, Oxon OX14 4RN

and by Routledge
711 Third Avenue, New York, NY 10017

Routledge is an imprint of the Taylor & Francis Group, an informa business

British Library Cataloguing in Publication Data
A catalogue record for this book is available from the British Library

Library of Congress Cataloging in Publication Data
Names: Jurrièens, Edwin, 1972– author.
Title: Visual media in Indonesia: video vanguard / Edwin Jurrièens.
Description: New York: Routledge, 2017. | Series: Routledge contemporary Southeast Asia series; 85 | Includes bibliographical references.
Identifiers: LCCN 2016044659| ISBN 9781138230019 (hardback) | ISBN 9781315302553 (ebook)
Subjects: LCSH: Video art–Indonesia. | New media art–Indonesia. | Technology and the arts–Indonesia. | Digital media–Social aspects–Indonesia.
Classification: LCC N6498.V53 J865 2017 | DDC 777.09598–dc23
LC record available at https://lccn.loc.gov/2016044659

ISBN: 978-1-138-23001-9 (hbk)
ISBN: 978-1-315-30255-3 (ebk)

Typeset in Times New Roman
by Wearset Ltd, Boldon, Tyne and Wear

This book is dedicated to the late Veven Sp. Wardhana, who taught me how to read the media, and to Krisna Murti, who taught me how to read new media art.

Contents

Figures

Acknowledgements

I would like to thank the Asia Institute and the Faculty of Arts at The University of Melbourne for their intellectual, institutional and financial support. Special thanks to Mark Considine, Simon Evans, Pookong Kee, Michael Ewing, Justin Wejak, Nani Pollard, Elisabeth Riharti, Dave McRae, Thomas Reuter, Tim Mann, John Murphy, Ana Dragojlovic, Aline Scott-Maxwell, Kate McGregor, Charles Coppel, Vedi Hadiz, Amanda Achmadi, Hannah Loney, Robyn Sloggett, Meredith Martin, Ken Lee, Hani Yulindrasari, Lewis Mayo, Muhammad Kamal, Anne McLaren, Claire Roberts, Charles Green, Kate Parsons, Robyn Borg, Leena Sookramanien, Morag Rees and Ramila Chanisheff.

This book would have been impossible without support from my Indonesian friends and counterparts, particularly Krisna Murti, Seno Gumira Ajidarma, Veven Sp. Wardhana, Aminudin Th. Siregar, Herra Pahlasari, Alfonzo Koapaha, Deden Durahman, Agung Hujatnikajennong, Vincensius Christiawan, Irene Agrivina, Tommy Suryo, Gustaff H. Iskandar, Reina Wulansari, Ade Darmawan, Hafiz, Benny Wicaksono, Jompet Kuswidananto, Tintin Wulia, Tisna Sanjaya, Darbotz, Hestu Nugroho, Wiyu Wahono, Cicilia Maharani, Zamzam Fauzanafi, Masduki, Muzayin Nazaruddin, Zaki Habibi, Anang Hermawan, Wahibur Rokhman, Akhmad Nasir, Ambar Sari, Bobby Guntarto, Amelia Virginia, Effendi Gazali, Tommy Taslim, Rachmah Ida, Made Bayak, Ngurah Suryawan, Ngurah Lengkonk Termana, Mudjijono Setropawiro, Laksmi Shitaresmi, Jumaldi Alfi, Mikke Susanto, Eddi Prabandono, Alia Swastika, Yoshi Fajar Kresno, Pitra Hutomo, Woto Wibowo, Antariksa, Edwina Brennan, Ferdiyansah Thajib, Kathleen Azali, Farah Wardani, Mella Jaarsma, Melani Budianta, Manneke Budiman, I Nyoman Darma Putra, Budi Subanar and Baskara Wardaya. I also acknowledge my colleagues from Timor Leste, Rosalia Soares, Jacky Ximines, Emilio Vicente and Luis Ximenes.

Special thanks to the various Indonesian art and media communities and institutions for their generous assistance and hospitality, particularly S.14, Video Lab, Common Room, The House of Natural Fiber (HONF), ruangrupa, Forum Lenteng, Ruang Mes 56, WAFT, Yayasan Pengembangan Media Anak (YPMA), KUNCI, Indonesian Visual Art Archive (IVAA), Cemeti, Selasar Sunaryo, Kampung Halaman, Combine Resource Institution (CRI), Angkringan, Sekolah mBrosot, Kineruku and Tobucil. In Melbourne, various people and institutions that play an important part in promoting Indonesian contemporary art to the Australian public have been supportive of my research, especially Bryan Collie, Mara Sison and Torey Karlin from MiFA/Melbourne Fine Art; Jill Morgan and Meg Larkin from Multicultural Arts Victoria; Lesley Alway, Jessica O'Brien and Louise Joel from AsiaLink Arts; Natalie King from the Victorian College of the Arts; Kelly Gellatly, Xanthe Jujnovich and Emily Lochowicz from the Ian Potter Museum; Tito Ambyo, Larissa Hjorth and Kristen Sharp from RMIT University; Megan Power from the Australia-Indonesia Centre; Channon Goodwin from Bus Projects; Barbara Hatley from the University of Tasmania; Julian Millie from Monash University; Max Lane from Victoria University; Monika Winarnita from LaTrobe University; Erwin Renaldi from the ABC; Sri Dean and Simon Williams from SBS Radio; Konfir Kabo and Denise Tsui. I also wish to acknowledge my PhD students Roger Nelson, Chui Fun Ho (Selina), Seng Yu Jin and Hellena Souisa for their inspiring conversations and impressive work on the arts and media in Asia.

During my research, I have been Adjunct Lecturer with the School of Humanities and Social Sciences at the University of New South Wales (UNSW) in Canberra, for which I want to extend my gratitude to David Lovell, Minako Sakai, Paul Tickell, Christopher Roberts, Jian Zhang and Shirley Ramsay. In the wider Canberra community, Amrih Widodo, Ross Tapsell, Michelle Antoinette, Caroline Turner, Ariel Heryanto, Emma Baulch, Roald Maliangkay, Amy Chan, Campbell Macknight, Gaik Cheng Khoo (now Kuala Lumpur) and Angie Bexley (now Jakarta) have been stimulating conversation partners. Other inspiring interlocutors include Francis Maravillas, Alexandra Crosby, Philip Kitley, Adrian Vickers, Audrey Low and Natali Pearson from Sydney; David Hill and Krishna Sen from Perth; Priyambudi Sulistiyanto from Adelaide; Amanda Rath from Frankfurt; Iola Lenzi from Singapore and Wendelien van Oldenborgh from Rotterdam.

I wish to acknowledge the International Institute for Asian Studies (IIAS), particularly Philippe Peycam and Titia van der Maas, for hosting me during a research stay in Leiden from January to March 2008, and involving me in the 'Artistic Interventions: Histories, Cartographies and Politics in Asia' project of the IIAS 'Rethinking Asian Studies in a Global Context' series. Also special thanks to Ben Arps, Suryadi, Patricia Spyer, Bart Barendregt, Els Bogaerts and Maya Liem from Leiden University; Henk Maier from the University of California in Riverside; Mikihiro Moriyama from Nanzan University in Nagoya; Jeroen de Kloet and Leonie Schmidt from the University of Amsterdam; Bram Hendrawan from the University of Utrecht; and Yiu Fai Chow from Hong Kong Baptist University for their friendship and ongoing support. Wulan Dirgantoro from LaSalle College in Singapore provided invaluable assistance with part of this research, and Dorothea Schaefter, Lily Brown and Richard Skipper from Routledge and Brett Hough kindly and professionally helped me with making the manuscript ready for publication.

Last but not least, many thanks to my family, Ken, Setia, Raphael, Marcel, Josepha, Ferdinand, Ingrid, Hersri, Ita, Syafiatudina, Khairunnisa and Nur Hilda, for their never failing love and understanding.

Chapter 2 is partially based on Edwin Jurriëns (2011), 'A call for media ecology: the study of Indonesian popular culture revisited', *Indonesia and the Malay World* 39(114): 197–219. Copyright © Editors, *Indonesia and the Malay World*, reprinted by permission of Taylor & Francis Ltd, www.tandfonline.com on behalf of Editors, *Indonesia and the Malay World*.

Chapter 3 is partially based on Edwin Jurriëns (2016), ' "TV or not TV": spelling the Indonesian media with Veven Sp. Wardhana', *Bijdragen tot de Taal-, Land- en Volkenkunde* 172(1): 33–65.

Chapter 4 is partially based on Edwin Jurriëns (2008), 'Television dreams: simulation, for a new reality of Indonesia', in Ariel Heryanto (ed.), *Popular culture in Indonesia: fluid identities in post-authoritarian politics*, London: Routledge, pp. 143–163.

Chapter 5 is partially based on Edwin Jurriëns (2016), 'Intimate video: creative bodies in the age of the selfie', *Continuum: Journal of Media and Cultural Studies* 30(1): 1–19. Reprinted by permission of Taylor & Francis Ltd, www.tandfonline.com.

Chapter 6 is partially based on Edwin Jurriëns (2010), 'Video spa: Krisna Murti's treatment of the senses', *Bijdragen tot de Taal-, Land- en Volkenkunde* 166(1): 1–24. It is also based on Edwin Jurriëns (2009), 'Motion and distortion: the media in the art of Jompet and Tintin', *Indonesia and the Malay World* 37(109): 277–297. Copyright © Editors, *Indonesia and the Malay World*, reprinted by permission of Taylor & Francis Ltd, www.tandfonline.com on behalf of Editors, *Indonesia and the Malay World*.

Chapter 7 is partially based on Edwin Jurriëns (2013), 'Social participation in Indonesian media and art: echoes from the past, visions for the future', *Bijdragen tot de Taal-, Land- en Volkenkunde* 169(1): 7–36.

Chapters 8 and 9 are partially based on Edwin Jurriëns (2015), 'Shaping spaces: video art communities in Indonesia', in Barbara Hatley with Brett Hough (eds), *Performing contemporary Indonesia: celebrating identity, constructing community*, Verhandeling van het Koninklijk Instituut voor Taal- Land- en Volkenkunde 297, Southeast Asia Mediated 6, Leiden and Boston: Brill, pp. 98–119. It is also based on Edwin Jurriëns (2013), 'Between utopia and the real world: Indonesia's avant-garde new media art', *Indonesia and the Malay World* 41(119): 48–75. Copyright © Editors, *Indonesia and the Malay World*, reprinted by permission of Taylor & Francis Ltd, www.tandfonline.com on behalf of Editors, *Indonesia and the Malay World*.

Chapter 10 is partially based on Edwin Jurriëns (2014), 'Mediating the metropolis: new media art as a laboratory for urban ecology in Indonesia', in Larissa Hjorth, Natalie King and Mami Kataoka (eds), *Art in the Asia-Pacific: intimate publics*, London and New York: Routledge, pp. 173–190.

Chapter 11 is partially based on Edwin Jurriëns (2014), 'From early warning system to trauma healing: alternative media and disaster relief in Central Java', in Minako Sakai, Edwin Jurriëns, Jian Zhang and Alec Thornton (eds), *Disaster relief in the Asia Pacific: agency and resilience*, London and New York: Routledge, pp. 147–168.

Abbreviations

ABC	Australian Broadcasting Corporation
ANTV	Andalas Televisi (Andalas Television)
ARC	Amatir Radio Club (Amateur Radio Club)
bavf-NAF	Bandung Video, Film and New Media Art Forum
BBM	Bahan Bakar Minyak (Fuel Oil)
BCCF	Bandung Creative City Forum
BCfNMA	Bandung Center for New Media Arts
BLBI	Bantuan Likuiditas Bank Indonesia (Bank Indonesia Liquidity Support)
BNPB	Badan Nasional Penanggulangan Bencana (National Agency for Disaster Management)
BOH	Bandung Oral History
BPPTK	Balai Penyelidikan dan Pengembangan Teknologi Kegunungapian (Research and Technology Development Agency for Vulcanology)
CC	Creative Commons
CCTV	Closed-Circuit Television
CD	Compact Disc
CEN	Creative Entrepreneur Network
CNN	Cable News Network
CRI	Combine Resource Institution
CT Corp	Chairul Tanjung Corp
DIY	Do-It-Yourself
DJ	Disc Jockey
DVD	Digital Versatile Disc
ECCD-RC	Early Childhood Care and Development-Resource Center
EFP	Education Focus Program
FKJ	Festival Kesenian Yogyakarta (Yogyakarta Art Festival)
Fokowati Forum	Komunikasi Warga Timbulharjo (Timbulharjo Citizens' Communication Forum)
FPI	Front Pembela Islam (Islamic Defenders Front)
GSRB	Gerakan Seni Rupa Baru (New Art Movement)

GTZ	Gesellschaft für Technische Zusammenarbeit (Corporation for Technical Cooperation)
HIVOS	Humanistisch Instituut voor Ontwikkelingssamenwerking (Humanist Institute for Development Cooperation)
HONF	The House of Natural Fiber
HTT	Hari Tanpa TV (Day Without TV)
ICT	Information and Communication Technology
IISIP	Institut Ilmu Sosial dan Ilmu Politik (Institute of Social and Political Sciences)
IKJ	Institut Kesenian Jakarta (Jakarta Institute of the Arts)
ISAI	Institut Studi Arus Informasi (Institute for the Studies on Free Flow of Information)
ISI	Institut Seni Indonesia (Indonesian Institute of the Arts)
ITB	Institut Teknologi Bandung (Bandung Institute of Technology)
IVAA	Indonesian Visual Art Archive
IWC	Integrated World Capitalism
IYCEY	International Young Creative Entrepreneur of the Year
Jalin Merapi	Jaringan Informasi Lingkar Merapi (Merapi Circle Information Network)
KIPPAS	Kajian Informasi, Pendidikan dan Penerbitan Sumatra (Sumatran Information, Education and Publishing Studies)
KPAI	Komisi Perlindungan Anak Indonesia (Indonesian Commission for the Protection of Children)
KPI	Komisi Penyiaran Indonesia (Indonesian Broadcasting Commission)
KRCB	Kelompok Riset Cekungan Bandung (Bandung Basin Research Group)
KTRI	Kelompok Teater Rakyat Indonesia (Indonesian People's Theatre Group)
Lativi	Latief Televisi (Latief Television)
LEAD	Centre for Learning and Advancing Experimental Democracy
LEKRA	Lembaga Kebudayaan Rakyat (The Institute of People's Culture)
LeSPI	Lembaga Studi Pers dan Informasi (The Press and Information Study Institute)
LIPI	Lembaga Ilmu Pengetahuan Indonesia (Indonesian Institute of Sciences)
LSF	Lembaga Sensor Film (Film Censorship Board)
MIT	Massachusetts Institute of Technology
MNCTV	Media Nusantara Citra Televisi (Archipelago Media Television Image)
MPEG	Moving Picture Experts Group
MPM	Masyarakat Peduli Media (Media Interest Society)

MRA	Media Mugi Rekso Abadi Media (Wish of Enduring Care Media)
MTV	Music Television
NasDem	Nasional Demokrat (National Democrat Party)
NGO	Non-Governmental Organisation
NPO	Non-Profit Organisation
NU	Nahdlatul Ulama (Association of Muslim Scholars)
ORARI	Organisasi Amatir Radio Indonesia (Indonesian Amateur Radio Organisation)
PAS NAD	Population Administration in Nanggroe Aceh Darussalam
PDI	Partai Demokrasi Indonesia (Indonesian Democratic Party)
PDI-P	Partai Demokrasi Indonesia-Perjuangan (Indonesian Democratic Party of Struggle)
Perfurbance	Performance Art Urban Festival
PETA	Philippine Educational Theater Association
PKI	Partai Komunis Indonesia (Indonesian Communist Party)
PKMBP	Pusat Kajian Media dan Budaya Populer (Centre for Media and Popular Culture Studies)
PPSJ	Pusat Penyelematan Satwa Jogjakarta (Wild Animal Rescue Centre Yogyakarta)
PTSD	Post-Traumatic Stress Disorder
RAPI	Radio Antar Penduduk Indonesia (Indonesian Inter-Population Radio)
RCTI	Rajawali Citra Televisi Indonesia (The Hawk Image of Indonesian Television)
Repelita	Rencana Pembangunan Lima Tahun (Five-Year Development Plan)
RRI	Radio Republik Indonesia (Radio of the Republic of Indonesia)
SCTV	Surya Citra Televisi (The Sun Image of Television)
SIUPP	Surat Izin Usaha Penerbitan Pers (Press Publication Business Licence)
SMS	Short Message Service
STPMD	Sekolah Tinggi Pembangunan Masyarakat Desa (Tertiary Institution for Village Community Development)
SWR	Strengthening Women's Civil Rights
TPI	Televisi Pendidikan Indonesia (Indonesian Education Television)
TVRI	Televisi Republik Indonesia (Television of the Republic of Indonesia)
UGM	Universitas Gadjah Mada (Gadjah Mada University)
UII	Universitas Islam Indonesia (Islamic University of Indonesia)
UNEP	United Nations Environment Programme
UNESCO	United Nations Educational, Scientific and Cultural Organisation

UU ITE	Undang-Undang Informasi dan Transaksi Elektronik (Information and Electronic Transaction Law)
VCD	Video Compact Disc
VJ	Video Jockey
WWW	World Wide Web
YIVF	Yogyakarta International Videowork Festival
YKAI	Yayasan Kesejahteraan Anak Indonesia (The Indonesian Child Welfare Foundation)
YPMA	Yayasan Pengembangan Media Anak (Foundation for the Development of Children's Media)
YSRK	Yayasan Seni Rupa Komunitas (Foundation of Community Art)

Part I

Media environments

1 Introduction

Media ecology

In the age of digital communication and Integrated World Capitalism (IWC; Guattari 1989), people's mental, social and natural environments are interconnected in complex and often unpredictable ways. Combining contemporary art and media theory with the detailed analysis of authentic texts and contexts, this book focuses on the visual media, one of the key factors in shaping the contemporary ecology of colliding environments. It specifically deals with creative actors, including video artists, community media activists, television programme makers and literary authors in the fourth most populous country in the world, Indonesia. The Indonesian artists and media workers reflect on, criticise and rework the multidimensional impact of the visual media in imaginative and innovative ways.

In line with Guattari (1989), who coined the idea of IWC, and various theorists of eco-aesthetics (Demos 2009; Brunner *et al.* 2013), this research seeks to demonstrate that Indonesian creative actors are part of a national and international social and creative vanguard, who create awareness about, alternative models for, and solutions to the interaction between mental, social and natural ecologies in the digital age. Their work, based on or inspired by video and other visual culture, attempts to provide alternatives to the increased commercialisation of the Indonesian media, arts and public life after the fall of President Suharto's authoritarian New Order regime (1967–1998). Video here refers not merely to a form of information and communication technology, but to a contemporary visual culture or ethos of Do-It-Yourself (DIY), citizen networks, and creative experimentation and collaboration beyond the main media industries and art institutions.

Some of the creative strategies covered in this book include an author who uses televisual devices for his essays and literary work to provide media literacy; the creators of a satirical television show, who analyse the connections between media and democracy by presenting hyperreal simulations of Indonesian society; a new media art collective exploring the interactions between virtual culture, material infrastructure and natural environment by promoting urban ecology as a sustainable alternative to the creative industry; and community media practitioners contributing to community resilience and trauma healing by rethinking and reshaping local culture, social structures and the built environment in anticipation of, during and after, natural and anthropogenic disasters.

The various creative actors discuss the state of the contemporary Indonesian media landscape, while also providing creative visions about what this landscape should ideally look like. Their ideas and practices feed into and redevelop media ecology as a field of study to map, analyse and possibly change the relation between people and their communication environments. According to Neil Postman (1970: 161), who coined the term, 'media ecology looks into the matter of how media of communication affect human perception, understanding, feeling, and value; and how our interaction with media facilitates or impedes our chances of survival'. Unlike Cultural Studies approaches, which are limited to analysing the texts, political economy or reception of the media, my idea of media ecology takes wider material and natural environments into account, and presents alternative information and communication models for social improvement and change. This book demonstrates that alternative visions for Indonesia's media present and future are relevant not only to the media as such, but also to many other, media-related aspects of Indonesia's new democracy such as consumer behaviour, political education, media literacy, environmental awareness, health care, urban design and disaster relief.

The Indonesian media landscape

In order to understand the trends, issues and creative interventions in contemporary Indonesian visual culture, it is necessary to put its most dominant medium, television, in a historical context. In just over five decades, Indonesian television has undergone some seemingly dramatic changes. Roughly, three different eras can be identified: government-controlled television from the mid-1960s to the late 1980s; the introduction and expansion of domestic commercial television in the late 1980s and early 2000s, respectively; and the media mergers and development of national and regional commercial networks since the late-2000s.

The first Indonesian television station, Televisi Republik Indonesia (Television of the Republic of Indonesia, TVRI), was established in 1962 under Sukarno's presidency (1945–1967). TVRI had a monopoly on Indonesian television broadcasting and was an important tool for government propaganda and nation building throughout most of the New Order regime of Sukarno's successor Suharto (Kitley 2000). In the late 1980s, Suharto gave in to the requests of his business partners and family members to expand their businesses in the growing media market, by allowing them to establish domestic commercial television stations (Kristiawan 2013: 6, 8). The first five commercial stations that started broadcasting were Rajawali Citra Televisi Indonesia (RCTI), Surya Citra Televisi (SCTV), Televisi Pendidikan Indonesia (TPI; since 2010 Media Nusantara Citra Televisi, MNCTV), Andalas Televisi (ANTV) and Indosiar. In the early 2000s, after the fall of Suharto, five more commercial stations with a nation-wide reach followed: Metro TV, TV7 (since 2006 Trans7), TransTV, Latief Televisi (Lativi; since 2008 TVOne) and Global TV. The increased decentralisation and commercialisation of the media in the late 2000s resulted in the mergers of media companies, the expansion of media networks across the archipelago, and the establishment of regional commercial television stations (Hendrawan 2015; Ida 2011).

Mainstream and alternative print, broadcast and digital media played an important part in the Indonesian reform movement of the late 1990s. One of the noticeable achievements of this democratic reform has been the increase in freedom of expression in and outside the media. This has been illustrated by the abolition of the notorious Departemen Penerangan (Ministry of Information), which was feared for its censorship practices; the ending of the intricate process of Surat Izin Usaha Penerbitan Pers (Press Publication Business License, SIUPP); the legalisation of news production by commercial radio and television; the official recognition of community media as a category in its own right; the formal transformation of state Radio Republik Indonesia (Radio of the Republic of Indonesia, RRI) and TVRI into public broadcasting organisations; and the establishment of an independent regulatory body, Komisi Penyiaran Indonesia (Indonesian Broadcasting Commission, KPI), to monitor the broadcast media in the public interest (Jurriëns 2009). The country now has a booming media industry with dozens of national and regional public and commercial television stations, thousands of radio stations, and even more print publications. The Indonesian government is no longer actively promoting depoliticised, decorative visual art, or censoring or banning social criticism in media and art. Social media, particularly video applications on mobile phones, has played an important role in the Indonesian reform, as it has done in other democratic movements around the globe, particularly the 2010–2012 Arab Spring (Castells 2012).

While at a formal level impressive steps have been made in less than 20 years after the fall of Suharto, at ground level media and art producers and consumers are still facing tremendous challenges. Old forms of surveillance have continued, and new restrictions on participation in public life have emerged. Although media organisations are now less likely to be censored or banned by the state, the more they have to fear from violent attacks by militant groups in society (Steele 2011: 97–98). Both journalists and artists have suffered physical and psychological intimidation by political and religious hardliners such as the fundamentalist Front Pembela Islam (Islamic Defenders Front, FPI; Lindsay 2011). The Indonesian contemporary art scene is increasingly steered by commercial rather than artistic or community interests, with top artists like Nyoman Masriadi selling for record prices at national and international art festivals and auction houses (Vickers 2012). In spite of the spectacular increase in the number of print and broadcast media, KPI's dual ideal of diversity of media content and ownership is still far beyond reach. Instead of a true decentralisation of the media, in line with the political ideal of regional autonomy, national players have simply usurped regional media businesses, while successful local players have expanded their businesses to other regions in the archipelago (Ida 2011: 14–18).

The logical result is concentration of media ownership and homogenisation of media content, against which KPI has not been able or willing to take clear measures. The print, broadcast and online media are dominated by only 12 media conglomerates (Lim 2012). These are MNC Group, Kompas Gramedia Group, Elang Mahkota Teknologi, Visi Media Asia, Jawa Pos Group, Mahaka Media, Chairul Tanjung (CT) Group, Beritasatu Media Holdings, Media Group, Mugi Rekso Abadi (MRA) Media, Femina Group and Tempo Inti Media (Nugroho *et al.* 2012: 4). The assets of these conglomerates cover a wide range of media and businesses. MNC group, for instance, has 3 free-to-air television channels, 20 local television networks and 22 radio networks; Jawa Pos Group controls 171 publishing companies; and KOMPAS owns 90 publishing businesses, 12 radio stations and a television network (Nugroho *et al.* 2012: 4).

The current oligopoly that controls the Indonesian media market threatens the post-Suharto democratic ideal of diversity of ownership and diversity of content (Jurriëns 2009: 35). Instead of representing the public cause, the commercial media companies serve the business and political interests of their owners. Two prominent examples are Visi Media Asia's Aburizal Bakrie, who is also Chairman of the Golkar political party, and Media Group's Surya Paloh, who is also Founder and Chairman of the Nasional Demokrat (NasDem) political party. Both media moguls have used their television stations and other media to give shape to their presidential ambitions (Haryanto 2011: 110–114; Tapsell 2012: 234–235). At the same time, media organisations that are supposed to provide an alternative on behalf of the general public or specific groups and communities in society, such as public and community radio and television, are still struggling to establish or reinvent themselves.

While audiences in contemporary Indonesia have easier access to a larger quantity of media than before the period of democratic reform, they are not exposed to forms of information, entertainment and artistic expression of substantially greater variety or socio-political relevance. Nugroho *et al.* (2012: 14) rightly argue that the Indonesian media oligopoly and the entanglement of business and politics impede the civil right of access to the media as formulated by international organisations such as the United Nations Educational, Scientific and Cultural Organisation (UNESCO). This right includes access to information, access to media infrastructure, and access to the means of influencing media regulation. Organisations that are supposed to protect this right, such as KPI, have faced their own problems in monitoring Indonesian broadcasting companies.

The role of video

Frustrated by the lack of progress in Indonesia's democratic development, visual artists and community groups have attempted to use mobile and social media, particularly video, for the purpose of social, political and creative improvement.

Indonesian youth in the urban centres of Java and other islands have set up their own independent community media and new media art initiatives, such as ruangrupa ('space of shapes') in Jakarta, Common Room in Bandung and Kampung Halaman ('Home Village') and The House of Natural Fiber (HONF) in Yogyakarta. These groups consist of youth with diverse educational and social backgrounds, and interests ranging from art and media to politics and science. It is their multimedia and multidisciplinary approaches that make these initiatives stand out from the more conventional practices of the Indonesian art and media establishment.

The trend of using video and other potentially participatory media for social and creative purposes is the result of both local and global developments, including the post-New Order democratic reform and the worldwide growth in consumer technology and DIY culture. While the role of the mainstream print and broadcast media (Heryanto 2008; Kitley 2000; Sen and Hill 2000, 2011) and conventional categories of contemporary art (Vickers 2012; Knol *et al.* 2009 Wright 1994) in Indonesia have been well documented, there is a lack of studies on alternative media. There are chapters in monographs and edited volumes on video and video art in Southeast Asia (McDaniel 1994; Tahir *et al.* 2011), but only a few important exceptions like Lowenthal (2009) discuss art and media in a combined analytical framework. This book deals with a rich variety of alternative creative genres, especially video art and community video, which have enabled Indonesians to critically express themselves about art and media related issues; establish or participate in civic networks of local, national and international scope; and break with past and present practices of political, social and economic surveillance.

Video art is a form of contemporary art that utilises video and other related technology. In Indonesia and elsewhere, it is also commonly referred to as *seni media baru* (new media art), a broader category of electronic and digital technology-based art (Murti 2009). Similar to community media, it has enabled forms of civic engagement and creative exploration in the Indonesian public sphere that did not exist or were seriously restricted before the democratic reform of 1998. A telling example is the 2004 'Beyond Panopticon' exhibition by the Bandung-based new media art collective Video Lab, which displayed video art in a local shopping mall to signal the end of the New Order's use of television and satellite for panopticon-like surveillance purposes (Siregar 2004).

In Indonesia, community media, including community video, is usually described as media *dari, oleh dan untuk rakyat* (from, by and for the people; Nazaruddin and Hermanto 2009). This type of media enables local communities not only to receive media content, but also to actively participate in media production and management. Community media has been included in Indonesia's 2002 Broadcasting Law as an official category besides public, commercial and subscription broadcast media. It is meant to give media access to groups in society that are normally not or only rarely represented in and by the mainstream media. This book addresses a wide range of pressing topical issues that have been represented and discussed in Indonesian community video, video art and other alternative creative media, including the state of the Indonesian media, consumer culture, the body, gender, sexuality, historiography, health care, education, urban development and the environment.

In spite of their different aims and focus points, it is not uncommon for the various video-related initiatives to comment on and be inspired by the same social phenomena, or to share the same practitioners and audiences. Considering the fluid nature of the Indonesian media and art worlds, in which actors, ideas and practices move across genres, my research utilises an interdisciplinary framework of visual culture that derives from various academic fields, including Cultural Studies, Art History, Anthropology, Sociology and Literature. I follow Indonesian video art pioneer Murti's (2009) argument that the study of the aesthetics and other characteristics of Indonesian contemporary visual culture cannot be limited to the field of conventional art history, but should also include the study of influential domestic and international media and popular cultures.

Structure of the book

The four parts of this book – media environments, media reflexivity, media utopia and media ecologies – each approach media, art and related social developments as interlinked components of a complex ecological whole. In the first part, Media Environments, I map dominant trends in the contemporary Indonesian visual media landscape and the study and critique thereof.

In Chapter 2, I focus on the relevance of media ecology, eco-aesthetics and Cultural Studies for the study and critique of contemporary trends in visual culture in Indonesia and beyond. In line with Postman (1970), media ecology is used as a tool to study how the media create virtual environments that affect people in almost every aspect of their lives, including the shape of their natural environments. I utilise Guattari's (1989) work for identifying the dynamic and political linkages between mental, social and natural ecologies, and exploring creative laboratories and alternative forms of subjectification that counter the forces of IWC. I also engage with Brunner *et al.*'s (2013) concept of eco-art, which addresses the complex cultural condition of IWC and goes beyond the narrow environmentalist ideology of 'green art' or art of the Green movement. I also distinguish my media ecological approach from approaches to the study of Indonesian visual culture that tend to celebrate the emancipatory potential of this culture at the expense of engaging with local forms of socio-cultural critique. The diversity of activities and actors, and the multiple roles and identities of the actors in the various fields of Indonesian television critique, transgress simple distinctions between 'the elite' and 'the ordinary people', between professionals and amateurs, and between producers and consumers of media and art.

Chapter 3 analyses how one important aspect of media ecology – media literacy – has been promoted in the pioneering work of the late Indonesian cultural analyst Veven Sp. Wardhana (1959–2013). Wardhana wrote numerous essays and books, including fiction, which criticised and creatively re-appropriated aspects of the broadcast media. In line with Postman's idea of media ecology, he conceptualised the mass media as a politically and commercially controlled environment shaping Indonesian culture and social behaviour. My chapter provides a biography of the author and examines the broader context of the political economy of the media to which his oeuvre responded. I specifically focus on the similarities and differences between Wardhana's work and the initiatives of the broader Indonesian media watch and media literacy movement. I also address the importance of not merely the content, but also the style of his writings, and critically examine whether or not his own work perpetuated some aspects of the Indonesian media world that it criticised.

Part II on media reflexivity deals with various types of media critique that can be found within the world of Indonesian visual media. Chapter 4 discusses the television show *Newsdotcom*, broadcast from 2006 to 2008, which was a rare form of creative self-reflexivity on Indonesian national commercial television. The show illustrated the interrelation between the state of the Indonesian media and Indonesian democracy. It used visual strategies, including hyper-real and humorous representations of the Indonesian president and other political figures, to promote media literacy as well as alternative visions of Indonesian politics and society. I will describe *Newsdotcom*'s use of imagery to project an alternative reality as an act of simulation, but one substantially different from French philosopher Jean Baudrillard's (2004) idea of simulation, or Heryanto's (2006) application of the concept to New Order strategies of rule. The programme linked illusion to reality by combining simulation with parody, switching between the worlds of the Republic of Dreams and Indonesia, and instructing the viewers about the ideological mechanisms behind media production.

Chapter 5 pays attention to video, which in academic literature is commonly referred to as 'the reflexive medium' (Spielmann 2007). I use David Teh's (2011) idea of 'the programme of video', which takes not only individual works and practitioners into account, but also more structural issues such as the accessibility and distribution of video, the interaction between newer and older media, the innovative quality of video, and the local conventions and histories that have shaped video and other alternative media. By analysing various video genres and developments in Indonesia, I explore to what extent video enables or obstructs people to have access to information and communication, reflect on social and personal issues, and engage in aesthetic exploration. It examines these three different aspects of agency and intimacy by looking at bodily (self-)representations in commercial, home and artistic video genres, including music videos, amateur pornography and new media art. I focus on work of the Indonesian video art pioneer Krisna Murti (b. 1957), in which representations of the artist's own body constitute a central theme. While Murti's early work fully explored the creative possibilities of video technology, his more recent art takes some critical distance from the medium. I argue that the artist puts forward the aesthetic modulation of video as a way of safeguarding or recuperating agency and intimacy in contemporary information and communication society.

Interactivity is a key strategy of alternative media practitioners to create intimate, personalised and process – rather than product – oriented relationships with their audiences. The new media art discussed in Chapter 6 distinguishes itself from the mass media not because of its interactivity as such, but because of its creative and critical reflections on processes of mediation and interactivity. The chapter focuses on the work of three internationally renowned Indonesian new media artists: Murti, Jompet Kuswidananto (b. 1976) and Tintin Wulia (b. 1972). The works of the three artists draw transversal connections between various ecologies, particularly those of politics, visual media, and social and mental life. They unveil the politics of information and communication media as well as the ideological dimensions of other forms of mediation, ranging from history-writing to the demarcation of geopolitical space and the mobilisation and modification of bodies. The three artists enable comparisons between different forms of mediation and interactivity in different areas of social life, and also provide creative and intimate alternatives to the problems addressed by their work.

Media literacy and reflexivity are the foundations of another key aspect of an ecological approach to the media, namely the invention of alternative media models and solutions. Part III on media utopia analyses some of the imaginative models and solutions that can be found in Indonesian new media art and community media. Chapter 7 uses a critical and historical perspective to examine some of the achievements of Indonesian community art and media, the problems they have encountered, as well as the solutions they are offering. I analyse the similarities and differences with earlier genres with an explicit participatory agenda, including certain forms of literature and art by Lembaga Kebudayaan Rakyat (The Institute of People's Culture, LEKRA) of the 1950s and 1960s, 'people's theatre' since the 1970s, and 'conscientisation art' since the 1980s. I also focus on media activists who have been at the forefront of the development of community media in Indonesia since the early 2000s. These activists have engaged in a variety of media, ranging from print bulletins to radio and the Internet. One of the main challenges for contemporary community art and media has been reconciling class differences in the collaboration between media or art facilitators and local communities. These and other factors have affected the accessibility, distribution, sustainability and reach of their ideas, activities and outputs. I demonstrate how facilitators and practitioners have tried to solve some of these problems through the exploration of alternative art and media networks, formats and content.

Chapter 8 discusses various Indonesian new media art groups that have created inclusive and interdisciplinary art works, communities, festivals and networks as alternatives to the relatively exclusive and monodisciplinary ideas and practices of established commercial or state-run galleries and academies. I discuss and seek to balance some of the local and international interpretations and critiques of new media art, by examining to what extent Indonesian new media art communities can be considered avant-garde. I critically engage with noted Indonesian art critic and curator Agung Hujatnikajennong's (2006) argument that Indonesian video artists constitute a 'post-avant-garde', who are able to undermine, but not completely escape, the structures of global capitalism or

IWC. I examine how or to what extent the Indonesian video groups reflect characteristics of the international historical avant-garde of the 1920s and the neo-avant-garde of the 1960s in their attempts to engage with the praxis of life; break with the modernist ideal of the autonomy of art as promoted in Indonesia's major art academies; provide aesthetic innovation; and present alternative, micro-utopian scenarios for the present and the future (Berghaus 2005; Bourriaud 2002; Bürger 1984). In Chapter 8, the main focus is on new media art communities attempting to re-engage with the praxis of life and break with the autonomy of art by collaborating with international and local universities, schools, Non-Governmental Organisations (NGOs) and social groups.

Chapter 9's focus is on Indonesian contemporary art as a historically and socially specific interpretation of the third and fourth key avant-garde principles: to provide utopian visions and present aesthetic innovation. HONF, one of Indonesia's pioneering new media art collectives, not only reflects on the tremendous impact of communication media and other technology on social and natural environments, but also provides scenarios for alternative ways of dealing with these environments. Aesthetically, the collective is innovative in using and developing presentational modes such as pastiche, interactivity and virtual reality. The HONF projects can be classified in three broad categories: performance art; VJ presentations and dance parties; and laboratory experiments and installations. All three categories contain visions of existing and/or preferred interactions between people and their social environments. I argue that the utopia presented in these types of contemporary art has a different character than the utopia of the historical and neo-avant-gardes, as it is less concerned with grand, evolutionary and explicitly political visions of the future, and more focused on better ways to deal with everyday life in the present (Bourriaud 2002).

The final part of the book analyses concrete examples of media ecologies. It demonstrates how the contemporary Indonesian visual vanguard, particularly in new media art and community media, provides innovative scenarios for people's interaction with their surroundings. Chapter 10 examines new media art communities with a special interest in urban life and infrastructure. I discuss collectives from Jakarta and Bandung, which use works of art, exhibitions, festivals and other activities to involve a diverse group of people and institutions, including artists, governments, businesses, NGOs and ordinary citizens, in rethinking, reimagining and, where possible, redesigning urban space. I demonstrate how their specific engagement with urban space can be seen as an aspect of a 'back to the city' movement in reaction to the socially disengaged elite urban development projects from the mid-1970s to the late 1990s. The main focus will be on the Bandung new media art collective Common Room, which has been a pioneer in introducing and developing the idea of the creative industry in Indonesia. Common Room's status as an independent art community has enabled it to simultaneously promote and take critical distance from creative industry projects and discourses, and explore these in the more comprehensive context of urban ecology.

Chapter 11 focuses on the role of visual and other media in rethinking urban and semi-rural life and infrastructure before, during and after the dramatic circumstances of disaster. In no other situation are the connections between virtual and physical environments, and mental, social and natural ecologies, more tight and urgent. The chapter deals with the role of community-based art and media – including community radio, popular theatre, performance art, and community video – in disaster relief and community resilience in the aftermath of the May 2006 earthquake in Yogyakarta Province. These art and media forms not only complement the material reconstruction efforts of disaster-hit communities, but also relate to an informational and spiritual domain that has been insufficiently covered by domestic and international public and commercial media. I argue that the mainstream media can learn from the alternative art and media, not only with regard to their coverage of dramatic events such as natural disasters, but also for their culture and communication-related practices in everyday life.

In the concluding chapter, I summarise some of the main media ecological interventions addressed in this book, and respond to eco-aesthetic scepticism, particularly by art historian Claire Bishop (2004, 2006). Bishop is sceptical about relational aesthetics and creative interactions between artists and audiences, criticising them for prioritising notions of collaboration over notions of aesthetics as such. Using Grant Kester's (2011) work about collaborative art, I argue that Bishop's examples of relational art are limited to the works of artists who predominantly work in the domain of established international art galleries and festivals. The Indonesian video and other new media art and activism provide aesthetic innovation and have social relevance not only because they facilitate various degrees of audience participation and interactivity, but also because they present, or are shaped in, the form of laboratories for the simulation of alternative, more sustainable mental, social, natural and other related ecologies. These multidisciplinary laboratories are strongly contextualised and feed back into everyday life, influencing the ideas and practices of media organisations and governments.

My research seeks to demonstrate that Indonesian visual culture is not at the margins, but at the centre of social and artistic innovation in the digital age. It builds on the work of academics analysing various types of creative networking throughout Asia (Antoinette and Turner 2014; Carroll 2005; Clark 2005), and explores to what extent the visual media practitioners adhere to a relational aesthetics (Bourriaud 2002) in which interpersonal connections constitute the actual work of art. Indonesian alternative media practitioners participate in and contribute to a global network society by travelling and creatively exploring the convergences between video and other communication media (Castells 1996, 2012; Jenkins 2006). Indonesian new media art festivals such as the Ok.Video (Jakarta), Nu-Substance (Bandung) and Yogyakarta International Videowork Festival (YIVF) attract impressive numbers of international participants and guests, while community media facilitators such as Kampung Halaman present their work to the international world through documentary film festivals and the Internet. This research is timely and urgent, as the innovative character of

Indonesian community media and new media art is slowly receiving international recognition. In 2011, Michelle Obama personally presented the International Spotlight Award of the US President's Committee on the Arts and Humanities to Kampung Halaman, while in the same year HONF won the prestigious Berlin transmediale.11 festival for new media art, which had 300 competing projects from 30 different countries.

The Indonesian new media artists are aware that contemporary practices of digital surveillance are not restricted to national borders either, and critically and creatively respond to such threats. Video artist Irwan Ahmett is known for criticising and artistically reworking the Closed-Circuit Television (CCTV) surveillance of public space in Indonesia and elsewhere. Another telling example was a collaborative new media art project ominously titled 'Put up a signal' by AsiaLink Arts (Melbourne), Ruang Mes 56 (Yogyakarta) and Bus Projects (Melbourne) in November 2013. The project took place only a few weeks before the political uproar over the Australian spying scandal, which involved the hacking of the mobile phones of Indonesia's presidential couple Susilo and Ani Bambang Yudhoyono. In a comment on the project, the Australian Broadcasting Corporation's (ABC) current affairs programme 'Newsline' (25 November 2013) confirmed the potential of new media artists 'to mend cultural fences'. This is not to deny that there are many other environmental dimensions to collaborative media and art projects than politics or soft diplomacy only, as this book seeks to demonstrate.

References

Antoinette, Michelle and Caroline Turner (eds). 2014. *Contemporary Asian art and exhibitions: connectivities and world-making*. Asian Studies series monographs 6. Canberra: Australian National University Press.

Baudrillard, Jean. 2004. *Simulacra and simulation*, translated by Sheila Faria Glaser. Ann Arbor, MI: The University of Michigan Press.

Berghaus, Günter. 2005. *Avant-garde performance: live events and electronic technologies*. Basingstoke: Palgrave Macmillan.

Bishop, Claire. 2004. 'Antagonism and relational aesthetics'. *October* 110 (Fall): 51–79.

Bishop, Claire. 2006. 'The social turn: collaboration and its discontents'. *Artforum* 44(6): 179–185.

Bourriaud, Nicolas. 2002. *Relational aesthetics*, translated by Simon Pleasance and Fonza Woods, with the participation of Mathieu Copeland. Dijon: Les presses du réel.

Brunner, Christoph, Roberto Nigro and Gerald Raunig. 2013. 'Post-media activism, social ecology and eco-art'. *Third Text* 27(1): 10–16.

Bürger, Peter. 1984. *Theory of the avant-garde*, translated by Michael Shaw. Minneapolis, MN: University of Minnesota Press.

Carroll, Alison. 2005. 'Arts Infrastructure and Networks in Asia'. In: Caroline Turner (ed.), *Art and social change: contemporary art in Asia and the Pacific*. Canberra: Pandanus Press, pp. 542–553.

Castells, Manuel. 1996. *The rise of the network society*. Oxford and Malden, MA: Blackwell Publishers.

Castells, Manuel. 2012. *Networks of outrage and hope: social movements in the internet age*. Cambridge and Malden, MA: Polity Press.

Clark, Christine. 2005. 'Distinctive voices: artist-initiated space and projects'. In: Caroline Turner (ed.), *Art and social change in Asia and the Pacific*. Canberra: Pandanus Books, pp. 554–568.

Demos, T. J. 2009. 'The politics of sustainability: contemporary art and ecology'. In: Francesco Manacorda (ed.), *Radical nature: art and architecture for a changing planet, 1969–2009*. London: Barbican Art Gallery, pp. 16–30.

Guattari, Félix. 1989. 'The three ecologies', translated by Chris Turner. *New Formations* 8 (Summer): 131–147.

Haryanto, Ignatius. 2011. 'Media ownership and its implications for journalists and journalism'. In: Krishna Sen and David T. Hill (eds), *Politics and the media in twenty-first century Indonesia: decade of democracy*. London and New York: Routledge, pp. 104–118.

Hendrawan, Bram. 2015. *Televising locality: industrial, historical and socio-cultural investigations of local television in post-authoritarian Indonesia*. PhD thesis, Universiteit Utrecht.

Heryanto, Ariel. 2006. *State terrorism and political identity in Indonesia: fatally belonging*. London and New York: Routledge.

Heryanto, Ariel (ed.). 2008. *Popular culture in Indonesia: fluid identities in post-authoritarian politics*. London and New York: Routledge.

Hujatnikajennong, Agung. 2006. 'Avant-gardeisme dalam seni: otonomi, resistensi, dan "sub-versi"' [Avant-gardism in art: autonomy, resistance, and 'sub-version']. In: Alfathri Adlin (ed.), *Resistensi gaya hidup: teori dan realitas* [Lifestyle resistance: theory and reality]. Yogyakarta: Jalasutra, pp. 175–183.

Ida, Rachmah. 2011. 'Reorganisation of media power in post-authoritarian Indonesia: ownership, power and influence of local media entrepreneurs'. In: Krishna Sen and David T. Hill (eds), *Politics and the media in twenty-first century Indonesia: decade of democracy*. London and New York: Routledge, pp. 13–25.

Jenkins, Henry. 2006. *Convergence culture: where old and new media collide*. New York and London: New York University Press.

Jurriëns, Edwin. 2009. *From monologue to dialogue: radio and reform in Indonesia*. Leiden: KITLV Press.

Kester, Grant. 2011. *The one and the many: contemporary collaborative art in a global context*. Durham, NC: Duke University Press.

Kitley, Philip. 2000. *Television, nation, and culture in Indonesia*. Research in International Studies. Southeast Asia Series 104. Athens, OH: Ohio University Center for International Studies.

Knol, Meta, Remco Raben and Kitty Zijlmans (eds). 2009. *Beyond the Dutch: Indonesië, Nederland en de beeldende kunsten van 1900 tot nu* [Beyond the Dutch: Indonesia, the Netherlands and the fine arts from 1900 until now]. Amsterdam and Utrecht: KIT Publisher and Centraal Museum.

Kristiawan, R. 2013. 'Prolog: publik yang terkepung' [Prologue: the besieged public]. In: Puji Rianto (ed.), *Model-model gerakan literasi media dan pemantauan media di Indonesia* [Media literacy movement models and the monitoring of the media in Indonesia]. Yogyakarta: Pusat Kajian Media dan Budaya Populer, pp. 1–12.

Lim, Merlyna. 2012. 'The league of thirteen: media concentration in Indonesia'. Research report. Tempe, AZ: Participatory Media Lab at Arizona State University. Available at: www.academia.edu/7282028/Lim_M._2012_The_League_of_Thirteen_Media_Concentration_in_Indonesia (accessed 27 August 2014).

Lindsay, Jennifer. 2011. 'Media and morality: pornography post Suharto'. In: Krishna

Sen and David T. Hill (eds), *Politics and the media in twenty-first century Indonesia: decade of democracy*. London and New York: Routledge, pp. 172–195.

Lowenthal, Andrew (ed.). 2009. *Videochronic: video activism and video distribution in Indonesia*. Research report by KUNCI Cultural Studies Center and EngageMedia. Collingwood: EngageMedia.

McDaniel, Drew O. 1994. *Broadcasting in the Malay world: radio, television, and video in Brunei, Indonesia, Malaysia, and Singapore*. New Jersey: Ablex.

Murti, Krisna. 2009. *Essays on video art and new media: Indonesia and beyond*. Yogyakarta: Indonesian Visual Art Archive.

Nazaruddin, Muzayin and Budhi Hermanto (eds). 2009. *Televisi komunitas: pemberdayaan dan media literasi* [Community television: empowerment and media literacy]. Jakarta: Ford Foundation, Combine Resource Institution, Program Studi Ilmu Komunikasi FPSB UII and Fakultas Film dan Televisi IKJ.

Nugroho, Yanuar, Dinita Andriani Putri and Shita Laksmi. 2012. *Mapping the landscape of the media industry in contemporary Indonesia*. Report series engaging media, empowering society: assessing media policy and governance in Indonesia through the lens of citizens' rights. Jakarta: CIPG and HIVOS.

Postman, Neil. 1970. 'The reformed English curriculum'. In: Alvin C. Eurich (ed.), *High school 1980: the shape of the future in American secondary education*. New York: Pitman Publishing Corporation.

Sen, Krishna and David T. Hill. 2000. *Media, culture and politics in Indonesia*. Melbourne: Oxford University Press.

Sen, Krishna and David T. Hill. (eds). 2011. *Politics and the media in twenty-first century Indonesia: decade of democracy*. London and New York: Routledge.

Siregar, Aminudin T. H. 2004. 'Melampaui kontrol pikiran lalu tubuh' [Exceeding control over thought, then the body]. In: Heru Hikayat and Herra Pahlasari (eds), *Beyond panopticon*. Bandung: Video Lab.

Spielmann, Yvonne. 2007. *Video: the reflexive medium*. Cambridge, MA and London: The MIT Press.

Steele, Janet. 2011. 'Indonesian journalism post-Suharto: changing ideals and professional practices'. In: Krishna Sen and David T. Hill (eds), *Politics and the media in twenty-first century Indonesia: decade of democracy*. London and New York: Routledge, pp. 85–103.

Tahir, Ibrahim, James Lui and Lindsay Davis (eds). 2011. *Video, an art, a history 1965–2010: a selection from the Centre Pompidou and Singapore Art Museum collection*. Singapore: Singapore Art Museum.

Tapsell, Ross. 2012. 'Old tricks in a new era: self-censorship in Indonesian journalism'. *Asian Studies Review* 36(2): 227–245.

Teh, David. 2011. 'Recalibrating media: three theses on video and media art in Southeast Asia'. In: Ibrahim Tahir, James Lui and Lindsay Davis (eds), *Video, an art, a history 1965–2010; a selection from the Centre Pompidou and Singapore Art Museum Collections*. Singapore: Singapore Art Museum, pp. 25–31.

Vickers, Adrian. 2012. *Balinese art: paintings and drawings of Bali 1800–2010*. Tokyo: Tuttle Publishing.

Wright, Astri. 1994. *Soul, spirit, and mountain: preoccupations of contemporary Indonesian painters*. Kuala Lumpur: Oxford University Press.

2 Media critique

Media ecology

The most common complaints about Indonesian television – as expressed in the essays of professional television critics; the letters of viewers to newspaper editors and KPI; media literacy campaigns; and video art and community media projects – concern the lack of diversity and the low quality of the programmes offered by national public and commercial stations. The complaints are typically about the abundance of non-educational entertainment such as *sinetron*,[1] 'infotainment' and reality shows. More specifically, the criticism concerns programmes containing violence (*kekerasan*), sexual references (*pornografi*) and unconventional religious practices (*mistik*). Some of these evaluation criteria are problematic, but they need to be taken seriously as the indicators of audience dissatisfaction with the current condition of Indonesian television.[2] Often the competition for audience share and the obsession of television companies to sell their programmes to advertisers is blamed for the low Indonesian television standards.

The various types of television critique respond to one of the pressing problems of contemporary Indonesian and global society, namely the cultural and environmental degradation caused by the media. Television and other electronic media build a dominant cultural environment that affects people's socialisation into the world. Unfortunately, the enormous potential of these media to create information and communication networks by, from and for citizens has been strongly curbed by international, national and regional political and commercial interests. Budd *et al.* (2004) rightly argue that television advertisements and programme content lead to intensified consumption with disastrous ecological consequences. The turnover of media equipment as consumer goods has increased dramatically, resulting in an overload of electronic waste (e-waste) dumped on developing countries such as Indonesia. Contemporary Indonesia is a prime example of how television causes the pollution of people's cultural as well as natural environments.

To tackle the problem of cultural pollution and moral degradation by the media, the late British Cultural Studies scholar Roger Silverstone (2007: 176–177, 180) pleaded for 'environmental standards of media practice' or 'the equivalent of a Kyoto for the media'. These environmental standards, involving media regulation as well as the promotion of media literacy, had to contribute to the strengthening of a 'media civics' and appeal to a sense of moral responsibility of both media producers and media consumers. In response to Silverstone's powerful argument, and acknowledging the complexity and problems of the Indonesian media experience, my book pleads for the reinvigoration of the idea of media ecology. This concept can be traced back to the work of several North American scholars of the 1960s and 1970s, such as Marshall McLuhan and Neil Postman, and is still being kept alive today by the international Media Ecology Association (Strate 2006). However, it has not spread widely as a field of academic study, and it has only rarely been applied to the ethnographic study of specific media environments.

Neil Postman reportedly coined the term in 1970, although he attributed some of the ideas and practices behind it to other scholars (Postman 1970: 161). Postman (1970: 161) defines media ecology as 'the study of media as environments':

> The word ecology implies the study of environments: their structure, content, and impact on people. An environment is, after all, a complex message system which imposes on human beings certain ways of thinking, feeling, and behaving. It structures what we can see and say and, therefore, do. It assigns roles to us and insists on our playing them. It specifies what we are permitted to do and what we are not. Sometimes, as in the case of a courtroom, or classroom, or business office, the specifications are explicit and formal. In the case of media environments (e.g., books, radio, film, television, etc), the specifications are more often implicit and informal, half concealed by our assumption that what we are dealing with is not an environment but merely a machine. Media ecology tries to make these specifications explicit. It tries to find out what roles media force us to play, how media structure what we are seeing, why media make us feel and act as we do.

In line with Postman, I suggest the project of (Southeast Asian) media ecology to be the study of how the media shape virtual environments that affect people in almost every aspect of their lives, including the form and structure of their natural environments. Postman prefers to call media ecology a 'field of inquiry' for 'the active pursuit of knowledge', rather than 'a subject', which implies 'replicating, memorizing, ventriloquizing someone else's well-established answers to someone else's well-formed questions' (Postman 1970: 163).

Postman argued for media ecology to replace the traditional subject of 'English' in the high school curriculum, which he believed was the product of a world predominantly formed by print culture, and not in line with the way in which the latest communication and information technology was shaping contemporary life. Now, 40 years later, traditional language and literature studies such as English have been expanded or replaced to a certain extent, and not always favourably, by Cultural Studies. Perhaps the new problem is that certain strands within Cultural Studies, such as the audience reception approach, have turned into relatively circumscribed and streamlined subjects themselves.

Media ecology, on the other hand, is still very much a field of inquiry, and perhaps will or should always be so. It has much to do with 'learn[ing] about that which is unknown' (Postman 1970: 164). The 'unknown' refers to the effects of the media on past and present life, which academics and the general public generally ignore or still have to come to terms with, as well as the social challenges of future media environments. This implies that media ecology is not only about describing and deconstructing cultural practices, but also about intervening and altering socio-cultural constructs. It has descriptive and normative aspects, but also gives space to the imagination and acknowledges the necessity of new utopian visions.

This is in line with Postman's observation that media ecology need not necessarily take the form of a text, but can be presented in other forms such as art. An excellent example is how Indonesian new media art collectives use a variety of media to express their feelings and ideas about the past, present and future of the interaction between social, virtual and natural environments. Postman went as far as projecting that in his revised curriculum and school system, 'the best contemporary art will come from high school students, if art is thought of as inseparable from contemporary technology' (Postman 1970: 168). Perhaps this prediction today is less far-fetched than it may have been 40 years ago, considering the spectacular growth of all sorts of DIY media for creative production. Postman's suggestions for the inquiries and projects of the high school group of the future (in his case, the 1980s) resonate with many of the ideas and activities of the various forms of Indonesian television critique that are discussed in this book, including monitoring the media, promoting media ethics, spreading media literacy, and providing community and artistic media alternatives.

Intertwined ecologies

Matthew Fuller (2005) identifies three different strands of media ecology. The first one refers to 'informational roles in organizations and in computer-supported collaborative work' (Fuller 2005: 3). This is a narrow definition, related to the information flows and management in a workplace. The second strand encompasses the environmentalist ideas of the school of Postman and McLuhan. Both Fuller and others, like Michael Goddard (2011: 7) and Niall Stephens (2014), have criticised this school of thought for conceptualising the human and natural environments as two clearly separate domains. The third strand includes the literary work and other writings of figures such as N. Katherine Hayles, Friedrich Kittler and Joseph Tabbi. The merit of their work is that it establishes connections between creativity, science and cultural analysis (Fuller 2005: 4–5). Fuller also commends Guattari's work for identifying the dynamic and political linkages between mental, social and environmental ecologies, and stresses the need for creative laboratories for alternative forms of subjectification (Fuller 2005: 5).

According to Stephens (2014: 2039), Postman's 'interest in the response of the conscious self to technology distracted him from how the mutual influences of consciousness and technology are increasingly taking place through interventions in physiology'. Especially in the contemporary context of Information and Communication Technology (ICT), the production, distribution, use and disposal of media hardware and software has, indeed, direct material impact on the environment. In global information and communication society, distinctions between the material and the immaterial, nature and culture, and the human and the nonhuman have also become blurred. Moreover, digital automation and artificial intelligence have made it possible for machines to become active agents of communication, and require non-human-centric forms of analysis (Stephens 2014: 2030). In Stephens' (2014: 2041) view, 'recognition and analysis of diverse aspects of the physical and metaphysical dimensions of media technologies' constitutes 'a necessary component of the kind of epistemological and ethical attitude made necessary by ongoing technological transformations of humanity and communication, and by the urgent need to mitigate the destruction of the Earth's ecosystems'.

I believe, however, that Postman's basic concept of media as an environment remains fruitful for identifying the cultural dynamics that shape people's thoughts and actions. The idea of 'environment' suggests the ambient or spatial, temporal and ethico-aesthetic dimensions of the media that partially condition the nature and quality of people's lives. It shows that the media, more than merely being tools or technologies for exchanging information and communication, encompass complex and interrelated processes of production, consumption and distribution.

I also believe that the concept taken from Biology and other sciences is not meant as a metaphor only, but has political relevance. It alludes to the often overlooked role of culture, art and the media in the destruction of various types of environments as well as their potential for providing creative alternatives or solutions to such destruction. Based on Guattari's work, Brunner *et al.* (2013: 16) rightly argue that 'ecology cannot but be mental and social, since it involves the reinvention of new ways of being with the world and new forms of sociability'. This idea of ecology forces us to think beyond technological or technocratic solutions, and adopt a multi-perspective approach instead.

In his essay 'The three ecologies', Guattari (1989) argues that contemporary society is dominated by IWC, which has moved away from the production of goods and services to the production of signs and discourses. IWC and its main tool of control, the media, not only influences social ecology, or the dynamic and interrelated processes shaping society, but also impacts on the mental ecology of individuals,[3] to the extent of 'the introjection of repressive power by the oppressed themselves' (Guattari 1989: 138). Environmental deterioration, on the other hand, is due not only to the destruction of nature as such, but also to distortions in and between social and mental ecologies. For instance, the marginalisation of the Third World is an ecological disaster in social and cultural terms, but also has negative impact on the natural environment and human immune systems (Guattari 1989: 135). In other words, people need to recognise and act on the interrelatedness of, or 'transversal'[4] connections between, the three different types of ecologies (Guattari 1989: 134).

Guattari (1989: 142) believes IWC has promoted both ignorance and apathy about environmental issues among individuals and society as a whole. Apart from the fact that people cannot, or no longer, rely on the welfare state and bureaucracy for protection or action, measures like 'censure and contention' or 'top-down reforms, laws, decrees, or bureaucratic programs' are in no way sufficient for a radical reconstruction of mental and social ecologies. Instead, creative interventions are needed that can open up each of the three ecological fields into processes or praxes that are 'inhabitable by human projects'. This means that people can escape the dominant capitalist subjectivity, and activate isolated and repressed singularities, by making pragmatic interventions in their own lives (Pindar and Sutton 2000: 9). These ecological praxes, or 'the art of the eco', can be seen as a quest for 'dissident vectors of subjectification', which go against 'the normal order of things' (Guattari 1989: 136, 140–141). They are not about preserving predetermined or pre-existent principles or wholes, but about creating the conditions for unprecedented formations of subjectivity (Genosko 2000: 152–153). As the following chapters will show, the human body often functions as an arena where the transversal connections and struggles between mental, social and natural ecologies and the impact of IWC become manifest. At the same time, the body is also an important site for creative interventions and shaping and representing alternative forms of subjectification.

Creative proliferation is posed here against the mental and social closure instigated by the media and public institutions. Guattari (1989: 146) sees it as the task of researchers and artists to promote non-capitalist forms of value exchange, which in the short run may not produce any benefit, but in the long run may become 'vehicles of processual enrichment'. They need to produce alternative and innovative experiments with 'the materials of expression', among others, which are meant to revaluate and revalorise labour and social activities based on criteria other than capitalist productivity and profit, and to produce 'a subjectivity that is simultaneously autonomous, yet articulates itself in relation to the rest of society' (Guattari 1989: 142, 146). Guattari (1989: 139) here envisages 'heterogenesis' in which large-scale struggle and the micro-political practices of desire, solidarity and gentleness mutually influence each other, in spite, or rather because, of not being in synchrony with each other. Considering the delocalising and deterritorialising power of IWC itself, mass movements based on ideological consensus are unrealistic and insufficient.

Specifically referring to the dominant and destructive role of the media in society, Guattari (1989: 144) believes that any ecological programme should attempt 'to shift capitalist societies out of the era of the mass media and into a post-media age in which the media will be reappropriated by a multitude of subject-groups'. Writing in the late 1980s, he recognised the potential of the then steadily growing development and deployment of computerised, mobile and affordable communication technology for creative interventions in the media and society at large (Guattari 1989: 144, 146). The engagement with these types of media in Indonesian new media art constitutes one of the central themes of this book. At the same time, we should be careful of feeling too optimistic about the singularising potential of contemporary ICTs. The Internet and social media comprise a domain that itself has become highly commercialised and ingrained in IWC. One could argue that IWC through ITCs has become even more successful than the conventional mass media in reaching and interfering with people's deepest levels of subjectivity.

The emphasis on subjectivity and singularisation also raises questions about the roles of community and collaborative art (Kester 2011; Pindar and Sutton 2000: 13). Guattari himself suggests that forms of collectivity are possible and necessary, but not in the shape of a mass movement aiming at consensus. Instead, collectivity should be seen as a gathering of dissident subjectivities, who, in the words of the translators of Guattari's work, come together in 'fluidarity', a 'unified disunity' or 'pragmatic solidarity without solidity' (Pindar and Sutton 2000: 15). In this sense, the various creative collaborations that are discussed in this book can be seen as instances of singularised subjectivity and dissensus, produced and symbolised by collectives of more or less disparate individuals, who are able to momentarily break with the homogenisation promoted by IWC.

At the same time, Guattari's subjectivity is not synonymous with individuality, but closely linked to ideas and practices of connectivity and relationality. For instance, in his writings with Gilles Deleuze, he uses the trope of the 'rhizome' to propose a new type of lateral networking involving both human and non-human actors. The rhizome brings together different types of elements, and by doing so, also change the nature of these elements (Deleuze and Guattari 1987: 21):

> [U]nlike trees or their roots, the rhizome connects any point to any other point, and its traits are not necessarily linked to traits of the same nature; it brings into play very different regimes of signs, and even nonsign states. [...] It is composed not of units but of dimensions, or rather directions in motion. It has neither beginning nor end, but always a middle (milieu) from which it grows and which it overspills.

The lateral rhizome reflects not only the realities of organic and mental growth, but also provides a model for democratic interaction. It is meant as an alternative to vertical, hierarchical 'arborescent' systems in societies, which use the model of the tree, towering high with its roots firmly in the soil, to install 'centers of signifiance and subjectification' (Deleuze and Guattari 1987: 16). Nicolas Bourriaud (2002: 89) uses Guattari's 'effort to de-naturalize and deterritorialize subjectivity' also as a model for his relational aesthetics (see Chapter 8). According to Bourriaud (2002: 92), 'this determination to handle existence like a network of interdependent factors, stemming from a unifying ecology, defines Guattari's relationship with the art thing: it is just one field of sensibility among others, associated with a global system'.

Eco-aesthetics

The work of Deleuze and Guattari is popular in the world of contemporary art and has reached Indonesian artists in one form or another through their active participation in numerous international festivals and networks. It provides a framework for understanding the special interest of art communities like HONF in combining machines and human bodies into cyborg-like installations, and using science and technology for producing prosthetics and manipulating the growth of plants (see Chapter 9). It also helps to explain why they make use of biological concepts and metaphors in a foreign language, such as a 'fibre' ('The House of Natural Fiber') and 'cells' (HONF's 'Cellsbutton' new media art festival).

Because of the interconnected nature of mental, social and natural environments, the field of study is literally endless. This book does not go into a psychoanalytical analysis of the mind, or a scientific investigation of environmental issues. Instead, it carefully restricts its scope to the subset of the media, the field that is instrumental to IWC and greatly influences the shape of the various ecologies. Media ecology here refers to the analysis of social, media-related processes and structures as well as the examination of creative and other interventions that map, critique and possibly change and improve such processes and structures. I focus on creative practices because of their potential to provide imaginary ideas and practical solutions that are less likely to emerge from within the constraints of formal institutions and discourses, including those of government, business and academia.

In his article 'The politics of sustainability: art and ecology', T. J. Demos (2009) gives a succinct overview of artistic engagements with ecological issues from as early as the 1960s. One of the strands of environmentalist art concerns 'restorationist eco-aesthetics'. Demos (2009: 20) criticises this strand for separating nature from culture, or objectifying nature 'as an ontology divorced from social, political and technological processes'. In that sense, restorationist eco-aesthetics is based on the same depoliticised grounds that have facilitated the relentless exploitation of nature by capitalism.

A different, arguably more complex strand of eco-aesthetics is represented by artists whose work, since the 1960s, can be understood in terms of cybernetics, or the interdisciplinary analysis of regulatory systems developed by figures like the British anthropologist and social scientist Gregory Bateson (Demos 2009: 21). According to Demos (2009: 21), the artists working in this tradition, including Hans Haacke (b. 1936), Les Levine (b. 1935) and Robert Barry (b. 1936), addressed the 'complex interlinking of biological, technological, social and political ecologies that construct an "environment" that can no longer be considered simply as "natural"'. At the same time, some of the work can be criticised for limiting direct audience participation.

More direct audience interaction was facilitated by another group of artists in the 1970s, including Dan Graham (b. 1942), Peter Campus (b. 1937), Bruce Nauman (b. 1941) and Joan Jones (b. 1936), who used the media of video and community cable television to explore the connections between technology, communication, sociability and affect. Some of their work can be seen as the antecedent of the Indonesian video art and community television experiments since the 1990s, although the links are usually only indirect and fragmentary. Working in yet another model of cultural ecology in the 1970s, the interdisciplinary Pulsa group attempted to bridge the gap between socio-technological and bio-political systems by experimenting with interactive sound and video installations, communal living and agricultural self-sufficiency projects (Demos 2009: 23).

In relation to the various types of eco-aesthetics, Demos (2009: 27) makes a crucial distinction between the practical and the speculative, and between the pragmatic/problem-solving and the ironic-subversive. He refers to projects like Nils Norman's (b. 1966) 'Ideal city, research/play sector' (2005), which combine 'a deep scepticism about the motivations, aims and results of pragmatic environmental art' with 'imaginative alternatives to the reality of everyday neo-liberal urbanism with which it competes' (Demos 2009: 27). The importance of conceptual and anti-pragmatic projects is that they demonstrate 'the ultimate impossibility of a local sustainable practice within a globally unsustainable system of ecologies' (Demos 2009: 28). The art projects in this book are all playful, critical and imaginative, while some of them also provide practical solutions to urban and rural development and disaster relief.

Demos (2009: 19) rightly points to the interdependence of environmental issues and questions of global geopolitics, class, gender, ethnicity and various other problems related to power and identity. This implies that ecological sustainability is not synonymous with ecological justice, as illustrated by the export of polluting industries from the global North to the global South. There is even the irony of eco-art exhibitions addressing some of these issues, while simultaneously producing their own carbon footprint because of the transportation of art works, the climate control in exhibition spaces, and the printing of catalogues (Demos 2009: 19).

According to Demos (2009: 24), the challenges for eco-aesthetics in today's world are manifold:

> How can artistic practices, operating at the juncture of art institutions, activism and non-governmental policies, challenge the emergence of neo-liberal eco-governmentality? How can art oppose the commercialisation of nature, packaged as economic resource, or redirect commercial forces in favour of alternative ways of defining the environment and sustainability with a focus on global justice? How might artists, furthermore, animate an 'environmentalism of the poor' – meaning environmental justice viewed from the perspective of those who have the least access to resources, job protection, socio-political and economic equality and governmental and media

representation – to avoid the exclusivity of 'environmentalism born of affluence' in Western capitalist societies?

An example of an art exhibition that engaged with some of these issues was *Beyond green: toward a sustainable art*, curated by Stephanie Smith in Chicago and New York in 2005. Art projects included creative experiments with recycling, community activism, sustainable fuels and alternative land use (Smith 2005; Demos 2009: 25). In curating the show, Smith (2005: 14) made the critical distinction between 'sustainable development' and the 'development of sustainment', based on her correspondence with theorist Tony Fry. The first term refers to 'the reform of the existing methods of development, but retaining its fundamental objectives'. The second idea demonstrates a stronger engagement with political ecology and social and environmental justice, as it aims at 'redirecting development towards a very different basis for the creation of economy, society, and a relation between human beings, the artificial worlds they create, and the biosphere' (Smith 2005: 14).

The Indonesian creative practices discussed in the following chapters are predominantly concerned with the 'development of sustainment' from a media ecological point of view. This means that this study is not exclusively or specifically focused on art projects that deal with the natural environment. As Brunner *et al.* (2013: 10) rightly argue, eco-art should be distinguished from 'green art', or art of the Green movement or a Green party. 'Conceiving of such art simply as an effect of a new ideology constitutes a problematic and instrumentally restricted relation between art and (environmental) politics' (Brunner *et al.* 2013: 10). Instead, I focus on creative experiments with and about the media, which are meant to show, analyse and where possible change the way in which the media, as the main force of IWC, interact with and shape other environments.

The creative interventions examined in my book encompass various media and outlets, from literature and television to video and computer technology in the specific locale of late twentieth and early twenty-first century Indonesia. These interventions have in common that they reflect on the media as an environment that is interlinked with other, material and natural, environments. They cover various types of micro-politics, ranging from the analysis and critique of the Indonesian media landscape, the promotion of media literacy, and alternative simulations or scenarios for a better present or future, to direct interventions in urban infrastructure, disaster-struck areas, and the creative industry.

The study of Indonesian popular culture

The focus on creative interventions in the overlapping contexts of Cultural Studies and Area Studies sets the media ecological approach apart from other approaches to the study of the media and popular culture. It also foregrounds and problematises notions of agency. David Morley (1992: 1–58), one of the pioneers of the Audience Reception approach, describes how Cultural Studies has gone through various phases, from an emphasis on 'media effects' to a focus on 'uses and gratifications', and more recently, 'interpretation'. Generally, in the 'media effects' approach, the impact of the media on audiences is determined by the content of the media; in the 'uses and gratifications' or 'functionalist' approach the impact or meaning of the media is shaped by, or a function of, the social category to which an audience belongs; while the 'interpretative' approach treats the audience as agents or actors who have the ability to give highly diverse and individualised meanings to the media. The last approach has instigated the so-called 'ethnographic turn' in Cultural Studies, which uses and promotes anthropological fieldwork as a means to mapping the specific socio-cultural situations in which audiences produce their interpretations.

Morley is one of the main exponents of the interpretative approach, but shares some of the criticism of this form of audience research. He acknowledges that certain trends in media research have such a narrow focus on 'interpretation' that they lose sight of the political economy of the media. They may even serve 'a populist neo-liberal rhetoric which would abandon any concern with cultural values – or 'quality' television – and functions to justify the positions of the deregulators who would destroy any version of public service broadcasting' (Morley 1992: 26).[5]

In the study of Indonesian popular culture, the divide between a political economy approach and an interpretative approach has not been as dramatic as in Cultural Studies with a more theoretical focus on other, predominantly Anglo-American, media. Indonesian popular culture studies have integrated both approaches relatively well, by generally providing extensive background on the history, institutions and politics of the Indonesian media. Ethnographic research is usually an integral part of studies of Indonesian society, including detailed accounts of the production and consumption contexts of the Indonesian media.

The role of television during the New Order and early Reformasi periods has been well documented by scholars like Philip Kitley (2000, 2003), Klarijn Loven (2008), Ariel Heryanto (2008b, 2014), Mark Hobart and Richard Fox (2008), and Krishna Sen and David Hill (2000, 2011). These authors have delivered important contributions to the acceptance of Cultural Studies in the field of Indonesian and Southeast Asian Area studies. However, the studies have largely left unaddressed the growing body of Indonesian television critique pioneered since the 1980s by Indonesian cultural analysts such as Veven Sp. Wardhana (1997, 2001, 2002), Idi Subandy Ibrahim (1997, 2007, 2011), Arswendo Atmowiloto (1986), Garin Nugroho (2002, 2004, 2005) and Ashadi Siregar (1995, 2001, 2005). Before the fall of Suharto, this type of television critique was one of the few public forums that offered television producers and consumers the opportunity for critical (self-)reflection. Together with other forms of television critique that developed in the late 1990s, including various genres of audio-visual experimentation, it constitutes an important tool for monitoring the media and its contribution to Indonesia's new democracy (Jurriëns 2011).

The paucity of academic discussion about television and other media critique is the result of specific conceptualisations of Indonesian popular culture and critical and creative agency. Hobart (2008: 44), for instance, explains that 'popular' genres of entertainment television are 'about ordinary people and aimed at a popular or mass market'. This rather circular description does not specify the similarities or differences between popular and mass markets and, by extension, between popular and mass cultures. I agree with Strinati (1995: 40) that popular culture consists of 'a diverse and varied set of genres, texts, images and representations which can be found across a range of different media' and is 'open to diverse uses and interpretations by different groups in society'. Mass culture is but one of the many forms of popular culture and it often has the negative connotations of standardised production and commoditisation, commercial and/or ideological manipulation, as well as uncritical or passive consumption (Storey 1993: 10–11; Strinati 1995: 5–21).

According to Stuart Hall (1981, 2005: 288), one of the pioneers of Cultural Studies, popular culture contrasts with elite culture, and is a site of ideological struggle. In the case of Indonesian popular culture, Heryanto (2008a: 7) makes distinctions between popular culture and 'so-called traditional or ethnic cultures', 'the state-sanctioned "official" version of national cultures', and 'the "avant-garde" or "high" cultures of the nation's intelligentsia'. He also explains that 'ordinary people' are people who are 'neither members of the philosophical, aesthetic, or political elites, nor ... of the new proletariat or under-classes' (Heryanto 2008a: 8). To bring in the idea of class – either in a strict Marxist sense or Heryanto's (2008a: 26) preferred Weberian sense – is valid and in certain cases highly relevant in the study of Indonesian society. At the same time, however, it may go against the very idea of 'fluid identities' (as in the subtitle of Heryanto's (2008b) publication) that are supposed to be represented in, or instigated by, popular culture. From the various case studies in Heryanto (2008b) it becomes clear that certain types of culture have a large circulation precisely because they have the ability to transcend class distinctions and appeal to people with otherwise very different outlooks and interests. Popular culture is certainly more than just an affair of the Indonesian lower and middle classes.

My own preferred definition of the 'popular' in popular culture is close to its third meaning in the *Oxford advanced learner's dictionary* (Hornby 2000), namely '*shared* by a large number of people' (my italics). This definition has no specific class connotations, goes beyond the idea of 'accessibility', and does not imply that popular culture has to be 'well liked'. I see popular culture as material and virtual objects and signifying practices that are shared by a relatively large number of people. In that sense, they influence people's discourse and leave an imprint in people's memory, regardless of whether they are liked or not. Some forms of popular culture create strong emotional bonds between people and remain fixed in collective memory, while other forms have a more instant character and only leave vague or individual impressions.[6] This conceptualisation acknowledges that popular culture has important impact on the way people talk and connect with each other, but also that people have the power to interpret or reject the cultural messages they are confronted with. It illustrates what Hall (1981: 228), with specific reference to the British working classes, has called 'the double-stake in popular culture', or 'the movement between containment and resistance'.

Cultural elite versus ordinary people?

Related to Hall's last point, Hobart (2008: 55) rightly argues that 'ordinary people' are 'working, suffering, thinking, feeling and engaging with the world through the mass media as part of often complex lives with histories' and constitute 'subjects who reflect on, and try to change, the conditions of their lives through various practices, including television-watching'. In that sense, television is important, because it 'is not just an industry but comprises overlapping cultural conversations, in the details of which viewers recognize or learn about themselves and others' (Hobart 2008: 56). Hobart believes that this point has been ignored or misunderstood by the Indonesian elite.

While I fully support Hobart's argument about the diverse ways in which people can and do engage with the media, it remains unclear who exactly is included or excluded from his category of the elite. Does the elite only consist of television critics, or does it also encompass media owners, media producers, journalists, visual artists, academics, or just anyone who is rich and/or educated? At some point, Hobart (2008: 55) specifies that his analysis is about the 'intellectual elite as it constitutes itself in the print media'. Perhaps this should read 'as *constituted* in the print media', since his analysis relies on the ways in which the elite and their comments are represented in the media.

There is indeed evidence from newspaper and magazine articles that Indonesian television critics sometimes speak about and on behalf of others – the ordinary people – in ignorant and authoritative, if not outright arrogant, ways (Hobart 2008; Weintraub 2008). I am unconvinced, however, that the media reports do complete justice to the knowledge and intentions of the television critics. While Hobart rightly assumes the heterogeneity of 'ordinary' viewers' responses to the media, the responses to television by 'the elite' are presented as surprisingly homogenous as well as outdated.

An example of alleged elite arrogance and ignorance in Hobart's (2008: 54) study is Universitas Indonesia (University of Indonesia, UI, Jakarta) scholar Effendi Gazali, who was quoted in an interview with the *Kompas* newspaper as saying that supernatural reality shows give children the false impression that their lives can improve without the need for studying or working hard. This remark would show disdain for the real-life situation of poor children, whose lives are unlikely to change no matter how hard they study or work, and for whom 'the supernatural arguably offers at least as rational and realistic a change of success' (Hobart 2008: 54). The remark would also be an illustration of the Indonesian intellectual, who in spite of his or her insufficient knowledge of 'media theory' (Hobart 2008: 54), presents 'as the knowing subject who, by mysterious means, understands those who are incapable of knowing themselves' (Hobart 2008: 52). For Hobart (2008: 52–55), such intellectuals strategically position themselves outside the category of *masyarakat*, but appropriate the authority and skill to predict and explain the impact of the media on this undifferentiated mass of people.

While Hobart (2008: 52) equates *masyarakat* as 'ordinary people' or 'the populace', and sees it as a euphemistic substitute for the more politically laden and previously popular term *rakyat* – the public at large or the masses – according to any standard Indonesian-English dictionary, *masyarakat* can also be translated with the more neutral words 'society' or 'community'. A third Indonesian word not mentioned in this context, *massa*, would more unambiguously refer to 'the masses'. Even if Gazali's conclusion was 'wrong' according to the standards of contemporary media theory, this does not necessarily mean that he distances himself from, and is not sincerely interested in, the lives and conditions of people with different social and educational backgrounds. Perhaps his main objective was to express his concern about the fate of children – generally considered the future of the community or the nation – in contemporary, media-saturated Indonesian society.

Gazali's own specific background, ideas and projects, beyond the media quotes, also reveal a different and more complex story of the Indonesian elite and the Indonesian media landscape. It is unlikely that Gazali is unfamiliar with the media theories favoured by Hobart, since he holds tertiary degrees in Political Science and Communications from American (Cornell) and Dutch (Nijmegen) universities, respectively. More importantly, besides his work as a university lecturer, he has been involved in various media projects, based on relevant media theory, and developed for and in collaboration with local communities.

Elsewhere I have described how Gazali established a 'Depok School' of thought, based on the Habermasian idea of the public sphere.[7] Within this conceptual framework, he organised workshops in dozens of Indonesian villages to promote the idea of community media, particularly low-cost community radio, as an alternative to commercial, state and public media. He has also created highly popular and innovative television shows, which discuss political, social and media issues in both critical and humorous ways (see Chapter 4). He thus shares his knowledge and engages in discussions about the media with large sectors of the Indonesian population. All these illustrate a different side of Indonesian intellectuals – be they academics, journalists or artists – who often much more than their western counterparts, myself included, feel the need and have the energy to participate in social projects outside their normal jobs. The fact that these activities sometimes also provide the organisers with fame, prestige and/or financial benefits does not necessarily diminish the humanitarian motives by which the activities are driven.

According to Heryanto (2005: 6–7), the great social engagement of intellectuals – whether spontaneous or imposed by external pressure – is one of the factors that has contributed to a lack of time for teaching and research in Cultural Studies at Indonesian universities, and has come at the expense of intellectual depth in the Social Sciences and Humanities more broadly. While the academic institutionalisation of Cultural Studies is indeed a problem in Indonesia, I believe the phenomenon of 'public intellectuals' in itself can be a fascinating *object* or even *method* of Cultural Studies, and can steer the discipline to previously unknown, perhaps more 'Southeast Asian', directions.

Heryanto (2003: 26) notes the strong diversity within the group of intellectuals, with attitudes ranging from opportunism and apathy to idealism and progressiveness. This diversity, and the fact that many intellectuals enjoy intense media consumption as part of their middle-class lifestyles, contradicts the assumption that they would all share a homogenous, negative elite judgement of popular culture. The Cultural Studies project in Indonesia also relies heavily on the initiatives of media institutions, NGOs and transnational communication and collaborative platforms with an interest in the politics of culture and everyday life (Heryanto 2005: 7–9). The engagement of the local media and NGO management and staff with the dynamics of daily life is another indication of the blurred boundaries between 'the elite' and 'the ordinary people' in Indonesia.

Both Hobart and Heryanto rightfully mention approaches to the study of popular culture that take into account more immediate production and consumption contexts. Hobart (2008: 57) recommends 'critical anthropological approaches' to the study of audience reception, and Heryanto (2008a: 4) stresses the necessity for researchers 'to go beyond close reading of a particular work of pop culture', to engage in 'qualitative' rather than 'quantitative' analysis, and to conduct 'ethnographic fieldwork'. However, these approaches which are crucial to a better understanding of popular culture in Indonesia have left out an important section of 'elite' audience reception, namely that of the Indonesian popular culture critique. This is characteristic of an approach in Cultural Studies more generally, which is concerned with audience reception and the emancipatory potential of popular culture, but shies away from providing evaluative statements about such culture.

The diversity of activities and actors, and the multiple roles or identities of the actors in the various fields of Indonesian television critique, are proof that in popular culture, no simple distinctions can be made between 'the elite' on the one hand and 'the ordinary people' on the other. At the same time, there are also no longer clear distinctions between professionals and amateurs, and between producers and consumers of media and art. Some of the creative producers discussed in this book do not have a formal art education, but started off as interested consumers of media and/or art. In particular, the introduction of digital video cameras in the late 1990s made it possible for larger segments of the Indonesian population not only to consume existing materials, but also to record their own videos (Thajib *et al.* 2011: 180). Hand-held cameras and, later, video recording applications on computers and mobile phones enabled people to become 'prosumers' (producer-consumers) or 'pro-am' (professional-amateur) creators of moving images (Willett 2009: 1–2, 12). Rather than continuing the dichotomy between ordinary people and the cultural elite, I prefer to explore the idea of a new creative vanguard which draws on many different groups, concepts, practices and materials (see Chapter 8).

My book uses a broad approach to television critique – arguably the main form of popular culture critique – which includes but goes beyond media watch activities by professional organisations such as KPI and media literacy campaigns of NGOs such as Yayasan Pengembangan Media Anak (Foundation for the Development of Children's Media, YPMA; see Chapter 3). It specifically focuses on creative genres that intervene in the Indonesian mainstream television landscape, such as the novel and essays about television by cultural analyst Veven Sp. Wardhana (Chapter 3); self-reflexive television programmes, or so-called televisual metadiscourse, such as *Newsdotcom* (Chapter 4); video art and new media art alternatives to public and commercial television by individual artists and art communities (Chapters 5, 6, 8, 9 and 10); and community media alternatives to public and commercial television by non-governmental and other grassroots organisations (Chapters 7 and 11).

The international networks to which many, if not all, of these media activists are linked confirm that media ecological issues and solutions transcend the borders of individual nation-states. My own preferred media ecology approach seeks active collaboration with the various agents in order to strengthen their cause, recommend, and contribute to more balanced and transparent structures and power relations in the Indonesian audio-visual landscape. This implies a normative and partisan stand, which can be accommodated in a media ecological approach, but is unusual in other strands of Cultural Studies. This approach is based on the principles of dialogue and collaboration between researchers and local communities in 'Participatory Action Research' and 'Ethnographic Action Research' (Hearn *et al.* 2008; Skuse *et al.* 2007; Tacchi and Kiran 2008), and in line with the argument that Cultural Studies in Indonesia 'has to strive to maintain contacts with the transnationally circulated intellectual discourses and individuals' (Heryanto 2005: 7). Due to advances in communication technology and the internationalisation of the various fields of interest, this type of partnership seems sustainable and likely to further increase in the near future.

Notes

1 *Sinetron* is an abbreviation for *sinema elektronik*, or electronic cinema. It should not be equated with Western-style soap opera. *Sinetron* has a rich history, dating back to the 1980s, and initially encompassed films made for television. Although they would sometimes consist of more than one episode, they were not intended as television serials. They included social criticism and displayed variation in genre, ranging from comedy to satire, but rarely had the melodramatic character of the majority of soap operas and more recent *sinetron* (Wardhana 2006: xxiii–iv).

2 Arguably the best indicator of this dissatisfaction is the dozens of viewer complaints received daily by KPI. Lembaga Ilmu Pengetahuan Indonesia (Indonesian Institute of Sciences, LIPI) has also published a series of small-scale quantitative and qualitative surveys of audience perceptions of television in several provincial capitals (including Bandung, Makassar, Palembang, Semarang, Pontianak, Medan and Yogyakarta), which draw the same negative conclusions about the state of contemporary Indonesian television (Hanim 2005, 2006; Hanim and Astuti 2007).

3 Subjectivity should be distinguished here from individuality. If mental ecology is the arena where the primary subjectivity of an individual is produced, the individual today

constitutes a 'terminal for processes involving human groups, socio-economic ensembles, data-processing machines' (Guattari 1989: 131, 141).

4 Genosko (2000: 146–147, 151) explains that transversality refers to a line 'across strata in an ontological dimension, or in relation to one of more dimensions'. It rejects 'the individual-social distinction' and 'the givenness or preformedness' of subjectivity. Instead, it has a deterritorialising character, involves social and political experimentation, and steers subjectivity and enunciation. It seems to suggest that plural dimensions are not merely linked to each other, but also work on and through each other.

5 Morley, and various other critics of this type of audience research, particularly criticise aspects of the work on audience interpretation by the cultural analyst John Fiske.

6 This is symptomatic of the media saturation of our contemporary information and communication society. Various authors (Cruz and Guins 2005; Hall 1981; Storey 1993; Strinati 1995) have shown how different times and societies have produced different ideas and practices of popular culture. My definition of popular culture is based on my view of the contemporary social condition, and is equally susceptible to criticism and change. See Williams (1976: 76) for a useful genealogy of the word 'culture', one of 'the two or three most complicated words in the English language'.

7 Depok is the location of the University of Indonesia's main campus in south Jakarta. Depok School is also a reference to the Frankfurt School, the school of thought of which Habermas is considered to be a late representative (Jurriëns 2009: 25–27).

References

Atmowiloto, Arswendo. 1986. *Telaah tentang televisi* [A research about television]. Jakarta: Gramedia.

Bourriaud, Nicolas. 2002. *Relational aesthetics*, translated by Simon Pleasance and Fonza Woods, with the participation of Mathieu Copeland. Dijon: Les presses du réel.

Brunner, Christoph, Roberto Nigro and Gerald Raunig. 2013. 'Post-media activism, social ecology and eco-art'. *Third Text* 27(1): 10–16.

Budd, Mike, Steve Craig and Clay Steinman. 2004. *Consuming environments: television and commercial culture.* Piscataway, NJ: Rutgers University Press.

Cruz, Omayra Zaragoza and Raiford Guins. 2005. 'Entangling the popular: an introduction to *Popular culture: a reader*'. In: Raiford Guins and Omayra Zaragoza Cruz (eds), *Popular culture: a reader*. London: Sage Publications, pp. 1–18.

Deleuze, Gilles and Felix Guattari. 1987. *A thousand plateaus: capitalism and schizophrenia*, translated by Brian Massumi. Minneapolis, MN: University of Minnesota Press.

Demos, T. J. 2009. 'The politics of sustainability: contemporary art and ecology'. In: Francesco Manacorda (ed.), *Radical nature: art and architecture for a changing planet 1969–2009*. London: Barbican Art Gallery, pp. 16–30.

Fuller, Matthew. 2005. *Media ecologies: materialist energies in art and technoculture.* Cambridge, MA: MIT Press.

Genosko, Gary. 2000. 'The life and work of Félix Guattari: from transversality to ecosophy'. In: Félix Guattari, *The three ecologies*, translated by Ian Pindar and Paul Sutton. London and New Brunswick, NJ: The Athlone Press, pp. 106–159.

Goddard, Michael. 2011. 'Towards an archaeology of media ecologies: "media ecology", political subjectivation and free radios'. *The Fibreculture Journal* 17. Available at: http://seventeen.fibreculturejournal.org/fcj-114-towards-an-archaeology-of-media-ecologies-%E2%80%98media-ecology%E2%80%99-political-subjectivation-and-free-radios/ (accessed 23 May 2016).

Guattari, Félix. 1989. 'The three ecologies', translated by Chris Turner. *New Formations* 8 (Summer): 131–147.

Hall, Stuart. 1981. 'Notes on deconstructing "the popular"'. In: Raphael Samuel (ed.), *People's history and socialist theory*. London: Routledge and Kegan Paul, pp. 227–240.

Hall, Stuart. 2005. 'What is this "black" in black popular culture?'. In: Raiford Guins and Omayra Zaragoza Cruz (eds), *Popular culture: a reader*. London: Sage Publications, pp. 285–293.

Hanim, Masayu S. (ed.). 2005. *Persepsi masyarakat terhadap tayangan pornografi, kekerasan dan mistik di televisi* [Society's perception of the screening of pornography, violence and mysticism on television]. Jakarta: Lembaga Ilmu Pengetahuan Indonesia.

Hanim, Masayu S. (ed.). 2006. *Dampak tayangan pornografi, kekerasan dan mistik di televisi di Palembang dan Semarang* [The impact of the screening of pornography, violence and mysticism on television in Palembang and Semarang]. Jakarta: Lembaga Ilmu Pengetahuan Indonesia.

Hanim, Masayu S. and Santi Indra Astuti. 2007. *Media literacy sebagai upaya mengatasi dampak negatif media televisi* [Media literacy as an effort to overcome the negative impact of the medium of television]. Jakarta: Lembaga Ilmu Pengetahuan Indonesia.

Hearn, Gregory N., Jo A. Tacchi, Marcus Foth and June Lennie. 2008. *Action research and new media: concepts, methods and cases*. Cresskill, NJ: Hampton Press.

Heryanto, Ariel. 2003. 'Public intellectuals, media and democratization: cultural politics of the middle classes in Indonesia'. In: Ariel Heryanto and Sumit K. Mandal (eds), *Challenging authoritarianism in Southeast Asia*. London: Routledge, pp. 24–59.

Heryanto, Ariel. 2005. 'Cultural Studies' significant others: the case of Indonesia'. *Antropologi Indonesia* 29(1): 1–15.

Heryanto, Ariel. 2008a. 'Pop culture and competing identities'. In: Ariel Heryanto (ed.), *Popular culture in Indonesia: fluid identities in post-authoritarian politics*. London and New York: Routledge, pp. 1–36.

Heryanto, Ariel (ed.). 2008b. *Popular culture in Indonesia: fluid identities in post-authoritarian politics*. London and New York: Routledge.

Heryanto, Ariel. 2014. *Identity and pleasure: the politics of Indonesian screen culture*. Kyoto CSEAS series on Asian Studies. Singapore: NUS Press.

Hobart, Mark. 2008. 'Entertaining illusions: how Indonesian elites imagine reality TV affects the masses'. In: Mark Hobart and Richard Fox (eds), *Entertainment media in Indonesia*. London: Routledge, pp. 42–59.

Hobart, Mark and Richard Fox (eds). 2008. *Entertainment media in Indonesia*. London: Routledge.

Hornby, A. S. 2000. *Oxford advanced learner's dictionary of current English*, edited by Sally Wehmeier, with phonetics editor Michael Ashby. Oxford, UK: Oxford University Press.

Ibrahim, Idi Subandy (ed.). 1997. *Ecstasy gaya hidup: kebudayaan pop dalam masyarakat komoditas Indonesia* [The ecstasy of lifestyle: pop culture in the Indonesian commodity society]. Bandung: Mizan.

Ibrahim, Idi Subandy. 2007. *Budaya popular sebagai komunikasi: dinamika popscape dan mediascape di Indonesia kontemporer* [Popular culture as a commodity: the dynamics of the popscape and mediascape in contemporary Indonesia]. Yogyakarta: Jalasutra.

Ibrahim, Idi Subandy. 2011. *Kritik budaya komunikasi: budaya, media, dan gaya hidup dalam proses demokratisasi di Indonesia* [A communication culture critique: culture, media and lifestyle in the democratisation process in Indonesia]. Yogyakarta: Jalasutra.

Jurriëns, Edwin. 2009. *From monologue to dialogue: radio and reform in Indonesia.* Leiden: KITLV Press.

Jurriëns, Edwin. 2011. 'A call for media ecology: the study of Indonesian popular culture revisited'. *Indonesia and the Malay World* 39(114): 197–219.

Kester, Grant. 2011. *The one and the many: contemporary collaborative art in a global context.* Durham, NC: Duke University Press.

Kitley, Philip. 2000. *Television, nation, and culture in Indonesia.* Research in International Studies. Southeast Asia Series 104. Athens, OH: Ohio University Center for International Studies.

Kitley, Philip (ed.). 2003. *Television, regulation and civil society in Asia.* London and New York: RoutledgeCurzon.

Loven, Klarijn. 2008. *Watching si Doel: television, language, and cultural identity in contemporary Indonesia.* Leiden: KITLV Press.

Morley, David. 1992. *Television, audiences, and cultural studies.* London: Routledge.

Nugroho, Garin (ed.). 2002. *TV publik: menggagas media demokratis di Indonesia* [Public TV: conceptualising democratic media in Indonesia]. Jakarta: SET and KTVPI.

Nugroho, Garin. 2004. *Opera sabun SBY: televisi dan komunikasi politik* [The SBY soap opera: television and political communication]. Rawamangun, Jakarta: Nastiti.

Nugroho, Garin. 2005. *Seni merayu massa* [The art of seducing the masses]. Jakarta: Kompas.

Pindar, Ian and Paul Sutton. 2000. 'Translators' introduction'. In: Félix Guattari, *The three ecologies*, translated by Ian Pindar and Paul Sutton. London and New Brunswick, NJ: The Athlone Press, pp. 1–20.

Postman, Neil. 1970. 'The reformed English curriculum'. In: Alvin C. Eurich (ed.), *High school 1980: the shape of the future in American secondary education.* New York: Pitman Publishing Corporation, pp. 160–168.

Sen, Krishna and David T. Hill. 2000. *Media, culture and politics in Indonesia.* Melbourne: Oxford University Press.

Sen, Krishna and David T. Hill (eds). 2011. *Politics and the media in twenty-first century Indonesia: decade of democracy.* London and New York: Routledge.

Silverstone, Roger. 2007. *Media and morality: on the rise of the mediapolis.* Malden, MA: Polity Press.

Siregar, Ashadi. 1995. *Media massa: sketsa-sketsa* [Mass media: sketches]. Yogyakarta: Yayasan Benteng Budaya.

Siregar, Ashadi. 2001. *Menyingkap media penyiaran: membaca televisi, melihat radio* [Revealing the broadcasting media: reading television, seeing radio]. Sleman, Yogyakarta: Lembaga Penelitian Pendidikan Penerbitan Yogya.

Siregar, Ashadi. 2005. *Sinetron Indonesia untuk pasar dan budaya* [Indonesian *sinetron* for the market and culture]. Sleman, Yogyakarta: Lembaga Penelitian Pendidikan Penerbitan Yogya.

Skuse, Andrew, Joann Fildes, Jo Tacchi, Kristy Martin and Emma Baulch. 2007. *Poverty and digital inclusion: preliminary findings of Finding a Voice project.* New Dehli: UNESCO.

Smith, Stephanie. 2005. 'Beyond green'. In: Stephanie Smith (ed.), *Beyond green: toward a sustainable art.* Chicago and New York: Smart Museum of Art and Independent Curators International, pp. 12–19.

Stephens, Niall P. 2014. 'Towards a more substantive media ecology: Postman's metaphor versus posthuman futures'. *International Journal of Communication* 8: 2027–2045.

Storey, John. 1993. *An introductory guide to cultural theory and popular culture*. New York: Harvester Wheatsheaf.

Strate, Lance. 2006. *Echoes and reflections: on media ecology as a field of study*. Cresskill, NJ: Hampton Press.

Strinati, Dominic. 1995. *An introduction to theories of popular culture*. London: Routledge.

Tacchi, Jo and M. S. Kiran (eds). 2008. *Finding a voice: themes and discussions*. New Dehli: UNESCO.

Thajib, Ferdiansyah, Nuraini Juliastuti, Andrew Lowenthal and Alexandra Crosby. 2011. 'A chronicle of video activism and online distribution in post-New Order Indonesia'. In: Geert Lovink and Rachel Somers Miles (eds), *Video vortex reader II: moving images beyond Youtube*. Inc Reader #6. Amsterdam: Institute of Network Culture, pp. 178–193.

Wardhana, Veven Sp. 1997. *Kapitalisme televisi dan strategi budaya massa* [Television capitalism and mass culture strategies]. Yogyakarta: Pustaka Pelajar.

Wardhana, Veven Sp. 2001. *Televisi dan prasangka budaya massa* [Television and mass culture prejudice]. Jakarta: Media Lintas Inti Nusantara and Institut Studi Arus Informasi.

Wardhana, Veven Sp. 2002. *Dari Barbar sampai Timor Timur: mengeja budaya massa* [From Barbarians to East Timor: spelling the mass media]. Yogyakarta: Galang Press.

Wardhana, Veven Sp. 2006. 'Lebih dari sekadar migrasi orang Barat ke/di Jawa Barat' [More than just the migration of a Westerner in/to West Java]. In: Edwin Jurriëns, *Ekspresi lokal dalam fenomena global: safari budaya dan migransi* [Local expression in global phenomena: cultural travel and migrancy]. Jakarta: LP3ES and KITLV-Jakarta, pp. xv–xxv.

Weintraub, Andrew N. 2008. 'Dangdut soul: who are "the people" in Indonesian popular music?'. In: Mark Hobart and Richard Fox (eds), *Entertainment media in Indonesia*. London: Routledge, pp. 60–80.

Willett, Rebekah. 2009. 'In the frame: mapping camcorder cultures'. In: David Buckingham and Rebekah Willett (eds), *Video cultures: media technology and everyday creativity*. Basingstoke: Palgrave Macmillan, pp. 1–22.

Williams, Raymond. 1976. *Keywords: a vocabulary of culture and society*. London: Croom Helm.

3 Media literacy

The first creative, ecological intervention in the Indonesian media to be discussed in detail is the oeuvre of journalist, essayist and literary author Veven Sp. Wardhana (1959–2013). His corpus of writings, which numbers thousands of pages, includes both fiction and non-fiction, covers seemingly ephemeral phenomena, and is situated in a field that is not strongly embedded in institutional structures or academic traditions (Jurriëns 2016). This chapter is an attempt at writing a biography of an influential, but in academic discourse relatively neglected, public figure and creative actor, as well as providing an analysis of structural problems in the Indonesian media landscape and the study thereof.

I argue that Wardhana's work is an important complement to the activities of KPI and other media watch and media literacy organisations, as it identifies recurring issues in media ownership, journalism and entertainment; offers a cultural conceptualisation of Indonesia as a televised world; and tries to provide alternatives to mainstream television by creatively reworking aspects of the medium. In line with Postman's idea of media ecology, it conceptualises the mass media as a politically and commercially controlled environment shaping Indonesian culture and social behaviour. Unlike Guattari's analysis, however, it does not discuss direct links between human and natural environments. Its merit is in providing detailed insight into some of the key problems of Indonesia's televisual ecology to which the work of other creative actors, including video artists and community media practitioners, has also responded.

My strategy to deal with the sheer volume and wide genre diversity of Wardhana's writings is four-fold. First, I provide a biography of the author, including a short bibliography and a short analysis of some of the key themes in his work. Second, I examine the broader context of the political economy of the media to which his writings are responding. This section specifically focuses on the similarities and differences between Wardhana's work and the initiatives of KPI, the main institution for monitoring the broadcast media in Indonesia, and the broader Indonesian media watch and media literacy movement. Third, I address the importance of not merely the content, but also the style of Wardhana's writings, including his novel. In the fourth and final part of this chapter, I discuss various contentious points in the creative work and position it in the nascent field of Indonesian Media and Cultural Studies. I critically examine whether or not

Wardhana's own work perpetuates some aspects of the Indonesian media world that it criticises; to what extent it goes beyond the media and celebrity culture of the Jakartan middle class shaped by gender bias and sensationalist accounts of sexuality; and if, or how, it is capable of influencing the Indonesian media world.

Veven Sp. Wardhana

On 17 May 2013, Wardhana passed away after a battle with lung cancer. He was married to Bastiana Thereskova Koraag, with whom he had three daughters. Together with his senior at the *Monitor* tabloid, Arswendo Atmowiloto (1986), author Ashadi Siregar (2006), film maker Garin Nugroho (2005) and cultural analyst Idi Subandy Ibrahim (1997), Wardhana stood out as one of the most productive, creative and consistent Indonesian television critics. Perhaps because it deals with seemingly ephemeral phenomena, or because of its sheer volume, Wardhana's work is yet to be explored to its full extent.

Wardhana was born Effendy Agus Hariyanto on 21 January 1959 in Malang, East Java.[1] He studied at Gadjah Mada University in Yogyakarta, graduating in 1984 with a degree in Literature. After his studies, he was on the editorial boards of various print and electronic media, including the tabloids *Hai* (1986–1987), *Monitor* (1987–1990), *Bintang* (1990), *Citra* (1991–1995) and *Tiara* (1995–1999), and the current affairs magazines *Tempo Interaktif* (1996–1997) and *Gramedia-Majalah Online* (1999–2003).[2]

In 1999, he was the Media Watch Programme Coordinator of the Jakarta-based Institut Studi Arus Informasi (Institute for the Studies on Free Flow of Information, ISAI) and one of the coordinators of the election media monitoring programme of the London-based independent organisation Article XIX (Diani 2014). From 2003 to 2012, he was editor at the Jakarta-based Prima Media Pustaka publishing company. From 2005 to 2012, he worked in various roles for the German NGO Deutsche Gesellschaft für Technische Zusammenarbeit (Corporation for Technical Cooperation, GTZ), including those of Senior advisor for Good Governance in the Population Administration programme, Senior advisor for Reconstruction and Development in the Population Administration in Nanggroe Aceh Darussalam (PAS NAD) programme, and Senior advisor for the Strengthening Women's Civil Rights (SWR) programme. Shortly before his death, he worked as media advisor for Hatta Rajasa, then Coordinating Minister for Economics.

Wardhana's writings covered the socio-cultural dimensions of the mass media, gender, ethnicity, politics and business in Indonesia. His creative work consisted of one novel, *Stamboel selebritas* ('The celebrity spectacle', 2004b), and various volumes of short stories, including *Perempuan yang gagal jadi kelelawar* ('The woman who failed to become a cave bat', 2013b), *Dari mana datangnya mata* ('From where came the eye', 2004a), *Panggil aku Peng Hwa* ('Call me Pheng Hwa', 2002d)[3] and *Centeng: matahari malam hari* ('Watchman: the sun of the night', 2002b). He also wrote the scripts of various television programmes, such as the television film (*telesinema*) *Xiao Qing* (broadcast by the commercial television station RCTI on 22 January 2004), the series *Puan* ('Madam', broadcast weekly by TVRI from 2003 to 2004), the miniseries *Nyai Dessy, Nyai Imah* ('Concubine Dessy, Concubine Imah', broadcast by TVRI in 1999 and 2001), the film review programme *Lintasan sinema Indonesia* ('Indonesian cinema newsflash', broadcast monthly by TVRI from 1997 to 2000), the television bulletin *RCTI-RCTI* (broadcast fortnightly by RCTI from 1996 to 1998) and the *sinetron Sang pengibar, sang pengobar* ('The flag waver, the inspirer', broadcast by TVRI in 1997).

He published his investigative essays in various volumes including *Budaya massa, agama, wanita* ('Mass culture, religion, women', published posthumously – see Wardhana 2013a), *Dari Barbar sampai Timor Timur: mengeja budaya massa* ('From Barbarians to East Timor: spelling mass culture', 2002c), *Televisi dan prasangka budaya massa* ('Television and the prejudice of mass culture', 2001), *Geger santet Banyuwangi* ('The tumult of the Banyuwangi black magic', 2001, with Abdul Manan and Imam Suma Atmadja), *Para superkaya Indonesia: sebuah dokumentasi gaya hidup* ('The superrich of Indonesia: a documentation of lifestyle', 1999, with Herry Barus), *Kemelut PDI di layar televisi: survey jurnalisme Indonesia* ('The crisis of the PDI [Partai Demokrasi Indonesia, Indonesian Democratic Party] on television: a survey of Indonesian journalism', 1997b), *Kapitalisme televisi dan strategi budaya massa* ('Television capitalism and the strategy of mass culture', 1997a) and *Budaya massa dan pergeseran masyarakat* ('Mass culture and the shift of society', 1995). He also edited and co-edited several books authored by others.

In a 24 October 2004 article in *The Jakarta Post*, journalist Hera Diani (2004) characterised Wardhana and his work as follows:

> Amid the grandstanding and clamoring for position in the colorful media jungle, Veven S.P. Wardhana stands out as a voice of understated reason. From the issue of press coverage of the May 1998 riots, to the broadcasting bill, government-press relations and the glut of TV gossip shows, Veven can tell it like it is.

Arswendo Atmowiloto (2013), his senior at *Monitor*, also praised Wardhana's sharp, personal and to-the-point writing style. *Detik.Com*, one of Indonesia's premier online news sites, referred to Wardhana as 'one of the pioneers of media studies in Indonesia' (Mujiarso 2013).

Wardhana's career shows a development from direct involvement in the news and entertainment industry to a more research-focused approach to the media world. Over the years, he also broadened his working experiences from the print and broadcast media to international NGOs working on gender and ethnicity-related issues. Moreover, he expanded his professional skills and interests from journalistic writing to more creative forms like short stories and a novel. A respected member of prestigious organisations like ISAI and Gramedia, he felt increasingly limited in his critical and creative potential within the structures of formal institutions. In the final years of his life, he decided to become an independent writer. After receiving the news about his death, a group of famous journalists, literary authors, film makers, activist and artists, including Seno Gumira Ajidarma, Butet Kertaradjasa, Leila S. Chudori, Ayu Utami, Jajang C. Noer, Mira Lesmana, Rotua Valentina Sagala, Bre Redana and Arswendo Atmowiloto spontaneously organised a respectful tribute of music and readings of his work (Andarnuswari 2013).

Identifying recurring issues: media concentration, 'spit journalism', 'the show must bloon'

Wardhana's critical media essays demonstrate that certain trends in the relatively ephemeral medium of television, such as lack of diversity of ownership and content, are not isolated and one-off phenomena. Instead, it shows that they are interrelated and recurring themes, which over time create specific, usually business-manipulated, social and mental ecologies. This critical and historical dimension is often absent in the initiatives of formal institutions dealing with the monitoring of the broadcast media, like KPI. Wardhana's essays normally use examples of specific television programmes or other media content to tell stories about the broader socio-political conditions shaping the Indonesian media industry. They are generally two to four pages in length and have the character of editorials that use a mix of journalistic analysis and personal opinion to invite readers and fellow television viewers to comment on topical media-related issues. Some of the recurring themes have been problems surrounding TVRI, commercial television, the film industry, television journalism, *sinetron*, infotainment, children's programmes, advertising, censorship and media representations of gender, nationalism, religion and ethnicity. I will focus in this section on themes relating to the political economy of the media, particularly media ownership, as well as media content, particularly journalism and entertainment.

In one of his essays, Wardhana (2002c: 149–152) used the example of the television station TPI, which stood for Televisi Pendidikan Indonesia (Indonesian Education Television), to demonstrate the roots of the unfair competition and lack of diversity in ownership and content in the Indonesian media. TPI was established by Suharto's eldest daughter Siti Hardiyanti Rukmana in the early 1990s (Kitley 2000). Because of its supposedly educational purpose, the station received privileges over other commercial stations that were established around the same time. These privileges included the right to broadcast nationally and the right to make use of the facilities of state television (TVRI). Within a few years, however, TPI's broadcasting schedule was not any different from that of its competitors (Wardhana 2002c: 151, 507–508). Other television stations also breached the conditions of their broadcasting licenses, including the prohibition to broadcast nationally (Wardhana 2002c: 193–196, 507). Until today, media owners have managed to escape legal sanctions due to a lack of law enforcement as well as their ingenuity in diversifying and rebranding their businesses (Ida 2011).

Wardhana also observed recurring issues in Indonesian journalism. In spite of the seemingly dramatic political and social changes of 1998, one of the continuities has been the lack of investigative reporting in the print and broadcast media. According to Janet Steele (2011: 89), many Indonesian 'investigative' newspaper articles are 'episodic' rather than 'thematic', as they focus on 'specific individuals or occurrences' rather than 'the broader social and political forces behind the news'. Wardhana (2002c: 226, 438, 440, 446) observed that the news media also continued publishing the statements (*pernyataan*) of high-ranked officials as the facts (*kenyataan*) of a news event rather than reporting and analysing reality in an objective manner. This lacuna had its roots in state control over the media, including TVRI's monopoly on television journalism from the 1960s until the early 1990s. The TVRI news of the time was dominated by the symbolic gestures of the bureaucracy, such as the official openings of new buildings, and rarely represented the daily reality of ordinary people (Wardhana 2002c: 33; see also Kitley 2000).

One of the studies in which Wardhana came to this conclusion was his 1997 research project conducted on behalf of ISAI. This study was about the events leading up to, during and after the attacks on the PDI headquarters in Jakarta on 27 July 1996.[4] Wardhana (1997b: 29–31) found that both TVRI and the four commercial television stations offering news coverage at the time (RCTI, SCTV, TPI and ANTV) were far from the ideal of investigative journalism. Instead of reporting the empirical facts (*kenyataan*) of the events, they relied on the statements (*pernyataan*) of interviewees, who were generally in favour of the government-supported faction of PDI (Wardhana 1997b: 32–37).

Nevertheless, the television coverage marked a new era in Indonesian television broadcasting in which news production was no longer monopolised and sanitised by the state, but had become a field of competition for the domestic commercial television stations (Sen and Hill 2000: 128–130). The news broadcasts were even more remarkable for presenting images of political demonstrations and riots to a nation-wide audience. They also contained juxtapositions between the statements made by officials, journalists and television hosts on the one hand, and the television images on the other.[5] Sen and Hill (2000: 130) referred to this phenomenon in terms of the 'politics of pictures'. By informing audiences that mass protests were happening around the country, the media contributed to the fall of Suharto in May 1998. Apart from providing his own analysis of television journalism, Wardhana (1997b: 49–67) also included transcripts of his interviews with the editors-in-chief of the television stations that had covered the PDI-related sequences of events. Although the answers to his questions were not particularly enlightening, Wardhana's effort to conduct and publish these interviews had a pioneering and performative quality in encouraging the development of journalistic accountability in a climate of authoritarianism.

According to Wardhana (2002c: 351–355), after the fall of the New Order, television news was still often characterised by bias and irrelevant issues. He also observed the rise of what he called 'spit journalism' (*jurnalisme [cipratan] ludah*), in which 'what was talked about (*yang dilidahkan*), the essential, became marginalised; and what was spat on (*yang terludahkan*), the "sensational", was continued endlessly' (Wardhana 2002c: 353). Although Indonesian commercial television introduced new approaches and styles of news reporting, Wardhana observed that it was still far from the ideal of critical and objective broadcast journalism. For instance, the post-New Order trend of interactive journalism (*jurnalisme interaktif*, see Jurriëns 2009) gave television viewers an opportunity to express their own opinion, but did not provide substantial contributions to investigative journalism (Wardhana 2002c: 457–459). Both public and commercial television rarely presented live coverage of news events, and if they did, their information was not necessarily correct or without manipulation (Wardhana 2002c: 223, 293).

Wardhana elaborated not only on how the commercialisation of the media in the post-authoritarian era impacted on Indonesian journalism, but also on how it shaped fictional genres such as *sinetron*. He criticised the majority of Indonesian television comedy for disregarding and dumbing down (*membloonkan*) their audiences by presenting 'stupid' (*bloon*) characters and stories (Wardhana 2002c: 87–90). He also used the pun 'The show must bloon' (pronounced as 'blo-on'), rhyming with the expression 'The show must go on', to refer to the low quality of Indonesian television shows (Wardhana 2002c: 87). He observed that it was difficult to distinguish the one *sinetron* from the other, as many of them shared the same actors and storylines (Wardhana 2002c: 133). He called these 'me too products', created by television producers who simply imitated television programmes that had proven to be commercially successful. The television producers used cheap comedy to keep up their television ratings, attract advertisers, and fulfil their requirement to broadcast at least 80 per cent of Indonesian content and a maximum of 20 per cent of foreign content (Wardhana 2001: 135, 188–189, 411). As noted by Hobart (2008: 56), television, including its entertainment, is important, because viewers can 'recognise or learn about themselves and others'. However, this should not preclude a critical examination of the broader political economy of the media, and the impact it has on media content and media consumption, including representations of gender.

According to Wardhana (2002c: 365–366), one of the results of the increased commercialisation of television and the lack of independence for scriptwriters was the stereotypical representation of gender in Indonesian *sinetron*. Scriptwriters depended on television producers, who believed that the perpetuation of stereotypical gender roles was in the best financial interests of their media companies. The title of one of his essays (Wardhana 2002c: 125), 'History, his story: Hiss! Ssst …', illustrated that Indonesian film and television reinforced authoritative male-dominated historiography ('his story') and silenced both alternative versions of history ('Hiss!') and the representation of historical facts that were considered shameful ('Ssst …'). If there were any films and *sinetron* focusing on historical themes, they tended to be of low quality and exclusively focusing on the epic heroes of official historiography rather than the daily reality of social life (Wardhana 2002c: 125–128). Also in his 2004b novel *Stamboel selebritas* ('The celebrity spectacle'), which will be analysed later in this chapter, Wardhana criticised the production mechanisms and gender dimensions of Indonesian *sinetron*.

The Indonesian Broadcasting Commission

In order to put Wardhana's work in a critical context, it is necessary not only to identify the political economy and content of the Indonesian media, but also the broader environment of media watch initiatives to which Wardhana belongs. The most authoritative institution in charge of monitoring broadcast content is the independent KPI. This commission is a product of the 2002 Broadcasting Law (Undang-Undang Penyiaran). Unlike the first Indonesian Broadcasting Law of 1997, which mentioned that the government was in charge of media regulation, the 2002 Broadcasting Law stated that broadcasting had to be monitored by an independent organisation in the public interest (Jurriëns 2009: 35).[6]

According to the law, KPI's main task is to guarantee that Indonesian broadcast media adhere to two basic principles: diversity of ownership and diversity of content. In practice, KPI has mainly focused on the latter. This is reflected by the fact that its largest division is Tim Bidang Isi Siaran (Broadcast Content Division Team). In addition to the 24/7 monitoring of Indonesia's 11 nationwide television networks, the broadcast content team also processes suggestions and complaints by ordinary television viewers (Armando *et al.* 2012: iii). Viewers can submit their views to KPI by phone, email, Short Message Service (SMS) or Twitter (Armando *et al.* 2012: 10–21). Based on the viewers' input, KPI can issue recommendations and warnings to radio and television stations, or take administrative sanctions against them (Armando *et al.* 2012: iii). There have been cases of up to 29,000 viewers' complaints about a single television programme. In order to increase the quality of Indonesian broadcasting, KPI has also inaugurated its own Anugerah KPI (KPI Awards) and developed educational programmes for media professionals and consumers (Armando *et al.* 2012: iv, 1–2).

In 2011, KPI issued 55 sanctions against broadcasting organisations, and in 2012 the number of sanctions even increased to 100 (Armando *et al.* 2012: 4). These measures have proven far from effective, however, as broadcasting organisations tend to ignore the instructions received from KPI. For instance, when TRANS7 was urged to stop broadcasting their controversial talk show *Empat mata* ('Face to face'), they continued the same broadcast content by simply adjusting the programme title to *Bukan empat mata* ('Not face to face') (Armando *et al.* 2012: 6). In addition to conflicting or limited media legislation and disregard from media producers, KPI has also had problems with safeguarding its image, maintaining neutrality, and warding off threats from disgruntled media consumers (Armando *et al.* 2012: 3–4).

According to Nugroho *et al.* (2012: 77–78, 102), one of KPI's main weaknesses is that it focuses on media content at the expense of monitoring media ownership. They quote Indonesian media analyst Ignatius Haryanto, who blames the commission for ignoring that undesirable, market-focused media content is a product of the 'structural problem' of the concentration of ownership. According to Haryanto, what is needed to improve the Indonesian broadcasting industry is 'to first fix the structure, then contents will follow' (Nugroho *et al.* 2012: 77–78). For instance, the 2002 Broadcasting Law promotes regional diversification of television by restricting the broadcasting reach of television stations. Instead of working with regional stations as a network (*berjaringan*), in line with the Broadcasting Law (article 60), Jakarta-based stations have continued to broadcast nationally without sharing income and other resources with the regions.

Gareth Barkin (2013: 46) observed that 'the lack of cooperation from national stations has led regional television to languish in obscurity'. At the same time, the regional stations, because of their lack of resources, 'depend on information from the same national news organizations to which they are ostensibly the alternative'. Barkin (2013: 47) argued that some regional stations, like Pacific TV in Manado, North Sulawesi, did succeed in providing alternative content and securing a certain degree of independence. Ironically, due to its success, Pacific TV eventually became part of a conglomerate, namely Kompas TV. Non-commercial community television (*televisi komunitas*) stations were officially acknowledged by the 2002 Broadcasting Law, but have since struggled with resistance from the commercial sector as well as bureaucratic hurdles for receiving broadcasting licences and frequencies (Nazaruddin and Hermanto 2009).

Wardhana (2012) wondered why KPI had not imposed any financial sanctions on media institutions that ignored the official guidelines, as such sanctions would directly impact on their core business of profit-making. I believe another problem of KPI's approach to media content is that it is predominantly reactive and limited to individual cases. The four most common objections against media content published by KPI on behalf of the public are representations of sex, violence and superstitious beliefs, and lack of objectivity in news reporting (Jurriëns 2009: 37). It is unclear, however, what exactly is covered by these categories, and why or in which circumstances any of these should be objected to.

For instance, in 2012, a 'kiss on the lips' (*ciuman bibir*) and 'sexuality' (*seksualitas*) were among the most frequent 'offences' (Armando *et al.* 2012: 10). The problem is that in the KPI reporting, scenes seem to be targeted in isolation, regardless of their style or visual representation, their function in a narrative or genre, or the classification or broadcasting time of the programmes in which they appeared. This also applies to broadcasts including (non-mainstream) religion, violence and topical information, which are often rejected on the basis of stereotypical categorisations such as SARA,[7] *horror* ('horror') or *mistik* ('mystical [that is, non-mainstream] beliefs') (cf. Armando *et al.* 2012: 6). Lack of clear criteria, critical debate, and contextual and conceptual understanding has caused the continuation of stereotypes and leaves the very issue of quality control unsolved or even unaddressed. Rather than seeing Indonesian television as an environment or ecological system, KPI seems to approach it mainly as a medium or technology for conveying information and entertainment.

Conceptualising Indonesia as a world of television

In Wardhana's work, on the other hand, the idea of television is not restricted to media organisations and their programmes, but also refers to television as an environment, and Indonesia as a televised society, or a world of television in its own right. It addresses the broader Indonesian cultural ecology that shapes, and is being shaped by, media production and consumption. Wardhana (2002a) explained this idea in one of his longer essays (16 pages), 'Budaya massa, budaya televisi, (tele)vision du monde: TV or not TV …' ('Mass media, television culture, *(tele)vision du monde*: TV or not TV …'). The essay puts forward two fundamental questions that underlie Wardhana's corpus of television-related writings: one about the type of television culture that can be found in Indonesia, and the other about the way in which this culture has shaped Indonesian society (Wardhana 2002a: 15). By attempting to answer these questions, which are yet to be fully addressed by organisations like KPI, this and several of his other essays provide a useful entry-point to analysing and potentially improving the Indonesian television landscape.

Wardhana (2002c: 47) argued that a television culture had taken root in Indonesia, and that the country had been fundamentally influenced and changed by the medium. This television culture would only continue to grow in the future, to the extent that people would be left with no other choice than the neo-Shakespearean '[to be with] TV or not [to be with] TV'. This existential condition would, unavoidably, determine people's *(tele)vision du monde* or television-shaped world view. According to Wardhana (2002c: 105), Indonesians, particularly youth, had become the children of television culture (*anak-anak kebudayaan televisi*), including its celebrity culture. Television did not merely fulfil the role of occasional babysitter or nanny, but had 'taken over the role of parents in educating and developing the character of children' (Wardhana 2002c: 105).

Although television had, indeed, become a matter of 'to be or not to be', Wardhana (2002c: 30) argued that parents should not prevent children from knowing reality (*realitas*) through television. If reality or 'the facts' (*fakta*) were considered undesirable, it was the world that had to be changed, not television as such. It was better for parents not to rely on formal institutions like KPI to provide media education to their children, but to actively contribute to monitoring and improving the cultural environment in which their children were watching television (Wardhana 2002c: 30, 175). In one of his articles from the mid-1990s, Wardhana (2002c: 106–107) agreed with scientific recommendations to limit children's television consumption to a maximum of one to four hours per day, and to encourage them to also engage in other activities. He believed it was the duty of parents to decide what their children watched on television, when, and for how long (Wardhana 2002c: 29, 73). This is in line with the message of Indonesian NGOs focusing on media literacy today.

Wardhana not only conceptualised the idea of Indonesia as a world of television, but also identified the factors shaping and sustaining this world. His writings showed that certain behaviour and practices, such as the discourse used by media producers to justify the commercialisation of Indonesian television, or the emotional reactions of Indonesian viewers to television content, were not new but recurring phenomena (Wardhana 2002a: 9–10). In Wardhana's (2002a: 25) view, the lack of interest in in-depth media analysis meant that even in the early 2000s television was still very much a new phenomenon or 'baby' (*bayi*) to the Indonesian public, television producers and policy makers. Wardhana's (2002a: 14–15) own work was an effort to chronicle and analyse developments that would otherwise remain unnoticed and undocumented. His analysis was not limited to a case-by-case approach, like KPI's, but tried to identify larger issues over a longer period of time. It constituted more than a series of topical and relatively ephemeral writings on equally ephemeral issues, and is still relevant today.

The media watch and media literacy movement

Both Wardhana (2002a: 11) himself and others (Siregar 2001: xxiv; Atmowiloto 2013; Mujiarso 2013; Diani 2004) rightly saw his work as the start of an Indonesian media watch and media literacy movement. This movement consists of NGOs, which, unlike KPI, cannot take any direct administrative action against media companies. At the same time, their smaller scale or grassroots character may put them in a better position than KPI for interacting with audiences and providing education and creating debate about the quality criteria of television and other media. These organisations deserve some attention here, as they form another relevant context for critically discussing Wardhana's work.

Roughly, media watch organisations focus on media producers, while media literacy organisations deal with media consumers (Rianto 2013b: 24, 181). In practice, the first is strongly related to the analysis and regulation of media companies and their products, while the second has a stronger commitment to the education of media audiences. Media literacy organisations seek to train media consumers to actively find, sort and analyse media information, and use this information in a way that is beneficial to their own lives (Hendriyani and Guntarto 2011: 10; Rianto 2013b: 15, 2013a: 201). Ideally, they base their pedagogical methods on the composition and media needs of the communities they work with (Rianto 2013b: 186). Media watch organisations focus on media research rather than pedagogy.

Yayasan Pengembangan Media Anak (Foundation for the Development of Children's Media, YPMA), established in 2004, is one of the pioneering organisations promoting media literacy in Indonesia (Jurriëns 2011). It was founded by people previously involved in Yayasan Kesejahteraan Anak Indonesia (Indonesian Child Welfare Foundation, YKAI), which in the early 1990s already had programmes focusing on media and children (Hendriyani and Guntarto 2011: 4; Rianto 2013a: 193). YPMA's partners include KPI, Komisi Perlindungan Anak Indonesia (Indonesian Commission for the Protection of Children, KPAI), Kementrian Komunikasi dan Informatika (Department of Communication and

Informatics), and several other state departments, NGOs, media organisations and tertiary education institutions (*Kidia* 2010c).

In recent years, the media literacy movement has considerably expanded. For instance, the Jakarta-based NGO Tifa Foundation alone sponsors eight organisations providing media literacy training on three different islands (Java, Sumatra and Sulawesi), including Kajian Informasi, Pendidikan dan Penerbitan Sumatra (Sumatran Information, Education and Publishing Studies, KIPPAS) in Medan, Yayasan Sahabat Cahaya (The Friends of the Light Foundation) and Remotivi in Jakarta, Lembaga Studi Pers dan Informasi (The Press and Information Study Institute, LeSPI) in Semarang, Jurnal Celebes (Celebes Journal) in Makassar, and Masyarakat Peduli Media (Media Interest Society, MPM), Early Childhood Care and Development-Resource Center (ECCD-RC), and Centre for Learning and Advancing Experimental Democracy (LEAD) in Yogyakarta (Poerwaningtias 2013: 3). According to Hendiyani and Guntarto (2011: 11–12), the broader field includes at least five different types of actors: NGOs and foundations, schools, universities, community groups, and government and other national and international organisations. To this list I add the often ignored group of creative actors, including media producers, artists, and writers like Wardhana.

One important aspect of the media literacy movement is the exploration of the idea of 'qualitative rating'. YPMA in particular presents itself as an institute that uses qualitative rating (*rating kualitatif*) for the collection and analysis of information about the media (Jurriëns 2011). This qualitative rating is meant as both a complement and alternative to the activities of organisations such as Nielsen Audience Measurement,[8] which are mainly concerned with collecting quantitative data about broadcasting institutions, genres and audience behaviour on behalf of the media industry. YPMA, on the other hand, attempts to raise media awareness in Indonesian society with a specific focus on media that are directed at or enjoyed by children and young adults, such as television, magazines, video games and mobile phones (*Kidia* 2010a).

Since 2004, YPMA has developed its own 'Kritis! Media untuk anak' ('Critical! Media for children' or 'Kidia') media awareness campaign for children, parents, teachers, government institutions, advertisers, advertising agencies and media organisations (*Kidia* 2010d). This campaign is meant to 'raise the critical awareness of children and parents' as well as to 'push for media policy changes that take the interests of children more into account' (*Kidia* 2010a). According to YPMA, a critical media attitude enables people to restrict their hours of media consumption, to better choose and understand media content, and to take personal benefit from media consumption (*Kidia* 2010b). Two of YPMA's main activities to reach the general public and achieve its campaign goals are the publication of the bimonthly media analysis journal *Kidia*, and the organisation of the annual media awareness event 'Hari Tanpa TV' ('Day without TV', HTT).

Kidia is a richly illustrated journal, which analyses television programmes and, since the twelfth edition (January–March 2008), has included other contemporary media that are relevant to Indonesian children and young adults, such as video games, magazines, books, films on Digital Versatile Disc (DVD) and

Video Compact Disc (VCD), Internet sites and mobile phone applications. The first two pages of the magazine contain an editorial and letters with comments and suggestions from readers, often concerned parents (predominantly mothers) or people who work professionally with children such as teachers. Each edition also has up to ten short articles on specific television programmes and other media products, and several longer articles on more general media-related issues, for instance bullying practices that are represented or instigated in the media.

In its analyses of specific media products, the journal distinguishes between three different media categories: (a) media that are 'safe' (*aman*) for children; (b) media with which children have to 'be careful' (*hati-hati*); and (c) media that are 'dangerous' (*bahaya*) for children. This form of categorisation is far from objective and contains some highly problematic criteria, similar to those used by KPI. The concept of 'superstitious beliefs' or *mistik*, for instance, in practice often means anything that goes against mainstream religious doctrine.[9] Nevertheless, *Kidia*'s classification should not be dismissed as just another example of elite judgement about media content and consumer behaviour.

First, YPMA, although embedded in a culture of 'high' national and international organisational forms, does not have strong preconceptions about 'low' television and its genres and impact on people. It promotes educational activities that *make* people think about the content of the medium and their own attitudes and behaviour as viewers. Second, *Kidia* provides relatively balanced evaluations rather than black-and-white pictures of specific media products. Controversial themes such as violence, sexuality and superstitious beliefs are accepted as long as their contributions to the main narrative can be demonstrated. Third, *Kidia* makes its own, subjective judgements, but also accepts that audiences make their own interpretations of media messages. *Kidia* advises parents to co-view certain media content with their children and to keep their children away from other media products, but has never called for a specific media product to be banned by the government or any other interested party. Fourth, if the role of parents and educators is generally accepted as a constitutive part of children's upbringing and socialisation into the world, it would be fallacious to assume that an organisation such as YPMA, comprising mainly parents and teachers, would be unable to provide a useful contribution to the media education of the younger generation. YPMA does not work in isolation either, but engages in dialogue and shares its findings with many other organisations, groups and individuals in society.

Apart from its journal, YPMA also has other ways to communicate with the Indonesian public, such as research projects, seminars and street rallies. The activity that gives YPMA most public exposure is HTT, which tries to raise critical awareness about media consumption by urging Indonesian families and individuals to abstain from watching television for a whole day (*Kidia* 2009). HTT has been an annual event since 2006, and consists of several days of press conferences, street marches, seminars and children's activities in various Indonesian cities. The events are specifically meant to encourage pre-school and primary school children to reduce television consumption, to be selective with programmes, and to engage more in other social activities.

The main demonstrations at the busy Hotel Indonesia roundabout in central Jakarta attract the participation of an average of 60 to 90 school children, university students, and representatives of NGOs and other organisations. Amongst the slow and heavy traffic, the participants usually display banners, stage short performances, and distribute flyers, stickers and posters, to attract media attention and inform the public about the impact of television and the purpose of HTT. Children's activities meant as alternatives to watching television, such as reading, drawing, dancing and singing, are also organised at public and symbolic places such as Medan Merdeka (Freedom Square) and Monumen Nasional (National Monument, Monas) in Jakarta. Every year, the organisers receive hundreds of messages of support via SMS, email and Facebook (*Kidia* 2009).

In 2009, the steering committee consisted of Bobi Guntarto (YPMA), Hendriyani (Faculty of Social and Political Sciences, Universitas Indonesia, Jakarta), Dr Sudjatmiko (Ikatan Dokter Anak Indonesia, Indonesian Association of Paediatricians), Tatty Elmir (Forum Indonesia Muda, Forum of Young Indonesians) and Santi Indra Astuti (Bascomms). The organisers had the ambitious goal of attracting the participation of approximately a million Indonesian households and of making a clear statement to the media industry that certain television offerings were not acceptable to a large part of Indonesian society (*Kidia* 2009). They emphasised that they were not anti-television, but attempting to raise awareness about the medium and its impact on television viewers (*Kidia* 2009). They specifically referred to the case of a 9-year-old boy in Bandung, who died in November 2006 after imitating fighting scenes from *SmackDown*, a US wrestling show broadcast on Indonesian commercial television. This case received attention in the national press for several days, but was only one in a series of fatal or near-fatal accidents related to violent television content.

Through the 'Day without TV' and its other activities, YPMA and its counterparts attempt to inform parents and their children that there are certain 'rules' (*aturan*) for media consumption (*Kidia* 2009). These could be seen as a translation on a micro-level of Silverstone's (2007: 176–177, 180) idea of a 'Kyoto for the media'. The rules are about the types of media children have access to, at what times, and for how long. YPMA argues that television, as the main source of family entertainment, is often consumed indiscriminately for many hours a day due to a lack of a 'healthy television watching routine' (*Kidia* 2009). The organisation also notices that broadcasting regulations and their implementation are still weak in Indonesia. According to YPMA, the key to developing a critical television culture in Indonesia is media education (*pendidikan media*), which should be provided to children by their parents at home and their teachers at school (*Kidia* 2009).

Creatively reworking the medium

According to Puji Rianto (2013a: 200–201, 205), Director of the Yogyakarta-based Pusat Kajian Media dan Budaya Populer (Centre for Media and Popular Culture Studies, PKMBP), media literacy should not be restricted to the analysis of media content, but also include critical perspectives on the political economy of the media, particularly the interaction between media, politics and business. Organisations like Remotivi also acknowledge that both fields are interlinked and should be addressed simultaneously (Rianto 2013b: 57). I agree that an approach that separates media watch from media literacy, and focuses on individual categories and cases, is too narrow and rigid. It may lose sight of the broader structures of the Indonesian media industry as well as the dynamic and interrelated nature of media production, distribution and consumption cultures.

As mentioned in Chapter 2, Silverstone (2007: 176–177, 180) pleaded for 'environmental standards of media practice' to tackle problems of cultural pollution and moral degradation. These environmental standards, involving media regulation as well as the promotion of media literacy, should contribute to the strengthening of a 'media civics' and appeal to a sense of moral responsibility of both media producers and media consumers. In the Indonesian case, however, the examples of KPI and the various NGOs show that regulation does not sufficiently cover issues of media ownership, while the promotion of media literacy is not necessarily interlinked with the critical observation of media organisations.

The Tifa research team also identified three practical problems faced by Indonesian media literacy organisations. First, their programmes tend to focus on the transfer of knowledge about the media, but have difficulty in triggering genuine concern about media-related issues, and are even less successful in changing media consumption behaviour. Second, they suffer from a lack of resources. Third, their funding depends largely on donor organisations (Rianto 2013b: 183–185).

It is important to acknowledge the role of creative actors like Wardhana in the context of media quality control, precisely because of their potential to engage with the media and audiences in innovative and alluring ways. Normally, they also create some artistic and critical distance from their funding sources. In addition, some of these actors use a more comprehensive approach to the media, by exploring them as cultural environments rather than mere technological tools, institutional forms or genre types. Their approach cannot be explained in terms of media watch or media literacy only, but come closer to Guattari's (1989: 136, 140–141) idea of 'dissident vectors of subjectification'.

By trying to uncover the underlying structures and recurring issues in the Indonesian media world, Wardhana's work demonstrates a media ecological desire to 'learn about that which is unknown' (Postman 1970: 164). Postman (1970: 168) also argued that media ecology does not necessarily need to take the form of text in order to facilitate the production of imaginative ideas about the present and the future, but may also, and perhaps preferably, be presented in other forms, such as art. Wardhana's own work is not in the form of conventional texts either, but presents an innovative form of intermediality. His writings were partially inspired by the conventions of television programmes, and reversed the traditional hierarchy of script and visual output as known from the film and television industry. His readers were encouraged not to ignore or be overwhelmed by television, but to creatively use and manipulate the medium for their own benefit. While KPI and the media watch and media literacy NGOs have, each in their own right, delivered important contributions to monitoring and criticising Indonesian television, Wardhana is different in also using experimental writing to creatively engage with and reflect on the medium.

Two of Wardhana's signature style devices were the use of wordplay and humour. The titles of his essays often contained a play on existing abbreviations and acronyms, or a humorous combination of Indonesian and English words. Examples include 'TVRI(S) dan TV(S)RI: TVRI Swasta atau Televisi Sangat Rindu Iklan' (Wardhana 1997a: 10), 'SCTV atawa Saluran Cerita Telenovela' (Wardhana 1997a: 23) and, of course, 'The show must bloon' (Wardhana 2002c: 87). The first two puns translate as 'TVRI(S) and TV(S)RI: Commercial TVRI or Television That Longs For Advertisements', 'SCTV or the Telenovela Stories Channel', respectively. The first pun referred to the banning of advertising on state television from the early 1980s until the late 1990s; the second pun to the popularity of imported soap operas on commercial television in the 1990s. The essays were usually concluded with equally engaging and humorous statements or questions. They were meant to make the readers think for themselves, and to encourage them to continue reading Wardhana's essays, not unlike cliff hangers in a television series that encourage audiences to continue watching a sequence of episodes.

It is fruitful to compare Wardhana's approach with that of his contemporary, colleague and prolific essayist, Goenawan Mohamad (b. 1941), who is known for his *Catatan pinggir* ('Sidelines') columns in the *Tempo* magazine. Mohamad and Wardhana were both involved in *Tempo Interaktif*, when the print version of the magazine was officially banned. While Mohamad (2002: viii) sought 'recourse to the realm of images or to poetry and its ambiguities' in his fight 'against the acronym-studded columns of bureaucratese that made New Order Indonesia', Wardhana stretched the New Order language to its limits, thus showing its ridicule while simultaneously making it suitable for humorous, creative and critical re-use.

One aspect of Indonesian television entertainment in which Wardhana had a special interest was celebrity culture. His main work to address how celebrity culture had entered Indonesian life and shaped contemporary Indonesian ways of being, including notions of gender and sexuality was the novel *Stamboel Selebritas* (2004b). This novel can be considered the first Indonesian literary work that had television culture as its main topic. It was also Wardhana's only writing in which he used fiction to discuss the cultural condition of Indonesia as a televised society. The novel reflected on television not only through its content, but also through its structure.

The celebrity spectacle

Stamboel Selebritas (2004b) was originally meant as a novel. However, when Wardhana (2004b: 538–539, 542) received an offer to have it published as a serial in *Media Indonesia*, he revised the structure of his manuscript in accordance with the format of the newspaper. In this way, he established a link between his creative work and a long tradition of Indonesian 'newspaper literature' (*sastra koran*; Lindsay 1998: 130–131), which has a degree of accessibility similar to other creative media, including television shows.

Wardhana (2004b: 539) tried to give each episode of his story a 'cliff-hanger', modelled on the structure of soap operas, to encourage readers to wait for, and then continue reading, the next newspaper edition. He approached the time-lag between two consecutive episodes as if it was a commercial break in the middle of a television programme. He also compared the newspaper instalments of his story with the individual broadcasts that make up a television serial, while he thought of his novel as a whole in terms of a relatively uninterrupted film on DVD or VCD (Wardhana 2004b: 542).

The reworking of the newspaper serial back into a novel forced Wardhana (2004b: 543) to make some new adjustments to his writing. Similar to soap opera and *sinetron*, this novel of more than 500 pages seems to meander and expand endlessly, without ever reaching closure. That is perhaps the reason the novel never received a literary review. However, the experience of reading the novel should be seen as watching and skipping parts of a soap opera, without adhering strictly to a defined collection of episodes in a specified order. It allows readers to enter and exit the story at relatively random points, or even skip certain parts of it, without losing the main thread of the narrative. In that sense, the novel offers a form of intermediality, reversing the hierarchy of writing and audio-visual communication, as the written script was not the basis, but the outcome of audio-visual culture.

In the title, the neologism *selebritas*[10] is combined with an older word, *stamboel*. I translate *stamboel* as 'spectacle' here, as it resonates with what the French philosopher and filmmaker Guy Debord (1994) calls a 'society of the spectacle', or a world where social relations between people are mediated by images. The historical *stamboel* was a performing arts genre, in which a travelling troupe of artists told a story over several consecutive nights. This genre was popular in the Dutch East Indies in the late nineteenth and early twentieth centuries (Cohen 2006). The artists in Wardhana's home region of East Java often performed stories from the *One thousand and one nights* epic in Malay to the accompaniment of Middle Eastern music (Wardhana 2004b: 540). Wardhana (2004b: 543) explained that the global glamour of contemporary celebrities shared characteristics with the cosmopolitan character of the historical *stamboel* touring group.[11] Similar to some of the most famous *stamboel* performers, many modern Indonesian film and television stars have an Indo-European background; are married to foreigners; seem to stand above the masses; make headlines because of their supposedly promiscuous behaviour; and wander around in society with much fanfare.

In his short guide to the novel, Wardhana (2004b: 543) explained with typical irony that he wanted to explore the inner world and character of celebrities, without turning them into cult figures. The novel played on the names and lives of real-life celebrities. For instance, Raiyya Rayhan was modelled on the

Indonesian female actor Ria Irawan, Harry Harsugitomo Tamtomo on Hutomo Mandala Putra ('Tommy Suharto'), criminal convict and the youngest son of former president Suharto, and Mintutilun on the female *dangdut* singer Inul. Wardhana (2004b: 543) added a list to his novel, giving the names of the main characters, because he often 'forgot' or 'interchanged' them while writing the story. This was an ironic reference to the ephemerality and interchangeability of celebrities in contemporary media and consumer society. The novel performs and reiterates the spectacle of a televised society, rather than merely recounting it.

The novel starts with the story of the discovery of the dead body of Ardisoma Sunarkaputra, or Ardy, in the house of his former lover Raiyya Rayhan. Ardy died because of an overdose of *shabu* or methamphetamine. This was based on the real-life story of Rivaldi Sukarno, who was found dead because of an overdose of drugs in Ria Irawan's home in Jakarta in 1993. By tracing the lives of other artists that are directly or indirectly connected to Raiyya, the novel uncovers the politics and mechanisms of the Indonesian news and entertainment industry. In addressing and criticising aspects of both media production and media consumption, it constitutes an important documentation of a specific, media-dominated time in Indonesia's history.

Some of the most hilarious scenes in the novel centre on the character of Pri. Pri is presented as a prototype celebrity, as someone who is known for being known and not necessarily for being a star (*bintang*) in something.[12] Pri uses both her oratorical and sexual talents to convince media personnel to destroy Raiyya and strengthen her own position in the show business. One of the central scenes in the novel is about Pri organising a huge media event for herself, in which numerous television representatives and celebrities participate without prior knowledge about the purpose of the event. Pri is granted a live interview with one of the television stations, which, in a pun on the abundance of hollow talk in Indonesian infotainment shows, goes on for hours but fails to disclose any relevant information about Pri's background or the purpose of her function (Wardhana 2004b: 173–197).

Apart from engaging with the production side of television, the novel also addresses the rights and responsibilities of media consumers. Reiterating some of the key points in Wardhana's essays on television, Raiyya mentions that newspaper readers and television viewers do not always realise that what is presented as fact or reality (*kenyataan*) in the media is often merely based on the unchecked, personal statements from informants (Wardhana 2004b: 86). According to some of the journalists in the story, media consumers are oversensitive and tend to react aggressively if they disagree with media content, such as nudity (Wardhana 2004b: 35–38). In the novel, mention is made of the real case of Atmowiloto, Wardhana's former editor-in-chief at *Monitor*, who received death threats and was imprisoned for five years because of a popularity poll he ran in his tabloid (Wardhana 2004b: 39). In the poll, the Prophet Muhammad came out as less popular than Indonesian political figures and celebrities, including Suharto and Atmowiloto himself (Aspinall 2005: 134).

The final part of the novel pays attention to the notorious case of *dangdut* performer Inul, who is represented by the character of Mintutilun. Inul caused a lot of heated debate in Indonesia in the early to mid-2000s because of the supposedly sexually suggestive character of her dance moves. Her case was used in arguments in favour and against the introduction of the Indonesian (anti-) Pornography Bill. This bill was eventually ratified in 2008 (Heryanto 2008b; Lindsay 2011: 183).

The narrator makes the plausible but rarely publicised point that the debate around Inul had less to do with issues of religion and morality (Heryanto 2008b: 20) than with the business interests of commercial television stations (Wardhana 2004b: 499–507). He argues that the success of CSTV (a pun on the Indonesian commercial television station SCTV) in attracting advertisers with Inul broadcasts was a source of frustration for the other commercial television stations. To destroy the success of their competitor and safeguard their own businesses, the other stations decided to broadcast negative comments on Inul and urge viewers to boycott and protest television programmes and performances in which the controversial artist appeared. Referring to the blurred line between news and entertainment in contemporary Indonesian television, the narrator reports that items about Inul were ideally situated to cross the boundaries between the two genres (Wardhana 2004b: 500). He also makes the important observation that the majority of Indonesian television viewers ignored the call by the powerful media to reject Inul.

Conclusion

With his writings, media appearances and other engagement activities, Wardhana delivered an invaluable contribution to teaching Indonesians how their new media environment, dominated by television and increasingly also by other technology such as mobile phones and the Internet, functions and shapes their daily lives. His work complements the activities of KPI and related NGOs, which each have their own merits as well as problems. What is offered by creative actors like Wardhana, and often missing in the activities of the organisations mentioned, is a broader conceptualisation of the Indonesian television world, the identification of television-related issues recurring throughout history, and creative engagements with, and alternatives to, the medium of television.

At the same time, what also needs to be critically examined is whether Wardhana's oeuvre displays, or even promotes, some of the same features of the Indonesian media that it criticises. To what extent has it been able to radically change the television industry, and go beyond the culture of Jakarta-based, middle-class television producers and consumers, including its clichés relating to issues such as sexuality? One way to put his work into perspective is by following the critical distinction between media watch and media literacy made by Indonesian television observers themselves. It is clear that Wardhana did not provide media literacy training to local communities in a direct manner. The audience he had in mind for his writings was also not based on socio-demographic research of its composition or media needs. Because of these circumstances, his analysis may have missed out on important media and social developments in Indonesia's regional areas.[13] Wardhana was firmly based in Jakarta, where he monitored national television developments with an imagined middle-class, nation-wide audience in mind.

However, his self-positioning also had clear advantages. Being based in Jakarta, and with his background in journalism, he had the opportunity to be in direct touch with the centre of Indonesia's media, entertainment and advertising industry. It enabled him to critically comment on the political economy of the Indonesian television industry, which is an aspect of the Indonesian media that is often left out in media literacy training programmes. This means that Wardhana's writings and other activities, although closer to the media watch principles, are far from irrelevant to the Indonesian media literacy movement.

Wardhana's novel may also be criticised for exploiting sensationalist elements from the television world, as it presents numerous and lengthy sex scenes. At the same time, however, these scenes seem to be deliberately and strategically overdone. Wardhana may have included them to make a stand against the commotion about the proposed pornography bill, and the banning or distorted representations of sexuality on Indonesian television. The scenes are not conventional depictions of sexuality, but full of humorous metaphors and statements that have a provocative quality in Indonesia's legal and social contexts. For instance, they are not restricted to heteronormative sex, but also depict lesbian and gay couples. At one point it is mentioned that Pri, who is portrayed as a woman of unconventional female sexual aggression herself, 'respects' queer people, because they 'want to be honest about the choices of their heart' (Wardhana 2004b: 345).

In several of his essays, Wardhana (2002c: 426, 432, 474) also regretted that in debates about gender and sexuality no clear distinctions were made between (the art of) eroticism (*erotisme/erotikagrafi*) and the representation of obscenity (*cabulisme/cabulografi*). Instead, 'pornografi' was often used by politicians as an argument to exercise censorship and restrict the freedom of the media. According to Wardhana (2002c: 426–428), there was no direct connection between media freedom and an increase in pornographic images in the print and broadcast media. Some media with relatively mild content, including his own *Citra* magazine in 1991, had been subject to scrutiny or challenged in court, while blatantly vulgar and exploitative media had been circulating without any difficulties (Wardhana 2002c: 426, 431). Even during the strong media repression of the Suharto regime, magazines, videos and other media displaying nudity and sexuality were relatively easy to access (Sen 1994: 154–155). Wardhana, on the other hand, presented the human body, especially the celebrity body, as the interface of struggles between mental and social ecologies, including the exploitation of women. For some of the characters in his novel, the body also functioned as a site for exploring new forms of creativity, dissonance and subjectivity in response to the overwhelming power of the mass media.

The third critical question relates to what extent creative actors like Wardhana can make more immediate changes to the television industry. The media industry has great economic and political power, and it is unlikely that its actors will change their behaviour and practices in the short run. The government and KPI have regulatory power, but are also struggling to effectively implement legal tools like the 2002 Broadcasting Law. Creative actors like Wardhana are void of any regulatory power, but their strength lies in addressing the consumption side of the media, and teaching television viewers about the interconnections between media ownership and media content as well as the wider ecology of the Indonesian media. If television consumers decide to follow the example of cultural activists such as television critics, video artists and community media groups, and subsequently change their viewing behaviour or even create their own media products, it would certainly affect the television establishment.

Although Wardhana had a reasonable outreach through his newspaper publications and media appearances, his efforts and those of some of his colleagues would have a much bigger impact on future generations of television viewers and critics if they were used as a resource in Media and Cultural Studies courses at schools and universities. Unfortunately, the Indonesian education system is struggling with a gap in Media and Cultural Studies curriculums and departments. Programmes and subjects focusing on the media normally use a practical, Communications-oriented method, and often lack theoretical and historical approaches to media and culture (Heryanto 2005: 6–7). This is partially due to a lack of time for research by Indonesian academics, who are often burdened by many administrative and non-scholarly obligations. Many of them are exemplary in showing their social commitment, including promoting media literacy among local communities, which sometimes comes at the cost of their own academic career.

Postman's (1970) suggestions for the inquiries and projects of 'the high school group of the future' resonate with the ideas and activities of Indonesian creative actors involved in monitoring the media and spreading media literacy, including Wardhana and the various video art and community television practitioners discussed in this book. Considering that the availability of suitable textbooks in Indonesian is an issue teachers and lecturers are struggling with, the work of these creative actors can constitute an accessible and attractive resource for introducing Indonesian students to critical perspectives in Media and Cultural Studies, making them rethink and reshape the media environments with which they are surrounded.

Notes

1 Veven is based on Effendy. The middle initials of his pseudonym refer to the names of his father (Soesanto) and mother (Piani). Wardhana may refer to Wikrama Wardhana, who was king of the historical Madjapahit kingdom from AD 1389 to 1429. The centre of this kingdom was located in today's East Java, the province where Wardhana was born. I wish to thank Wardhana's wife, Thereskova Koraag, and his fellow author and friend, Seno Gumira Ajidarma, for this information (personal e-mail communications, 24 August and 11 September 2014, respectively).

2 This short biography is primarily based on Taman Ismail Marzuki (2013) and the biographical information in Wardhana's published books.

3 According to Paul Tickell (2009: 280), the importance of Wardhana's collection of short stories *Panggil aku Pheng Hwa* ('Call me Pheng Hwa', 2002d) was that it explored the interconnections between naming, absence, identity, place, arbitrary authority, violence, personal uncertainty and insecurity from the perspective of the Indonesian Chinese minority during the New Order. See also Allen (2003: 67, 71) and Heryanto (2008a: 75).

4 During the late New Order, PDI and its leader Megawati Soekarnoputri were an important part of the growing opposition movement against Suharto (Vickers 2005: 202). From 20–22 June 1996, a congress was organised in Medan by government-supported members of the party, who, in an attempt to break with Megawati, declared themselves the only legitimate PDI. On 27 July, supporters of this initiative, protected and assisted by thugs, the military and police, used physical violence to claim the party head office in Jakarta and oust the party members loyal to Megawati (Wardhana 1997b: 18–24; see also Vickers 2005: 202).

5 For instance, the TVRI hosts would mention that protesters were attacking the police, whereas the visuals, in fact, showed the reverse (Wardhana 1997b: 40).

6 The 2002 Broadcasting Law and several of its by-laws, especially the 2005 Peraturan Pemerintah (Government Regulations) 49 to 52, were ambiguous, however, in stating that 'the state' (*negara*) was responsible for issuing broadcasting licenses. According to KPI, 'the state' here referred to KPI, while the Susilo Bambang Yudhono government (2004–14) believed that broadcasting licenses were the responsibility of the Minister of Communications and Informatics (Jurriëns 2009: 34). This ambiguity restricted the mandate of KPI.

7 SARA stands for restrictions on media representations of *suku* (ethnicity), *agama* (religion), *ras* (race) and *antar-golongan* (intergroup relations, relating to class or ideology). These restrictions are a legacy of the New Order regime, which implemented SARA to 'limit news reporting of ethno-religious tensions and control the public interpretation of all socio-political conflicts, to exclude (as in the case of the Chinese) and to restrict languages used in the media in various ways' (Sen and Hill 2000: 12).

8 Nielsen Audience Measurement is an international company that collects quantitative audience data on behalf of the television industry. The Indonesian branch publishes monthly newsletters that contain short opinion pieces on Indonesian television by the company's own data analysts as well as independent academics.

9 Unfortunately, the highly politicised and legal debates around the Anti-Pornography Law since 2002 (Lindsay 2011) have obscured and hampered a more nuanced and open public debate on pressing contemporary issues such as the ethics of the media. So far, YPMA has operated outside the realm of practical politics, and tries to achieve cultural change by appealing to people's individual sense of responsibility.

10 For the title of his novel, Wardhana used *selebritas* instead of the more common Indonesian word *selebriti* in order to refer to 'celebrities' or famous people. He believed *selebritas* was more consistent with Indonesian words of similar English derivation, such as *komunitas* (from 'community'), *komoditas* ('commodity') and *seksualitas* ('sexuality'; see also Coutas 2008: 113).

11 Perhaps to give expression to *tempo doeloe*, or nostalgia for the time in which *stamboel* was performed, Wardhana (2004b: 541) used the style of the pre-1972 official Indonesian spelling reform ('oe' instead of modern-day 'u'). The use of mixed spelling in the title may also signal a continuation between past and present social phenomena and refer to the 'otherworldliness' of present-day celebrities.

12 See Coutas 2008 for a critical discussion of the differences between *bintang*, *selebritas* and *Idola*. The third concept refers to the contestants ('Idols') in talent shows, who derive their stardom partially from their own qualities as performers and partially from the media marketing mechanisms for producing celebrities.

13 Academic publications that have focused on television programmes on regional culture include Hendrawan (2015), Barkin (2013), Loven (2008), Jurriëns (2004), Mrázek (2002) and Hobart (2002).

References

Allen, Pamela. 2003. 'Contemporary literature from the Chinese "diaspora" in Indonesia'. *Asian Ethnicity* 4(3): 383–401.

Andarnuswari, Ninus D. 2013. 'Malam kenangan untuk Veven Sp. Wardhana' [A night of remembrance for Veven Sp. Wardhana]. *Alinea TV*, 24 May. Available at: http://alineatv.com/2013/05/24/malam-kenangan-untuk-veven-sp-wardhana/#sthash.JRN-LAAhs.dpbs (accessed 17 October 2013).

Armando, Nina Mutmainnah, Hiski Darmayana, Fredy Wansyah Putra, Ardinanda Sinulingga and Ezki Tri Rezeki Widianti. 2012. *Demi frekuensi milik publik* [For the sake of frequencies owned by the public]. Jakarta: Komisi Penyiaran Indonesia Pusat Bidang Isi Siaran.

Aspinall, Edward. 2005. *Opposing Suharto: compromise, resistance, and regime change in Indonesia*. Stanford, CA: Stanford University Press.

Atmowiloto, Arswendo. 1986. *Telaah tentang televisi* [A research about television]. Jakarta: Gramedia.

Atmowiloto, Arswendo. 2013. 'Veven: generasi haus budaya' [Veven: the generation thirsty for culture]. *Kompas.com*, 20 May. Available at: http://oase.kompas.com/read/2013/05/20/22014665/Veven.Generasi.Haus.Budaya (accessed 27 August 2014).

Barkin, Gareth. 2013. 'Reterritorialization in the micromediascape: Indonesian regional television amidst the rise of normative media-Islam'. *Visual Anthropology Review* 29(1): 42–56.

Cohen, Matthew. 2006. *The Komedie Stamboel: popular theater in colonial Indonesia, 1891–1903*. Athens, OH: Ohio University Press.

Coutas, Penelope. 2008. 'Fame, fortune, *Fantasi*: *Indonesian Idol* and the new celebrity'. In: Ariel Heryanto (ed.), *Popular culture in Indonesia: fluid identities in post-authoritarian politics*. London and New York: Routledge, pp. 111–129.

Debord, Guy. 1994. *The society of the spectacle*, translated by Donald Nicholson-Smith. New York: Zone Books.

Diani, Hera. 2004. 'In the media glare with observer Veven'. *The Jakarta Post*, 24 October. Available at: http://m.thejakartapost.com/news/2004/10/24/media-glare-observer-veven.html (accessed 27 August 2014).

Guattari, Félix. 1989. 'The three ecologies', translated by Chris Turner. *New Formations* 8 (Summer): 131–147.

Hendrawan, Bram. 2015. *Televising locality: industrial, historical and socio-cultural investigations of local television in post-authoritarian Indonesia*. PhD thesis, Universiteit Utrecht.

Hendriyani and B. Guntarto. 2011. 'Defining media literacy in Indonesia'. Paper presented at the International Association for Media and Communication Research Conference, Kadir Has University, Istanbul, 13–17 July.

Heryanto, Ariel. 2005. 'Cultural studies' significant others: the case of Indonesia'. *Antropologi Indonesia* 29(1): 1–15.

Heryanto, Ariel. 2008a. 'Citizenship and Indonesian ethnic Chinese in post-1998 films'. In: Ariel Heryanto (ed.), *Popular culture in Indonesia: fluid identities in post-authoritarian politics*. London and New York: Routledge, pp. 70–92.

Heryanto, Ariel. 2008b. 'Pop culture and competing identities'. In: Ariel Heryanto (ed.), *Popular culture in Indonesia: fluid identities in post-authoritarian politics*. London and New York: Routledge, pp. 1–36.

Hobart, Mark. 2002. 'Live or dead? Televising theatre in Bali'. In: Faye Ginsburg, Lila Abu-Lughod and Brian Larkin (eds), *Media worlds: anthropology on new terrain*. Berkeley, Los Angeles and London: University of California Press, pp. 370–382.

Hobart, Mark. 2008. 'Entertaining illusions: how Indonesian elites imagine reality TV affects the masses'. In: Mark Hobart and Richard Fox (eds), *Entertainment media in Indonesia*. London: Routledge, pp. 42–59.

Ibrahim, Idi Subandy (ed.). 1997. *Ecstasy gaya hidup: kebudayaan pop dalam masyarakat komoditas Indonesia* [The ecstasy of lifestyle: pop culture in the Indonesian commodity society]. Bandung: Mizan.

Ida, Rachmah. 2011. 'Reorganisation of media power in post-authoritarian Indonesia: ownership, power and influence of local media entrepreneurs'. In: Krishna Sen and David T. Hill (eds), *Politics and the media in twenty-first century Indonesia: decade of democracy*. London and New York: Routledge, pp. 13–25.

Jurriëns, Edwin. 2004. *Cultural travel and migrancy: the artistic representation of globalization in the electronic media of West Java*. Leiden: KITLV Press.

Jurriëns, Edwin. 2009. *From monologue to dialogue: radio and reform in Indonesia*. Leiden: KITLV Press.

Jurriëns, Edwin. 2011. 'A call for media ecology: the study of Indonesian popular culture revisited'. *Indonesia and the Malay World* 39(114): 197–219.

Jurriëns, Edwin. 2016. '"TV or not TV": spelling the Indonesian media with Veven Sp. Wardhana'. *Bijdragen tot de Taal-, Land- en Volkenkunde* 172(1): 33–65.

Kidia. 2009. 'Info lengkap Hari Tanpa TV [Comprehensive information on the Day Without TV], Week of 26 July 2009'. Available at: www.kidia.org/tahun/2009/bulan/07/tanggal/01/id/114 (accessed 19 April 2010).

Kidia. 2010a. 'Kegiatan utama' [Main activity]. Available at: www.kidia.org/profile/4/ (accessed 19 April 2010).

Kidia. 2010b. 'Kritis! Media untuk anak ("Kidia")' [Kritis! Media for children ("Kidia")]. Available at: www.kidia.org/profile/3/ (accessed 19 April 2010).

Kidia. 2010c. 'Latar belakang' [Background]. Available at: www.kidia.org/profile/1/ (accessed 19 April 2010).

Kidia. 2010d. 'Mitra kerja' [Working partners]. Available at: www.kidia.org/profile/7/ (accessed 19 April 2010).

Kitley, Philip. 2000. *Television, nation, and culture in Indonesia*. Research in International Studies. Southeast Asia Series 104. Athens, OH: Ohio University Center for International Studies.

Lindsay, Jennifer. 1998. 'Essays'. In: John H. McGlynn (ed.), *Indonesian heritage 10: language and literature*. Singapore: Archipelago Press, pp. 130–131.

Lindsay, Jennifer. 2011. 'Media and morality: pornography post Suharto'. In: Krishna Sen and David T. Hill (eds), *Politics and the media in twenty-first century Indonesia: decade of democracy*. London and New York: Routledge, pp. 172–195.

Loven, Klarijn. 2008. *Watching Si Doel: television, language, and cultural identity in contemporary Indonesia*. Leiden: KITLV Press.

Mohamad, Goenawan. 2002. 'Foreword'. In: Goenawan Mohamad, *Conversations with difference: essays from Tempo magazine*, translated by Jennifer Lindsay. Jakarta: Tempo Inti Media, pp. vii–ix.

Mrázek, Jan. 2002. 'To be or not to be there: watching theatrical performances on television'. In: Jan Mrázek (ed.), *Puppet theatre in contemporary Indonesia: new approaches to performance events*. Ann Arbor, MI: University of Michigan, Center for South and Southeast Asian Studies, pp. 330–361.

Mujiarso, Is. 2013. 'Sastrawan Veven Sp Wardhana meninggal dunia' [Literary author Veven Sp Wardhana has passed away]. *Detikcom*, 17 Mei. Available at: http://hot.detik.com/art/2248797/sastrawan-veven-sp-wardhana-meninggal-dunia (accessed 17 June 2016).

Nazaruddin, Muzayin and Budhi Hermanto (eds). 2009. *Televisi komunitas: pemberdayaan dan media literasi* [Community television: empowerment and media literacy]. Jakarta: Ford Foundation, Combine Resource Institution, Program Studi Ilmu Komunikasi FPSB UII and Fakultas Film dan Televisi IKJ.

Nugroho, Garin. 2005. *Seni merayu massa* [The art of seducing the masses]. Jakarta: Kompas.

Nugroho, Yanuar, Dinita Andriani Putri and Shita Laksmi. 2012. *Mapping the landscape of the media industry in contemporary Indonesia*. Report series engaging media, empowering society: assessing media policy and governance in Indonesia through the lens of citizens' rights. Jakarta: CIPG and HIVOS.

Poerwaningtias. 2013. 'Pengantar' [Introduction]. In: Puji Rianto (ed.), *Model-model gerakan literasi media dan pemantauan media di Indonesia* [Media literacy models and the monitoring of the media in Indonesia]. Yogyakarta: Pusat Kajian Media dan Budaya Populer, pp. iii–vi.

Postman, Neil. 1970. 'The reformed English curriculum'. In: Alvin C. Eurich (ed.), *High school 1980: the shape of the future in American secondary education*. New York: Pitman Publishing Corporation, pp. 160–168.

Rianto, Puji. 2013a. 'Epilog: menimbang kontribusi literasi media bagi penguatan demokrasi' [Epilogue: considering the contributions of media literacy to strengthening democracy]. In: Puji Rianto (ed.), *Model-model gerakan literasi media dan pemantauan media di Indonesia* [Media literacy models and the monitoring of the media in Indonesia]. Yogyakarta: Pusat Kajian Media dan Budaya Populer, pp. 193–210.

Rianto, Puji. (ed.). 2013b. *Model-model gerakan literasi media dan pemantauan media di Indonesia* [Media literacy models and the monitoring of the media in Indonesia]. Yogyakarta: Pusat Kajian Media dan Budaya Populer.

Sen, Krishna. 1994. *Indonesian cinema: framing the New Order*. London and New Jersey: Zed Books.

Sen, Krishna and David T. Hill. 2000. *Media, culture and politics in Indonesia*. Melbourne: Oxford University Press.

Silverstone, Roger. 2007. *Media and morality: on the rise of the mediapolis*. Malden, MA: Polity Press.

Siregar, Ashadi. 2001. 'Pengantar' [Introduction]. In: Veven Sp Wardhana, *Televisi dan prasangka budaya massa* [Television and the prejudice of mass culture]. Jakarta: Media Lintas Inti Nusantara and Institut Studi Arus Informasi, pp. xi–xxiv.

Siregar, Ashadi. 2006. *Etika komunikasi* [Communication ethics]. Yogyakarta: Pustaka Book Publisher.

Steele, Janet. 2011. 'Indonesian journalism post-Suharto: changing ideals and professional practices'. In: Krishna Sen and David T. Hill (eds), *Politics and the media in twenty-first century Indonesia: decade of democracy*. London and New York: Routledge, pp. 85–103.

Taman Ismail Marzuki. 2013. 'Penulis Veven Sp. Wardhana' [The author Veven Sp. Wardhana]. Available at: http://tamanismailmarzuki.co.id/tokoh/veven.html (accessed 27 August 2014).

Tickell, Paul. 2009. 'Indonesian identity after the dictatorship: imagining Chineseness in recent literature and film'. In: Minako Sakai, Glenn Banks and John H. Walker (eds), *The politics of the periphery in Indonesia: social and geographical perspectives*. Singapore: NUS Press, pp. 274–295.

Vickers, Adrian. 2005. *A history of modern Indonesia*. Cambridge, UK: Cambridge University Press.

Wardhana, Veven Sp. 1995. *Budaya massa dan pergeseran masyarakat* [Mass culture and the shift of society]. Yogyakarta: Yayasan Bentang Budaya.

Wardhana, Veven Sp. 1997a. *Kapitalisme televisi dan strategi budaya massa* [Television capitalism and the strategy of mass culture]. Yogyakarta: Pustaka Pelajar.

Wardhana, Veven Sp. 1997b. *Kemelut PDI di layar televisi: survey jurnalisme Indonesia* [The crisis of the PDI on television: a survey of Indonesian journalism]. Jakarta: Institut Studi Arus Informasi.

Wardhana, Veven Sp. 2001. *Televisi dan prasangka budaya massa* [Television and the prejudice of mass culture]. Jakarta: Media Lintas Inti Nusantara and Institut Studi Arus Informasi.

Wardhana, Veven Sp. 2002a. 'Budaya massa, budaya televisi, (tele)vision du monde: TV or not TV…' [Mass media, television culture, *(tele)vision du monde*: TV or not TV…]. In: Veven Sp. Wardhana, *Dari Barbar sampai Timor Timur: mengeja budaya massa* [From Barbarians to East Timor: spelling the mass media]. Yogyakarta: Galang Press, pp. 9–26.

Wardhana, Veven Sp. 2002b. *Centeng: matahari malam hari* [Watchmen: sun of the night]. Jakarta: Gramedia Media Sarana Indonesia.

Wardhana, Veven Sp. 2002c. *Dari Barbar sampai Timor Timur: mengeja budaya massa* [From Barbarians to East Timor: spelling the mass media]. Yogyakarta: Galang Press.

Wardhana, Veven Sp. 2002d. *Panggil aku Peng Hwa* [Call me Pheng Hwa]. Jakarta: Kepustakaan Populer Gramedia.

Wardhana, Veven Sp. 2004a. *Dari mana datangnya mata* [From where came the eye]. Jakarta: Gramedia Pustaka Utama.

Wardhana, Veven Sp. 2004b. *Stamboel selebritas* [The celebrity spectacle]. Jakarta: Kepustakaan Populer Gramedia.

Wardhana, Veven Sp. 2012. 'Kebebasan pers' [Press freedom]. *Tempo.co*, 10 May. Available at: https://m.tempo.co/read/kolom/2012/05/10/581/kebebasan-media (accessed 12 August 2016).

Wardhana, Veven Sp. 2013a. *Budaya massa, agama, wanita* [Mass culture, religion, women]. Jakarta: Kepustakaan Populer Gramedia.

Wardhana, Veven Sp. 2013b. *Perempuan yang gagal jadi kelelawar* [The woman who failed to become a cave bat]. Jakarta: Kepustakaan Populer Gramedia.

Wardhana, Veven Sp. and Herry Barus. 1999. *Para superkaya Indonesia: Sebuah dokumentasi gaya hidup* [The superrich of Indonesia: a documentation of life style]. Yogyakarta: Galang Press.

Wardhana, Veven Sp., Abdul Manan and Imam Suma Atmadja. 2001. *Geger santet Banyuwangi* [The tumult of the Banyuwangi black magic]. Jakarta: Institut Studi Arus Informasi.

Part II

Media reflexivity

4 Media democracy

Wardhana tried to give his novel televisual characteristics in order to critically comment on Indonesian media culture. Although rare in Indonesia and elsewhere, creative interventions in the media can also be found in mainstream television itself, in the form of televisual self-reflections or 'meta-discourse'. One example is *Dewan Pers kita* ('Our Press Council'), broadcast on TVRI. This media watch programme is hosted by Dewan Pers (Indonesian Press Council) and focuses on press-related issues, including Indonesian broadcast journalism.

The most creative and provocative programmes reflecting on Indonesian television have been a series of shows invented by Communications and Political Science scholar Effendi Gazali and his fellow staff from the University of Indonesia's 'Depok School' in Jakarta (see Chapter 2). These programmes were emblematic of the transition from authoritarianism to democratic reform in the first decade of the twenty-first century. As well as providing media literacy, they also provided information about Indonesian politics (especially its leadership) and people's rights and obligations in the new climate of free speech. They pioneered microscopic or hyperreal detail of political figures and their policies to a nationwide audience on a medium that for its entire existence had restrained itself from, and been censored for, any direct political engagement, let alone criticism.

This chapter focuses on arguably the most popular and successful of these shows, *Newsdotcom*, which was broadcast weekly from 2006 until 2008 on Metro TV (Jurriëns 2008). The name referred to the news agency of a fictional country called Republik Mimpi or Republic of Dreams.[1] The idea of the programme was not developed by the television industry, but came from a relatively independent group of academics and theatre performers. As a creative form of televisual meta-discourse, it attempted to provide an alternative to mainstream television and thus increase the diversity and sustainability of the Indonesian media. Most importantly, the programme gave its creative producers access to the television audience, the main target of their media literacy efforts. In a media ecological sense, it established communication between various environments in Indonesia, particularly the worlds of media, politics and civil society. After more than ten years, there are still spin-off programmes on Indonesian national television with similar formats and some of the same actors, such as *Sentilan-Sentilun* ('Scolding'), which has been broadcast on Metro TV since 2010.

Newsdotcom made use of parody, which had been a representational strategy during the New Order to express criticism in a humorous and thus relatively indirect and safe way. In the television show, it functioned to critically examine and, where necessary, undermine Indonesian socio-political realities. At the same time, the programme went beyond parody, and the representation of existing realities, by simulating scenarios for an alternative and better present or future. While the representational mode of parody to a certain extent was the cultural counterstrategy of the past, and the hyperreal functioned as a breaking point with authoritarianism, the presentational strategy of simulation could be seen as an avant-garde strategy for searching for micro-utopian solutions in the digital age. Simulation illustrates a new type of citizen engagement with politics and the media, including interactive audience participation, in which media imagery is used to overlay and manipulate, rather than represent, reality. In that sense, *Newsdotcom* shares similarities with the creative video experiments that will be explained in detail later in this book.

In this chapter, I describe *Newsdotcom*'s use of imagery to project an alternative reality as an act of simulation, but one substantially different from French philosopher Jean Baudrillard's (2004) idea of simulation, or Heryanto's (2006) application of the concept to New Order strategies of rule. Both the original concept and the New Order practices of simulation were intrinsically and negatively linked with simulacra, or signs without referents, designed to keep illusions intact, and turning simulation into an all-encompassing, inescapable condition controlled and manipulated by the media and the political leadership. *Newsdotcom*, on the other hand, reformulated simulation as a strategy for creative and critical interventions.

The programme linked illusion to reality by combining simulation with parody, switching between the worlds of the Republic of Dreams and Indonesia, and instructing the viewers about the ideological mechanisms behind media production. The show confirmed the idea of utopia as imaginative visions about the future that are firmly grounded in critical evaluations of the present and the past (Noble 2009: 14). In the final part of this chapter, I argue that the former Minister of Communications and Informatics's distress about *Newsdotcom* may have been stirred by nostalgia for a New Order-style of simulation, used for spreading propaganda, creating fear, and installing authority.

Realigning the media with politics and society

Newsdotcom grew out of a unique trend of mimetic representations of political figures on Indonesian television in the mid-2000s. This trend was set into motion by a programme called *Republik BBM* (The BBM Republic), which was also invented by Gazali and broadcast on the commercial channel Indosiar in 26 episodes between December 2005 and June 2006. The programmes gave their viewers an unprecedentedly intimate, up-close look at the bodies and policies of their political leaders. By imitating political figures not just in a realistic, but microscopic, hyperreal manner, the programme makers seemed to confirm that politics in the era of democratic reform had come within the reach of ordinary people, and that it was something that needed to be engaged with and commented on by all members of society.

BBM stood for *Benar-Benar Mabuk* ('Truly Drunken'), a play on the acronym for *Bahan Bakar Minyak* (Fuel Oil), which could be frequently found on the front-pages of Indonesian newspapers, due to the controversial decision by the government to raise the price of BBM soon after Susilo Bambang Yudhoyono came to power in 2004. Similar to the Republic of Dreams in *Newsdotcom*, the 'Truly Drunken' Republic was presented as a never-never land (*negeri antah-berantah*) with many similarities with its neighbouring country (*negara tetangga*) Indonesia. The fictional country had a President (played by Taufik Savalas), Vice-President (played by Kelik Pelipur Lara), State Secretary (played by Denny Chandra) and Presidential Advisor (played by Gazali himself).

In every episode they tackled the task of finding a suitable candidate for a ministerial post or other high position in society. They were assisted by members of the audience, including groups of students from different universities. Usually two candidates were invited to present their ideas and compete for a position. The contestants were public figures, including artists, politicians and high-profile professionals. The format, selection of guests and studio setting confirmed a new, democratic vision about the Indonesian media, politics and society, in which direct interaction and open, critical discussion between all three parties was possible and encouraged.

Some political leaders, media owners and members of the general public had difficulties with aspects of Indonesia's new or envisaged democratic reality. Controversy over *Republik BBM* rose after a meeting between Indonesian Vice-President Yusuf Kalla and the owners of seven commercial television stations on 8 April 2006. In the meeting Kalla urged for the reduction of graphic contents in television programmes. Several television owners attempted to rescue their own broadcasting interests by pointing the finger at *Republik BBM*, alleging that 'it crossed the line in poking fun at the country's leaders and went against local cultural norms' (Hotland 2006).

In June 2006, Indosiar made the shock-announcement that it would discontinue broadcasting *Republik BBM*. According to Gazali, since Kalla's meeting with the television owners, Indosiar had provided the programme producers with a list of 'dos and don'ts' that put many limitations on their creative freedom. In response, Gazali and Pelipur Lara refused to appear in the programme's final six episodes. Indosiar spokesman Ghufron Sakaril denied corporate pressure had been responsible for the decision to discontinue the show. According to Sakaril, it had been agreed from the outset that *Republik BBM* would only last for 26 episodes (Taufiqurrahman 2006).

Following the closure of *Republik BBM*, the people previously involved in the show split into two groups, each inventing their own spin-off programme. The first group, including Savalas and Chandra, created *Istana BBM* (The BBM Palace, or 'The Truly Drunken Palace'; BBM here also stood for *Benar-Benar Mabuk*), a situation comedy about the President's daily routine at the presidential palace. The second group, including Gazali and Pelipur Lara, started *Newsdotcom*. According to the creators of *The BBM Palace*, their programme had a 'human-comical' (*komedi-manusiawi*) approach (Indosiar 2006). The programme, which was also broadcast by Indosiar and still dealt with the fictional BBM Republic, explored the individual characters and behaviour of the President (Taufiq Savalas) and his staff members. Institutions and symbols of state power were not treated as objects of veneration, but presented in humorous contexts to become topics of critical discussion.

During the 2006 Islamic fasting month of Ramadhan, the producers of *Istana BBM* created another spin-off programme called *Ramadhan di Istana* (Fasting Month in the Palace; Ivvaty 2006). This variety show was broadcast daily during the time of *sahur*, the meal eaten before daybreak. It included discussions on current affairs between the President and his staff with invited guests, including comedians, dancers, actors and other public figures. It also had quizzes and religious teachings by Islamic scholars and leaders. The studio audience, consisting of groups of university students, had the opportunity to ask questions about religious issues to the presidential Islamic teacher (*ustadz*).

A special segment of the show was *BBC: BBM Broadcasting Center*. BBC was presented as the BBM Palace's centre of radio and television services, or 'a direct communications means between the BBM Republic government and its citizenry, as well as the people of the neighbouring country' [that is, Indonesia] (Hartanto 2006). This humorous reflection on the news media, which included sketches with fictional programme producers, was probably inspired by the example of *Newsdotdom*, which, more than *Republik BBM* and *Istana BBM*, focused on the role of the media in representing and constructing politics.

The Republic of Dreams and Indonesia

In every episode, the *Newsdotcom* news agency offered a forum for discussion to the residents of the Republic of Dreams. This usually produced humorous but critical discussions on Indonesia, which was portrayed as the Republic of Dreams' neighbouring country (*negara tetangga*). The Republic's capital was Yaharta, an obvious reference to Indonesia's Jakarta. Its residents included the President Si Butet Yogya ('SBY', played by Butet Kertaredjasa), Vice-President Jarwo Kuat (also spelled Kwat, played by Jarwo), Presidential Advisor (played by Gazali) and their honorary guests. The guests were usually former presidents such as Gus Pur (played by Handoyo), Megakarti (played by Megakarti), Habudi (played by Budi Setiawan) and Suharta (played by Burhan Uemuluk, with his voice dubbed by Butet Kertaredjasa). The characters all had uncanny similarities in name, appearance and speech with their real-life Indonesian counterparts Susilo Bambang Yudhoyono (also known as SBY), Yusuf Kalla, Gus Dur, Megawati, Habibie and Suharto.

Each episode started with the house band performing the programme's theme song, which urged people to accept that 'criticism is normal' (*kritik itu biasa*). After this, the band, fictional characters and studio audience sung the Republic's national anthem together. During the show, the Presidential Advisor offered topics for discussion by providing short summaries of front-page stories from the Indonesian newspapers, confirming the discursive links between politics and the media. Former heads of state in the Republic and other guests then started joking and debating about the news. The studio guests always included groups of students from two or more Indonesian universities and several other invitees, such as politicians, actors, journalists, NGO activists and representatives of other social groups. They were sometimes selected for a specific, fictional ministerial position, related to the show's main discussion topic.

The show constantly switched in a creative and strategic manner between fantasy and reality, future and present, aspirations and doubts, humour and criticism, and ideas and actions. The Republic of Dreams itself was presented as a 'country in the clouds' (*negeri di awan*) and a never-never land. While 'neighbouring country' expressed difference, but spatial proximity, with Indonesia, 'never-never land' implied more radical differences between the two countries in terms of space and time. Although both references seemed to indicate that the Republic of Dreams was *not* Indonesia, if not entirely fictional, my interpretation of the Republic of Dreams' national anthem and *Newsdotcom*'s theme song will suggest a different relationship between simulation and reality.

The national anthem, composed by the Indonesian pop musician Katon Bagaskara, followed the programme's theme song at the start of each episode. It was performed by the *Newsdotcom* house band, singing together with the Republic of Dreams residents, their special guests and the audience members. The song's introduction of the Republic of Dreams as 'a country in the clouds, where peace is the palace' (*sebuah negeri di awan, di mana kedamaian menjadi istananya*) referred to the imaginary character of the country, or to the role of the medium of television in shaping such imagination. Its portrayal as a peaceful, democratic place alluded to an ideal picture of the progress of Indonesia's democratic reform. It was as if the studio guests and viewers at home were lured into visiting the dreamlike place, and encouraged to try to realise the peaceful and democratic ideals in their own country, Indonesia.

The lyrics of *Newsdotcom*'s theme song, on the other hand, were not about a fictional country, but about the Indonesia as known by the audience. The song addressed the studio guests and viewers at home by talking about 'we' (*kita*, including both the speaker and the addressee) and 'this country' (*negeri ini*, that is, Indonesia), and using different types of imperative to provoke concrete action, such as 'don't' (*jangan*) and 'come on' (*ayo*). Although it welcomed the audience to the Republic of Dreams, at the same time it admonished the listeners 'to wake up from dreaming', and start acting quickly, that is, 'to do something as small as it may be', even in a situation where 'this country is still in deep trouble'.

These were references to *Reformasi*, in scholarly literature often portrayed as a troublesome, transitional period from totalitarianism to democracy (Schulte Nordholt 2002: 1–24). One of the main agendas of *Reformasi* addressed in the song was the implementation of democratic rule, asserting that politicians as well as ordinary citizens agree that 'criticism is normal'. The studio guests and audience members always stood and put their hand on their breast when singing the Republic of Dreams' national anthem, as if making a pledge to stick to the principles of Indonesia's new democracy.

Characters, themes and setting

After the singing of the anthem, the show's guests would be introduced by the host, Olga Lydia, in her position as Cabinet Secretary. Lydia also welcomed the viewers at home and the studio audience, including the university students. Government officials and former presidents of the Republic of Dreams sat opposite, but in close proximity, to the studio audience in a circular arena. A second host, Presidential Secretary Anya Dwinov, even sat in the audience in order to conduct on-the-spot interviews with the students and special guests. Another regular *Newsdotcom* member sitting in the audience was Iwel Wel, a nickname for Welnadi, one of the producers of the show. He was usually introduced either in his fictional role of 'young Republic of Dreams intellectual' or in his 'real' capacity of 'Indonesia's first stand-up comedian'. During the show, Iwel Wel interviewed audience members and was sometimes asked to give his views about certain matters to the Republic's government members.

The whole setting did not merely represent an ideal picture of the interaction between government and civil society in a democratic public sphere, but allowed the studio guests, and by extension, the viewers at home, to experience democracy in a physical, bodily manner. It exploited interactive and experiential modes that are characteristic of the 'post-representational' age of social media and digital culture (see Chapter 9). One of the show's popular characters, who usually appeared in the audience near the end of the programme, was specifically designed to convey messages to the government on behalf of the common people. This character, Isa, or the Republic's 'Spokesperson for the Less Affluent People', was known for constructing grammatically incorrect sentences in his efforts to be polite. He also had the habit of conveying his messages in self-made poetry, which was funny in form as well as content.

For instance, in one of his dialogues with the government members, Isa expressed his concern about the highly controversial Peraturan Pemerintah (Government Regulation) no. 37 of 2006/07, which put into effect an increase in the allowances for members of the Dewan Perwakilan Rakyat Daerah (Regional Parliaments, DPRD). In a meandering introduction, with sentences full of loops, he politely asked for permission to talk with the President about this issue. However, he was interrupted by Vice-President Jarwo Kuat, who made comments on Isa's speech pattern while unintentionally displaying his own ineffective communication skills.

In her work on the relation between politics and the press during the New Order, Angela Romano (2003: 141) explains that the common people were almost never accessed as a source of information or opinion. Suharto and other political figures engaged with the media 'in a fashion that prevented direct accountability through public interrogation of his [Suharto's] actions or policies' (Romano 2003: 117–118). Business leaders were also often reluctant to share information with journalists, and documentary information was hard to obtain (Romano 2003: 134). The only people that were relatively easy to approach and obtain information from were NGO activists, academics, religious leaders and certain retired generals (Romano 2003: 138). The New Order leaders could not permit the media to present alternative representations of themselves or the people, as this would threaten their own constructed idea or simulation of Indonesian politics, society and the state.

Newsdotcom, on the other hand, suggested that the actors and terms of political debate had changed since *Reformasi*, and that simulation with the aim of control and intimidation no longer had a place in contemporary Indonesia. The show's creation of characters, selection of studio guests and spatial organisation of the studio set all projected a vision of reform in which students and other groups from civil society had the opportunity to get into direct dialogue with politicians, whether impersonated or real, and were acknowledged as alternative sources of authority. The visibility of the students in the audience could be explained by the involvement of UI academics in the production of the programme, but also confirmed the prominent position of student activism in both scholarly and non-scholarly narratives on key events in Indonesian history.[2]

The show brought high politics closer to daily life by presenting characters that not only had physical similarities with their Indonesian counterparts, but also strong resemblances in voice and personal or political attitude. These hyperrealist techniques confirmed that the Republic of Dreams did not consist of empty, meaningless signs, but invited the Indonesian audience to know their political leaders better, and identify some of the ideological motives behind their decision making. At the same time, the hyperreal representations of authoritative bodies as well as the bodily configurations in the television studio also presented the human body as a site for exploring alternative socio-political directions for the present and the future.

Similar to Susilo Bambang Yudhoyono, for instance, Si Butet Yogyakarta often made dutiful but empty promises to take action and tackle a problem by starting his statements with *Saya akan* ('I will …'). Similar to Yusuf Kalla, Jarwo Kuat often used Arabic expressions such as *Alhamdulillah* ('Praise be to God') and switched codes between Indonesian and English. Sometimes he made a statement in Indonesian, before continuing with an idiosyncratic translation into English, as in '*karena apa*, because what …'. His more politically oriented discourse included the important-sounding but hollow phrase 'relevant and significant' (*relevan dan signifikan*). Gus Pur, one of the most popular characters in the show, had the same seemingly indifferent, down-to-earth attitude as the late Gus Dur, reflected in his preference for using expressions such as 'For me, it is all easy' (*Buat saya sih gampang aja*) and 'Why worry?' (*Gitu aja kok repot*). Megakarti often started with a short statement by exclaiming the nationalist phrase *Merdeka!* ('Freedom!'), which referred to Megawati's attempts to increase her popularity by building on the revolutionary past of her father and

Indonesia's first President, Sukarno. Habudi reflected Habibie's obsession with technology by offering 'high-tech' as the solution to any problem, irrespective of its nature. Suharta's speech was interspersed with Suharto-type Javanese speech and symbolism.

The President's political behaviour was clearly depicted in scenes of a conflict between Si Butet Yogya and Megakarti. The scenes were an ironic reaction to Megawati's comments in the Indonesian press that Susilo Bambang Yudhoyono was only 'spreading around charm' (*tebar pesona*), but had no real policies or solutions to problems. In a guest appearance of the *Newsdotcom* actors in Metro TV's talk show *Kick Andy*[3] on 25 January 2007, Megakarti advised the President 'not too much spread around charm, but rather spread around more work'. The President replied that it was better 'to let the people decide which between them was talking nonsense, and who was working day and night'.[4]

Arguably the most ground-breaking and controversial sketches in *Newsdotcom* involved Suharta impersonating former president Suharto. Suharta was played by an amateur actor with a strong physical resemblance to Suharto, while his voice was dubbed by Butet Kartaredjasa. Kartaredjasa is a master of mimicking Suharto's low voice, slow speech and quasi-ceremonial idiosyncrasies, which include the use of the verbal suffix -ken (instead of -kan), the adjective clause *yang mana* ('in such a manner') and the preposition *daripada* in ways that are stylistically old-fashioned. Interviews between Gazali and Suharta were pre-recorded, situated outside the usual *Newsdotcom* studio setting, in a place that resembled the presidential palace. The pre-recording technique enabled the producer to dub Suharta's voice before the programme was broadcast, although Gazali explained to the viewers in an interview on 28 January 2007 that the recording technique was needed because of Suharta's bad 'health situation'. Suharta, unlike the real Suharto, expressed his sympathy for the student protests in 1998, and even declared he would have joined the protests if he had been a student himself. He was also prepared to go to trial, but, just like Suharto, demanded that the trial be stopped if he were to fall ill again.

Parody, hyperrealism, simulacra and simulation

One of the antecedents of the various post-New Order political talk shows was Kartaredjasa's series of theatre monologues, which had begun in 1987, but only increased in popularity after 1998 (Emond 2007). During the New Order it would have been unthinkable, however, to have the same embodiments of political figures on national television. The New Order leaders would have considered these creations to be in conflict with their own idea of a 'free but responsible' press and broadcast media.[5]

At the same time, both media producers and consumers found creative and effective ways to circumvent the government repression, or turn it on its head. A counter-strategy used by journalists from the print media was to invite their readers to 'read between the lines' (McDaniel 1994: 289). For instance, they would visibly juxtapose contradictory statements of government officials, but refrain from drawing any explicit conclusions, thus conveying political analysis while reducing the risk of censorship or worse. Another popular counter-strategy in the media, the arts and popular culture was so-called *plesetan*, a specific type of parody. *Plesetan* literally means 'slip of the tongue', but also refers to punning or word games, in which humorous effects are achieved by interchanging words and their meanings on the basis of sound association (Jurriëns 2004: 154).

Heryanto (1996) identified three types of *plesetan* that circulated in society during the New Order. The first type was word play for entertainment, not serving any explicit ideological goals. The second type aimed at reversing hierarchies and power relations, for instance by turning around names of official institutions or making a curse sound respectful. It was used as a counter-strategy by or on behalf of the weak, poor or suppressed in society. The third type was *plesetan* as a radical and serious discipline, which was not merely oriented towards laughter or the reversal of social power relations, but questioned and undermined grand narratives with truth claims (Heryanto 1996: 102–103). This last type is similar to poststructuralist traditions that work to 'de-doxify cultural representations and their undeniable political import' (Hutcheon 1989: 3).

The various genres of *plesetan* remained popular during the era of democratic reform and could also be found in *Republik BBM*, *Istana BBM* and *Newsdotcom*. All three programmes contained entertaining word play, as manifested in the alternative use of the acronym BBM (the first type of *plesetan*); reversed social hierarchies by making fun of people in power (the second type); while, in particular, *Newsdotcom* also structurally discussed the national media, and aimed at enhancing the media literacy of its audience (the third type).

At the same time, these programmes went beyond the reversal and deconstruction techniques of parody and *plesetan*, by also presenting hyperreality, and inventing and validating alternative realities. This was confirmed by a producer statement on the Indosiar website (Indosiar 2006):

> In Indonesia, the phenomenon of hyper-reality has spread via the programme *The BBM* (*Truly Drunken*) *Republic*. Apparently *The BBM Republic* is accepted as a friendly country that really exists, as if the people are presented with a reality – which is in fact only an illusion.

As shown, the hyperreal representations of political figures and situations in *The BBM Republic* and the other political variety shows desacralised officialdom, brought it closer to the people, and turned it into a topic for public discussion. The television shows also went beyond hyperrealism, however, by presenting dream-like countries that were tied to, but further removed from, real social and political life. The various fantasy countries and palaces created critical, imaginative space and distance for exploring scenarios that would be beneficial for Indonesia's democratic present and future.

In that sense, the hyperreality that started on Indonesian television with *Republik BBM*, as described in the quote, was both similar to and different from Baudrillard's concept. According to Baudrillard (2004), hyperreality is symptomatic of the contemporary world being dominated by an 'ecstasy of communication', or an abundance of sounds, images and other sensations produced by modern media technology such as television. This audio-visual overload has not only made people readily accept the imaginary, but has caused the imaginary to take over reality as such. One of Baudrillard's (1995) examples was the 1991 Gulf War, which was transmitted 'live', in real time, for almost 24 hours a day by the US-based international broadcaster Cable News Network (CNN). Although this media coverage suggested accuracy and proximity, Baudrillard (1995) argued that it did not bring the viewers any closer to what was actually happening on the battleground. The viewers had no option but to rely on the images on the screen, which seemed to provide microscopic detail but in fact took the war out of sight, as if it was not taking place, and were only there to confirm the ideological message of a 'clean war'.

Baudrillard (2004: 1) uses the idea of simulation to refer to the state of contemporary life, in which the hyperreal has preceded and replaced the real, and the laws of causality have been reversed and undermined. The elements that keep the process of simulation going, so-called simulacra, consist of images without realities, signs without referents, or copies without originals (Baudrillard 2004: 6). The example of the Gulf War showed, however, that simulacra can also be deliberately used for specific political and ideological purposes. Hyperreality then is no longer a description of contemporary society's general condition, but rather functions as a discursive tool or device to be used and manipulated by political actors. Heryanto (2006: 12) argues that simulacra prevailed during the New Order rule, and mediated 'the inevitable discrepancies between the ambitious claims of the dominant discourse and what they can actually achieve'.

An example of a New Order simulacrum was the film *Pengkhianatan G30S/PKI* (The Treason of G30S/PKI [the 30 September Movement/Indonesian Communist Party]). This film, which was shown annually on national television and at schools around the country, was the officially sanctioned version of the alleged communist coup attempt on 30 September 1965, in the aftermath of which Suharto came to power, and hundreds of thousands, if not millions, of people designated as communists were imprisoned or killed. According to Heryanto (2006: 13), the point about this film and other simulacra used by the Suharto regime was not to make sure people really believed them, but rather to create and keep intact the illusion of New Order's total dominance and control. The practices of *plesetan* discussed previously were signs that the regime's dominance and control was in fact far from total.

While the Bush Sr. and Suharto governments attempted to keep simulation intact and ward off any threats by which it could be disrupted, including any parody or 'ironic voice' (Heryanto 2006: 11), the producers of *Republik BBM*, *Istana BBM* and *Newsdotcom* made such disruptions an integral part of their simulation. In the three television shows, various manifestations of *plesetan* could be found as well as other elements that destabilised the imaginary, such as explanations about the workings of the media, and a constant switching between the dreamlike countries and real-life Indonesia. These creative interventions could be seen as humorous and critical reflections on the types of simulation instigated by the Baudrillardian over-abundance of the media in contemporary life, or the more specific manipulations of signs for political dominance and control by the former US and Indonesian governments. At the same time, the creative producers partially decoupled simulation from simulacra, and used it as a, far from meaningless or void, tool for creative imagination, including scenarios for more sustainable interactions between the Indonesian media, politics and social life.

Televisual meta-discourse and social action

Apart from the use of *plesetan* and the constant switching between the Republic of Dreams and real-life Indonesia, *Newsdotcom* also disrupted the imaginary character of the programme and television in general by providing media education to its viewers. Gazali explained that he created the programme to 'educate people to watch the news' and give 'political education in a humorous package' (Andri 2006a). He said he was inspired by current affairs shows from the US, such as the *Jon Stewart Daily Show*, *Jay Leno* and *David Letterman* (Andri 2006a), although his show also displayed similarities with programmes such as *Spitting Image* (UK), *Les Guignols* (France) and *Kopspijkers* (The Netherlands), which used puppets or human actors in their mimetic portrayal of political figures.

Newsdotcom was also meant as an alternative to the abundance of infotainment, *sinetron* and superstition in *horror, misteri* and *mistik* shows on Indonesian television (Andri 2006b). While these mainstream genres and programmes hardly contain any critical reflection on their own processes of simulation, *Newsdotcom* exposed what the French sociologist Pierre Bourdieu (1998: 20–21) calls the 'structural corruption' of television. According to Bourdieu (1998: 20–21), this corruption has manifested itself in the 'symbolic violence' of genres that cater for large audiences and steer away from any political controversy. Another symptom is the 'circular circulation of information', or the phenomenon that the same news item is digested over and over again by media institutions that decide on the newsworthiness of something primarily by measuring its coverage by other media institutions (Bourdieu 1998: 30–31).

Newsdotcom referred to the symbolic violence of melodramatic *sinetron* and the circular circulation of 'news' items in endless runs of infotainment shows, amongst others. The US media scholar Robert Stam (1985: 16; see also Stam *et al.* 1992: 202–203) positively applies this type of reflexivity to literature and film, arguing that television's reflexivity is 'of a peculiarly ambiguous and often debased kind'.[6] *Newsdotcom* proves, however, that 'quality television' (Elsaesser *et al.* 1994) may also achieve the aesthetic and critical sophistication found and admired by Stam in film and literature. Bourdieu (1998: 13, 64) briefly addresses the benefits of 'on-screen criticism of the screen', but restricts his analysis almost entirely to television journalism. When the broader idea of 'televisual meta-discourse' is applied, video art and other media that make use of television's discursive devices of language, sound and vision also need to be included, even if they do not belong to the world of television as such.

One of the genres regularly analysed and ridiculed in *Newsdotcom* was infotainment. For instance, in the 14 January 2007 episode an article from the popular tabloid *Cek n Ricek* (Check 'n' Re-Check) about the all-girl band Trio Macan (Tiger Trio), known for their sensual performances including tiger-like costumes and movements, was ironically presented as 'intellectual, scholarly news' (*berita ilmiah, intelek*). In the same episode Gus Pur also made an ironic remark about a clumsy headline of the much more serious newspaper *Media Indonesia*. In other episodes (21 January 2007 and 18 February 2007), the benefits and disadvantages of the system of television ratings were explained to the viewers.

The 21 January 2007 episode paid comprehensive attention to the relation between politics and the press. The special guest was political scientist and Susilo Bambang Yudhoyono's spokesperson, Andi Mallarangeng. Mallarangeng was interviewed about his role in informing the press about the President, and also asked about the President's opinion on the new phenomenon of political commentary on Indonesian television. Mallarangeng declared that the Indonesian President found *Newsdotcom* refreshing and constructive, but emphasised that politicians and critics should have a sense of mutual tolerance, and know about the 'legal framework' of what was legally acceptable, and what not. Gazali reacted to Mallarangeng's comments by explaining the benefits of constructive criticism generally and *Newsdotcom*'s attempts to offer 'elegant criticism' particularly. Later in the show, Gazali also remarked that it could no longer be denied that 'modern politics nowadays was a politics of imagery', implying that simulation was not only an integral part of the media industry, but politics as well, and that the two discursive forms were interconnected.

The producer also regularly invited members of the ordinary public in order to recount their personal stories related to the effects of (incompetent) government action. These stories immediately brought the audience back from the simulated realm of the Republic of Dreams to the Indonesian reality. For instance, the 28 January 2007 episode featured two survivors of the sunken Senopati Nusantara passenger ferry, while the 11 February 2007 episode had three homeless people from flood-struck Jakarta.

In the first case, the Republic of Dreams politicians expressed their disapproval about the financial compensation arrangements for relatives of the victims of the sunken passenger ferry. They believed class action was called for, as had been applied to the predominantly middle-class victims of the Adam Air airplane crash. In the case of the latter, 500 million Rupiah (approx. US$50,000) was paid per person, while only 5 million Rupiah (approx. US$500) was offered to the predominantly low-income class victims of the passenger ferry disaster. With regard to the Jakarta floods, they blamed Jakarta's governor Sutiyoso, whose impersonated character appeared on the show, for having called the floods a 'natural phenomenon' (*fenomena alam*). They argued that the floods were annual disasters that could and should have been better anticipated.

In February 2007 broadcasts, the *Newsdotcom* team started an energy saving campaign, by reminding the audience neither to steal electricity nor use more than two lights at home between 5 and 10 p.m. They also expressed their support for several small-scale development projects in Indonesia. For instance, in the 18 and 25 February broadcasts the invited guest was Tri Mumpuni, who was involved in developing alternative, water-powered electricity facilities in villages whose needs were not served by Indonesia's national electricity company. In the 25 February episode, an official Memorandum of Understanding was signed between Mumpuni and a representative of a cooperation that was prepared to invest money in the facilities. In a remarkable television moment, in which the distinction between simulation and reality entirely dissolved, the Memorandum was signed with a fictional character, President Si Butet Yogya, as the official legal witness. Sometimes the *Newsdotcom* team itself descended from the realm of dreams to real-life Indonesia, as in the 18 March episode that showed footage of a visit to mud-struck Sidoarjo. During the visit the team interviewed, entertained and expressed their solidarity with the victims of the disaster.

Reflections on simulations of the past

Indonesia's former Minister of Communications and Informatics, Sofyan Djalil, could not appreciate *Newsdotcom*'s play with and comments on the politics of simulation and the simulation of politics. On 1 March 2007, Djalil told journalists that he had considered issuing a legal notice (*somasi*) against *Newsdotcom*, as he did not agree with 'the President being mocked' (Hayid 2007). Only a day after the *somasi* statement, the producers were confronted with another blow, when their main sponsor, the cigarette company Sampoerna, announced its intent to terminate its sponsorship contract that had expired at the end of February, and redirect its sponsorship to sports and music events (Fadil 2007b). The company explained there had been internal agreement on the decision on 28 February, implying that it had not been influenced by Djalil's comments (Fadil 2007a).

I argue that the Minister's discourse could be seen as an expression of nostalgia for 'the reign of simulacra' (Heryanto 2006: 140) during the New Order period. At the same time, the television producers employed a creative counter-discourse as a form of protest against the various threats. In the 4 March 2007 episode, for instance, the *Newsdotcom* team changed the name of their republic into a monarchy, The Kingdom of Dreams. While 'President SBY' in the Republic of Dreams was a democratically elected and fair leader, 'King SBY' (still played by Butet Kartaredjasa) in The Kingdom of Dreams was portrayed as someone who stood above the law, immune to any criticism, similar to President Suharto during the New Order. In anticipation of a fierce legal battle, and in an attempt to prompt support from different sections in society, the on-air debates in this and following shows centred heavily on the ministerial threats, the function of *Newsdotcom*, and the nature of democracy generally.

The 4 March programme opened with Si Butet Yogya giving a video conference in which he read out a decree changing the republic into a kingdom. He gave three reasons for the change: it was nicer to be a king than a president; unlike presidents, kings were not allowed to be criticised; and unlike the presidential institution, the royal institution could not be delegitimised. According to King SBY, the change would affect the bureaucratic system accordingly: high officials would receive high salaries, low officials would receive low salaries, and the people would be subjected to higher prices for rice. He concluded by stating that 'this decree was based on the irritation that had arisen in the commotion about the legal notice, as there was a minister who did not yet understand democracy'. In other words, the decree was presented as a token serving the ambition of total dominance and control, in a humorous but critical allusion to the Minister's more serious attempts at simulating such dominance and control.

During the episode the new king cynically joked that he preferred living in a kingdom, as 'everything was comfortable and nice'. Jarwo Kuat, now Prime Minister instead of Vice-President, made a *plesetan* of his own name, saying he was feeling 'stronger and stronger' because of the political threats. Gus Pur applauded Gazali for never considering a career in politics. He believed that creativity would never die and that 'many great works had come into being from behind iron bars'. He also thought the Department of Communications and Informatics was of no use, and should be abolished or restricted to purely technological issues, as the public was capable of assessing what they saw. Iwel Wel gave examples of political parody in other countries, arguing that even an 'arrogant' George W. Bush accepted being parodied by actors such as Steve Bridges. Students and fellow journalists in the audience, showing their media literacy, wondered why *Newsdotcom* was under political threat, while programmes that contained nudity, superstition and violence were allowed. The protests against the *somasi* statement developed into discussion and explanation about the role of the media – exactly the type of purpose the programme was designed for by its creators.

The Republic of Dreams government made it clear that the Indonesian political landscape had undergone major changes since *Reformasi* by citing support from real Indonesian politicians, including the ones parodied in the programme. In newspaper articles or in person, Gus Dur, Megawati, Habibie and, astonishingly, even members of the Suharto family had all declared they enjoyed the programme and did not feel offended by it (Tresnawati 2007). During the show, the previously broadcast interview with Yudhoyono's spokesperson Mallarangeng was repeated, reminding viewers that Indonesia's President did not object to the programme. Special studio guest Amien Rais, a *Reformasi* figure and co-founder of Partai Amanat Nasional (National Mandate Party, PAN), argued that politicians who could not deal with parody and criticism needed more self-confidence and a better understanding that there was always room for improvement. Referring to a similar example of political parody from US television, *D.C. Follies*, which was broadcast with few restrictions, Rais believed that 'governments that exercised censorship perhaps signalled that they would not last much longer'.

The *Newsdotcom* team suspected that references to a corruption case in the episode of 25 February were the main trigger for the *somasi* comments. The case was presented by Isa, the Spokesperson for Less-Affluent People, in the form of a riddle (*teka-teki*). In his characteristically indirect way Isa suggested that the perpetrators of *Bantuan Likuiditas Bank Indonesia* (Bank Indonesia Liquidity Support, BLBI) corruption case, where trillions of Rupiah in state-funds had been embezzled, were welcomed as honorary guests at the Presidential palace.[7] This referred to a government decision that eight of the corruptors would not be sentenced if they were prepared to return the stolen money to the state (Shaleh 2006).

In the 11 March 2007 episode, Gus Pur, still angry that the programme was under *somasi* threats, re-emphasised that the change from a republic into a kingdom was an act of resistance. Anya Dwinov showed information from surveys that confirmed that the majority of the public supported *Newsdotcom*. Fragments from an Arte France TV feature on *Newsdotcom* were played to demonstrate that the show had also received international attention.[8] Special guests on the programme were musicians and women activists, including Sinta Nuriyah Wahid, Gus Dur's wife, who were invited in the context of Indonesia's Music Day (9 March) and International Women's Day (8 March). In newspaper interviews, Sinta Wahid explained her husband had no problem about being parodied in *Newsdotcom*, and believed the humour in the programme served the political education of the people (Tresnawati 2007).

The Kingdom of Dreams lasted for only two episodes before it reverted to a republic, as officially confirmed by public decree of King SBY, 18 March 2007. After reading the decree, Si Butet Yogya exchanged his crown for an Indonesian-styled Muslim cap, and Jarwo Kuat removed his prime-ministerial decorations to become Vice-President again. The President and Vice-President declared that the symbolic return to republican status was meant as a sign of self-confidence and a stand against political threat. It could be read as a reminder to Indonesia's contemporary political leaders to refrain from using 'royal', New Order-like simulacra for exercising and legitimising their power.

The 18 March episode became an even more unique television event when immediately following the reading of the decree, the real Djalil made a brave guest appearance. In a remarkably open conversation, the Republic of Dreams government gave the minister the opportunity to explain why he had considered taking action against *Newsdotcom*. Djalil emphasised that he had spoken as a private citizen, not as the Minister of Communications and Informatics. He thought the programme set a bad example, ridiculing rather than confirming political and social figures as models for society. Djalil's statement expressed nostalgia for order based on simulacra-driven simulation, that is, a New Order-like ambition to create a country where social and political leaders enjoyed untouchable positions, detached from and controlling the common people. It showed the minister's anxiety about losing this order, of seeing it disrupted and replaced by unstable simulations that are less dependent on simulacra and open to *plesetan*. It also seemed to express an anxiety about the uncertainties and ambitions of the *Reformasi* in general.

In a typical courageous and humorous reaction, Gus Pur disagreed with the Minister by saying that 'true leadership cannot be mocked [...] why bother just because of that?'. This was a *plesetan* for saying that true leadership *can* be mocked, and *accepts* being mocked. Djalil was also challenged by a representative of the Nahdlatul Ulama (Association of Muslim Scholars, NU), who argued the issuing of a legal notice against *Newsdotcom* would look a bad political move, and questioned why the Minister did nothing about programmes containing violence and nudity.

Djalil responded that he, together with KPI, would act to ensure violence and nudity would no longer be tolerated on Indonesian television between 6 a.m. and 9 p.m. Thus, by the end of the programme, the focus of ministerial attention seemed to have shifted, peace between the *Newsdotcom* team and Djalil temporarily restored. It was unclear, however, whether this was a short reprieve for the programme, or a sign of the Indonesian leadership's sincere and enduring acceptance of its country's new social and political realities.

Conclusion

Newsdotcom presented an alternative to the predominant genres on Indonesian mainstream television in the second half of the 2000s, such as *sinetron* and infotainment. It also provided media literacy to its viewers by addressing topical issues related to the Indonesian press and entertainment industry. It included hyperreal representations of politicians as a statement that politics and the media in post-authoritarian Indonesia had become, and should remain, topics and instruments of public discussion, instead of being limited to, and serving the ideological and commercial interests of, a small and powerful elite.

The show also facilitated the exploration of alternative, micro-utopian scenarios for the present and future of the Indonesian media, politics and society, as well as the initiation of humanitarian projects and concrete action. It brought together representatives of various fields in a setting that projected an ideal version of a democratic Indonesian public sphere. The socio-political scenarios offered by *Newsdotcom* constituted a reflection on, and alternative to, the simulations of power and control of the New Order as well as the general hyperreal condition of media-saturated contemporary society. They exploited the creative and critical possibilities of interactive, experiential modes of presentation that are characteristic of contemporary digital and social media culture. They also confirmed that Indonesians no longer had to rely on relatively indirect means of expression, such as parody or *plesetan*, to give their opinion in public.

One important restriction to *Newsdotcom* and related shows was that they had to operate in the challenging context of commercial television, and IWC more generally. These surroundings posed serious demands on the programme makers and even resulted in the discontinuation of various shows. Gazali acknowledged, with regret, that *Newsdotcom* was interspersed with commercials, which made the programme financially viable but were at the expense of prolonged, in-depth discussion and analysis (Hartiningsih and Khoiri 2007). He also pointed to the irony that he and his fellow-actors had become celebrities themselves, while trying to present an alternative to the consumerism and celebrity-culture promoted on Indonesian television. He was confident, however, he would never be co-opted by the celebrity culture of Indonesian media and politics, by keeping his critical distance as an academic and creative producer: 'Whoever enters [the political system] will be completely pulverised. For me, it is more interesting to remain what I am, a lecturer' (Hartiningsih and Khoiri 2007).

Notes

1 The programme's theme song called it 'Dreaming Country'.

2 Heryanto (2006) is sceptical about these narratives, including those that emphasise the involvement of the student movement in the overthrow of Suharto. He acknowledges that 'successive governments have been irritated by student activists and have repeatedly punished them with considerable severity for criticizing the status quo', but at the same time argues that 'Indonesian student activism has political significance insofar as it enjoys the special privilege rendered to it by the dominant discourse' (Heryanto 2006: 70).

3 This weekly show is presented by the journalist Andy F. Noya. It addresses topical issues in a mix of entertainment and critical discussion.

4 In the *Newsdotcom* episode of 14 January 2007, Gazali referred to a news article from the 11 January 2007 edition of the *Media Indonesia* newspaper. It reported that Megawati had made her *tebar pesona* comments during the celebration of the thirty-fourth anniversary of her political party, Partai Demokrasi Indonesia-Perjuangan (Indonesian Democratic Party of Struggle, PDI-P). In humorous sketches in the programme, Si Butet Yogya showed his predilection for dutiful promises and lack of action by stating that he 'would solve' problems related to the rebuilding of tsunami-struck Aceh and the rescue of people in the Sidoarjo region, who were hit by large flows of hot mud erupting from the soil.

5 A 'free but responsible' press, in contrast to the 'libertine' and 'irresponsible' Western press, meant that it had to act as the guardian of the national Pancasila ideology and avoid sensational reporting about issues related to ethnicity, religion, race and intergroup relations (SARA, see Chapter 2). The print as well as electronic media were obliged to have licences, while their employees had to become members of government-ruled professional associations. The government could withdraw media licences at its discretion, while dissident journalists ran the risk of imprisonment or worse. Many media institutions were forced to self-censorship, while others were simply banned, as happened in 1994 with the news magazines *Tempo*, *Editor* and *DeTik* (Romano 2003: 40–46; Sen and Hill 2000: 56, 67–69; Hill 1995: 37–54).

6 In more recent work, Stam has been more positive about the critical potential of television. Stam and Shohat (2007: 247) praise Jon Stewart's *Daily Show* for critically deconstructing US politics, in a way that 'serves up more of the truth than the conventional serious news'.

7 From August 1997 to early 1999, the Indonesian government, via the state bank Bank Indonesia, provided liquidity support amounting to Rp.144.5 trillion (approx. US$14.45 billion) to assist 48 commercial banks in coping with massive runs during the monetary crisis. An estimated 95 per cent of the money was eventually embezzled (Saraswati 2002).

8 In the episodes of 4 and 18 March 2007, other film crews and journalists from Australia, Japan and Singapore were visibly present in the studio.

References

Andri, Aulia. 2006a. 'Republik Mimpi News Dot Com diluncurkan di Metro TV' [Republik Mimpi News Dot Com launched at Metro TV]. Available at: www.republikmimpi.com/content/view/28/28/ (accessed 10 August 2006).

Andri, Aulia. 2006b. 'Tayangan perdana Newsdotcom di Metro TV' [The first Newsdotcom broadcast on Metro TV]. Available at: www.republikmimpi.com/content/view/32/28/ (accessed 15 August 2006).

Baudrillard, Jean. 1995. *The Gulf War did not take place*, translated by Paul Patton. Sydney: Power Publications.

Baudrillard, Jean. 2004. *Simulacra and simulation*, translated by Sheila Faria Glaser. Ann Arbor, MI: The University of Michigan Press.

Bourdieu, Pierre. 1998. *Over televisie* [About television], translated by Rokus Hostede. Amsterdam: Boom.

Elsaesser, Thomas, Jan Simons and Lucette Bronk (eds). 1994. *Writing for the medium: television in transition*. Amsterdam: Amsterdam University Press.

Emond, Bruce. 2007. 'Not just going for laughs'. *The Jakarta Post*, 8 February. Available at: www.thejakartapost.com/weekender/cover.asp (accessed 8 February 2007).

Fadil, Iqbal. 2007a. 'Republik Mimpi stop tayang?' [Will Republik Mimpi broadcasts stop?]. *Detikcom*, 2 March. Available at: www.detiknews.com/index.php/detik.read/tahun/2007/bulan/03/tgl/02/time/110535/idnews/748960/idkanal/10 (accessed 2 March 2007).

Fadil, Iqbal. 2007b. 'Sampoerna tak perpanjang kontrak sponsor utama Republik Mimpi' [Sampoerna is not extending its main sponsor contract with Republik Mimpi]. *Detikcom*, 2 March. Available at: www.detiknews.com/index.php/detik.read/tahun/2007/bulan/03/tgl/02/time/132142/idnews/749026/idkanal/10 (accessed 2 March 2007).

Hartanto, Budi. 2006. 'BBC (Bi Bi Si)'. Available at: http://program.indosiar.com/prog_read?.htm?id=54871 (accessed 14 September 2006).

Hartiningsih, Maria and Ilham Khoiri. 2007. 'Effendi Gazali di antara tiga C' [Effendi Gazali amidst the three C's]. *Kompas*, 3 June, p. 12.

Hayid, Muhammad Nur. 2007. 'Republik Mimpi terancam disomasi Menkominfo Sofyan Djalil' [Republik Mimpi under threat of a legal notice from Communications and Informatics Minister Sofyan Djalil]. *Detikcom*, 1 March. Available at: www.detiknews.com/index.php/detik.read/tahun/2007/bulan/03/tgl/01/time/165727/idnews/748699/idkanal/10 (accessed 1 March 2007).

Heryanto, Ariel. 1996. 'Bahasa dan kuasa: tatapan posmodernisme' [Language and power: observing postmodernism]. In: Yudi Latif and Idi Subandy Ibrahim (eds), *Bahasa dan kekuasaan: politik wacana di panggung Orde Baru* [Language and power: discourse politics on the New Order stage]. Bandung: Mizan, pp. 94–103.

Heryanto, Ariel. 2006. *State terrorism and political identity in Indonesia: fatally belonging*. London and New York: Routledge.

Hill, David T. 1995. *The Press in New Order Indonesia*. Jakarta: Sinar Harapan.

Hotland, Tony. 2006. 'Kalla tells "Republik BBM" no hard feelings'. *The Jakarta Post.com*, 27 April. Available at: www.thejakartapost.com/yesterdaydetail.asp?fileid=20060427.A03 (accessed 27 April 2006).

Hutcheon, Linda. 1989. *The politics of postmodernism*. London: Routledge.

Indosiar. 2006. 'Istana BBM' [The BBM Palace]. Available at: http://program.indosiar.com/prog_read.htm?id=53787 (accessed 7 August 2006).

Ivvaty, Susi. 2006. 'Lelucon sambil menanti Imsak' [Joking while waiting for the morning start of fasting]. *Kompas*, 15 October. Available at: http://kompas.com/kompas-cetak/0610/15/hiburan/3024808 (accessed 15 October 2006).

Jurriëns, Edwin. 2004. *Cultural travel and migrancy: the artistic representation of globalization in the electronic media of West Java*. Leiden: KITLV Press.

Jurriëns, Edwin. 2008. 'Television dreams: simulation, for a new reality of Indonesia'. In: Ariel Heryanto (ed.), *Popular culture in Indonesia: fluid identities in post-authoritarian politics*. London: Routledge, pp. 143–163.

McDaniel, Drew O. 1994. *Broadcasting in the Malay world: radio, television, and video in Brunei, Indonesia, Malaysia, and Singapore*. New Jersey: Ablex.

Noble, Richard. 2009. 'Introduction: the utopian impulse in contemporary art'. In: Richard Noble (ed.), *Utopias: documents of contemporary art*. London and Cambridge, MA: Whitechapel Gallery and The MIT Press, pp. 12–19.

Romano, Angela. 2003. *Politics and the press in Indonesia: understanding an evolving political culture*. London and New York: RoutledgeCurzon.

Saraswati, Muninggar Sri. 2002. 'Controversial verdicts issued in BLBI cases'. *The Jakarta Post.com*, 23 August. Available at: www.thejakartapost.com/yesterdaydetail.asp?fileid=20020823.B08 (accessed 21 March 2006).

Schulte Nordholt, Henk. 2002. 'Introduction'. In: Henk Schulte Nordholt and Gusti Asnan (eds), *Indonesia in transition: work in progress*. Yogyakarta: Pustaka Pelajar, pp. 1–24.

Sen, Krishna and David T. Hill. 2000. *Media, culture and politics in Indonesia*. Melbourne: Oxford University Press.

Shaleh, Habieb. 2006. 'Pengampunan hukum pengemplang BLBI menyinggung rasa keadilan' [Legal clemency over BLBI insults sense of justice]. *Suara Merdeka CyberNews*, 21 March. Available at: www.suaramerdeka.com/cybernews/harian/0603/21/nas7.htm (accessed 21 March 2006).

Stam, Robert. 1985. *Reflexivity in film and literature: from Don Quixote to Jean-Luc Godard*. Ann Arbor, MI: UMI Research Press.

Stam, Robert and Ella Shohat. 2007. *Flagging patriotism: crises of narcissism and anti-Americanism*. New York and London: Routledge.

Stam, Robert, Robert Burgoyne and Sandy Flitterman-Lewis. 1992. *New vocabularies in film semiotics: structuralism, post-structuralism and beyond*. London and New York: Routledge.

Taufiqurrahman, M. 2006. 'Drunken masters of political show call it a day'. *The Jakarta Post.com*, 7 June 2006. Available at: www.thejakartapost.com/yesterdaydetail.asp?fileid=20060607.H01 (accessed 7 June 2006).

Tresnawati. 2007. 'Perjalanan Republik Mimpi: mendapat dukungan kaum perempuan' [The journey of Republik Mimpi: receiving the support of women]. *Suara Merdeka*, 12 March. Available at: http://suaramerdeka.com/harian/0703/12/nas20.htm (accessed 12 March 2007).

5 Video bodies

The programme of video

The case of *Newsdotcom* illustrated the limitations posed by government, sponsors and commercial television stations on dissonant programme makers. Video, the main medium of interest in this book, is widely used in Indonesia both within and outside the mainstream media. Together with other 'small' and mobile media such as cordless phones, video has significantly contributed to shaping a new paradigm of contemporary culture, creative production and social life, characterised by practices such as DIY, 'recycling', interactivity, networking and 'conviviality' (Coyer *et al.* 2007; Bourriaud 2002: 14, 26). These practices have both changed and gone beyond the parameters of the mass media.

Video is conceptualised here not merely as a technology or a tool of communication and information, but as a 'programme'. David Teh (2011a: 27) derived this idea from Vilém Flusser's (2000) concept of the 'programme of photography'. According to Teh (2011a: 27), the programme of video refers to 'a social process – a process of mediumship – that is, not merely a channel but a channelling that may be corporeal, social and spiritual'. This idea mirrors Wardhana's (2002) concept of television as a *television du monde* or a matter of 'TV or not TV'. It offers a comprehensive approach that is not restricted to the study of video images, but also addresses the accessibility, production, distribution and consumption of video, video's interaction and differences with other media, and the local conventions and histories of video in specific, including non-western, contexts (Teh 2011a: 30). In line with this idea, I acknowledge that the history of video in Indonesia is closely related to local styles and genres of corporeal, social and spiritual channelling (Jurriëns 2016).

Although video as a technological tool was not, or only to a limited extent, utilised by Wardhana and the *Newsdotcom* team, some of the features of the broader cultural paradigm or programme of video were reflected in their creative work and enabled them to critique, modify or leave behind the mechanisms of commercial television. Both Wardhana and the *Newsdotcom* team offered forms of corporeal, social and spiritual channelling through their focus on bodies in their representation of characters as well as their creation of forms of interactivity and intimacy with their readers, studio audiences or television viewers. Their work displayed features that are similar to the new forms of 'affective interpersonal intimacy' that Larissa Hjorth *et al.* (2014: 3, 6–7, 9) associate with the emergence of mobile media, including video applications, in contemporary life.

By analysing various video genres and developments in Indonesia, this chapter explores to what extent local video users obtain a sense of agency and intimacy in dealing with the medium and its related social practices and cultures. It specifically focuses on the way in which video enables people to, or obstructs people from, having access to information and communication, reflecting on social and personal issues, and engaging in aesthetic exploration. It examines these three different aspects of agency and intimacy by looking at bodily (self-) representations in commercial, home and artistic video genres, including music videos, amateur pornography and new media art. By demonstrating that bodily (self-)representations constitute a substantial part of the development of video in Indonesia, it attempts to fill in gaps in the largely unexplored site-specific history of the medium.

I describe how video has impacted on the way Indonesians have represented, perceived, shaped, criticised and changed their bodies, and also how features of their bodies have steered the use and development of the technology itself. Chapter 4 illustrated how *Newsdotcom* sought to make public and put under scrutiny previously unknown or untouched bodies, including those of distanced and authoritarian politicians. This chapter discusses other types of intimacy and addresses the precarious balance between the public and the private in media-saturated society. It shows how bodies mediated by video bear the imprint of IWC while also presenting unprecedented forms of subjectivity and alternative interactions between mental and social ecologies. Although it confirms that various types and degrees of reflexivity can be found in both mainstream and alternative video, special attention is paid to the role of avant-garde new media art in mapping and evaluating the past, present and future of video in Indonesian social life and creative production.

I focus on work of the Indonesian video art pioneer Krisna Murti, in which representations of the artist's own body constitute a central theme. The analysis of more general media developments in Indonesia aims to contextualise Murti's work, while the art work itself identifies some hitherto under-examined aspects of the social and creative implications of video production and consumption in Indonesia and elsewhere. While Murti's early work fully explored the creative possibilities of video technology (see Chapter 6), his more recent art takes some critical distance from the medium, without abandoning it. I argue that the artist puts forward the aesthetic modulation of video as a way of safeguarding or restoring agency and intimacy in contemporary information and communication society.

Intimate technology

Video was introduced in Indonesia around 1974 (Hafiz 2009: 13). It became a popular consumer item for the Indonesian middle class in the mid-1980s and emerged during the New Order's strong control over journalism and the media (Steele 2005). Until the late 1980s, state-owned TVRI was the only domestic television service available to the Indonesian public (Kitley 2000). TVRI was bound to censorship, compulsory and dull government broadcasts, and quota on programmes and imported materials (McDaniel 2002: 47). The government could broadcast its television messages to most parts of the archipelago via the domestic Palapa satellite, launched in 1976.[1]

During the Suharto period, video provided televisual content to those parts of the archipelago that did not have access to broadcast television (McDaniel 2002: 47). It also gave an alternative to the programmes of the state broadcaster and, later, the commercial television channels. According to Philip Kitley (2000: 218), video 'thrived on exogenous culture, challenging the government's construct of a distinct, and self-sufficient national culture'. Some videos contained messages that the New Order regime deemed politically subversive. In 1980, the Indonesian military launched the so-called *sapu jagad* ('complete wipe out') campaign in Bandung, which was directed against people accused of reviving the banned Indonesian communist party through the distribution of videos with ideological content (McDaniel 2002: 57).

Until the early 1990s, video was a luxury item, restricted to the Indonesian urban middle class (McDaniel 1994: 278). According to McDaniel (1994: 277–278), many middle-class consumers were 'light usage owners', who bought video recorders not only to watch films and television programmes, but also, and often predominantly, to show off their purchasing power and social status to others. Videos were not only watched at home, but also in public screenings in the Indonesian suburbs and villages (McDaniel 1994: 276–277). Other common settings for non-residential viewing included hotels and long-distance intercity buses (McDaniel 1994: 266; Kelana *et al.* 2009: 37–38).

The introduction of digital video cameras in the late 1990s made it possible for larger segments of the population not only to consume existing materials, but also to record their own videos (Thajib *et al.* 2011: 180). Hand-held cameras and, later, also video recording applications on computers and mobile phones, enabled people to become 'prosumers' (producer-consumers) or 'pro-am' (professional-amateur) creators of moving images (Willett 2009b: 1–2, 12). Since the mid-2000s, there has been a dramatic increase in the distribution of digital videos through mobile phone and the Internet (Thajib *et al.* 2011: 178). The accessibility and relatively easy recording, editing and distribution possibilities of digital video gave it an advantage over and, in a technological sense, more intimate character than the older medium of celluloid film (Sugiharto 2002: 10; Teh 2011a: 28).

Self-imagings of consuming bodies

The arrival of video coincided with and partly shaped the emergence of specific televisual genres in Indonesia, such as *sinetron*, commercials and music clips. These genres have been promoted by Music Television (MTV) and domestic commercial channels in Indonesia since the late 1980s. Apart from its technological features, it was the specific types of information, entertainment and aesthetics offered by (digital) video that gave the medium a greater accessibility and intimacy than the images shown on government-controlled TVRI.

While TVRI news programmes during the New Order were dominated by scenes of government officials at official events (Kitley 2000: 193–198; Romano 2003: 138, 141), other genres, especially those on domestic commercial television since the late 1980s, presented different types of 'bodies' (Hujatnikajennong 2011: 66). These alternative video bodies, including those of celebrities and ordinary people, have arguably had more potential than state television to appeal to viewers, trigger their imagination, and make them reflect on aspects of their own lives, including their bodies.

Apart from representing and criticising 'other' bodies, media professionals, artists and ordinary consumers have also used video to contemplate aspects of their 'own' bodies. These 'self-imagings'[2] or 'selfies', taken with various degrees of agency and intimacy, can be found in both mainstream and alternative video genres. Three of these genres, music clips, amateur pornography and video art are addressed in this chapter.

Emma Baulch (2007: 184–185) has demonstrated that Indonesian video clips have functioned not only as a medium to represent others in the there-and-then, but also as a mirror or surface for popular artists to look at themselves in the here-and-now. She observed these self-imagings in the music clips and video stills of the singer Kris Dayanti and the punk band 'Superman is Dead', whose rise to national superstardom coincided with the emergence of MTV in Indonesia (Baulch 2007: 185). By using video as a mirror, these artists have been able to evaluate and change their body, image and identity, and create models for an alternative future. Video reflections have assisted them with knowing, buying or modifying the right consumer goods, and in their struggle to the top of a capitalist 'hierarchical taste regime' (Baulch 2007: 191).

While the 'Superman is Dead' members attempt to restrict media coverage of their bodies in order to preserve their authenticity, Dayanti fully embraces media images of her own body in order to shape and express her 'transformative desires' (Baulch 2007: 194). An example is her appearance in an advertisement for blue contact lenses, meant to give Indonesian women a more Western appearance, and mirroring the bodily transformations and aspirations of the artist herself (Baulch 2007: 192). According to Baulch (2007: 198), media consumers to a certain extent 'define themselves and their place in the society in terms of which television programmes they watch', while artists like Kris Dayanti 'use their self-imagings like mirrors in their quests to discover their truly transformed, or self-realized, bourgeois selves' in post-authoritarian Indonesia.

In the context of the development of video in Indonesia, these examples show that video has been used not only as a medium of representation, but also as a medium of presentation. Moreover, they demonstrate that critical (self-)analysis is not restricted to avant-garde art and media, but can also be found in popular culture. They partially live up to video's potential of a 'reflexive medium' (Spielmann 2007).

The music clips and photographic stills, similar to the majority of *sinetron*, advertisements and other video-based genres on commercial television, however, are not reflexive in a more comprehensive way, as they normally do not address the broader social and political conditions surrounding the medium of video. By inspiring consumers to change the shape of their bodies, the heroes of these popular genres also introduce new forms of socio-political and economic control. They share a paradigm of monitoring, disciplining and acculturating individuals with other forms of contemporary video, including the Closed-Circuit Television (CCTV) surveillance of people in public spaces and the seemingly more private 'home mode' recordings of daily life activities and family ceremonies (Chalfen 1987; Buckingham 2009: 29; Willett 2009a: 212).

Bodies have also been disciplined in a more direct physical manner by the gestures that are necessary or desirable for recording or being recorded with video (Hujatnikajennong 2011: 64, 67). The arm and head gestures associated with taking selfies immediately come to mind. In cases like amateur pornography, as will be explained later, digital consumer video goes beyond representing the body, by also functioning as a physical extension of it. Although the self-imagings of pop stars may appear more intimate and appealing to ordinary television consumers than the images of government officials, they also remain relatively 'distant selves', with lifestyles beyond the reach of ordinary media consumers.

Intimate bodies and their discontents

At the same time, digital video has contributed to 'the proliferation of voices', 'the devolution of authorship' and the widening of 'the range of tones available to the individual' in Indonesia (Teh 2011b: 174). This is especially the case with consumer recording technology that enabled the creation of video genres outside the mainstream media. Apart from home video, various types of alternative or 'activist' video have emerged, such as grassroots video created for communal goals, tactical video for political purposes, and experimental video for artistic objectives (Thajib *et al.* 2011: 181–182).

The 1998 democratic reform movement, for instance, recognised the tactical potential of new media such as mainstream and alternative video, international satellite television and the Internet, to disturb the New Order attempts to control the Indonesian broadcast spectrum (Kitley 2000: 217–224; Sen and Hill 2000: 116–119; Hill and Sen 2005). More recently, in 2014, videos on social networks like Facebook importantly contributed to Joko Widodo's rise to the Indonesian presidency. In both cases, video enabled 'media participation and first-person storytelling' and confirmed 'the power of audiovisual representation and dissemination to generate extensive socio-political changes' (Thajib *et al.* 2011: 181; cf. Hafiz 2009: 13; Teh 2011a: 31, 2011b: 170–171).

The large increase in amateur or pro-am productions since the late 1990s reflect the extent to which video has provided an alternative to the mainstream media. The relatively affordable digital video camera has made it possible for individuals to record, show and reflect on almost every aspect of their daily lives, including their bodies. Video self-imagings or selfies are no longer restricted to pop stars like Dayanti and 'Superman is Dead' or professional video artists, but have come within the reach of ordinary media consumers.

The seemingly most intimate and, paradoxically, widely publicised home video genre in Indonesia is amateur pornography. In amateur pornography, people have tested video technology with their bodies, while their bodies have also been tested by the technology (Halim 2010: 55–56). Considering that the genre enables people to display their own bodies and witness the bodies of their peers in sexual acts, it is the case study par excellence to examine the nature and limits of accessibility, agency, connectivity, reflexivity and intimacy in the age of mobile and social media. Some of Murti's work discussed later in this chapter can be seen as a critique of and alternative to the broader socio-cultural developments – the programme of video – of which amateur pornography and other types of self-imaging form a considerable part.

There has been a long tradition of sexual innuendo and the sexualised representation of women in Indonesian visual culture, particularly in the national film productions of the 1970s and 1980s. However, due to censorship and cultural conventions, these films did not show explicit sexual acts or completely naked bodies (Sen 1994: 154–155). People's exposure to explicit pornography increased with the import and reproduction of illegal hard-core videos and laser discs from Europe, the US and other Asian countries. With the introduction of VCD and Moving Picture Experts Group (MPEG) files in the 1990s, there has been a growth in domestically produced professional and amateur videos (Set 2007: 6). These videos are usually referred to as *blue film* (blue films) or *video mesum* ('dirty or indecent videos'; Set 2007: 4, 9; Ida 2013: 21). In the early 2000s, local porn received mass attention with the wide circulation of a handful of amateur videos, predominantly created by students and other young, unmarried couples.

Undeniably problematic in many facets of its creation, distribution and consumption, Indonesian amateur porn is also rich in information about how Indonesians have interacted with video, and used the medium to represent and reflect on their own bodies as well as the bodies of others. Many of the early porn videos did not have a scenario but were meant for private documentation and consumption (Set 2007: 24). According to Set (2007: 23–25), the reason for their popularity was their use of local actors, whose looks, behaviour and language were very recognisable to the viewers, unlike those of foreign professional actors in imported porn. Some of the videos gave a realistic representation of the mix of curiosity and awkwardness of young people simultaneously exploring the new media equipment and their own bodies and sexuality. Set (2007: 30) also suggested that the videos could be seen as an expression of youth in search of new challenges and identities after their involvement in the heroic struggle for political reform in 1998.

Home videos of Indonesian celebrities engaging in sexual activities also became popular (Halim 2010). An infamous case that received much public attention in June 2010 was the online posting of several videos starring Nazril Ilham (better known as Ariel), the lead singer of the pop band 'Peterpan'. Television and documentary maker Syaiful Halim (2010) argued that the case was highly beneficial to mainstream television stations, which included sensationalist coverage in infotainment shows as well as supposedly more serious news programmes. In January 2011, Ilham was sentenced to three-and-a-half-years of prison under the 2008 Undang-Undang Informasi dan Transaksi Elektronik (Information and Electronic Transaction Law, UU ITE) for distributing pornography (Prakoso and Andriyanto 2012).

The amateur porn videos not only give some form of agency and intimacy to its creators, but also to other viewers. Rachmah Ida's (2013) research demonstrates how video has made *kampung* (urban village) residents in the city of Surabaya think about the bodies and sexual behaviour of others, and, ultimately, also of themselves. One of her surprise findings is that it is not uncommon for the neighbourhood dwellers to have communal porn viewing sessions. According to Ida (2013: 24), the communal viewing of films that were previously banned or unavailable on national television, such as critical political documentaries and pornography, has enabled the local citizens to 'expand their imaginative experience'. Examples include groups of housewives consuming Indonesian amateur porn in between their household and child caring duties (Ida 2013: 26). The communal watching of these videos has enabled the women to guard themselves from male interference and to comment on what they see.

Ida (2013: 24) uses the concept of 'privatised-communal mobility', based on a mix of Raymond Williams' 'mobile privatisation' and Lynn Spigel's 'privatised mobility', to refer to the way in which the video consumers 'share their private viewing experiences with neighbours and acquaintances'. Roughly, Williams' (1990: 26) idea of 'mobile privatisation' suggests that television gives mobility to viewers by bringing the outside world into their private living rooms, while Spigel's (2001: 72) idea of 'privatised mobility' explains how the increased mobility of the television set has made people's private viewing practices visible to the outside world.

To a certain extent, the porn videos give people access to information and communication media, and facilitate or strengthen a DIY ethos, interpersonal connectivity and reflexivity. However, these specific manifestations of agency and intimacy are often disrupted by deplorable production and distribution mechanisms. Some videos meant only for private consumption were leaked to the general public through VCD, mobile phone and the Internet by people involved in the digital recording or transferring process (Set 2007: 8–9).[3] Other videos were made with hidden cameras, without the consent of the people being filmed (Set 2007: 22). Although the Surabaya *kampung* women generally derive pleasure from watching and commenting on the bodies of the actors, which are often regarded as a standard of female beauty, they strongly object to the conditions under which some of the videos were made, such as the use of hidden cameras to spy on female models changing their clothes and underwear (Ida 2013: 26).

While the groups of video-viewing Surabaya housewives can be seen as 'intimate publics' (Hjorth *et al.* 2014: 3) that are 'tightly bound and share common emotional ground', the more general porn-viewing audience is, at most, a 'social public' that is 'broader' and 'less tightly bound' by 'emotional affinities'. The illegal distributors of private videos or the television producers covering the Ilham case, on the other hand, may be void of 'intimacy' and not be seen as a 'public' at all, in spite of the nature of the goods they disseminate or report on. They rather constitute a 'social network' of digital media users, who have the commercial exploitation of other people's intimacy as their sole objective, and 'are not constituted in common affect, but are instrumentally related in interconnected and ramified ego-based formations' (Hjorth *et al.* 2014: 3).

Bodily critique in video art

The Indonesian amateur porn demonstrates that in the complex, highly mediatised world of today, media savviness is not synonymous with media literacy. Being aware of the general lack of media literacy among Indonesian youth, the Indonesian television producer Sony Set (2007: 183, 199), together with colleagues from his Yogyakarta-based consultation firm for television programme production TVLab.Communications, launched the Internet campaign *Jangan bugil di depan kamera!* ('Don't get naked in front of the camera!') on 11 April 2007. It was similar to other initiatives promoting media literacy, like YPMA's annual *Hari tanpa TV* (see Chapter 3). Unlike other campaigns, however, it was specifically focused on warning youth about the far-reaching implications of recording private activities with media that have the potential of being mass distributed (Set 2007: 60). On 15 June 2007, the campaign took to the streets of Semarang in Central Java, targeting students from the local Diponegoro University and other young adults.

The impact of this type of campaign is difficult to measure. It may be seen as overtly didactic, and not engaging with or providing alternatives to the visual culture that is being criticised. In this respect, video or new media art deserves critical attention, as it appropriates the signs and languages of contemporary popular cultures and lifestyles, while simultaneously modifying and undermining them. Video art or new media art is closely related to performance art and pays attention, in many of its manifestations, to the human body. In that sense, it is similar to other video-based or -inspired genres such as music clips, *sinetron*, commercials and amateur porn, which have also enabled Indonesian viewers to contemplate their own or other people's bodies. More than mainstream and home video, however, it reflects not only on bodies as such, but also on the socio-political conditions that influence people's bodily shapes and idea(l)s.

The Bandung-based new media art community Video Lab, for instance, referred to television under the New Order as a Panopticon-type of state surveillance. It also argued that other types of civilian (body) control emerged in the late 1980s in the form of the promotion of consumer culture on the newly introduced domestic commercial television channels. In the mid-2000s, Video Lab itself presented experimental video as a tool to break with the legacy of these surveillance practices in Indonesia's post-1998 democracy (Siregar 2004; see also Thajib *et al.* 2011: 179).

The Jakarta-based new media initiative 'ruangrupa' explicitly engaged with the theme of the body in 'Flesh', the 2011 edition of their biennial OK.Video art festival.[4] According to the artistic director of the festival, Hafiz, the title referred to the 'flesh' or historical framework of video art in Indonesia. The aim of the festival was to document the state of Indonesian new media art and generate ideas for its future development (Hafiz 2011: 15). Similar to my book, it made direct connections between the human body and the history of video in Indonesia. It also referred to video-facilitated forms of interpersonal communication and interconnectedness, including new ways for people to produce and distribute images of themselves (Hafiz 2011: 15). According to Hafiz (2011: 14), this development had not been entirely positive, as some videos containing people's most intimate details were nothing less than 'visual garbage' (*sampah-sampah visual*).

Krisna Murti (b. 1957) is an Indonesian new media artist, who is best known for representing his own body and the bodies of fellow performers to comment on the impact of media and consumer culture on people's physical appearance and social and mental life. After his graduation from the prestigious Indonesian arts academy at Institut Teknologi Bandung (Bandung Institute of Technology, ITB) in 1981, he has experimented with a wide variety of genres, ranging from poetry, painting, printmaking and collage to photography, performance and installation art. In the early 1990s, he was one of the first Indonesian artists to explore the medium of video. In just over 20 years, he has created more than 50 video art projects. He has also written numerous essays and newspaper articles on video art and is a lecturer at the Yogyakarta-based Institut Seni Indonesia (Indonesian Institute of the Arts, ISI; Jurriëns 2010: 5).

Murti (2006: 61–66) makes a useful distinction between five different types of (Indonesian) video art:

1 video art as 'an extension of the body', based on artistic, realistic or socio-realistic recordings or real-time streaming of bodily activities in performance art;
2 video art as an alternative type of film, which presents various forms of narrative, such as biography, documentary and fiction;
3 video art as installation art, combining video with other artistic media, and containing a spatial, architectural dimension;
4 video art as new media art, in which video technology is combined with other electronic media such as computers, disc jockey equipment and mobile phones; and
5 video art as consumer culture, mainly deriving from popular genres such as MTV video clips. Murti's own work presents various types of bodily representation in predominantly the first, third and fourth categories of video art.

Some Indonesian art critics make a distinction between 'media art' and 'new media art' based on the specific type of technology that is being used. Within this framework, media art consists of analogue media such as photography and video, while new media art makes use of digital media, such as computers (Hujatnikajennong 2006: 15). Most Indonesian video art is a combination of both old and new media, in which analogue film and photo are often used as objects or models for the application of digital technology (Hujatnikajennong 2006: 18). Murti (2009: 20) rightly argues that the very name of the art form can be confusing and stand in the way of a more inclusive approach. 'New' may imply a hierarchical distinction from supposedly 'old' or 'outdated' forms of art; 'media' could be wrongly interpreted as a mere technology for maintaining and updating traditional art ideas and practices; while 'art' itself may embody a narrow idea of Indonesian art history that excludes relevant related fields of theory and practice, such as media studies and popular culture.

The work of Krisna Murti

Murti is an artist who strategically positions himself outside the institutional structures of the mainstream media industry, while at the same time appropriating technologies and discourses from this industry for his own work. In his creative work, lectures and writings, he has expressed his concern about how the mass media, particularly television, have influenced politics, culture and society, and changed people's notions of time, space, body and gender. In light of these concerns, Murti's work should be seen in a context that is broader than cutting-edge contemporary art. The work also relates to recent developments in media and society, such as viewers sending letters to newspaper editors complaining about the quality of Indonesian television; media scholars and observers writing books with titles such as *Matikan TV-mu!* ('Turn off your TV!'; Wirodono 2006); and KPI urging radio and television organisations to improve their production and broadcasting standards.

Murti's work engages viewers in a different, deeper way than journalistic forms of televisual metadiscourse. Media watch programmes such as *Dewan pers menjawab* ('The press council responds') on Indonesia's public channel TVRI, or the programmes *Media watch* and *De leugen regeert* ('The rule of lie') on Australian and Dutch public television, respectively, discuss the production mechanisms behind media discourse and the media industry in rational terms from political, economic or professional perspectives. While Murti's work provides similar insights, it pays special attention to media consumption – how recipients experience and are impacted upon by television and other media – and also attempts to offer aesthetic and conceptual alternatives to mass communication. The artist made a deliberate choice to work with alternative, attractive and accessible media such as video and performance, in order to be able to engage and educate the audience in matters related to contemporary consumer and communication culture.

One of Murti's main sources of inspiration is the Korean video art pioneer Nam June Paik (1932–2006), who in one of his iconic works attempted to turn the 'cold' and distanced medium of television into a 'hot' and interactive device by placing a magnet on a television screen. The magnet turned media consumers into media producers, as it allowed them to distort and reshape the images on the screen. This was meant as an alternative to the images reflecting the commercial and ideological interests of inaccessible, top-down-oriented institutions with a monopoly on television production and broadcasting (Murti 1999: 47).[5]

From the work and writings of another video art pioneer, the American Bill Viola (b. 1951), Murti (1999: 44) learned that video art is not about the use of advanced technology, but about sharing a vision or thought. Even though his creations often emphasise the senses, creative imagination and audience participation, he does not work impulsively, but conducts extensive research to develop an idea and express it in a piece of art (Murti 1999: 66).[6] He also agrees with Viola that the artistic media in video art are not the camera or the screen, but the human experiences and notions of time that are generated by this form of art (Murti 1999: 35). According to Murti (1999: 50), people's capacity to think, memorise and react intuitively steers their 'video sprouts' (*kecambah-kecambah video*), or the ability to edit, record and play images in their mind. Video art functions as a 'trigger' (*pemicu*) that stimulates people's imagination, and helps the video sprouts to develop into a full-grown 'tree of life' (*pohon hayat*; Murti 1999: 50). It is these analogies between the video camera and the human mind that make video art Murti's medium of preference.

The artist calls his own work *video publik* (public video), which unlike 'an art paradigm that focuses on the aesthetic factor' is meant 'to serve the public interest' (Murti 1999: 53). Emphasising his bond with and impact on the audience, he sees himself as 'mediator', 'stimulator' or 'provocateur' rather than 'creator' or virtuoso artist. He acknowledges that it is unlikely that video art can solve major social and political problems (Murti 1999: 54). He also believes that it is difficult or undesirable for this type of art to have the same reach as mainstream television (Murti 1999: 48, 59). He is convinced, however, of video art's potential to mediate and create awareness about socio-political transformations, to show and promote plural realities (*realitas plural*), and to provide an alternative to the general conservatism and one-sidedness of the mass media (Murti 1999: 54–55).

Apart from contextualising the disciplining of the body by media and consumption practices, Murti's art also attempts to offer aesthetic innovation and bodily alternatives. In several of his works, the artist explicitly refers to the role of advertising and the media in shaping people's thoughts and perceptions about the human body. In his video work 'Videohijab' (2011), he demonstrates how people's everyday presentation of their bodies to the outside world is determined by the complex intertwining of politics, religion, consumer culture and the media. This work consists of video projections of a dozen women, shown as larger than in real-life, standing in line next to each other. Each of the women is dressed in a different, colourful Indonesian version of the *hijab*, the Muslim veil for women. At the short commands of a recorded voice, which sounds harsh and loud as if uttered through a megaphone, the women turn their bodies around synchronically. The video suggests that women, in spite of displaying diversity in the way they dress, are confined in their bodily movements and identity choices by the socio-religious climate in which they live.

Self-imagings of critical bodies

Partially in resistance against the abundance and narcissism of celebrity self-imagings in the mass media and amateur selfies in social media, Murti has included representations of his own body in some of his recent work. This is remarkable, as most of his earlier work was based on recordings of the bodies of fellow performers, actors and models (Rath 2010: 42). The self-imagings in Murti's videos and digital prints bring to mind the models in advertisements, are posed in the mode of selfies familiar from Facebook and other social media, and in some cases constitute 'counter-selfies' by obstructing the gaze of others.

Examples of Murti's bodily self-representations were on display in his 'Mute! Theater' solo exhibition at the Bentara Budaya cultural centre in Jakarta from 13–17 July 2010. This exhibition consisted of the video installation 'Empty theater' (2010) and several digital prints, which represented characters, themes and images known from traditional Indonesian performing arts, particularly *wayang* puppet theatre. The works were the result of a creative collaboration between Murti, the *wayang wong* (performance with human actor-dancers) director Ngesti Pandowo and several professional photographers (Murti 2010: 6).

One of Murti's reasons for using his own body to present traditional dresses and characters was to share responsibility for the social and environmental problems that are the result of excessive (media) consumption behaviour. Rather than merely being an observer (*pengawas*), he wanted to be critically observed (*diawasi*) himself (Murti 2010: 8). One aspect of the problem was the negative impact of contemporary media and consumer culture on the state of the arts in Indonesia, particularly the traditional arts. The tiresome process of dressing up physically reminded Murti of the poor conditions in which many of his fellow artists live (Murti 2010: 7).

Murti (1999: 50) also draws analogies between *wayang*, video and the human mind. Rather than suggesting a break between puppet theatre and video, he attempts to demonstrate how both media have similar ways of creating a sense of illusion. By playing with shadows and other subtle, poetic or unconventional visual languages and materials, both are able to trigger the imagination of their audiences, and interrupt the mental ecologies resulting from the explicit imagery of the mass media (Jurriëns 2010: 14).

The video installation 'Empty theater' (2010) presents ten different *wayang* characters: Gareng, Petruk, Bagong, Srikandi, Pergiwati, Sinta, Kresna, Anoman, Arjuna and Gatotkaca, who are all played by Murti himself. Illusionary effects are created by *wayang* figures exploding or fading into nothingness, and the screen turning to black, which are all elements that urge the audience to reconsider or complete the story in their mind (Siregar 2010: 14). At some points, the digitally manipulated characters seem to explode into fragments as if they have a texture of porcelain, while at other points, they slowly fade into colourful, low-definition pixels.

The background of this and much of Murti's other art is the artist's nostalgia for the traditional Javanese dance and theatre performances he attended during his youth in Semarang in the 1960s (Murti 2010: 6). As a result, the video installation has been interpreted as symbolising a tension between tradition (*ketradisian/tradisionalitas*) and modernity (*kemodernan/modernitas*; Siregar 2010: 14). Art critic Amanda Rath (2010: 43) sees in it a reference to the museumisation of the Indonesian traditional arts by the Dutch colonial and Indonesian postcolonial regimes.

The bodies and characters in Murti's art are not merely the victims of the past and present, however, but also seem to take critical distance from, and provide alternatives to, socio-historical phenomena such as contemporary media and consumer culture. I believe that Murti does not merely re-enact the destruction of tradition by modernity, or the museumisation of tradition, but deliberately creates a distance between traditional and modern cultural expressions in order to be able to critically comment on both.

In 'Empty theater' (2010), the various 'modern' forms of digital manipulation do not necessarily oppose or destroy tradition, but rather constitute elements with which the *wayang* figures actively and playfully engage. The characters seem to retain a certain autonomy and to function as witnesses or bystanders, who perceive and react to the miracles of modern times without necessarily being deeply affected by them. Rath (2010: 15) confirms that Murti's donning of traditional outfits refers not only to the colonial practice and neo-colonial mimicry of collecting and archiving cultural phenomena, but also to playful and empowering 'masquerade and impersonations'.

In the video installation there are no direct references to modernity, other than the use of digital technology for aesthetic manipulation. The 21 digital prints from the same exhibition, on the other hand, contain clear juxtapositions between the traditional arts and modern consumer culture. Several of the prints, including 'Street theater' (2010), 'For odd for ever' (2010) and 'The old and the beauty' (2010) consist of *wayang* figures, all impersonated by Murti himself, photoshopped in front of billboard advertisements and shop windows (Figure 5.1). Some of the photos of shops and billboards contain clues that they were taken in metropolitan Southeast Asia, most likely Kuala Lumpur, while some of the other pictures are fairly generic. The prints can be seen as 'hybrid' spaces (Gordon and De Souza e Silva 2011: 86) which 'disrupt binary modes of co-presence such as virtual versus actual' and 'augment and simulate' aspects of everyday practices (Hjorth *et al.* 2014: 5).

The digital manipulation that makes the characters in the prints transgress the boundaries of space and time also confirm the potential of mobile digital technology as media of propinquity (Hjorth *et al.* 2014: 7). There is no total fusion between the traditional *wayang* figures and their modern surroundings, however. The other figures in the pictures, 'real' people walking by the shops and

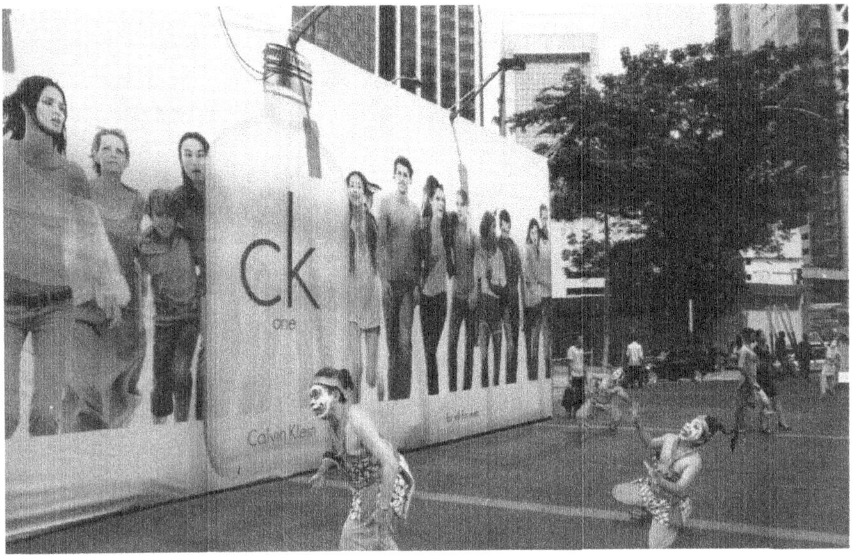

Figure 5.1 'For odd for ever' (Krisna Murti), digital photography, 2010.

Source: photo courtesy of the artist.

billboards, seem to completely ignore or be unable to see the various *wayang* characters in the street. The *wayang* figures themselves, on the other hand, are aware of and react to their unusual environment. Their reaction is not one of shock, surprise, admiration, fear or disgust, but of an open, natural and self-confident bodily assimilation or interpretation of the alien world with which they are confronted. Rather than merely mimicking the passers-by and the items in the advertisements and shop windows, their bodily gestures function as witness, documentation or counterbalance of these real-life people and goods.

The centrepiece of one print, 'Albino karabao #1' (2010), is a clownish *wayang* face in front of a perfume shop at an airport (Figure 5.2).

The figure, Murti's impersonation of the humorous *wayang* character Gareng, looks straight into the camera, addresses the viewers directly, and provides them with a mirror that shows the ridicule of their consumer behaviour. It also functions as a parody of contemporary social media culture, and could be seen as the world's first *wayang* selfie. The silly smile on the *wayang* face is mirrored by the facial expressions of the two albino water buffalos in the background, on each side of the Gareng figure. In some local Indonesian beliefs, albino buffalos are considered sacred (Siregar 2010: 15–16). Their out-of-placeness in the artwork could signal that religious values have been desacralised by consumer culture or, conversely, that commodities have become a contemporary form of religion. They could also signal a juxtaposition of man and nature, and the precarious balance between the two. The digital print as a whole functions as a video mirror

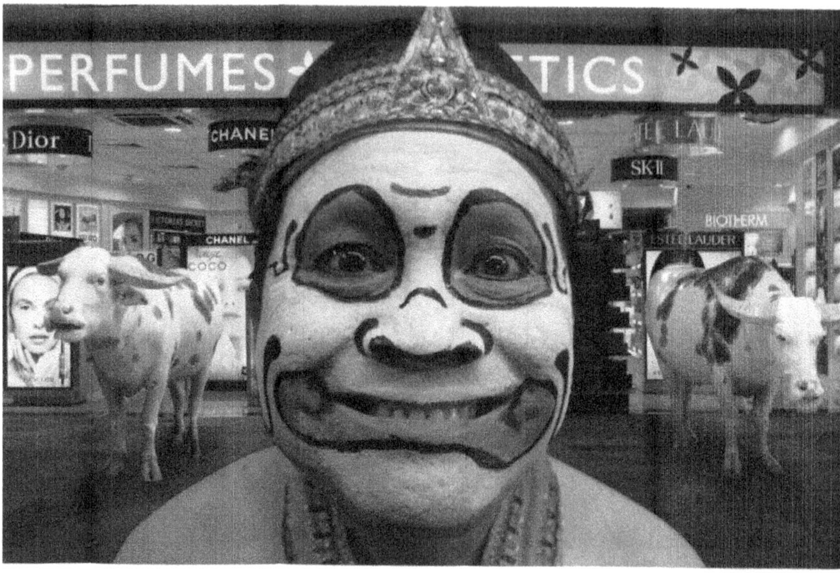

Figure 5.2 'Albino karabao # 1' (Krisna Murti), digital photography, 2010.
Source: photo courtesy of the artist.

that reflects and deconstructs the self-imaging by artists like Dayanti and 'Superman is Dead', as well as the standard selfies in social media.

In some of the digital prints, Murti is not dressed in Javanese *wayang* style, but in traditional costumes from Borneo, while posing against a grim background of deforested landscapes and container ships heavily loaded with black coal. The prints illustrate the transversal connections between mental, social and natural ecologies. They bear cynical titles like 'Tropical goddess #1' (2010), 'The guardian of the Mount Coal' (2010) and 'Pre-wedding photograph' (2010). The photos represent 'counter-selfies', in which the characters do not look at the viewer, but keep their eyes closed and do not look at all. They may signal that human greed has gone beyond limits, and environmental damage beyond repair. Their symbolical gesture suggests that only intense self-reflection and inner strength can help people to overcome shame and reverse the detrimental impact of their consumer behaviour.

In comparing video art in Thailand and Indonesia, Teh (2011b) characterises the differences between the two scenes as differences between the bystander (the Thai artist) and the observer (the Indonesian artist):

> The bystander is incidental to the action; the observer is more like a monitor, a feedback conduit, and never neutral. The former inevitably carries the pejorative connotation of a passive sort of viewing, while the observational stance may be considered a more active footing on which to make images.

The *wayang* figures in Murti's prints escape the dichotomy between bystander and observer by presenting a hybrid mix of the two. The characters need the dissociation of the bystander, symbolised by the far-away times and places from which they originate, to put contemporary cultural practices into perspective through juxtaposition. At the same time, they need the observational stance to be able to adapt to dramatic change and, where necessary, to protest against conditions that are deemed harmful and unsustainable. They denote the precarious balance between tradition and modernity, and remind the viewer of the tremendous impact of contemporary media and consumer culture on the state of people's bodies, minds, and social, cultural and natural environments.

Aesthetic intimacy beyond video

The example of Indonesian amateur pornography showed that the use of intimate technology for creating, distributing and consuming images of intimacy does not necessarily create intimate audiences. One could even argue that in times of informational abundance, sensory overload and visual detail and precision, intimacy seems to be harder to define, if not to find, than ever. This problem is not limited to interpersonal relations, but extends to aesthetic intimacy, or the bond between artist, work and viewer. It is the rethinking of this artistic relationship in the context of contemporary video and other mobile media that has inspired Murti's recent work. The work demonstrates that discussions about video should not be limited to the political economy, content and impact of video, but also address the aesthetic dimensions of the medium. It is Murti's specific modulation of video aesthetics that is meant to give back a sense of agency and intimacy to the viewer. It provides a space for interpersonal contact, reflection and re-subjectification to audiences, who may otherwise be overpowered and ultimately silenced and numbed by the noise of the media, advertisements and commoditised bodies they are confronted with on a daily basis.

It is telling that Murti's recent work is characterised by technologically uncomplicated, small-scale, intimate and poetic video projects, while his earlier new media art consisted of relatively large-scale multi-media installations that intensively explored and exploited the creative opportunities of video (see Chapter 6). An example of this new direction in Murti's career was his 'Art after drama' exhibition at the Salihara gallery in Jakarta from 20 July until 4 August 2013. Among various other works, it had the multi-channel video 'Dance of the unknown' (2012) and the video installation 'Eggology' (2013). The works involved collaboration with two female dancers, Indonesian Gita Kinanthi (b. 1986) in 'Dance of the unknown' (2012) and Polish Ewelina Eve Smereczynska (b. 1985) in 'Eggology' (2013).

In 'Dance of the unknown' (2012), Kinanthi's digitally modified dance movements represent the different stages of life (Murti 2013a: 12). The work demonstrates how technology has interfered with the most substantial aspects of human existence, including birth and death. It plays with video's ability to modify the appearance of bodies by changing their proportions, doubling them, mixing them with other bodies, or positioning them in a different time or space. It invites audiences to participate in the video dance and embark on an unknown journey by giving them not only a visual, but also a physical or bodily, experience. By presenting an elongated, double landscape view, it forces the viewers to stretch their necks and move their eyes in order to be able to follow the dance movements on the screen (Murti 2013a: 12). This could also refer to the acrobatics used by some people in order to capture the perfect angle for their selfies. In an experiential manner, the work illustrates the profound impact of the media on people's inner life as well as their bodies.

In 'Eggology' (2013), Murti seems to suggest a solution for art 'after' – highly mediatised – drama by returning to the origins of both life and art. This installation consists of the projections of the dance movements of Smereczynska on an egg-shaped structure. The structure and images suggest an unborn baby in its mother's womb. Similar to 'Dance of the unknown', the work seems to deal with the power of technology to enter and record the most private aspects of the human body. According to Murti (2013b: 16) himself, the video installation is primarily meant to capture the beauty of the most basic movements, of the most basic stages of life, in the most limited spaces of all. Rather than augmenting or distorting reality, video here works to document the essence of art and life before both are subject to life-long manipulations by politics, consumer culture and the media.

In his exhibition 'Poetshop' at Langgeng Gallery in Jakarta from 3–20 November 2011, Murti realigned video with other art forms, including local literature and performance traditions such as *mantra* and *rajah* (magical formulas and visual sign language, respectively); ordinary objects, including coffee tables, chairs and hand basins; and everyday practices, such as eating, drinking, washing and reading. One of his sources of inspiration for this exhibition was the multi-media experiments of the early twentieth century Dadaists and Surrealists. In 1978, when he was still an arts student at ITB, Murti (2011) contributed to a concrete poetry event of the well-known Indonesian writers Sutardji Calzoum Bachri (b. 1941) and Danarto (b. 1941). He learned from the international and Indonesian experimental artists that literature can derive its meaning not only from its style and content, but also from the material ('concrete') qualities of the typography of writing and the sound of performance (Murti 2011).

Murti's work confirms Philip Auslander's (1999) observation that the dichotomy between mediated and 'live' performances in contemporary information and communication society is largely arbitrary, notwithstanding the unique types of 'performativity' or ways of affecting audiences each medium may have. It is also important to note that Murti's art is not merely nostalgia for modernist conceptions of the autonomy of art and the artist. Although his work is interactive to only a limited degree and does not invite the audience members to become artistic collaborators, it does share the relational aesthetics of other forms of contemporary art that in their very conceptualisation and execution give prominence to various forms of audience engagement and agency (Bourriaud 2002).

In the 'Poetshop' exhibition, Murti (2011) wanted to share with the audience his old interest in poetry in order to 'return to the heart' (*kembali kepada hati*) and bring back 'a personal touch' (*sentuhan personal*), which he felt was often lost in the 'regime of no hearts' (*rezim non-hati*) of modern communication and information technology. Using various media, he presented poems and performances of the Chinese-Indonesian poet Hanna Fransisca (b. 1979). One of the works, 'Kursi merah mendaras' (Reciting red chair, 2011), consists of a red iron chair that integrates Fransisca's poems 'Rindu' (Longing) and 'Palung' (Pool) into its structure of metal. Attached to the chair are two mini-loudspeakers through which Francisca's own recitation of her poems can be heard. The installation is an example of Murti's use of the materiality of alternative media such as iron and voice recordings to give new expression to the idea of concrete poetry.[7]

Also, in several of the other 'Poetshop' works, Murti creatively combined and integrated the tactile qualities of poetry and performance with the tactile nature of contemporary media such as installation, video and other information and communication technology (Jeon 2013: 10). In the video installation 'Secangkir teh' (A cup of tea, 2011), Murti presented a video with a poem by Fransisca that bears the same title as the installation. In this installation, the video screen is placed at the bottom of a glass bowl on a white coffee table. The installation perfectly captures the poem's symbolism of the sea and the beach, by partially covering the video screen in sand and shells. The colours and waves of the sea are also suggested by the moving text and images in the video. The work softens video technology and creates a new, hybrid form of aesthetic intimacy by blurring the video images and reconnecting them with nature and literature.

Implicit in Murti's recent poetic work may be a revolt against, and an attempt to provide a media-ecological alternative to, the loss of agency, intimacy, beauty and ultimately meaning in highly mediatised genres such as video clips and pornography. Not unlike other international new media artists (Dixon 2007: 645–647), Murti may have reached a point in his career in which he is more interested in the art, rather than the medium, of video art, although technology and aesthetics, and modern media and traditional craft and performance, remain inextricably intertwined in his work.

Conclusion

At the time of its introduction in Indonesia (the 1970s), video, including pirated video, increased people's access to information and communication technology by providing an alternative to state television, which did not cover the entire archipelago and only offered specific types of programmes. Especially with the introduction of domestic commercial television in the late 1980s, video became an integral part of television production in genres such as music clips, advertisements and *sinetron*. These genres introduced the public to the bodies of ordinary people and celebrities, which were rarely found in the news programmes on state television that were dominated by reports on government officials.

Both in terms of its technology and its facilitation of interpersonal relations, video provided a seemingly even greater sense of agency and intimacy after the explosive growth in consumer recording technology, particularly digital cameras on computers and mobile phones, in the 1990s and 2000s. Mobile video played a role in key events in Indonesia's political history, such as the fall of Suharto in 1998 and Joko Widodo's rise to the presidency in 2014. It also further developed home genres such as amateur pornography, which enabled prosumers to witness and reflect on the bodies and identities, including sexual identities, of themselves and their peers.

Video's relative affordability, mobility and adaptability have also come at the cost of agency and intimacy. Both professional and amateur video have been shaped by the commercial demands of the video production and distribution industry. The self-imagings of pop stars seem to promote consumer culture as the key to fulfilling personal ideals, including bodily ambitions. Some amateur pornography has been produced and distributed without the consent of, and with far-reaching negative implications for, the actors involved in it. Digital video proves that media savviness is not synonymous with media literacy.

A video genre with a relatively high degree of reflexivity is video art or new media art. Murti started pioneering this genre in Indonesia in the early 1990s. He has used his art to comment on the impact of media and consumer culture on people's cultural and natural environments, including their self-perceptions, bodies and gender identities. He has engaged with traditional art forms such as *wayang* to create dialogue, juxtapositions and hybridity between different times and spaces, and to both critically and humorously reflect on contemporary (media) consumption practices. With his *wayang* selfies and other bodily representations of himself and his fellow performers, he provides a mirror for people's uncritical absorption in a hedonistic and, in that sense, far from intimate, commercial and social media culture.

While his early work fully explored the technological and aesthetic possibilities of video (see Chapter 6), in his more recent work Murti takes some critical distance from the medium. He attempts to bring back intimacy as an important aspect of people's social and mental ecologies, by combining video with elements from nature and other creative genres, particularly literature, drama and craft. As an avant-garde artist, he seems to indicate a new, personally and artistically more satisfying direction in dealing with the abundance and intensity of visual stimuli in the age of selfies. His works suggests that these contemporary challenges demand not only the monitoring of the political economy and the content of the media, but also the creation of a new type of aesthetics that gives space to audiences for reflection, interpersonal contact and intimate audio-visual experiences.

Notes

1 Indonesia was the third country in the world, after the US and Canada, to launch its own communication satellite. There were 54 ground stations for satellite reception established in various provincial capitals and industrial and agricultural centres around the archipelago (Kelana *et al.* 2009: 29–30).

2 This is derived from Baulch 2007. This neologism seems to refer to both the technological act of taking pictures or making a movie, and the symbolic act of creating a good impression of oneself. Both aspects also play a role in the creation of self-portraits or selfies for circulation in social media like Facebook.

3 One of the first and most widely circulated videos was popularly dubbed *Bandung lautan asmara* ('Bandung, ocean of love'), a pun on the so-called *Bandung lautan api* ('Bandung, ocean of fire') or scorched earth tactics in Bandung, 1946, during the Indonesian struggle for independence. This video was reportedly duplicated by the staff of an Internet café and distributed without prior knowledge or approval of the young couple. The video forced the couple to terminate their university studies, but was highly profitable for the Indonesian underground video market (Set 2007: 22).

4 Previous editions included 'OK. Video' (2003, about video art), 'Sub-Version' (2005, about visual counterstrategies), 'Militia' (2007, about video activism), and 'Comedy' (2009, about humour).

5 Nam June Paik used videos for many different art forms including installations, live performances and broadcasts. According to Meigh-Andrews (2006: 9–18), Paik and the German artist Wolf Vostell's (1932–1998) work in 'appropriating the television apparatus and presenting the domestic TV set as iconic, was crucial to the establishment of video art as discourse, and influential on subsequent generations of video artists'. Both Paik and Vostell were linked to the Fluxus movement, an international group of artists that was influential in the development of conceptual art from the late 1950s to the early 1970s.

6 As a result of the extensive research on which they are based, some of Murti's video films resemble short documentaries. An example is 'My ancestors are Sangiran man' (1997), which is about the discovery of an ancient Homo erectus fossil at Sangiran in Central Java. The film contains manipulated images of the Sangiran site and the fossil, and interviews with an Indonesian palaeontologist and local residents, including the excavator of the fossil. With this work, Murti attempts to address certain problems and ironies surrounding the discovery of the fossil. For instance, he provocatively asks whether the relatively poor excavator and other local residents will also have to wait thousands or millions of years, and turn into fossils themselves, before they will receive the same regard as the Homo erectus.

7 Murti himself prefers the term 'free poetry' (*puisi bebas*) to refer to this type of literary activity (personal communication, 21 June 2014).

References

Auslander, Philip. 1999. *Liveness: performance in a mediatized culture*. London and New York: Routledge.

Baulch, Emma. 2007. 'Cosmopatriots in Indonesian pop imagings'. In: Edwin Jurriëns and Jeroen de Kloet (eds), *Cosmopatriots: on distant belongings and close encounters*. Amsterdam and New York: Rodopi, pp. 177–203.

Bourriaud, Nicolas. 2002. *Relational aesthetics*, translated by Simon Pleasance and Fronza Woods with the participation of Mathieu Copeland. Dijon: Les presses du réel.

Buckingham, David. 2009. 'A commonplace art? Understanding amateur video production'. In: David Buckingham and Rebekah Willett (eds), *Video cultures: media technology and everyday creativity*. Basingstoke: Palgrave Macmillan, pp. 23–50.

Chalfen, Richard. 1987. *Snapshot versions of life*. Bowling Green, OH: Bowling Green State University Press.

Coyer, Kate, Tony Dowmunt and Alan Fountain (eds). 2007. *The alternative media handbook*. London and New York: Routledge.

Dixon, Steve. 2007. *Digital performance: a history of new media in theater, dance, performance art and installation*. Cambridge, MA: MIT Press.

Flusser, Vilém. 2000. *Towards a philosophy of photography*. London: Reaktion.

Gordon, Eric and Adriana De Souza e Silva. 2011. *Net locality: why location matters in a networked world*. Chichester, UK: Wiley-Blackwell.

Hafiz. 2009. 'Video base: melihat sejarah kita' [Video base: seeing our history]. In: Mirza Jaka Suryana (ed.), *Video base: video, sosial, historia* [Video base: video, social, history]. Jakarta: Pusat Informasi Data Penelitian dan Pengembangan Forum Lenteng, pp. 11–14.

Hafiz. 2011. 'Menghadirkan daging di hadapan pemirsa' [Presenting flesh in front of the viewers]. In: Deasy Elsara and Ibnu Rizal (eds), *Ok.Video Flesh: 5th Jakarta International Video Festival 6 – 17 October 2011*. Jakarta: ruangrupa, pp. 14–16.

Halim, Syaiful. 2010. *Tayangan video mirip artis: pertaruhan objektivitas dan kearifan media* [The screening of videos resembling artists: putting at stake objectivity and the wisdom of the media]. Jakarta: Gramata Publishing.

Hill, David T. and Krishna Sen. 2005. *The Internet in Indonesia's new democracy*. London and New York: Routledge.

Hjorth, Larissa, Natalie King and Mami Kataoka. 2014. 'Intimate publics: the place of art and media cultures in the Asia-Pacific region'. In: Larissa Hjorth, Natalie King and Mami Kataoka (eds), *Art in the Asia-Pacific: intimate publics*. London and New York: Routledge, pp. 1–20.

Hujatnikajennong, Agung. 2006. 'Avant-gardeisme dalam seni: otonomi, resistensi, dan "sub-versi"' [Avant-gardism in art: autonomy, resistance, and 'sub-version']. In: Alfathri Adlin (ed.), *Resistensi gaya hidup: teori dan realitas* [Lifestyle resistance: theory and reality]. Yogyakarta: Jalasutra, pp. 175–183.

Hujatnikajennong, Agung. 2011. '[In]corporeal: tubuh, video, seni' [(In)corporeal: body, video, art]. In: Deasy Elsara and Ibnu Rizal (eds), *Ok.Video Flesh: 5th Jakarta International Video Festival 6–17 October 2011*. Jakarta: ruangrupa, pp. 63–74.

Ida, Rachmah. 2013. 'Communal consumption of VCD/DVD and social change in the urban *kampung* community Indonesia'. *New Media and Mass Communication* 17: 20–28.

Jeon, Jeong-Ok. 2013. 'Art after drama: Krisna Murti'. In: Krisna Murti (ed.), *Art after drama: Krisna Murti videos*. Jakarta: Komunitas Salihara, pp. 5–11.

Jurriëns, Edwin. 2010. 'Video spa: Krisna Murti's treatment of the senses'. *Bijdragen tot de Taal-, Land- en Volkenkunde* 166(1): 1–24.

Jurriëns, Edwin. 2016. 'Intimate video: creative bodies in the age of the selfie'. *Continuum: Journal of Media and Cultural Studies* 30(1): 1–19.

Kelana, Andang, Mahardika Yudha and Mirza Jaka Suryana. 2009. 'Ikhtisar video Indonesia: masa analog' [Outline of Indonesian video: the analogue era]. In: Mirza Jaka Suryana (ed.), *Video base: video, sosial, historia* [Video base: video, social, history]. Jakarta: Pusat Informasi Data Penelitian dan Pengembangan Forum Lenteng, pp. 23–44.

Kitley, Philip. 2000. *Television, nation, and culture in Indonesia*. Research in International Studies, Southeast Asia Series 104. Athens, OH: Ohio University Center for International Studies.

McDaniel, Drew O. 1994. *Broadcasting in the Malay world: radio, television, and video in Brunei, Indonesia, Malaysia, and Singapore*. New Jersey: Ablex.

McDaniel, Drew. 2002. *Electronic tigers of Southeast Asia: the politics of media, technology, and national development*. International topics in media. Ames, IA: Iowa State University Press.

Meigh-Andrews, Chris. 2006. *A history of video art: the development of form and function*. Oxford, UK: Berg.

Murti, Krisna. 1999. *Video publik* [Public video]. Yogyakarta: Kanisius.

Murti, Krisna. 2006. 'Media baru: kultur gerilya hingga seni gadget' [New media: from guerilla culture to gadget art]. In: Direktorat Kesenian, *Apresiasi seni media baru* [New media art appreciation]. Jakarta: Direktorat Kesenian, Direktorat Jendral Nilai Budaya, Seni dan Film and Departemen Kebudayaan dan Pariwisata, pp. 45–66.

Murti, Krisna. 2009. *Essays on video art and new media: Indonesia and beyond*. Yogyakarta: Indonesian Visual Art Archive.

Murti, Krisna. 2010. 'Wayang wong, performativitas dan digitalisasi' [Wayang wong, performativity and digitalisation]. In: Krisna Murti (ed.), *Mute!Theater*. Jakarta: Bentara Budaya, pp. 6–8.

Murti, Krisna. 2011. *Poetshop*. Magelang: Langgeng Gallery.

Murti, Krisna. 2013a. 'Dance of the unknown'. In: Krisna Murti (ed.), *Art after drama: Krisna Murti videos*. Jakarta: Komunitas Salihara, p. 12.

Murti, Krisna. 2013b. 'Eggology'. In: Krisna Murti (ed.), *Art after drama: Krisna Murti videos*. Jakarta: Komunitas Salihara, p. 16.

Prakoso, Rangga and Heru Andriyanto. 2012. 'As Peterpan's Ariel leaves prison, some asked why he was ever there'. *The Jakarta Globe*, 23 July. Available at: http://thejakartaglobe.beritasatu.com/archive/as-peterpans-ariel-leaves-prison-some-ask-why-he-was-ever-there/ (accessed 20 October 2014).

Rath, Amanda Katherine. 2010. 'Krisna Murti's theatre'. In: Krisna Murti (ed.), *Mute!Theater*. Jakarta: Bentara Budaya, pp. 42–43.

Romano, Angela. 2003. *Politics and the press in Indonesia: understanding an evolving political culture*. London and New York: Routledge Curzon.

Sen, Krishna. 1994. *Indonesian cinema: framing the New Order*. London and New Jersey: Zed Books Ltd.

Sen, Krishna and David T. Hill. 2000. *Media, culture and politics in Indonesia*. Melbourne: Oxford University Press.

Set, Sony. 2007. *500+ gelombang video porno Indonesia: jangan bugil di depan kamera!* [500+ Indonesian porn video channels: don't get naked in front of the camera!]. Yogyakarta: Penerbit ANDI.

Siregar, Aminudin T. H. 2004. 'Melampaui kontrol pikiran lalu tubuh' [Exceeding control over thought, then the body]. In: Heru Hikayat and Herra Pahlasari (eds), *Beyond panopticon*. Bandung: Video Lab.

Siregar, Aminuddin T. H. 2010. 'Ketradisian versus kemodernan: kasus Krisna Murti' [The traditional versus the modern: the case of Krisna Murti]. In: Krisna Murti (ed.), *Mute!Theater*. Jakarta: Bentara Budaya, pp. 14–17.

Spielmann, Yvonne. 2007. *Video: the reflexive medium*. Cambridge, MA and London: The MIT Press.

Spigel, Lynn. 2001. *Welcome to the dreamhouse: popular media and postwar suburbs*. Durham, NC and London: Duke University Press.

Steele, Janet. 2005. *Wars within: the story of Tempo, an independent magazine in Soeharto's Indonesia*. Jakarta and Singapore: Equinox Publishing and Institute of Southeast Asian Studies.

Sugiharto, Bambang. 2002. 'Art without "ism"'. In: Wawan S. Husin (ed.), *bavf-NAF 1: Indonesia performance documentation*. Bandung: bavf-NAF, pp. 9–10.

Teh, David. 2011a. 'Recalibrating media: three theses on video and media art in Southeast Asia'. In: Ibrahim Tahir, James Lui and Lindsay Davis (eds), *Video, an art, a history 1965–2010: a selection from the Centre Pompidou and Singapore Art Museum collections*. Singapore: Singapore Art Museum, pp. 25–31.

Teh, David. 2011b. 'The video agenda in Southeast Asia, or, "digital, so not digital"'. In: Geert Lovink and Rachel Somer Miles (eds), *Video vortex reader I: moving images beyond Youtube Inc Reader #6*. Amsterdam: Institute of Network Culture, pp. 162–177.

Thajib, Ferdiansyah, Nuraini Juliastuti, Andrew Lowenthal and Alexandra Crosby. 2011. 'A chronicle of video activism and online distribution in post-New Order Indonesia'. In: Geert Lovink and Rachel Somer Miles (eds), *Video vortex reader I: moving images beyond Youtube Inc Reader #6*. Amsterdam: Institute of Network Culture, pp. 178–193.

Wardhana, Veven Sp. 2002. 'Budaya massa, budaya televisi, (tele)vision du monde: TV or not TV…' [Mass media, television culture, *(tele)vision du monde*: TV or not TV …]. In: Veven Sp. Wardhana, *Dari Barbar sampai Timor Timur: mengeja budaya massa* [From Barbarians to East Timor: spelling the mass media]. Yogyakarta: Galang Press, pp. 9–26.

Willett, Rebekah. 2009a. 'Always on: camera phones, video production and identity'. In: David Buckingham and Rebekah Willett (eds), *Video cultures: media technology and everyday creativity*. Basingstoke: Palgrave Macmillan, pp. 210–229.

Willett, Rebekah. 2009b. 'In the frame: mapping camcorder cultures'. In: David Buckingham and Rebekah Willett (eds), *Video cultures: media technology and everyday creativity*. Basingstoke: Palgrave Macmillan, pp. 1–22.

Williams, Raymond. 1990. *Television: technology and cultural form*. Second edition. London: Routledge.

Wirodono, Sunardian. 2006. *Matikan TV-mu! Teror media televisi di Indonesia* [Turn off your TV! The terror of the medium of television in Indonesia]. Yogyakarta: Resist Book.

6 Video interactivity

Interactivity is a key strategy of alternative media practitioners to create intimate, personalised and process- rather than product-oriented relationships with their audiences. It should be noted, however, that the same strategy is also integrated into highly commercialised and mass-produced contemporary media, in the form of Tweets on live television talk shows or games on computers and mobile phones, among others. In art, interactivity is to a lesser or larger extent controlled by the artist, gallery or museum, or the broader conventions and trends in the art world.

The new media art discussed in this chapter distinguishes itself from the mass media not because of its interactivity as such, but because of its creative and critical reflections on processes of mediation and interaction. These reflections are offered to audiences in aesthetically innovative, experiential and interactive ways. They also address a broader field of representational politics, related to pressing contemporary issues such as historiography, global geopolitics and the construction of religious and cultural identities.

This chapter focuses on the work of three internationally renowned Indonesian new media artists: Krisna Murti, Jompet Kuswidananto and Tintin Wulia. The examples of Murti's early work examine the political and commercial factors that have shaped contemporary media and lifestyle. Kuswidananto creatively explores the ethical dimensions of mediation and interactivity and the ideological representation of history, religion and culture. Wulia addresses the impact of the representational strategies of global geopolitics and national and international bureaucracies on people's mobility and identity.

The works of the three artists draw transversal connections between various ecologies, particularly those of politics, representational media, and social and mental life. They unveil the politics of information and communication media as well as the ideological dimensions of other forms of mediation, ranging from history-writing to the demarcation of geopolitical space and the mobilisation and modification of bodies. They enable creative comparisons between different forms of mediation and interactivity in different areas of social life.

The three artists, each in their own way, also provide creative and intimate alternatives to the problems they discuss in their work. This chapter describes how Murti has offered audio-visual catharsis as well as serene video treatments for the body, mind and senses; Kuswidananto has created a mobile installation for community television broadcasts; and Wulia has produced personalised video animations, passports, maps and national anthems, among others.

Videos of reform

Murti's early new media art, created during Indonesia's period of transition from authoritarianism to democratic reform in the late 1990s, combined comments on the media with criticism of the New Order regime, thus highlighting the interconnections between the ecologies of communication and politics. While his more recent work provides serenity as an alternative to the noise and vulgarity of contemporary media culture, Murti's earlier installations seemed to aim at catharsis by imitating and overstating the mechanisms of the mass media. Some of the early work used audio-visual 'terror' (*teror*) or sensory overload and bodily and mental shock-effects as a strategy to annoy or energise audiences, revive their senses and make them critically rethink the fanfare and fantasies presented by the mass media (Kuss 1999: 30). Three examples were 'The President brand panty liners' (1998), 'Learning to queue up to the ants or "status queue"' (1996) and 'Foodstuffs are ethnic, never racist' (1999).

The video 'The President brand panty liners' (1998) was a parody of commercials for sanitary towels, in reaction to the abundance of advertisements on Indonesian television as well as a controversy surrounding the 1999 race for the Indonesian presidency.[1] It made fun of the detailed and pseudo-scientific information of television commercials by showing the multi-functionality of the fictional 'President' panty liner, which could be used as blindfold, compress and tea bag (Murti 1999: 49, 65, 77). The central scene showed blood-stained panty liners inscribed with the texts *kekerasan* (violence) and *machoisme* as blindfolds over the eyes and face of then President Habibie. Following the resignation of Suharto, whom he had served as vice-president for several years, Habibie became Indonesia's third president in 1998. Merely functioning as a transition figure up to the 1999 elections, Indonesia's first democratic elections in more than 40 years, Habibie spoke out against the prospect of having a woman – that is, Megawati Sukarnoputri, leader of the popular opposition party PDI-P – as the next Indonesian president.

Murti's work suggested that the abundance of television commercials for women's products did not open the eyes of viewers, particularly men, to a better understanding of women, but rather reinforced female domestication and subordination in Indonesian society. President Habibie was branded 'a macho', someone who was an accomplice in the symbolic violence against women in politics and the media, and blind to the psychological and physical violence against women in daily life. The video also contained clips from a popular film about the female national hero Kartini, to demonstrate the paradox of a society that adored the image of this historical proponent of women's rights, but at the same time accepted imagery that showed, and even promoted, violence against women. In exhibitions, Murti showed the video on a television monitor that was hung above a urinal in an exhibition hall, to dramatically force males to bodily experience and rethink gender relations while imagining holding their penises.

The video installation 'Learning to queue up to the ants or "status queue"' (1996) also had presidential succession as one of its themes (Murti 1999: 72). It consisted of a video film, television monitors, pieces of cut wood and dried leaves, long pieces of cloths with words printed on them, and modified *petulangan* – wooden coffins that are burnt during Balinese Hindu cremation rituals – in the shape of lions. Murti made the lions with the help of Balinese artisans over a period of six months. The exhibition of the installation at Soemardja Gallery at ITB was opened with a performance by Wawan S. Hoesin and Ine Arini (Murti 1999: 72).

The lion *petulangan* were lined up in a queue, each of them with their head directed towards an individual television set, and standing with their feet on miniature television units surrounded by pieces of cut wood and dried leaves. This setting suggested that the lions were watching television. The video film shown on the television screens was about the communal behaviour of ants. The coffins, wooden logs and leaves were representations of a 'recycling process' (Murti 1999: 72), or more specifically, signs of the anticipated step-down and succession of Suharto. According to Murti (1999: 72), the lions were references to Indonesia's political leaders, who studied the discipline, hard labour and communal spirit of the Indonesian common people, represented by the ants. The long cloths, which were hung from the ceiling, had written on them Balinese aphorisms that admonished the elite to learn from their subordinates (Hujatnikajennong 2005: 52). At the same time, the political elite intended to crush the small people, as suggested by the miniature television monitors under the feet of the lion *petulangan*.

From a media point of view, the video installation referred to the Suharto government attempting to monitor and control the broadcast media, and secure Indonesia's social and political 'status quo'. These attempts turned out to be futile, as the media – like a nest of ants – were too diverse and dynamic to be monitored, and were an important contribution in Suharto's fall and the initiation of the process of democratic reform. In other words, the 'status queue' of control and order failed to produce the status quo desired by the New Order government. According to Hujatnikajennong (2005: 52–53), 'this work was something like a prophetic vision, suggesting that someday those in power would be brought down in part due to the power of those very technologies that ruling powers try to control'.

New Order media propaganda was one of the themes of the third video installation, 'Foodstuffs are ethnic, never racist' (1999). It presented an arrangement of pink toilet bowls, containing pictures of various dishes and explanations about the origins of the food. The toilets were surrounded by two walls with projections of enlarged 'Mooi Indië' style paintings,[2] and a third wall on which was shown the film *Pengkhianatan G30S-PKI* (about 'the treason of the 30 September [1965] movement of PKI') with segments inserted from Indonesian television cooking shows. During the opening of the exhibition at Cemeti Art House

Gallery in Yogyakarta, Murti offered the audience fresh food from street hawkers outside the gallery (Rath 2008: 8).

Similar to Murti's other video installations, 'Foodstuffs are ethnic, never racist' brought together various, seemingly unrelated, narratives. I believe the work demonstrated the ideological character of different versions of 'Indonesianness' by juxtaposing and mixing narratives from various media and areas of social life. The landscape painting genre showed an artistic vision, the *Pengkhianatan G30S-PKI* film a political account, and the food pictures and television cooking programmes commonly shared perceptions about Indonesian identity. The instructions on the toilet bowls explained that food, generally considered to originate from a specific Indonesian place or region, often turns out to have its roots outside Indonesia.

Murti seemed to question how it was possible that people, who easily accepted different types of foreign food as expressions of Indonesian identity, still used racial grounds to exclude certain groups, particularly Chinese-Indonesians, from participation in public life. By inviting the audience to eat food and look inside the toilet bowls, he not only suggested that the food, once digested, all looked the same, but also that solid and objective historical research was needed for tracing back the origins of and ideological motives behind powerful truth and identity claims shaping contemporary Indonesian society.

Murti's late New Order and early *Reformasi* work read as a reflection on the euphoria and confusion of a society celebrating democratic reform while trying to come to terms with the traumas of the past. Rath (2008: 7) confirmed the connection between artistic creation and the socio-political climate in Indonesia at the time:

> For about one year (between 1998 and 1999), artistic expression leaned towards euphoric paroxysms and vitriolic indictment. It was as if the corpse of Suharto's presidency was forcibly exorcised through vicious imagery, political satire, and propagandist art and literature. [...] It was during this period that Krisna made some of his most overtly political and aggressive work. [...] After this necessary period of collectively shared catharsis, many artists, like Krisna, began to weave constructive alternatives to the official version of national history and culture imposed by the New Order government.

In the early 2000s, Murti started to entertain the prospect of a more peaceful and stable future for Indonesia, by displaying a shift of focus from explicit political commentary to a media-ecological approach to interconnected issues of culture, communication and identity. While the totalitarianism of the New Order and the chaos of early *Reformasi* previously encouraged him to build large and overwhelming multimedia installations, he then switched to relatively small-scale video works for the in-depth exploration of ideas.

'Wayang machine' (2002), for instance, consisted of a video retelling the story of Bhisma, one of the main characters in the canonical *wayang* epic

Mahabharata. Murti prepared the script with Arya Sanjaya, a poet and theatre performer from Bandung. The video consisted of dance movements of the Balinese performer Made Sidia, which were manipulated to resemble the two-dimensional shape of the leather puppets in *wayang kulit*. The video performance had singing in *kawi* (Old Javanese) with voice-over versions in Indonesian and English (Utari 2002). During public screenings, it was shown on two or three screens, each measuring approximately 3 × 4 m.

Murti explained that Bhisma's internal conflict represented the tension between Indonesia's troubled past and its aspirations for an uncertain future (Wilson 2002). He also attempted to contrast the mechanisms of video and *wayang* theatre with those of the mass media. According to Murti, the shadows of *wayang* theatre stimulate the viewers' imagination and allow them to construct their own story, or 'play the video that is inside of them', while the mass media offer mere imagery, with little for the audience to think or fantasise about.[3] In 'Wayang machine' and his other, later video art, Murti found a successful fusion between the use of advanced technology on the one hand, and established styles and methods that promote contemplation and creativity on the other.

Video as health treatment

Murti's artistic type of televisual meta-discourse not only discusses the commercial and ideological mechanisms behind the mass media industry, but also provides insight into, and compares the cultural-technological features of, various media (video, film, literature, performing arts and painting); the historical dimensions of various genres of representation (such as landscape painting and government propaganda); the position of the artist and the audience in processes of mediation (illustrating the way the body, mind and senses are impacted by the mass media); and alternative forms of intermediality and interactivity (including audio-visual catharsis and poetic contemplation). The work engages with the field of media archaeology, or the socio-cultural histories of media use (Manovich 1998). At the same time, it also contributes to media ecology by presenting alternative visions for sustainable communication environments with reduced levels of audio-visual noise and pollution.

One of the most dramatic and convincing ways in which Murti used interactivity to comment on the interconnections of mental, social and natural ecologies was his work 'Video spa' (2004; Jurriëns 2010). This video installation was the result of a collaboration between Murti and the performers Surin Welangon and James Bennet, video editor Arifin M. Badruddin and sound artist Moro.

Characteristic of this work, and the installation genre in general, is that it combines various artistic media, stimulates and is shaped by the interaction between artist, work and audience and, as a consequence, does not have a fixed form, but takes different shapes under different circumstances. The work was presented at Galeri Nasional Indonesia (Indonesian National Gallery) in Jakarta from 16–23 December 2004 and at Gaya Fusion of Senses Gallery in Ubud from

16–18 March 2005. Both in Jakarta and Ubud, video images were projected from three different outputs onto three separate, although connected, 'larger-than-life' video screens (each measuring 2.5 × 3 m). On each of the screens the same or similar images were shown simultaneously, but with variations in camera angle and graphic modification.

In 'Video spa' as well as in much of Murti's other work, cultural traditions were explored through a specific lens, focusing on the mass-mediated character of contemporary life. The installation went beyond a simple portrayal of a clash between 'tradition' and 'modernity' and evoked a sense of cosmopolitanism or cosmopatriotism (Jurriëns and De Kloet 2007). Murti prefers spontaneous bonds between individuals with similar interests and ideas, to communal claims based on preconfigured notions of nationality, ethnicity or religion.[4] He himself has a mixed Javanese-Balinese background, which he sees as an advantage in freely adopting and achieving critical distance from both Islamic and Hindu-Buddhist traditions and other aspects of Javanese and Balinese cultures, like those represented in 'Wayang machine' (2002) and 'Empty theater' (2010). He is also a much-travelled artist, with residencies in Japan (1999) and Singapore (2006), public talks and guest lectures in Cuba (2001), Spain (2002) and Australia (2003, 2004, 2013), and numerous international solo and group exhibitions, including the prestigious Biennale in Venice (2005).

Murti (2004a, 2004b) presented 'Video spa' as a 'Videotherapy by Krisna Murti' and a 'Therapy for everyday living'.[5]

It offered its audiences therapeutic experiences through a mix of video images, performance elements and audience participation. It integrated Hindu-Buddhist elements with the technologies, cultural artefacts and social experiences that Murti brought back from his many journeys, such as video and computer technology, English-language poems and advertisements, beauty and health treatments and various recreational activities.

The video starts with computer-manipulated images of collaborator Surin Welangon, floating freely in meditating Buddha pose against a background of grassland and mountains (Figure 6.1). The accompanying sounds are high-pitched, monotonous and ceremonial, as if inviting its audience to participate in a ritual. The meditating figure disappears in a sea of fire, perhaps referring to the stress and heightened emotions of modern life, but also to the first phase of a cleansing process. The fire is replaced by the sounds and images of a waterfall and people swimming and enjoying the freshness of the water. The sounds of dripping water follow, alternating with the high, monotonous tune from the first scene. This could signify that people in the initial stage of the therapy are still moving back and forth between two conflicting states of mind, or between their 'old' and 'new' selves.

New images of the waterfall are shown, with a young, romantic couple sitting high on a rock. A poem in English is shown over three screens, containing strings of words of which the meanings and sounds refer to different feelings and sensations. The words slide down in sync with the movement of the waterfall, followed by images of bathing people and close-ups of stones in the water.

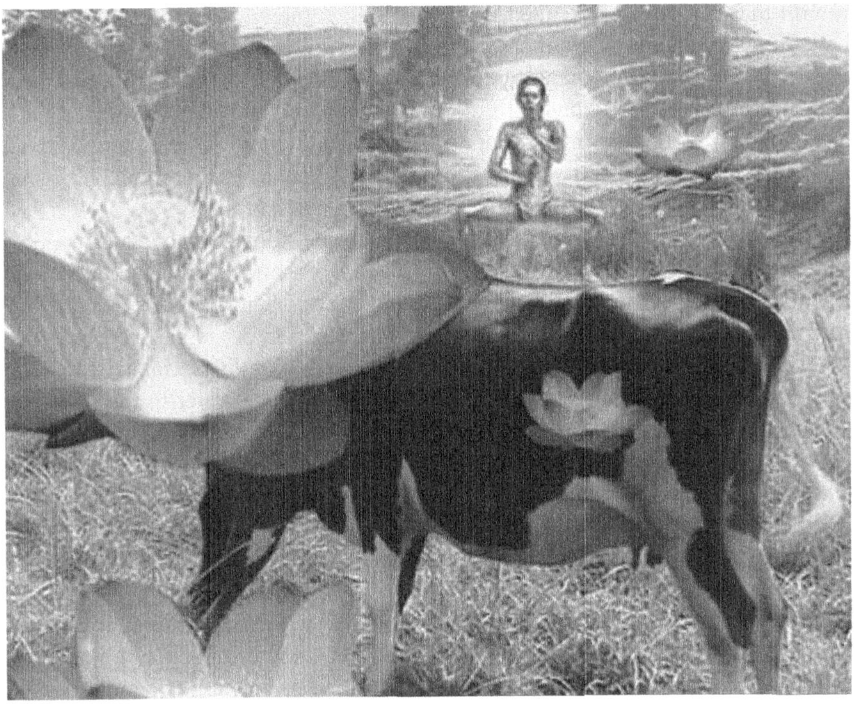

Figure 6.1 'Video spa' (Krisna Murti), video still. From: video therapy – an interactive installation, created by Krisna Murti, 2004–2005.

Source: photo courtesy of the artist.

Suddenly the screens turn black and the text 'Close your eyes' appears in white, accompanied by the high-pitched tune. This interlude offers the viewers a moment of rest, in which they can meditate and reflect on the video images, sounds and messages they have been confronted with.

After a fade-to-black of a few seconds, the text 'Open your eyes' is shown, which in conjunction with the sounds and images of water lilies signifies the final phase of the video therapy. Cows are grazing on a lush green field, and the high-pitched tune announces the return of the meditating figure, surrounded by colourful lotus flower animations. After a series of realistic lotus images, the meditating figure floats, on a computer-animated blue lotus, from the waterfall towards the audience, while making *mudra* gestures with his hands, representing the 'turning of the wheel' teachings which lead towards enlightenment in Buddhism.

Next are blurred images of a Buddhist monk, performed by James Bennet, in a desolate landscape. Subtitles and a voice in English represent the monk's wisdom, which includes the warning that 'the ocean of Samsara is full of sea monsters that constantly threaten us as we seek to cross to the other side'. This refers to the Buddhist concept of *samsara*, or the endless cycle of birth and rebirth that can only be escaped through enlightenment. The video presentation concludes with the images and sounds of birds in their natural setting of forest and grassland, and a montage of crowing roosters against a background of seas and beaches. The bird sounds are meant to awake the audience from their half-asleep state, dreaming or meditating to a state of full consciousness, and to signal that they have successfully gone through the spiritual journey and cleansing process.

Both in Jakarta and Ubud, the audience was only allowed to enter the exhibition space individually or in pairs, in order to enhance their personal video therapy experience and sense of participation. The visitors were positioned in relaxing chairs in front of the three screens and, in Ubud, masseuses even gave massages. The exhibition in Bali was opened with a night performance in which video screens were placed behind a swimming pool. The water in the pool was decorated with flowers, and several foreign and Indonesian female guests in swimsuits were given a footbath of water and flowers as well as a neck-and-shoulder massage. Once the projections started, the female participants were instructed to enter the pool and swim in front of the video screens. In this way, the video imagery was expanded from the flat video screens into the space where the audience was situated.

Murti's installation is a multilayered work that can be interpreted in various ways. There are many references to Hindu-Buddhist culture, such as the meditating figure, the Buddhist monk, the lotus flowers, the monotonous tune, the elements of water and fire, the cows and other animals. According to Murti (2004a), the element of water also represents the concept of *wudhu* in Islam, the ritual ablutions performed before praying. At the same time, he was inspired by international popular culture, particularly *The Blue Lagoon*, a US film from the 1980s about two shipwrecked children who eventually develop a romantic relationship with each other on a lush tropical island. Murti combined all these different elements to invite the audience on a journey to heaven or paradise (*tamasya ke surga*).

The catalogue presents 'Video spa' not only as an alternative spa treatment for the eyes (*mata*), but also for the mind (*mata hati*). This suggests that the installation links together three different human aspects: the senses, the body and the mind. This comprehensive approach is shaped by ideas from Balinese Hindu-Buddhist culture as well as the media-ecological reality of modern everyday life. Hujatnikajennong (2004) observes that 'the imaginary images in "Video Spa" address the problem of "physicality" in modern society, where the function of the "physical body" is no longer autonomous, but controlled by its psychological relations with the world of imagery'. This context explains Murti's combined treatment of the body, the senses and the mind as a remedy for the mental and physical disorders caused by the mass media.

The installation can be conceived as a form of media therapy, as it is not only about people trying to find enlightenment and escape *samsara* through reflection and meditation, but also about curing people of the ordeals of domestic and international television culture. The video with its slow, aesthetic and relaxing images and sounds of waterfalls, pools, flowers and animals is meant as an alternative to the fast, noisy and intimidating messages of contemporary television genres such as commercials, music shows and soap operas.

Murti is aware that a work like 'Video spa' does not stand a chance of appearing on television, as it does not meet the ideological and commercial dictates of the media market.[6] While the new generation of video artists has been brought up with satellite television, internet and mobile phones, he still remembers a time when the main media for information and entertainment were non-electronic forms such as *wayang* theatre. He is not cynical about these changes in the Indonesian visual landscape, but attempts to use his art and writings to search for collaborative strategies to understand and, if necessary, subvert the contemporary, media-dominated cultural condition.

The work of Jompet Kuswidananto and Tintin Wulia

Two examples of younger internationally renowned Indonesian new media artists are Jompet Kuswidananto[7] and Tintin Wulia.[8] While some work of the younger generation of Indonesian new media artists consists of short films in the style of MTV video clips, Kuswidananto and Wulia use installations to give a multimedia and multilayered critique of processes of representation and interactivity. In this respect, their artistic style is similar to that of Murti's (Jurriëns 2009).

Kuswidananto holds a BA in Communications from Gadjah Mada University, while Wulia holds a PhD in Fine Art from RMIT University, in addition to her degrees in Architecture and Music and working experiences as a music producer for television commercials. They both defected from their initial study and working interests, as they felt that the media production and broadcasting industry could not give them enough opportunity for creative and critical expression. When she was still working for the television advertising industry, Wulia made a personal vow to produce at least one truly creative, individual art work a month.[9] In addition to addressing how processes of mediation and interactivity are affected by politics, bureaucracy and commerce, the oeuvres of both artists also focus on related issues of culture and identity: 'Javaneseness' and syncretism in Kuswidananto's case and 'Sino-Indonesianness' and cosmopolitanism in Wulia's case.

Both artists have created interactive installations consisting of basic materials drawn from daily life and comprising a rich variety of media, ranging from video and sound to kites, passports, masks and bicycles. They are critical of media interactivity and try to bring technology, creativity and politics back to human, as opposed to distorted, proportions. Their installations do not celebrate or anticipate the latest developments in high technology, but express a personal approach to the media, comparable to Murti's methods in his recent poetic work.

Many of Kuswidananto's works are made of found objects, a technique also used by another pioneer of Indonesian new media art, Heri Dono (b. 1960).[10]

Some of his art presents the electronic media as integrated parts or extensions of the human body, which either enable people to transcend their physical limitations, or lead to miscommunication and abuse of power in restricting freedom. Wulia often has a physical presence in her video films, for example, by showing her hands and fingers moving and arranging objects. In this way, she gives a personal dimension to the use of media technology, and presents her art as an open process or work in progress rather than the finished and venerable product of the special skills, knowledge, and social, political and economic power associated with the professional art and media worlds. The media of communication, bureaucracy and geopolitical power in her art, such as passports, maps and walls, influence and are shaped by personal identities in a symbiotic process at best, and have their own trajectory completely detached from, and negatively impacting on, people's lives at worst.

The use of video and mechanical devices puts the installations of both artists in motion and gives them a temporal dimension. The use of these media also encourages audience participation and removes some of the fear or reluctance audience members may feel when engaging with modern technology. Kuswidananto and Wulia demonstrate to their audiences that different but interrelated processes of mediation, ranging from electronic communication to bureaucratic paperwork, are not inherently or ontologically good or bad, but steered by the ideological interests of their agents.

The politics and ethics of mediation and interactivity

Kuswidananto's creative career began as a member of the Yogyakarta-based performance art group Performance Fucktory (1998–2002), which also consisted of Marzuki and Ugoran Prasad (Marzuki 2009: 28; Suroto 2009: 10). Confirming the fluidity and interdisciplinary character of the Yogyakarta art scene, each of them would eventually become successful in a different field of art: Jompet in installation art; Marzuki, as founder of the Jogjakarta Hip Hop Foundation, in hip hop music; and Ugoran Prasad, as lead singer of Melancholic Bitch, in hard rock music.

With fellow Yogyakarta artist Vincensius Christiawan ('Venzha'), the current leader of the new media art community HONF (see Chapters 8 and 9), Jompet co-founded the experimental music group Garden of the Blind (2000–2002). Garden of the Blind used modified guitars, cassette players, bicycles, oxygen masks and other found objects to produce music and visual effects on stage.[11] Many of its performances displayed a certain euphoria about the possibilities of mediation, as reflected in titles such as 'Glorified' (2001) and 'Ultra-output' (2002). These titles, including Garden of the Blind, referred to people's capacity to transcend the restrictions of their sensory faculties via audio-visual media.[12]

In 'Glorified' (2001), the performer – either Kuswidananto or Christiawan – obtained a presence and aura that was larger-than-life from his upright position on a kind of mechanical throne consisting of numerous turning wheels, electronic devices and horns (Figure 6.2).

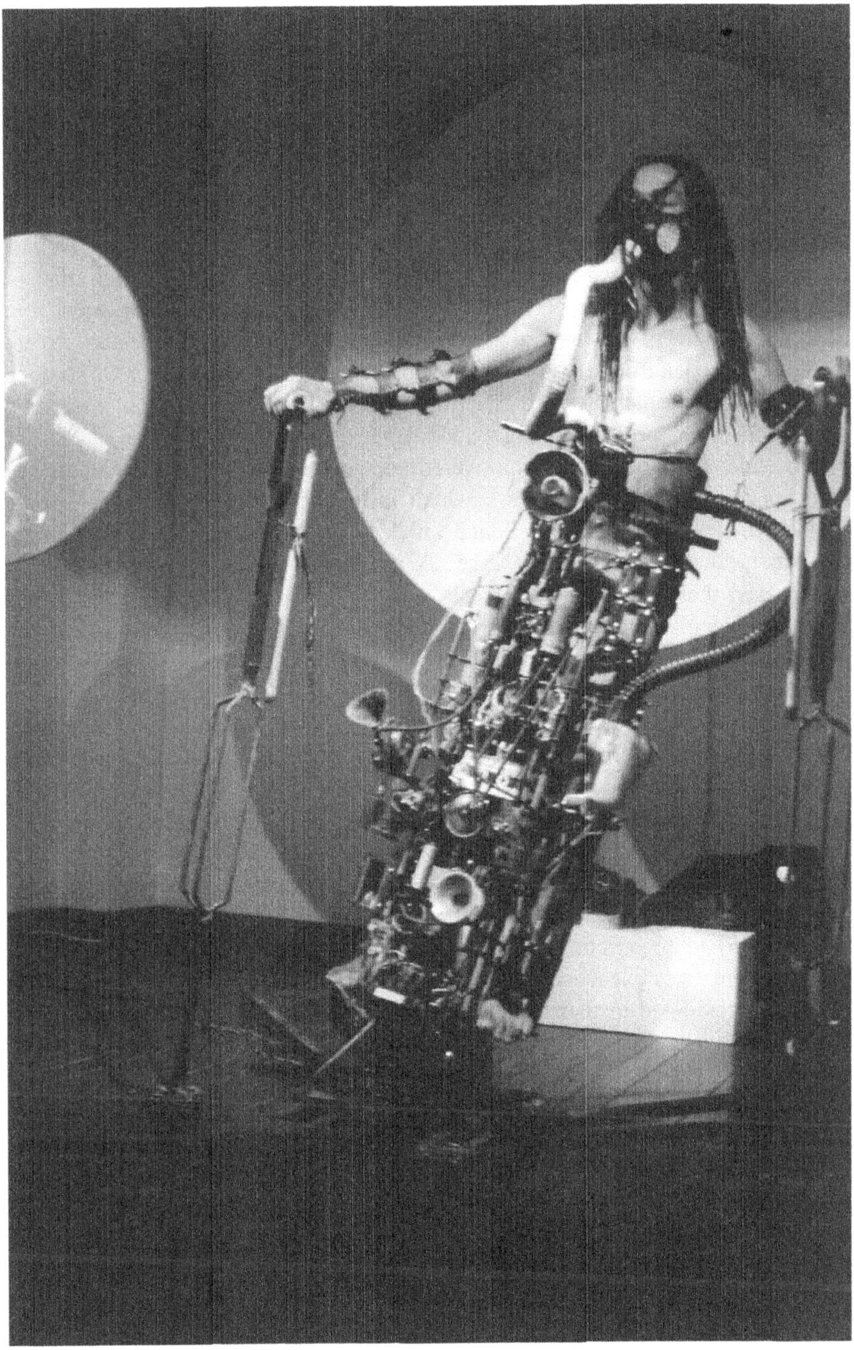

Figure 6.2 'Glorified' (The Garden of the Blind), multimedia installation, 2001.

Source: photo courtesy of Jompet Kuswidananto.

The performer was able to sway the throne sideways by moving two long sticks that were attached to his arms. He also wore an oxygen mask connected to the many other devices of the installation. The performer's swaying and breathing generated movements, which were mechanically processed and turned into experimental sounds.

In 'Ultra-output' (2002), Kuswidananto and Christiawan rode two vehicles which looked like bicycles. These were mounted in opposite directions on a stage and remained immobile during the pedalling. The modified bicycles had cassette players as gear handles. By increasing or decreasing the speed of their pedalling movements, the performers were able to manipulate the sounds from the cassette players. At intervals, their movements also triggered video projections on the background wall, which showed animations of a pair of running figures. Thus a triple intermediality took place, in which movement translated into sound, sound produced image, and image represented movement.

Kuswidananto and Christiawan were reluctant to elaborate on the meaning of their spectacular performance art, which is unique in Indonesia. Their works often gave art critics and the audience a high-tech and sci-fi impression, although the artists themselves were averse to advanced computer technology and emphasised their use of found objects and low-level mechanics.[13] Their works were also perceived to have a mystical quality (Iskandar 2002: 13), which could be indirectly related to Kuswidananto and Christiawan's syncretic Catholic background.[14] The performer-figure in 'Glorified', whose back and arms were supported by a cross-shaped wooden construction, did indeed evoke the image of a cyborg Christ on the cross. This image also signified that the Garden of the Blind performances and Kuswidananto's installations considered mediation in contemporary information and communication society not only in terms of glorification, but also loss and sacrifice.

Both 'Glorified' and 'Ultra-output' demonstrated that the media, as integral parts of daily life and extensions of the human body and mind, could be hard to control and had a restricting impact on people's personal freedom. The actors in both performances exceeded their worldly, human capabilities, but at the same time were restricted in their movements by the many devices attached to their bodies. Moreover, they did not have full control over the 'output', or the sounds and images produced by their movements. In other works, Garden of the Blind demonstrated that mediation was a delicate process, which could only be successful if the participants in the process understood the character and ethical dimensions of media use, and respected their interaction with other participants.

Two of Kuswidananto's other early artistic investigations into mediation and interactivity were 'One hour to be other' (or '1hour 2be oth3r', 2003–2005) and 'Cross personal respiratory' (2005). Both installations took the format of an electronic game to be played by two participants. In 'One hour to be other' (2003–2005), each of the two participants wore headgear with an integrated video screen. Attached to the headgear was a camera which sent images to the other participant's video screen. This meant that the participants did not have direct visual contact with the outside world, but relied on the camera view directed by the co-participant's head movements. In one version of the installation, the participants played a board game where they directed their cameras to a map of the city of Yogyakarta. By giving each other instructions, the participants had to try to meet at exactly the same location. Kuswidananto (2008) explained that the electronic exchange of eyesight was meant to make the participants feel 'disabled' and 'fully dependent' on each other. It caused their bodies to experience a lack of 'authority', and their identities to become 'blurred' (Kuswidananto 2008). The works pointed to both the difficulty and necessity of building interpersonal trust in highly mediatised social environments.

'Cross personal respiratory' (2005) also illustrated how mediation relied on, shaped and obstructed interdependency. It involved two participants, who were instructed to wear a mask and breathe from a single oxygen tube. A mechanical valve in the tube allowed only one person at a time to breathe. This forced the participants to communicate with each other and to control their respiration, as they had to take turns in breathing. While engaging in this type of 'risk management' (Kuswidananto 2008), the participants had to complete an electronic puzzle. Once the puzzle had been solved, the oxygen valve would switch off automatically so the two participants could breathe normally again. This game installation also demonstrated that interactivity was not inherently liberating or democratic, but depended on the ethical values and trustworthiness of the actors involved.[15] More dramatically, it showed that media-ecological imbalances can literally become a matter of life and death.

Kuswidananto produced an explicit critique of contemporary Indonesian television culture with 'Neighbours' (2002), which sat between video art and community video or community television. The title of the work referred to the Australian television drama hit *Neighbours*, but also to the real-life neighbours in a village community near Yogyakarta (Murti 2006: 64). Kuswidananto gave camera equipment and television training to the community members to facilitate the production of the local programme content. The artist broadcast the video recordings 'from, by and for' the community members by touring the village with a pick-up van modified with a giant television screen. He thus created a modern mobile version of the Indonesian outdoor cinema tradition of *layar tancep*. Underlying this work was a personal dissatisfaction with the Indonesian broadcasting world. The village programmes were meant as an alternative to the public and commercial television services on offer, which did not represent local interests and had neglected and underestimated the intellectual skills and informational needs of the Indonesian public for many years.

In another series of art works, Kuswidananto put into perspective the euphoria of media freedom in Indonesia following the fall of Suharto in 1998, particularly the political abuse of such potentially democratic tools as megaphones and mobile phones. The series included art installations about Javanese farmers, and was based on Kuswidananto's own experience when working for an NGO that defended the rights of farmers.[16] One of the works, 'Broken morse code' (2007), consisted of a small video screen that was connected by metal wires to a metal megaphone. The screen showed a female farmer expressing her anger about her miserable life. The megaphone gave the impression that her voice would be loud and clear to a mass of people. In the installation, however, her angry voice became completely distorted by the metal wires.

In another installation, 'Resistance is not around' (2007), a farmer's sickle was placed on the floor. At intervals, an image of Kuswidananto using a mobile phone was projected on a background wall. Each time the image appeared, the sickle started to vibrate. The work appeared to refer to the popular use of mobile phones in Indonesia. On the one hand, these mobile phones confirmed and expanded people's social contacts and information sources, but on the other hand, they did not necessarily change power structures in society. Kuswidananto's figure in the video, representing a government official or politician, used his mobile phone not for a democratic two-way communication, but for sending a message or order that could not be ignored. The sickle was thus left with no other option than to tremble in obedience. The installation was not merely about a conflict between modernity (technology) and tradition (farming) but, like many of Kuswidananto's other works, also about the politics of mediation and media interactivity (Murti 2007: 23, 30).

Kuswidananto's oeuvre as a whole comprises the possibilities and effects of mediation as well as the politics of Javanese religious and cultural history, identity and syncretism. His most iconic, and multiple international award-winning, work, which combines both themes, is a series that started with the 2008 exhibition *Java's machine: phantasmagoria* at Cemeti art house in Yogyakarta. The exhibition consisted of five different installations, all titled 'War of Java: do you remember?' (Fadjri 2008: 202), a reference to the local struggle against Dutch colonialism during the Java War (1825–1830).

The works referred to the need for recalling Java's past through the 'Do you remember?' admonitions from the installation titles and voice recordings, the display of Javanese military gear and drums, the projections of pages from a history book and the footage of archived colonial material (Figure 6.3).

In the exhibition catalogue (Cemeti Art House 2008), Kuswidananto explained that he drew his inspiration from the guards of the Javanese *kraton* (palaces). Today these guards have only a ceremonial role, for sight-seeing tourists. His art series attempted to reveal parts of the neglected history behind the colourful costumes, musical instruments and other attributes. According to Kuswidananto, the story of the guards intersected with that of Javanese syncretism, as for centuries the Javanese 'had been taught' to accept incoming cultures and beliefs and present them in a new synthesis of Javanese syncretism rather than opposing them. This syncretism has become the 'machine' (*mesin*), 'truth' (*kebenaran*) or 'cultural system' (*sistem budaya*) of Javaneseness (Cemeti Art House 2008). However, as implied by the title of the exhibition, it can also create 'phantasmagoria', spectres from the past that come to haunt a society that neglects its history.

The installations did not merely represent the past, but also attempted to bring it back to life through sound, video and mechanical devices, in a fashion similar to the frightening phantasmagoric projections of modified magical lanterns in the

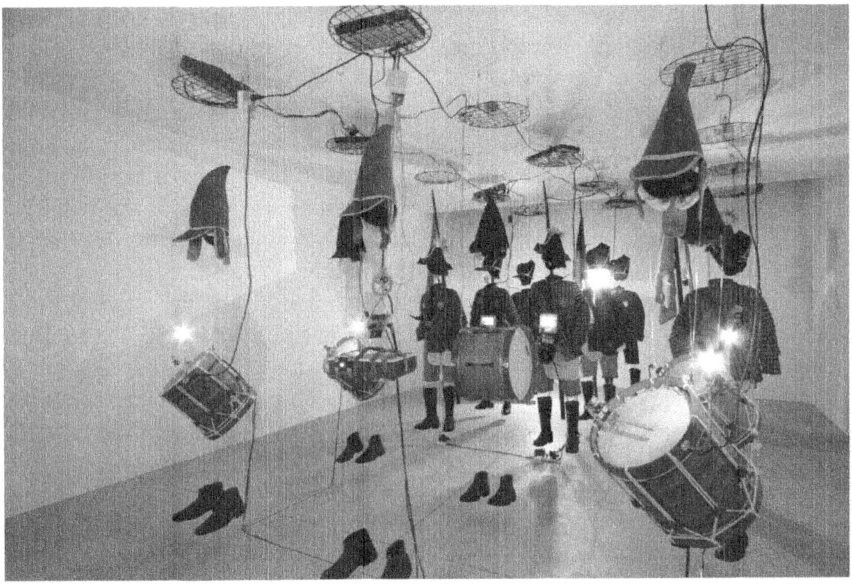

Figure 6.3 'War of Java: do you remember? # 3' (Jompet Kuswidananto), multimedia installation, 2008.

Source: photo courtesy of the artist.

Europe of the late eighteenth and nineteenth centuries. Without the recorded voices, the playing drums and the page projections, the displayed gear of the Javanese military would have been just that – a collection of hats, jackets, boots and guns. Without the inserted figure of a contemporary performer, the archival footage would also have been nothing more than old material. It was precisely the added sound and video that created an impression of wholeness and gave an almost uncanny presence to stories and figures from the past.

Kuswidananto's theatrical approach to sound, image and mechanics in his installations, enables him to unleash an unknown and enchanting dimension from the sheer materiality of the media being used. It is the sparks from this presentational dimension of the media, rather than its representational qualities, which figuratively, and often also literally, puts his installations in motion, and encourages the audience to participate in the art and reflect on the complex, conflicted and politicised mediations of history and identity.

Geopolitics and the mediation of borders and identity

Wulia's oeuvre comprises a critical approach to the various factors involved in creating and protecting geopolitical borders, including statecraft, individual agency, communication media and chance. Some of the key themes in her work include the trauma of the post-30 September 1965 mass killings in Indonesia, the violence against Chinese-Indonesians in 1998, and the broader geopolitical factors and mediation processes determining national borders and personal identities. She highlights and reworks the role of chance in border interactions, by recounting both personal experiences and news stories about the way in which coincidence mediates official policies and their impact. Her work not only represents, but also simulates, re-creates and disturbs the various agents and processes involved in the making, mediating and controlling of borders. Many of her works facilitate audience participation, enabling members of the public to directly experience and interfere with, rather than merely seeing, reading or hearing about, fundamental aspects of border politics.

Wulia has embodied her artistic concepts and practices by her ongoing travel and impressive record of international art projects and exhibitions. She continuously explores and amplifies the ambiguous character of media that function as distanced and ideological tools of border security on the one hand, and intimate memorabilia of people's life journeys and identities on the other. Conceptually, her art is situated in the intersections between Art History, Communications, Globalisation Studies and Games Studies. It engages with Gerard Toal's concept of critical geopolitics, Hegel's Standpoint theory, Anthony Giddens' individual agency as subversion at/of the border, Bruno Latour's Actor-Network-Theory, and Nikos Papastergiadis' aesthetic cosmopolitanism (Wulia 2013). It produces a new form of critical geopolitics that is shaped by conversations between various theoretical concepts and art practices.

Her art undermines the idea of fixed borders and fixed identities and increases the factor of chance by engaging audience members in 'aleatoric' play.[17] Aleatoric play, a concept derived from musicological discourse, refers to the relatively unpredictable outcomes of the interactions between individual agents, who are connected with and influenced by each other in a network of communication. Wulia's work presents and represents various icons of border politics, including passports, maps and walls, which are both individually and collectively reworked by audience members involved in artistic game-performances. Through these game-performances, Wulia integrates art into a new, creative form of critical geopolitics that explores the conditions of, and possible alternatives to, national and international border politics and communication strategies.

Many of her works explore the possibility and effect of the personalisation of officialdom by giving participants the opportunity to contribute writings or visual representations of their personal histories and experiences. In 'Terra Incognita' (2013), audience members could use paint, flowers and other organic and non-organic material to reconfigure wall and ground maps of countries and regions in the world. Other work has presented walls as spaces that can be accessed and modified through the manipulation of video projections and paintings. The various installations also often contain videos about the interactive process of creating and displaying art itself.

In '(Re)collection of togetherness' (2008–current), Wulia focuses on the possibilities and restrictions provided by a specific type of bureaucratic medium, the passport. The first version of this ongoing project, exhibited in 2008 at

Cemeti in Yogyakarta, displayed dozens of realistic copies of passports from various countries, based on internet samples and the official passports of Wulia's international friends (Simatupang 2008: 4). The passports contained the bloodstains and fake remains of mosquitoes, as if the bugs had been slammed between the passport pages and squashed to death. Next to the bloodstains in each passport were the real names and messages of people from various countries. On the tabletop there was also a television monitor showing the documentary about the Indonesian political exile Sobron,[18] while a glass flask for nurturing real mosquitoes had been placed on a pillar next to the table.

The installation appeared to show that passports provide individuals with the freedom to cross national borders and meet people from other countries. At the same time, it also demonstrated that passports confine people's identity to a single nation and do not cater for the thoughts and ideals of those who do not want to be tied to a single country and/or have emotional attachments to multiple places and communities. The latter type of people was represented by the mosquitoes, which sip blood from, and create close connections with, every person they come across, regardless of national, ethnic, racial or religious backgrounds. Within the bureaucratic system, such people are seen as outcasts who are ignored at best and squashed into silence at worst. Like the mosquitoes, they can grow in but not escape their glass house, which remains perfectly sealed from the ideal bureaucratic world of documents and rules.

In 'Study for wanton' (2008), also exhibited at Cemeti, Wulia deconstructed the idea of single national identity.

In this installation, exhibition visitors could walk through four open rooms in each of which a different short video was shown on a television monitor (Figure 6.4). One of the videos portrayed real mosquitoes being nurtured in a glass flask, the same symbol as used in '(Re)collection of togetherness'. Another video showed the view from a landing aeroplane, a representation of people travelling. A third video depicted hands opening and showing messages from Chinese fortune cookies. This symbolised mere chance, or people who were not entirely free to decide on their travel destination or their more general destiny in life, because of being tied to the rules of bureaucracy. A fourth video showed a black screen that had a passport-size image of a singing Wulia. The artist was shown singing four national anthems – Chinese, Dutch, Indonesian and Japanese – in karaoke style, as her eyes followed the lyrics above her in the top right corner of the screen.

The national anthems in the video represented the four countries that had an important impact on Wulia's family history: China as the land of ancestry, Indonesia as the home country, and The Netherlands and Japan as the former colonial powers. This family history showed the complexity that overrides a single national identity. 'Study for wanton' also deconstructed the national anthem as being an almost sacred song that can only be sung by those with the right national background and emotional disposition, into a medium that is not radically different from bureaucratic tools such as passports. It seemed to say that singing a national anthem by adhering to the standard melody and lyrics was no different from participation in a karaoke performance.

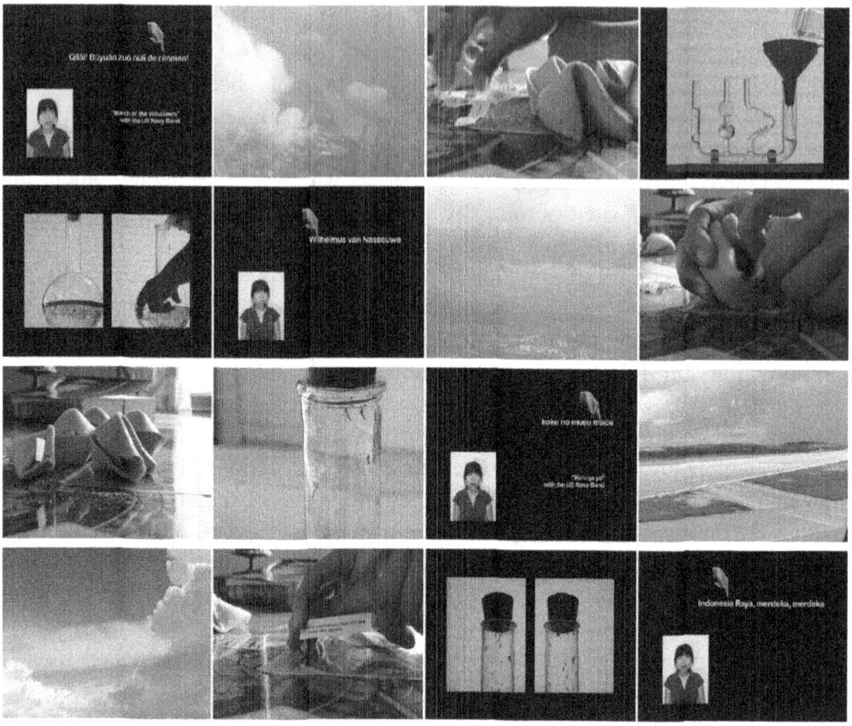

Figure 6.4 'Study for wanton' (Tintin Wulia), multimedia installation, 2008.
Source: photo courtesy of the artist.

Wulia also explored the politics of representation and interactivity in a conceptual sense and beyond the parameters and interests of the mass media by focusing on doors as a medium of communication. 'Slambangricketychuck' (2003) documented the different shapes, colours and sounds of front doors in a middle-class Melbourne suburb. It also contained interviews with residents standing at their front door. Written texts in the video referred to the various mediating functions of doors, such as protecting and connecting people and provoking thoughts.

Another video that contained doors as its main protagonist and focused on the post-30 September 1965 violence was 'Ketok' (Knocking, 2002). It illustrated the danger of media making a life of its own or media that can no longer be contextualised or resisted from complete domination by the ideological interests of a particular political entity. An example is the compulsory annual television broadcast of the New Order propaganda film *Pengkhianatan G30S/PKI*, also referred to in Murti's work. 'Ketok' (2002) included blackboard drawings of a house at night, the sounds and shadows of hands knocking on a door and photos from an old family album. For the occupants of the house, representing Wulia and her family members, the door became a medium of fear because of the unknown source and meaning of the knocks. By the end of the video, they realised that the knocking had nothing to do with the door, but was the sound of a gecko living in or near the house.

According to Wulia (2008; Somzé 2008: 38), the video related a funny family anecdote as well as parodying a popular Indonesian horror television series. However, many viewers also saw in it references to the evocation of fear from the mass imprisonment and killing following the 1965 events. One of those killed during these raids was Wulia's grandfather. 'Ketok' implied the climate of fear during the Suharto regime, which could turn any medium, from a film and a newspaper to a human body and possibly also a door, into a tool for instilling terror and controlling society (see also Heryanto 2006). It was impossible for people to preserve and share their memories and create a comprehensive picture of the past in the climate of fear, as re-animation showed in 'Ketok' (Somzé 2008: 38).

In an early short video, 'Violence against fruits' (2000), Wulia commented on the violence against Chinese-Indonesians in several Indonesian cities preceding the fall of Suharto in May 1998. The video showed a piece of fruit that was slowly being peeled and cut into pieces by a hand holding a kitchen knife. For Wulia (2008), the 1998 events helped her to understand and trace some of the previously inexplicable sources of fear and silence that had reigned over her family since 1965 and had also dominated parts of her own life.

Simatupang (2008) and Somzé (2008) both identify 'borders' separating the individual from the geopolitical as the central theme of Wulia's work. Somzé (2008: 38) argues that this theme is not only illustrated in the content but also the style of her multimedia art. She refers specifically to the 'stop-motion' animation technique used in the video films. This technique produces jerky movements and simplified gestures, which have a sense of 'childish innocence' and are reminiscent of the style of early cinema and experimental film making.

Coming to a slightly different conclusion, I believe that Wulia's installations emphasise the *mediated* character of social and political borders, and also comment on processes of mediation and interactivity in a more conceptual way. Her works presents video, music, writing, architecture, animation and other audio-visual media, which, similar to Kuswidananto's installations, are able to re-animate the past and engage audiences in interactive and experiential aesthetics. At the same time, the artist refers to mediation in terms of the tools of geopolitics and bureaucracy, such as passports, which can either set people literally and figuratively in motion, or restrict their physical mobility and emotional development.

Conclusion

The interactive installations of Murti, Kuswidananto and Wulia engage audiences in a relatively intimate manner. By stimulating their minds and senses, the art works encourage participants to rethink and physically experience issues relevant to contemporary Indonesian society. Mainstream television provides sensory experiences too, in order to appeal to audiences and stimulate them to consume the storylines, commodities and lifestyles promoted in programmes and commercials. The video installations, constructed outside the constraints of the media industry, provide a different type of intimacy, however, as it is combined with contextual information about and critique of the social topics addressed in the art works, including the issues of mediation and interactivity themselves.

Murti, Kuswidananto and Wulia express an interest in the politics of mediation and interactivity by offering unconventional media and innovative and personalised forms of audience participation. Similar to *Newsdotcom*, they also reflect on the interconnectivity between the political landscape and the information and communication infrastructure in pre- and post-1998 Indonesia. Moreover, they share a concern about historiography, or an attempt to readdress and rewrite aspects of Indonesian history as an essential foundation of the country's democratic present and future. Murti focuses on historical constructions of bodies, gender and ethnicity, Kuswidananto on the roots of cultural and religious syncretism, and Wulia on the social impact of the 1965 mass killings, among others.

Their juxtaposing and mixing of high technology, found objects and people's bodies facilitates comparisons between tradition and modernity as well as various media and art genres. Murti incorporates references to art and media history and offers video treatment for curing people of the ordeals of the mass media. Kuswidananto and Wulia have created interactive games which explore, test and expose people's capacity to communicate, collaborate and adhere to ethical standards in a highly mediatised environment. Through aleatoric play, Wulia addresses and recreates the impact of the media of bureaucracy and the politics of chance on people's mobility and identity. Kuswidananto has also created a form of community television that problematises and attempts to provide an alternative to the national public and commercial broadcast media.

Although the three artists work outside the confines of the media industry, to a certain extent they are confined to the commercial and ideological interests of other centres of power, those of the art world itself. The majority of their installations were created for and exhibited in art galleries and museums. Although they are often the product of collaboration with fellow artists or audience members, the art works also have a strong sense of individual authorship attached to them. In that sense, the works, with the exception of Kuswidananto's 'Neighbours' (2002), do not offer a radical alternative to conventional ways of creating and displaying art. The following two chapters will discuss participatory media, including community media and community art, which provide not only audience interactivity and experientiality, but also alternative forms of art and media ownership, management and institutional structures.

Notes

1 Murti, personal communication, Jakarta, 15 April 2008.
2 The 'Mooi Indië' or 'Beautiful Indies' style is a painting school of the late nineteenth and early twentieth centuries, depicting a colonial vision of the Dutch East Indies with idealised landscapes in an atmosphere of nostalgia. In the 1930s and 1940s, nationalist painters such as Sudjojono rejected this style for not representing the reality and hardship of daily life of the common people. For many decades thereafter, the landscape was discredited in the Indonesian modern art world because of its colonial connotations (Siregar 2010; Turner 2005). Murti is one of the first artists to revive interest in exploring and questioning the genre.
3 Murti, personal communication, Jakarta, 15 April 2008.
4 Murti, personal communication, Jakarta, 15 April 2008.
5 A flyer lured the audience to the exhibition through the following pun on advertisement slogans: 'Indulge yourself with a break from tiring modern activities. So why not choose now for Video spa as a 'cleansing' therapy and revitalisation of your daily life? [...] A therapy for the mind. Video spa is a treatment for those who have already tried a normal spa, but it is also recommended to everyone else, especially to all of those who are longing for freshness of mind' (Murti 2004a).
6 Personal communication, Jakarta, 15 April 2008.
7 Jompet (b. 1976, Yogyakarta, now Denpasar) is his nickname. His full name is Agustinus Kuswidananto and he is also known as Kus Widananto.
8 Wulia's (b. 1972, Denpasar, now Brisbane) full name is Maria Clementine Wulia. Tintin is derived from Clementine.
9 Personal communication, Canberra, 2 September 2008.
10 In Dono's work (Hujatnikajennong 2006b: 23; Barry 2006: 77; Iskandar 2006: 117; Hujatnikajennong 2006a: 56), the use of found objects represents the creativity of ordinary Indonesians in recycling and re-appropriating different forms of 'media waste'. The work also contains a critique of the disjunctions in Indonesian society between those who have the economic and educational means to engage with the latest technology, and those who do not. It also shows the juxtaposition between the electronic media and non-electronic objects from daily life rather than a symbiotic relationship between the two.
11 Christiawan had his own metal workshop and originally trained as an interior designer. When Kuswidananto and Christiawan began collaborating, they used materials and skilled labour from the workshop, and recycled metal and other found objects into integrated parts of their works of art (Iskandar 2002: 15).
12 Garden of the Blind may also be a reference to 'opera for the blind', an informal name for 'Symphonie pour l'homme seul' (1949), the first large-scale composition of *musique concrète* by Pierre Schaeffer, Pierre Henry and Jacques Pollin (Meigh-Andrews 2006: 89–90). This composition, consisting of recordings of everyday environmental sounds, had an important impact on the development of installation and video art.
13 Kuswidananto, personal communication, Yogyakarta, 19 December 2008; Iskandar 2002: 12–17.
14 In his video installation 'Nobody's body' (2005), Kuswidananto (2005: 47), explicitly commented on his Catholic background, where he felt the politics of monotheism promoted by the Indonesian state did not reflect the more complex, syncretic realities of religion in Java. Perhaps Kuswidananto's involvement in (interactive) art can be seen as an attempt to liberate himself from his formal religious identity that was mediated by the Indonesian bureaucracy and to explore spiritual as well as other possibilities of the body.
15 Kuswidananto's collaborative performance with Marzuki, currently lead singer of the successful Jogja Hiphop Foundation, 'I'm sorry I'm fucking sorry – ISIFS' (1999),

showed in an immediate and confrontational manner that interactivity can lead to abuse (Murti 2007: 22). In this performance, Marzuki's body was wrapped in long ropes. Members of the audience were invited to move the performer's body in different directions by pulling the ropes. As anticipated by the artists, this inflicted physical wounds on Marzuki. The performance demonstrated that interpersonal communication included interdependence, involved people in vulnerable situations, and required mutual trust and respect.

16 Kuswidananto, personal communication, Yogyakarta, 19 December 2008.

17 This is based on Wulia's 2013 thesis and art exhibition in completion of her PhD at RMIT University in Melbourne.

18 In the video documentary 'Pulang' (Returning home, 2008–current), Wulia documents periods of Sobron's life in exile. Sobron was the younger brother of Aidit, leader of PKI in the 1950s and 1960s. After the 1965 coup, Sobron, who was on an official cultural mission in China, could not return to Indonesia, and he and his family were forced into exile. The documentary, which is still in the final stage of editing, shows Sobron and his family in France and the Netherlands – their two countries of exile after a 17-year stay in China – shortly before his death in early 2007. A key scene in the documentary is where Sobron shows his *titre de voyage*, a travel document specifically for stateless people and refugees, issued by the French government in 1984. The document allowed Sobron and his family to leave France for the first time in two years. They could use it for travel anywhere except the country they longed to return to: Indonesia.

References

Barry, Syamsul. 2006. 'Seni media (kebiasaan) baru kemajuan teknologi informasi dan seni' [New (habit) media art is the progress of information and art]. In: Direktorat Kesenian, *Apresiasi seni media baru* [Appreciation of new media art]. Jakarta: Direktorat Kesenian, Direktorat Jendral Nilai Budaya, Seni dan Film and Departemen Kebudayaan dan Pariwisata, pp. 71–85.

Cemeti Art House. 2008. *Jompet Kuswidananto, Java's machine: phantasmagoria.* Yogyakarta: Cemeti Art House.

Fadjri, Raihul. 2008. 'Gerak kinetik penaklukan Jawa' [Kinetic movement of the subjection of Java]. *Tempo*, 28 December, p. 202.

Heryanto, Ariel. 2006. *State terrorism and political identity in Indonesia: fatally belonging.* London and New York: Routledge.

Hujatnikajennong, Agung. 2004. 'Video spa: immaterialitas tubuh dan substansi citraan bergerak' [Video spa: the immateriality of the body and the substance of moving imagery]. In: Krisna Murti (ed.), *Video spa: videotherapy by Krisna Murti.* Bandung: Studio Krisna Murti.

Hujatnikajennong, Agung. 2005. 'Everything true melts through the screen: an overview of Indonesian video art practice'. In: Amanda Rath (ed.), *Taboo and transgression in contemporary Indonesian art.* Ithaca, NY: Herbert F. Johnson Museum, Cornell University, pp. 51–57.

Hujatnikajennong, Agung. 2006a. 'Highlighting Indonesian new media art'. In: Marie Le Sourd, Septina Ferniati, Lioni Beatrik Tobing, Mirna Adzania and Tarlen Handayani (eds), *The 3rd Asia-Europe art camp 2005: artist initiative spaces and new media arts post-event publication.* Singapore and Bandung: Asia-Europe Foundation and Bandung Center for New Media Arts, pp. 53–57.

Hujatnikajennong, Agung. 2006b. 'Tentang seni media baru: catatan perkembangan' [About new media art: notes on its development]. In: Direktorat Kesenian, *Apresiasi seni media baru* [Appreciation of new media art]. Jakarta: Direktorat Kesenian, Direktorat Jendral Nilai Budaya, Seni dan Film and Departemen Kebudayaan dan Pariwisata, pp. 11–27.

Iskandar, Gustaff Harriman. 2002. 'Garden of the blind'. *Trolley* 9(2): 12–17.

Iskandar, Gustaff Harriman. 2006. 'Rekomendasi kebijakan pengembangan praktik seni media di Indonesia' [Policy recommendations for the development of media art practice in Indonesia]. In: Direktorat Kesenian, *Apresiasi seni media baru* [Appreciation of new media art]. Jakarta: Direktorat Kesenian, Direktorat Jendral Nilai Budaya, Seni dan Film and Departemen Kebudayaan dan Pariwisata, pp. 103–130.

Jurriëns, Edwin. 2009. 'Motion and distortion: the media in the art of Jompet and Tintin'. *Indonesia and the Malay World* 37(109): 277–297.

Jurriëns, Edwin. 2010. 'Video spa: Krisna Murti's treatment of the senses'. *Bijdragen tot de Taal-, Land- en Volkenkunde* 166(1): 1–24.

Jurriëns, Edwin and Jeroen De Kloet (eds). 2007. *Cosmopatriots; on distant belongings and close encounters*. Thamyris/Intersecting: Place, Sex, and Race 16. Amsterdam and New York: Rodopi.

Kuss, Alexandra P. 1999. 'Mengetuk pintu ruang publik' [Knocking on the door of public space]. In: Krisna Murti (ed.), *Video publik* [Public video]. Yogyakarta: Kanisius, pp. 25–34.

Kuswidananto, Jompet. 2005. 'Nobody's body'. In: ruangrupa, *OK. Video sub/version: Jakarta video festival 2005*. Jakarta: ruangrupa, p. 47.

Kuswidananto, Jompet. 2008. Artist's portfolio, Yogyakarta.

Manovich, Lev. 1998. 'Towards an archaeology of the computer screen'. In: Thomas Elsaesser and Kay Hoffman (eds), *Cinema futures, Cain, Abel or cable: the screen arts in the digital age*. Amsterdam: Amsterdam University Press, pp. 27–43.

Marzuki. 2009. 'Marzuki: jadi seniman, craftsmanship saja tak cukup' [Marzuki: to become an artist, craftsmanship alone is not enough]. *Gong: Majalah Seni Budaya* 113(10): 28–29.

Meigh-Andrews, Chris. 2006. *A history of video art: the development of form and function*. Oxford, UK: Berg.

Murti, Krisna. 1999. *Video publik* [Public video]. Yogyakarta: Kanisius.

Murti, Krisna (ed.). 2004a. *Video spa: therapy for everyday living*. Exhibition brochure. Bandung: Studio Krisna Murti.

Murti, Krisna (ed.). 2004b. *Video spa: videotherapy by Krisna Murti*. Bandung: Studio Krisna Murti.

Murti, Krisna. 2006. 'Media baru: kultur gerilya hingga seni gadget' [New media: from guerrilla culture to gadget art]. In: Direktorat Kesenian, *Apresiasi seni media baru* [New media art appreciation]. Jakarta: Direktorat Kesenian, Direktorat Jendral Nilai Budaya, Seni dan Film and Departemen Kebudayaan dan Pariwisata, pp. 45–69.

Murti, Krisna. 2007. 'Jompet's exploration, mbah Poni's testimony; Penjelajahan Jompet, kesaksian mbah Poni'. In: Mella Jaarsma and Nindityo Adipurnomo (eds), *Landing soon 4: Jompet*. Yogyakarta: Cemeti Art House and Heden, pp. 22–30.

Rath, Amanda. 2008. 'Talking back to the landscape: trajectories of an Indonesian discourse in the video art of Krisna Murti'. In: Krisna Murti (ed.), *Forbidden zone*. Semarang: Rumah Seni Yaitu, pp. 4–21.

Simatupang, Landung. 2008. 'Let's consider: mosquito! Impressions and a bit of reflection'. In: Tintin Wulia, Mella Jaarsma and Nindityo Adipurnomo (eds), *Landing soon 5: Tintin Wulia*. Yogyakarta: Cemeti Art House and Heden, pp. 2–7.

Siregar, Aminuddin T. H. 2010. 'Ketradisian versus kemodernan: kasus Krisna Murti'

[The traditional versus the modern: the case of Krisna Murti]. In: Krisna Murti (ed.), *Mute!Theater*. Jakarta: Bentara Budaya, pp. 14–17.

Somzé, Catherine. 2008. 'Borders in (stop-)motion'. In: Tintin Wulia, Mella Jaarsma and Nindityo Adipurnomo (eds), *Landing soon 5: Tintin Wulia*. Yogyakarta: Cemeti Art House and Heden, pp. 36–39.

Suroto, Pincuk. 2009. 'Seni media yang terbuka' [Accessible media art]. *Gong: Majalah Seni Budaya* 113(10): 6–17.

Turner, Caroline. 2005. 'Indonesia: art, freedom, human rights and engagement with the West'. In: Caroline Turner (ed.), *Art and social change: contemporary art in Asia and the Pacific*. Canberra: Pandanus Books, pp. 196–217.

Utari, Dewi Ria. 2002. 'Romantisme Bhisma di instalasi video Krisna Murti' [The romanticism of Bhisma in Krisna Murti's video installation]. *Koran Tempo*, 31 January, p. B8.

Wilson, Alex. 2002. 'Artist Krisna Murti experiments with technology'. *The Jakarta Post*, 2 February, p. 15.

Wulia, Tintin. 2008. 'The name game: or, the years of living with no one to blame'. *Inside Indonesia* 93 (July–September). Available at: www.insideindonesia.org/the-name-game?highlight=WyJ3dWxpYSIsInRpbnRpbiIsInd1bGlhIHRpbnRpbiJd (accessed 13 August 2016).

Wulia, Tintin. 2013. *Aleatoric geopolitics: art, chance and critical play on the border*. PhD thesis, RMIT University, Melbourne.

Part III

Media utopia

7 Participatory media

Community art and media

This chapter focuses on the development of community art and media in Indonesia. Community art and media are independent, grassroots-based initiatives, which have an activist agenda of community cohesion or change, and are meant as an alternative to the mainstream art world or public and commercial print and broadcast media. In that sense, they are different from other interactive genres, such as social media focusing on individual expression and consumption, or traditional art genres with non-activist modes of social participation and community building.

In Indonesia, community media or *media komunitas* have been described as media 'from, by and for the people' (*dari, oleh dan untuk rakyat*; Nazaruddin and Hermanto 2009; Jurriëns 2009a: 141–158, 2013; Birowo 2010). According to this definition, community media are a type of participatory media in which 'ordinary' people, that is, non-media professionals, can contribute to content, management and ownership. Following Raymond Williams (1980), Atton (2002: 4, 25) describes community media as a form of alternative media, comprising various degrees of the 'decapitalisation', 'deprofessionalisation' and 'deinstitutionalisation' of communication. Alternative media would facilitate a more democratic form of communication, as they give access to media production, distribution and consumption to people who are excluded by the financial, professional and institutional structures of the mainstream media (Dowmunt with Coyer 2007: 1; Howley 2010a: 4, 2010b: 16, 2010c: 75). They are not limited to media with an explicit or radical political agenda, but include any media that enable people to reflect on and transform processes of communication in relation to their specific social circumstances (Atton 2002: 7, 30; Howley 2010b: 17–19; Dowmunt with Coyer 2007: 3–4).

Community media have their international roots in groups using pamphlets, radio, audio- and videocassettes and other media for a specific cause. For instance, community radio has been used for demanding better working conditions for Bolivian and Columbian miners in the late 1940s; for fighting government broadcasting monopolies in Europe in the 1960s and 1970s; and for promoting democracy in South Africa after the fall of the Apartheid regime in the early 1990s (Fraser and Estrada 2001: 6). Nowadays community art and media in Indonesia and elsewhere are seen and used as a tool in the struggle against the intensified commercialisation, monopolisation and homogenisation of the mainstream art world, and print and broadcast media.

Ideas about the history and concept of community media spread to Indonesia through the educational and practical training programmes of international organisations such as UNESCO.[1] Initially only involving a dozen pioneering print bulletins and radio stations in predominantly Central and West Java, nowadays hundreds of community radios can be found throughout the country. Since the early 2000s, Indonesian community media initiatives have also incorporated other technologies, such as video, television and the Internet. The 2002 Indonesian Broadcasting Law (particularly part 6, paragraphs 21 to 24) includes community media as a fourth official broadcasting category, besides public, commercial and subscription broadcasting services.

I use a critical and historical perspective to examine some of the achievements of Indonesian community art and media, the problems they have encountered, as well as the solutions they are offering. The various participatory genres can be seen as an aspect of the renewed freedom of expression since the fall of the New Order regime, and a reflection of the trends and cultures of interactivity and interconnectivity that have been rapidly developing with the World Wide Web (www) and mobile technologies since the early 1990s. At the same time, they have their roots in a long tradition of social commitment and participation in a variety of Indonesian cultural genres (Jurriëns 2013).

First, I analyse the similarities and differences with earlier genres with an explicit participatory agenda, including certain forms of LEKRA literature and art of the 1950s and 1960s; 'people's theatre' (*teater rakyat*) since the 1970s; and 'conscientisation art' (*seni rupa penyadaran*) since the 1980s. Then I focus on the various initiatives of media activists in the village of Timbulharjo, Central Java, as an example of contemporary community media. These activists have not only been at the forefront of the development of community media in Indonesia since the early 2000s, but have also covered a variety of media, ranging from print bulletins to radio and the Internet. Their experiences illustrate both the potential and the limits of community media in Indonesia and resonate with some of the characteristics of the historical participatory genres.

One of the main challenges for contemporary community art and media has been to reconcile class differences in the collaboration between media or art facilitators and local communities. These and other factors have affected the accessibility, distribution, sustainability and reach of their ideas, activities and outputs. The final part of this chapter demonstrates how facilitators and practitioners have tried to solve some of these problems through the exploration of alternative art and media networks, formats and content.

Social engagement in art: The Institute of People's Culture 1950–1965

No other institution in Indonesian history has put the issue of social commitment in culture and art higher on the agenda than LEKRA, The Institute of People's Culture. LEKRA, which existed from 1950 until 1965, was informally linked to Partai Komunis Indonesia (Indonesian Communist Party, PKI), and encouraged artists to demonstrate social commitment in their works and activities. LEKRA also introduced participatory genres and methods, although in its literature and other art there was a stronger tendency to represent local people rather than engage and work with them directly.

In that sense, contemporary community media are less ambiguous: social engagement is something not only to be represented, but also to be demonstrated or performed through the actual participation of local communities. The relation between the intentions and interests of local communities on the one hand, and the creation and distribution of art and media works on the other, is usually mediated by third parties with their own approaches and agendas. Although its practical application is often characterised by conflict, the concept of community media suggests coherence between content (social issues) and format or style (social participation).

Keith Foulcher (1986) has observed various conflicts between content and format or style in LEKRA literature and other art. Reflecting President Sukarno's discourse on the Indonesian post-colonial state and its position in the world, LEKRA promoted a combination of nationalism, anti-imperialism and modernisation that was rooted in the reality and ambitions of the *rakyat* ('society' or 'the people'; Foulcher 1986: 28), a term also commonly used in the context of contemporary community media. Initially, in LEKRA's Mukadimah ('Preamble') founding statement of 1950, 'the people' referred to class and material interests, but in the mid-1950s the idea was formulated by the institute in terms of an emotional commitment to values that went beyond class divisions, such as nationalism, anti-imperialism, modernisation, justice and equality (Foulcher 1986: 29). Artists were supposed to share this 'state of awareness' or 'state of mind' and reflect it in their creative works. Foulcher (1986: 25) argues that this type of social commitment was restricted predominantly to the 'content' of art, but never really translated into a distinct aesthetic theory, style or production method.

LEKRA promoted an idea of socialist realism that was based on the work of the Russian author Maxim Gorki (1868–1936). This socialist realism was a form of realism in its attempt to represent the nature, essence or truth of society and everyday life; it was socialist in presenting an idealist, revolutionary vision of the future with suggestions, changes and solutions for a better Indonesia (Foulcher 1986: 23, 37–39, 50, 121, 141). Usually, there was no explicit concern with the construction of a political form of socialism, however, but rather a 'revolutionary realist' focus on 'immediate, concrete issues, and 'the struggle for justice in a radical nationalist context' (Bodden 2012: 463–464).

In terms of style, the socialist or revolutionary realism of LEKRA-related artists shared many characteristics with the modern, if not modernist, outlook of the rival 'universal humanist' camp.[2] The creation and evaluation of LEKRA art was generally based on the same criteria of originality and individuality, although in terms of content and attitude towards reality the work rejected the a-historical and a-social general values of the universal humanist artists. According to Foulcher (1986: 41–51, 122–123, 134–137), the paradoxical and theoretically problematic combinations of modern western styles, such as realism and expressionism, and people-oriented (*kerakyatan*) content remained largely ignored or unsolved by the LEKRA artists and art critics.[3] Although the integration between message and approach or presentation is at the heart of contemporary community media theory, in practice incongruities remain, as shown by the analysis of the Timbulharjo alternative media initiatives later in this chapter.

This is not to say that LEKRA did not promote innovative artistic methods or formats, distinct from the universal humanist tradition and partially continued in today's community media. For instance, LEKRA provided material, organisational and promotional support to painters and other visual artists that were part of so-called *sanggar* (Holt 1967: 218; Foulcher 1986: 41–42). In *sanggar*, which originated from the time of the Revolution (1945–1949), a senior artist taught painting and other creative skills to young aspiring artists. The artists normally worked as a cooperative and lived as a commune in an *asrama*.[4] They also organised art exhibitions and workshops in the open air that were accessible to the general public (Spanjaard 1998: 120; Foulcher 1986: 140). Examples of these communities were the Pelukis Rakyat ('People's Painters'), who used the slogan *Seni untuk rakyat* ('Art for the people'), and the Seniman Indonesia Muda ('Young Indonesian Artists') of the 1940s and 1950s.

LEKRA also published reportage-style short stories by ordinary people who normally would not present themselves as literary authors in the cultural affairs section of the PKI daily *Harian Rakyat* ('The People's Daily'). In terms of content, these stories can be seen as early examples of media 'from and for the people', although the newspaper itself was not managed or owned 'by the people', as would be the case in more recent community media. The stories were not published in their original regional languages, but translated into the national language. Most likely, they were also extensively edited and rewritten in other ways. According to Foulcher (1986: 54), this genre remained 'a minor tendency overshadowed by the direction of the movement as a whole, and its "proletarian" character is still mitigated by the fundamental "modernising" and "national culture" elements of LEKRA ideology'.

In the early 1960s, when LEKRA became more directly involved in party and state politics, it demanded a stronger social commitment of artists and cultural activists by encouraging them to 'move down' (*turun ke bawah* or *turba*) and live, work and otherwise fully participate in local communities.[5] The usually urban-based artists and activists were to undergo a personal transformation as a result of the physical deprivations and psychological hardships of living in the countryside. They were also prompted to conduct research about the revolutionary potential of regional art forms and culture.

Shackford-Bradley (2000) argues that 'the very concept of "descent from above" is based on a spatial configuration of class that is uncompromisingly hierarchical'. Ironically, the term itself continued to be used by state officials during the New Order to refer to their official visits to the Indonesian slums, villages and outer regions (Shackford-Bradley 2000). The aspect of class division would not be solved by the people's theatre and conscientisation art of the following decades, and it still poses a real challenge to today's community media facilitators. In general, community media facilitators have a higher education than their target groups and the length and depth of their immersion in local societies is relatively limited.

Early participatory media: people's theatre since the 1970s

After Suharto took over power from Sukarno in 1965, LEKRA and the PKI were banned, and hundreds of thousands of their real or alleged members were imprisoned or killed in a series of violent events that took place in Java and other islands. The universal humanist approach of individual expression and international and decorative styles became the officially approved creative practice, while socially and politically engaged art and media were discredited, censored or banned. This does not mean, however, that artists and media practitioners did not attempt to express socio-political commitment in various other, often innovative ways.

Gerakan Seni Rupa Baru (New Art Movement, GSRB), for instance, deliberately distanced themselves from academic, politically accepted and socially distanced or universal styles, such as abstract modernism, post-impressionism and classical realism. They were influenced by the 1960s Pop Art movement in the United Kingdom and the United States, the West German sculptor Joseph Beuys (1921–1986) and early twentieth century Dadaism and surrealism, and adopted and reinvented genres such as performance art, happenings, installations, mixed media, found objects and photorealism (Hardi 1979: 14–15; Miklouho-Maklai 1991: 2, 25; Harsono 2009a: 50, 2009c: 69; Supangkat 1979: 99–103). They engaged with the daily realities of contemporary consumer culture and sought to level:

> the aesthetic distance between the art of urban mass culture – such as *becak* decoration, folk arts, or *seni rupa di kaki lima* ('street' art, comprising such expressions as posters, T-shirts, bumper stickers, comics and the many other articles commonly found for sale in urban street stalls and shops) – and contemporary art as practiced by graduates of art academies.
>
> (Miklouho-Maklai 1991: 1)

According to FX Harsono (2009e), co-founder of GSRB and prolific artist and essayist, the movement had a different, broader idea of people's issues (*kerakyatan*) than the previous generations of socially engaged artists. In their works and statements, the young artists, children of both the New Order regime and the era of globalisation, gave expression to issues of national and international concern, such as 'the environment, displacement, labour, humanity, war, the culture of violence and the conflict between traditional and modern culture' (Harsono 2009e: 106). Brita Miklouho-Maklai (1991: 26) observed that GSRB attached equal importance to form and content for expressing their ideas, whereas earlier movements such as LEKRA focused on content rather than form. However, similar to the majority of LEKRA literature and visual art, GSRB was about representing social commitment rather than enabling direct social participation. The decision of artist-activist Moelyono (1997b: 124) to create 'conscientisation art' in the 1980s was also partly in protest against GSRB's practice of speaking on behalf of the 'ordinary people' rather than engaging in real dialogue with them.

The principles and sources of social engagement of another art form during the early New Order regime, people's theatre, were much closer to those of the community media of the late twentieth and early twenty-first centuries. An institution that illustrates the connections between people's theatre and modern community media is the Yogyakarta-based catholic media production centre Studio Audio Visual Puskat (Puskat Audio-Visual Studio). Puskat has contributed to the development of Indonesian people's theatre through its involvement with the Arena theatre group since 1971 (Hatley 2008: 134–137; Bodden 2010: 58). In the 1980s and 1990s, it gradually expanded its activities to other art, media and topics, including religion, youth, regional culture, agriculture and ecotourism. In 1995, it established its own community radio station Balai Budaya Minomartani (Minomartani Cultural House; Jurriëns 2009a: 153–154), which focuses on children's programmes and Javanese arts including *wayang kulit* and *gamelan*, and is based on principles similar to those of people's theatre, such as accessibility, participation and 'conscientisation' or creating social awareness through education.[6]

Arena's version of people's theatre was influenced by various international sources, particularly the work of the Brazilian educator and philosopher Paolo Freire, the Brazilian theatre director Augusto Boal, the Philippine Educational Theater Association (PETA), the German playwright Bertold Brecht and the Canadian theatre activist Ross Kidd (Erven 1992: 187; Bodden 2010: 59–62, 68). Aspects of these sources, especially Freire's idea of conscientisation, are reflected in the people's theatre theory as formulated by Fred Wibowo (Bodden 2010: 80–81), who was the artistic leader of Arena from the early 1970s to the early 1990s, and later became the managing director of Puskat. This theory comprises the following six points:

1 The stories of performances must have their origins in local social conditions.
2 The scripts of performances should be created and arranged by the local people themselves.

3 Performances should be kept simple and make use of easily accessible, locally available resources.
4 They should break down the barriers between performers and audiences and avoid the use of professional actors.
5 They should aim not at catharsis, but at raising awareness about social problems.
6 They have to effect change and create conditions for a better world by building dialogue between people.

If these six criteria are followed, people's theatre can become, in Wibowo's words, a true 'people's feast' (*pesta rakyat*) and a 'rehearsal' for complete social change, including material improvement (Bodden 2010: 80–81). Puskat has based its community radio station and community media training workshops on similar ideas. The members of another Yogyakarta-based group, Kelompok Teater Rakyat Indonesia (Indonesian People's Theatre Group, KTRI; established in 1989) took the idea of people's theatre to a more radical end than Arena, by living and working full-time, in *turba*-like fashion, with local communities (Hatley 2008: 136; Bodden 2010: 74–76).

Community media facilitators such as Puskat have not only worked with local groups, but also trained NGOs to combine their development programmes with theatrical and other cultural techniques for informal education and social conscientisation (Bodden 2010: 74). It is in this complex interaction between cultural workers, NGO activists and local communities in people's theatre and other cultural activities at the grassroots where conflicts of class and other interests have arisen. One issue that emerged in various forms of 'workers' theatre' (*teater buruh*) in the 1990s was that well-educated, middle-class NGO activists valorised theatre groups more in terms of their contribution to a labour movement than in terms of their own artistic development. For the workers themselves, theatre was a medium for not only representing the reality of everyday life, providing education and building solidarity, but also enjoying the pleasures of association, recreation and relaxation (Bodden 2010: 227–229). Middle-class artists, art critics and journalists, for their part, often ignored or criticised the artistic value of workers and other grassroots theatre. The performances were primarily seen as tools for creating awareness, not for providing aesthetic sophistication or innovation (Bodden 2010: 239–242, 256–258).

This type of criticism echoed the conflict between style and content in the creation and discussion of LEKRA art during the 1950s and 1960s. I argue, however, that rather than suffering from a lack of artistic quality, grassroots theatre and, following from it, other community media present a specific type of aesthetics. This aesthetics, in line with the content and production mechanism of grassroots performances, has a strong contextual, interactive and dialogical character. It constitutes an important alternative to the universal humanist aesthetics of time- and space-transcending originality and individuality, which became the dominant and politically endorsed line after the abolition of LEKRA in 1965.

According to Michael Bodden (2010: 241):

> rather than searching for universal values, workers' theatre embraced the local, specific issues of its primary audience and did so in a way that allowed the audience to join in the fun. This 'intimacy' was then joined with modern notions of theatre as an educational medium.

In the current age of computer-mediated interactivity and connectivity, aspects of this alternative aesthetics have moved to the centre of creative production and consumption, although, both in Indonesia and elsewhere, community media as a whole is still battling to find social and political acceptance.

Creating awareness: conscientisation art since the 1980s

Indonesian artists have applied Freire's idea of conscientisation not only to theatre, but also to drawing, installation and other visual art. The Indonesian pioneer of such participatory visual art is Moelyono. According to Moelyono (1997a, 1997b), art, as a means of education, expression and dialogue, can make people critically aware of their position and role in society, and encourage them to voice their aspirations and alter their prospects for the future. He has used various names for his art, which all refer to social participation, social awareness and social change, including 'conscientisation art' (*seni rupa penyadaran*), 'renewal art' (*seni rupa pembaruan*), 'virtuous art' (*seni rupa kagunan*),[7] 'public art' (*seni rupa publik*), 'community art' (*seni rupa komunitas*), 'art at the margins' (*seni pinggiran*) and 'Village Unit Art' (*Kesenian Unit Desa*).[8]

Since the mid-1980s, Moelyono has promoted his thoughts about art and education through his work as an art teacher at a Catholic high school in the town of Tulungagung, a teachers' training college in the town of Kediri, an art institute in Surabaya, and a small elementary school serving the tiny fishing villages of Brumbun and Nggerangan in the Tulungagung regency, all in East Java (Wright 1994: 216). Since 1993, Moelyono has also run his own art foundation in the town of Tulungagung, called Yayasan Seni Rupa Komunitas (Foundation of Community Art, YSRK). The foundation provides art education, documentation, workshops, discussions, and children's art festivals and exhibitions (Brangwetan 2011). Moelyono (2005: 5) has also brought his art programmes to provinces outside Java, including Aceh and Papua.

Moelyono has used his art classes as a means to improve and create awareness about the material, mental and physical wellbeing of his students (Wright 1994: 214–216; Harsono 2009d: 57–62). While drawing is his preferred medium, he also uses other three-dimensional media such as rattan sculptures as interactive tools for play and instruction (Aditjondro 2005: 87). He tries to provide education and social change 'from below' by asking children and, directly or indirectly, also their parents, questions about everyday matters such as the importance of clean drinking water.[9] By encouraging them to give expression to these issues in art, he hopes that his students can break away from habitual ways of observing and behaving, and produce imaginative ideas and practical solutions (Wright 1994: 217–218).

In August 1988, Moelyono organised an exhibition in Jakarta with drawings from the East Javanese fishing village children, which, in line with his idea of *seni rupa penyadaran*, was titled 'Transformative Dialogue'. The exhibition catalogue was not a conventional art catalogue, but included texts, maps, statistics and photographs that presented a geographical and social portrait of the villages (Wright 1994: 216–217). The money from the art works sold at the exhibition was used to fund local projects such as water storage facilities (Harsono 2009d: 61). Moelyono (1997b: 86–91) has done projects with both rural communities and urban groups. On 12 August 1993, he used installation art as a medium to mobilise a group of factory workers in Surabaya for an event at the Surabaya Art Council, called 'An Art Exhibition for Marsinah'. This courageous exhibition, which commemorated the first 100 days since the rape and murder of local worker-activist Marsinah, was closed by the police soon after its opening (Moelyono 1997b: 98; Fakih 1997: xxix).

It may be difficult to find the same degree of social commitment as shown by Moelyono among other community media facilitators. However, even his supporters question certain aspects of his approach. In an essay for one of Moelyono's books (2005), the Indonesian sociologist George Junus Aditjondro tried to make Moelyono, as well as community media facilitators, local residents and academics, re-evaluate their own position in various forms of social interaction. Aditjondro's critical questions included the following: (1) How can the oversimplification and confusion of categories such as 'poor people', 'people with problems', 'villagers' and 'children' be avoided?; (2) Considering the variety of problems faced by local residents, who decides on the selection of key themes for public display and discussion with the outside world?; and (3) What are the target audiences for exhibitions that take place outside the local communities, and what is their connection with the communities and/or community media facilitators? (Aditjondro 2005: 85–104).

Aditjondro (2005: 84–85) wondered, for instance, why Moelyono (1997b: 79–82), for an exhibition touring Java in 1989, highlighted the theme of the diversion of village land and resources for tourism purposes in Nggerangan and Brumbun, while many other issues could have been raised from the art works produced by the local villagers. Referring to the sale of art works at the 1998 'Transformative Dialogue' exhibition, he also warned of the risk of diverting projects from their original pedagogical and emancipatory purposes to merely becoming fund raising events. Similar to the lessons drawn from the *teater buruh* initiatives, and equally relevant to various forms of contemporary community media, this suggests that the interests of an outside party, no matter the sincerity of its social commitment, do not necessarily match those of the target communities. Aditjondro (2005: 92–94) also referred to the basic problem of community art and media activists needing to decide on the right moment to leave their target group and consider their mission of supporting community independence and emancipation accomplished.

Contemporary community media: the case of Timbulharjo

A more recent example of similar issues is the range of local media initiatives in the Central Javanese village of Timbulharjo. In 2000, young people from the Dadapan area in Timbulharjo made use of the relaxed media regulations of the reform era to start a print bulletin, called *Angkringan*.[10] The village youth believed the bulletin would be an effective means of: assisting people in communicating their thoughts and organising and monitoring themselves; strengthening the role of local people in controlling corruption in their village administration; giving specific interest groups a stronger bargaining position in negotiations with other groups; and uniting the various village factions (Sulistyowati *et al.* 2005: 171–172).

The *Angkringan* bulletin is published four times a month and costs only Rp.750 (approximately US$0.08) per copy. Apart from the income from sales, the production costs are covered with the money from advertisements for local small trade. In addition to local news, the bulletin publishes national news of local relevance, for instance about an outbreak of a virus. The first edition of the bulletin, published on 14 January 2000, critically discussed the way in which the village government had handled money for a poverty reduction project. Partly as a result of the publication of stories about the mismanagement of the poverty reduction funds, the village head was forced to step down.

In July 2000, the *Angkringan* bulletin was the only community initiative to receive one of the annual media awards of the Jakarta-based ISAI. The prize money of Rp.2,500,000 (approx. US$450) was invested in the establishment of a community radio station, also called Angkringan. The station started broadcasting in August 2000 (Sulistyowati *et al.* 2005: 171–173; Jurriëns 2009a: 147–149). Its advantage over the print bulletin is that it has a larger reach and can also be understood by illiterate people. As the villagers are usually busy with their normal work and other activities during the day, the broadcasts take place every evening from 8 to 11 p.m. The broadcasts discuss issues such as land certificates, social insurances and public housing (Sulistyowati *et al.* 2005: 174).

Since 2007, the Timbulharjo citizens have also used the community radio infrastructure to broadcast internet signals. The advantage of this system is that users do not have to pay individual internet connection fees, but can share the costs with each other, which amount only to several thousand Rupiah (less than US$1) per household per month. To receive the internet signals, the Timbulharjo citizens use so-called ‘wajanbolic’, or modified *wajan* or frying pans, which are not only cheap but also have symbolic value as basic cookware that can be found in almost every Indonesian household and *warung* (food stall). The wireless internet service, called AngkringaNet, provides the local people with internet links to the outside world as well as an intranet exclusively for the community. The AngkringaNet website contains various Open Source software programmes for general use, and also enables people to access and contribute to a Village Database with information about local governance, economy, health and other issues. Community members are also trying to use the internet service for the local production, broadcasting and reception of television programmes (Jurriëns 2009b).

The various Angkringan community media receive operational support from the Yogyakarta-based Combine Resource Institution (CRI), which itself receives financial support from The Ford Foundation. As The Ford Foundation requires that every partner organisation of CRI has legal status, the Timbulharjo community established the Forum Komunikasi Warga Timbulharjo (Timbulharjo Citizens' Communication Forum, Fokowati), an official body for the coordination of the local media initiatives, on 27 May 2001. Fokowati aims to contribute to a 'participatory, transparent and accountable governance of the Timbulharjo village', and tries to maintain its independence by not accepting any members of the village government (Sulistyowati *et al.* 2005: 174–175).

The Angkringan community media discuss issues that were raised during workshops organised by Fokowati and involving representatives of all the major interest groups in the village, including women and young people. The five key problems highlighted during the workshops were the mismanagement of land certificates, students leaving high school prematurely, unemployment, the lack of financial support for local businesses and inadequacies in the village's material infrastructure. With support from CRI, Fokowati was relatively successful in bringing these issues to the attention of the village government. Initially the Angkringan community radio station was even provided with a space at the village meeting hall. After a while, however, their phone connection began to be interrupted by members of the village government who disagreed with some of the broadcast content, in particular about the government's mismanagement of land certificates (Sulistyowati *et al.* 2005: 196).

According to a detailed study of the Communications Studies programme at Sekolah Tinggi Pembangunan Masyarakat Desa (Tertiary Institution for Village Community Development, STPMD) in Yogyakarta, the availability of community media and other public institutions in Timbulharjo has not sufficiently improved people's political participation in terms of 'voice', 'access' and 'control' (Sulistyowati *et al.* 2005: 183). 'Voice' here means to be able to express one's opinion about issues related to governance and development; 'access' to be able to influence and participate in the creation of government policies and public services; and 'control' to be able to monitor the operations, policies and financial situation of the government (Sulistyowati *et al.* 2005: 168–169). Although community media can serve a broader spectrum of more subtle types of politics – the politics of local identity, gender or the media, for instance – the focus on administrative politics is useful for testing the reach, depth and strength of the ideal of social empowerment through community media.

According to the STPMD report, one of the problems directly impacting the Angkringan community media has been Fokowati's lack of initiatives after the partnership with CRI formally expired. The only people willing to participate in the activities are the local educated elite. The majority of the Timbulharjo population does not understand the idea and function of Fokowati, due to a perceived lack of media literacy, or an antagonism towards a communication forum that was introduced by an external organisation. While the total population of Timbulharjo numbers more than 16,000 people, the discussion forums are attended by an average of only 20 to 40 villagers. Because of technical and financial problems, there have also been interruptions in the publication of the *Angkringan* bulletin (Sulistyowati *et al.* 2005: 196–200).

Based on the Timbulharjo experience, the STPMD research team published three recommendations to improve the effectiveness of community media. First, local citizens should be made aware of the presence, function and benefit of community media, and be given a sense of ownership of these media. Second, community media should be supported by 'transformative' leadership that is able to formulate and put into operation democratic policies. Third, education should be provided to help people transform themselves and become the subjects rather than the objects of communication practices and, consequently, also the initiators rather than the targets of local policies (Sulistyowati *et al.* 2005: 201). In short, some of the main issues have been accessibility and participation, political support and reach, and media education. Indonesian community media facilitators and practitioners are aware of these and other difficulties in their work, and are in a continuous process of self-reflection and improvement.

Media distribution and institution building

As the previous discussion has demonstrated, collaboration between art or media activists and local communities typically involves a complex negotiation of conflicting interests and class differences. The success of these negotiations depends on the transparency of the arrangements and the depth and length of dialogue between the various participants. The failure of some aspects of these negotiations puts the idea of media 'from, by and for the people' in critical perspective. At the same time, however, community media initiatives should be credited with publishing stories and creative ideas to the outside world that normally would not reach the mainstream media.

For the participants in community media initiatives, the distribution of media content is usually a bigger challenge than the production of content. Indonesian community video facilitators and practitioners, for instance, do not have access to the mainstream channels for the distribution of films and DVDs. In commercial cinemas, there is a lack of digital projection facilities that allow the screening of film as well as video (Lowenthal 2009: 39). Commercial DVD outlets such as Disc Tarra only distribute videos that meet the required minimum number of copies (usually 1,000 copies or more) and carry a tax ribbon issued by the Lembaga Sensor Film (Film Censorship Board, LSF; Lowenthal 2009: 41). A problem for video artists is that they may not be invited to exhibitions and festivals if their work is already available on the Internet. The organisers of video festivals themselves are often confronted with complex organisational problems and copyright and censorship issues (Lowenthal 2009: 39).

Many video activists also refuse to have their work broadcast on public or commercial television, because they feel this would compromise the independent or radical character of their activities. Those who do not object to working with mainstream television institutions often miss out on receiving royalties, because their work is regarded as non-profit in nature (Lowenthal 2009: 40). Community television is still in its early phase of development in Indonesia (Nazaruddin and Hermanto 2009), and video activists and community television practitioners are often not aware of the complementary values of their activities and ideas.

Faced with these challenges, Indonesian alternative video practitioners have come up with many creative solutions to make their work accessible to the public. These solutions include screenings at alternative venues such as independent cinemas, foreign cultural institutes, art galleries, campuses, political centres, village halls, boarding schools and family homes. Films and videos are also shown outdoors, continuing an Indonesian cinema tradition of projecting movies on mobile, temporary screens or *layar tancap* (literally, 'screens that are stuck in the ground'; Lowenthal 2009: 38). Another form of distribution is the sale of DVDs or VCDs in alternative bookshops, on promotional internet sites, and in so-called *distro* or small 'distribution' shops for independently produced fashion, music, video and other creative work (Iskandar 2006: 106–107; Uttu 2006).

Support for the distribution of alternative video is also provided by the Australia and Indonesia-based NGO EngageMedia, which has been building an online network of video activism in the Asia-Pacific region. The network is meant as a site where facilitators and practitioners can easily get in touch and exchange materials and ideas with each other. One of its outcomes has been an open source video-sharing platform called Plumi. The system makes it possible for local organisations to set up video archives:

> which run on a server hosted locally in the office of the organisation, making uploading and downloading to the archive extremely rapid. Videos can be watched by anyone on the local area network and easily copied to USB sticks, DVDs and CDs.
>
> (Lowenthal 2009: 49)

EngageMedia expects the organisations that make use of its facilities to publish their work under Creative Commons (CC), which is an alternative copyright system to 'help authors share their work while keeping their copyright and specifying certain conditions' (Lowenthal 2009: 51).

One of EngageMedia's counterparts and a forerunner in the exploration and application of alternative video distribution is the Yogyakarta-based community video facilitator Kampung Halaman ('Home Village'). Kampung Halaman (2010c), founded in 2006 by Cicilia Maharani, Dian Herdiany, Elanvito, Zamzam Fauzanafi and M. Abduh Azis, focuses on young people as the key to social transformation. It tries to make young people aware of their role as 'agents of change', and assists them in telling, recording and screening stories that are rarely covered in the mainstream public and commercial media (Kampung Halaman 2010c).

Its main programme, the Youth Media Community Lab, provides participants with training about how to conduct research, make videos, organise video screenings, and set up creative media businesses and local media centres. The participating groups receive assistance from Kampung Halaman for approximately two years, after which they are expected to continue their activities independently (Kampung Halaman 2010c). In November 2011, Michelle Obama presented the International Spotlight Award from the US President's Committee on the Arts and Humanities to Kampung Halaman for its engagement programmes with local youth (Youth Program Awards 2011).

In collaboration with EngageMedia, Kampung Halaman has developed Depot Video, a Plumi-inspired facility that enables students, academics and the general public to easily download and save community videos. It also publishes community videos in the form of DVDs, which are distributed for free to local communities, NGOs, schools, universities and national and international film festivals. Another distribution strategy is monthly community video screenings, called 'Nonton bareng di kampung' ('Let's watch together in the neighbourhood'). The screenings always take place in different communities to the ones that created the videos, in order to facilitate the inter-local exchange of materials and ideas (Lowenthal 2009: 38). Kampung Halaman has also been involved in documentary film competitions as a means to produce and distribute community videos (Kampung Halaman 2010a).

Two of its special annual events are the Indonesian Youth Media Camp and Jalan Remaja 1208 ('Youth Street/Path 1208'). The Indonesian Youth Media Camp provides media training to young community leaders, while Jalan Remaja 1208 teaches local young people how to create and share their own videos and video blogs (Kampung Halaman 2010b, 2010e). Kampung Halaman has also attempted to give a more sustainable character to community video production and distribution by facilitating the establishment of community media centres. An example is Opak House, which consists of a library, theatre and activity room, and is situated near the Opak river in the Karang Ploso village in Bantul, Central Java. The purpose of the centre is to make the local young people aware of both the problems and the assets of their communities, and to help them find a balance between individual and communal interests, and between modern and traditional communication and information media (Kampung Halaman 2010d).

Some local groups refuse Kampung Halaman's offer to install internet facilities in their villages, because of fear of exposure to pornography and other unwanted materials (Lowenthal 2009: 45). EngageMedia's plans for building an on-line community video network are not always received well either. Some communities have ideological objections against collaboration with other interest groups as a single network, while others fear a lack of human resources for maintaining such a network (Lowenthal 2009: 34). There are also groups who prefer to communicate directly with other community members rather than to try to address a relatively abstract and unknown internet audience (Lowenthal 2009:

46). EngageMedia itself rightly acknowledges that 'the fact that the technology exists and certain groups have an affinity for video is not enough to form effective networks. Networks must begin from common political goals and shared understandings' (Lowenthal 2009: 64).

Creating common ground

Community media facilitators and practitioners have tried to meet, exchange thoughts and materials, and create common ground not only through on-line communication, but also through face-to-face encounters. Both on- and off-line meetings provide public visibility to and education about community media, and give these media a stronger position in dealing with the competition and resistance from the social, political and business establishment. More than just being two of the buzzwords of our time, connectivity and networking can function as effective strategies for community media initiatives to increase their accessibility and social and political reach.

An example of a face-to-face meeting that was specifically designed to create common goals and shared understanding was the community media festival Jagongan Media Rakyat, or 'Social Gathering of People's Media', held in Yogyakarta from 22 to 25 July 2010. The festival was organised by CRI with support from The Ford Foundation, the Humanistisch Instituut voor Ontwikkelingssamenwerking (Humanist Institute for Development Cooperation, HIVOS) and several other institutions.[11] In addition to practitioners from public, commercial, community, campus and school media, it attracted the participation of civil society activists, community leaders, academics, artists, and primary and secondary school teachers and pupils (Jagongan Media Rakyat 2010a). The festival events comprised a national seminar on village poverty; workshops about handicraft, art, technology and Open Source software; local music, dance and theatre performances; and presentations and discussions about community media and other socio-political issues, including environmental sustainability and the rights of women and workers (Jagongan Media Rakyat 2010b).

The participation of organisations such as Sekolah mBrosot illustrated that the festival organisers acknowledged the importance of education in advancing the development of community media. Sekolah mBrosot is an informal education and activity centre in the village of Brosot, located in the Bantul area south of Yogyakarta. The centre organises many activities, especially for children and women, ranging from theatre and literature to handicraft and cooking workshops. It also comprises a professionally run library with an impressive array of local, national and international literary and academic texts.[12] These references provide the community with a means of contextualising historically, socio-politically and/or theoretically their self-representations in artistic and other activity. The library is not only an invaluable source of knowledge for the Brosot community, but also attracts scholars and students from Yogyakarta and beyond. Although the favourable material and intellectual conditions of Sekolah mBrosot may not be available to the majority of other alternative art and media initiatives, the school could nevertheless serve as a model for the integration of community media in a wider educational context.

The central event of the Jagongan Media Rakyat, the national seminar of 22 July 2010, was meant to identify and find solutions for problems with the collection of correct data about poverty levels in Indonesia. These problems include the use of different interpretations and variables for measuring poverty as well as delays in information updates. An example was the 2008 Bantuan Tunai Langsung ('Direct Cash Help') government programme for the distribution of money to poor people, which, due to a lack of reliable information, resulted in the unequal allocation of funds. The seminar aimed at developing a national information system for the collection and comparison of micro-data and statistics from various Indonesian regions. The discussions drew participants from national and regional government institutions, aid organisations, NGOs and universities (Jagongan Media Rakyat 2010c).

In the context of the development of community media in Indonesia, Jagongan Media Rakyat stood out for two reasons: first, an effort was made at building networks of community media and other, governmental and non-governmental, organisations; and second, the discussion of community media was directly linked to providing education about and finding solutions for specific socio-political issues. The festival can be seen as one of the first focused attempts to strengthen the impact of community media beyond individual institutions and communities.

The use of the concept of 'people's media' rather than 'community media' in the festival's title may also signal a re-orientation from the general principles of alternative media to the more explicit political agenda of 'tactical' or radical media, which are aimed at directly influencing the opinion of the general public and key decision makers. In a research conducted by EngageMedia with the Yogyakarta-based Kunci ('Key') Cultural Studies Center, tactical video is distinguished from two other categories of 'video activism', experimental video and grassroots video.[13] I regard tactical video as a subgenre or an approach rather than a category of its own, as it moves, by its very nature, between different forms of alternative media (Garcia 2007: 6–7).

Jagongan Media Rakyat also seemed to be moving community media in the direction of creative or experimental activism by welcoming the participation of visual artists. This combined focus on education, politics and creative imagination may strengthen community media's effort to break through the dominant paradigms of the mainstream media and to expand its reach to policy makers and the general public.

Conclusion

Indonesian community media confirm Edward Aspinall's (2012) argument that after the destruction of the PKI in 1965, leftist ideas and activities of 'commitment to the interests of the "little people", hostility to "the elite", and the high value placed on mass action as a form of political engagement' has continued to exist, in various form and degrees, during and after the New Order. This means that community media are not purely a post-New Order phenomenon, but build on and diverge from the ideas and activities of earlier socially engaged movements and genres. However, for the majority of the post-1965 art and media initiatives analysed in this chapter it is irrelevant to talk in terms of 'left' or 'right', as they do not express explicit politico-ideological thought.

Movements such as LEKRA and GSRB showed their social commitment predominantly by representing socio-political issues and talking on behalf of specific groups. Forms of workers' theatre, Moelyono's conscientisation art and contemporary community media, on the other hand, not only provide socio-political content, but also allow social groups to directly participate in creative production, management and ownership. In these cases, there is a correlation between media content and approach or style.

This means that the analysis of social engagement in media and art needs to differentiate between social commitment and social participation. The difficulty of genres of social participation lies in the mediation of the different and often conflicting interests of art and media facilitators on the one hand, and local communities and other social groups on the other. Some of the problems include the limited accessibility to, and social participation in, media initiatives, the lack of education about community media, and the limited distribution, political reach and sustainability of works, ideas and activities.

One of the overarching problems of the community media initiatives has been their fragmentation. According to Aspinall (2012), fragmentation is symptomatic of the Indonesian radical movement at large and caused by the activists' over-reliance on NGOs. He acknowledges, however, that activists in post-New Order Indonesia have played an important role in putting pressing social issues on the political agenda such as health care and social security schemes (Aspinall 2012). Similarly, community media initiatives have not only brought to the surface some of the major flaws in the mainstream media system, especially the lack of diversity in ownership and content, but also tried to provide ecological solutions in the form of alternative media programmes and structures.

The Jagongan Media Rakyat is a promising initiative to bring NGOs, local communities, government parties, artists and others together, create a more focused socio-political agenda, and strengthen the viability and expand the reach of community media. The video archives of Kampung Halaman and Engage-Media serve similar purposes, and try to build connectivity between various community media initiatives by exploring and developing on-line technologies. While these initiatives may not be capable of, or aim at creating, a mass movement according to the principles of the old Left, they have partly succeeded in recommending, and providing alternatives for, a more equitable, diverse and sustainable Indonesian information and communication landscape.

Notes

1 In September 2001, UNESCO organised an influential seminar on community radio in Jakarta and Yogyakarta and distributed a handbook on community radio (Fraser and Estrada 2001) in Indonesian and English to radio practitioners nationwide.

2 An important statement explaining the Indonesian notion of universal humanism, without using the actual term, is the Surat Kepercayaan Gelanggang (Letter of Gelanggang Beliefs) of October 1950. This statement, issued by the nationalist, non-Communist art collective Gelanggang ('Arena'), expressed the belief that the development of a modern national culture and literature in Indonesia would not be fundamentally different from that in Europe or other parts of the world (Foulcher 1986: 2–3).

3 Michael Bodden (2012: 455) has nuanced Foulcher's observation by pointing out that in various theatre and dance genres of the time 'potentially radical aesthetic ideas [...] were being formulated and developed through practice on a variety of local "stages"'. These included mobile theatre and dance groups and so-called sendratari dance drama spectacles that were meant to be more accessible to the ordinary people than classical performing art genres. Nevertheless, even in these cases, direct and relatively spontaneous audience participation in performances was limited, and often only allowed after a rigorous review process guided by the PKI cadres (Bodden 2012: 468–469).

4 A large main house with smaller nearby structures (Holt 1967: 218; Wright 1994: 21; Harsono 2009b: 129–131, 2009e: 101).

5 The concept of turba was influenced by Maoist thought, particularly the idea of *xia fang* ('to go out into the countryside'), and marked LEKRA's growing orientation towards Chinese communism since the late 1950s (Shackford-Bradley 2000). This new orientation also influenced the introduction of the slogan Politik adalah Panglima, or 'Politics is the Commander', which not only urged artists to retain their socio-political commitment, but also implied that LEKRA would become increasingly involved in state politics as a means to further develop Indonesian art and culture. Only from 1964 to 1965, did a stronger, direct impact of PKI on LEKRA became manifest (Foulcher 1986: 107–108, 110).

6 This idea of conscientisation has been developed in Paolo Freire's *Pedagogy of the oppressed* (1970). This book also inspired Augusto Boal's version of community theatre, called the 'Theater of the Oppressed' (1979).

7 *Kagunan* here means 'a skill, a technique, and a practice that can be controlled and practiced by all people' (Moelyono 1997a: 128–129). In Old Javanese, *guna*, the base word of *kagunan*, has the connotations of 'goodness, good characteristics, character, virtue, ability, skill, expertise, capability, holiness, use, benefit, service, charity, power' (Moelyono 1997a: 124). For Moelyono (1997a: 129), these characteristics confirm that art is not restricted to the practices and judgments of an educated and/or wealthy elite, but forms 'an inalienable aspect of everyday life' and implies deeply rooted (Javanese) communitarian values.

8 Kesenian Unit Desa is a play on Koperasi Unit Desa, or Village Unit Cooperation, a New Order government economic initiative to improve the living standard of farmers (Moelyono 1997a: 93). One of the purposes of Moelyono's Village Unit Art was to provide a platform for protecting and reviving local art traditions, such as traditional horse dance (*jaranan* or *kuda lumping*) and glass painting (*lukisan kaca*) in East Java (Moelyono 1997a: 92–106).

9 Moelyono (1997a: 95–96) decided to work predominantly with children, not only for pedagogical reasons, but also out of pragmatic and safety considerations. While living in the Nggerangan and Brumbun villages, he was constantly interrogated by the local bureaucracy and security forces about his background and motives for working with isolated and poor communities. One of the constant, intimidating questions was about his familiarity with the Indonesian political events of 1965. This was a warning that

Moelyono should avoid any suggestions he was trying to revive communist ideology and the ideas and practices of LEKRA.

10 *Angkringan* is Javanese for a small outdoor food stall where people come together to eat and chat. Typically, it consists of a bamboo carrying pole with baskets or chests on either end for storing and presenting food.

11 The idea of the festival was developed by Akhmad Nasir, then Head of CRI and a Social and Political Sciences graduate from Yogyakarta's Universitas Gadjah Mada (Gadjah Mada University, UGM). Nasir originates from Timbulharjo and was the main force behind the various Angkringan community media initiatives.

12 It consists of the collections of the founders of Sekolah mBrosot, the public intellectuals and human rights activists Hersri Setiawan and Ita F. Nadia, and also includes donations from the Indonesian publishing company Gramedia and one of the Monash University libraries in Melbourne. In the 1960s, Setiawan was Head of the Central Javanese branch of LEKRA. After years of imprisonment in Indonesia and exile in the Netherlands, he returned to Indonesia in 2004 to re-engage with cultural activities and young people in his home village. Although Sekolah mBrosot does not espouse any particular political ideology or art theory, the community-based character of its library and creative activities is not surprising considering Setiawan's background.

13 According to this study, experimental video tries to change the relationship between the medium and its audience through aesthetic and technological experimentation and the deconstruction of imagery, while grassroots video attempts to transform communities by involving them in the process of media production (Lowenthal 2009: 26). Grassroots video is synonymous with the, in Indonesia, more common concept of community video (*video komunitas*), while experimental video is normally referred to as video art (*seni video*) or (new) media art (*seni media [baru]*; Jurriëns 2009c).

References

Aditjondro, George. 2005. 'Membongkar Moel guru nggambar' [Uncovering Moel the drawing teacher]. In: Moelyono (ed.), *Pak Moel: guru nggambar* [Mr Moel: the drawing teacher]. Yogyakarta: InsistPress, pp. 81–104.

Aspinall, Edward. 2012. 'Still an age of activism: left-wing politics are fragmented, but left-wing ideas are surprisingly influential'. *Inside Indonesia* 107 (January–March). Available at: www.insideindonesia.org/still-an-age-of-activism (accessed 15 February 2012).

Atton, Chris. 2002. *Alternative media*. London: Sage.

Birowo, A. B. 2010. 'The use of community radio in managing natural disaster in Indonesia'. *Bulletin of the American Society for Information Science and Technology*, June–July, pp. 18–21.

Boal, Augusto. 1979. *Theater of the oppressed*. New York: Urizen Books.

Bodden, Michael. 2010. *Resistance on the national stage: modern theatre and politics in late New Order Indonesia*. Ohio University Research in International Studies, Southeast Asia Series 123. Athens, OH: Ohio University Press.

Bodden, Michael. 2012. 'Dynamics and tensions of LEKRA's modern national theatre, 1959–1965'. In: Jennifer Lindsay and Maya H. T. Liem (eds), *Heirs to world culture: being Indonesian 1950–1965*. Verhandelingen van het Koninklijk Instituut voor Taal-, Land- en Volkenkunde 274. Leiden: KITLV Press, pp. 453–484.

Brangwetan. 2011. 'Direktori aktivis kesenian Tulungagung' [Directory of Tulungagung arts activists]. Available at: http://brangwetan.wordpress.com/2007/10/04/direktori-aktivis-kesenian-tulungagung (accessed 8 November 2011).

Dowmunt, Tony, with Kate Coyer. 2007. 'Introduction'. In: Kate Coyer, Tony Dowmunt and Alan Fountain (eds), *The alternative media handbook*. London and New York: Routledge, pp. 1–12.

Erven, Eugene van. 1992. *The playful revolution*. Bloomington, IN: Indiana University Press.

Fakih. 1997. 'Aksi kultural untuk transformasi sosial' [Cultural action for social transformation]. In: Moelyono, *Seni rupa penyadaran* [Conscientisation art]. Yogyakarta: Yayasan Bentang Budaya, pp. ix–xxxvi.

Foulcher, Keith. 1986. *Social commitment in literature and the arts: the Indonesian 'Institute of People's Culture' 1950–1965*. Clayton: Centre of Southeast Asian Studies, Monash University.

Fraser, Colin and Sonia Restrepo Estrada. 2001. *Buku panduan radio komunitas* [Guidebook of community radio]. Jakarta: UNESCO Jakarta Office.

Freire, Paolo. 1970. *Pedagogy of the oppressed*. New York: Herder and Herder.

Garcia, David. 2007. 'Tactical media'. In: Kate Coyer, Tony Dowmunt and Alan Fountain (eds), *The alternative media handbook*. London and New York: Routledge, pp. 6–7.

Hardi. 1979. 'Catatan-catatan I' [Notes I]. In: Jim Supangkat (ed.), *Gerakan Seni Rupa Baru Indonesia: kumpulan karangan* [Indonesian New Art Movement: collection of writings]. Jakarta: Gramedia, pp. 14–19.

Harsono, F. X. 2009a. 'Gerakan-gerakan baru dalam seni rupa Indonesia sejak 1974 hingga kini' [New movements in the Indonesian fine arts from 1974 until now]. In: F. X. Harsono, *Seni rupa, perubahan, politik* [The fine arts, change, politics]. Magelang: Langgeng Gallery, pp. 45–56.

Harsono, F. X. 2009b. 'Meraba peta komunitas seni rupa Indonesia'. In: F. X. Harsono, *Seni rupa, perubahan, politik* [The fine arts, change, politics]. Magelang: Langgeng Gallery, pp. 129–137.

Harsono, F. X. 2009c. 'Perkembangan seni rupa kontemporer di Indonesia: tinjauan problematik' [The development of contemporary art in Indonesia: a survey of its set of problems]. In: F. X. Harsono, *Seni rupa, perubahan, politik* [The fine arts, change, politics]. Magelang: Langgeng Gallery, pp. 63–81.

Harsono, F. X. 2009d. 'Seni rupa dukuh Brumbun Nggerangan' [The arts of the Brumbun Nggerangan hamlet]. In: F. X. Harsono, *Seni rupa, perubahan, politik* [The fine arts, change, politics]. Magelang: Langgeng Gallery, pp. 57–62.

Harsono, F. X. 2009e. 'Tema kerakyatan dalam seni lukis Indonesia: perbandingan masa Persagi dan Orde Baru' [The theme of the people in Indonesian painting: a comparison between the Persagi period and the New Order]. In: F. X. Harsono, *Seni rupa, perubahan, politik* [The fine arts, change, politics]. Magelang: Langgeng Gallery, pp. 96–114.

Hatley, Barbara. 2008. *Javanese performances on an Indonesian stage: contesting culture, embracing change*. Singapore: Asian Studies Association of Australia with NUS Press.

Holt, Claire. 1967. *Art in Indonesia: continuities and change*. Ithaca, NY: Cornell University Press.

Howley, Kevin. 2010a. 'Introduction'. In: Kevin Howley (ed.), *Understanding community media*. Los Angeles: Sage.

Howley, Kevin. 2010b. 'Part 1: theoretical issues and perspectives'. In: Kevin Howley (ed.), *Understanding community media*. Los Angeles: Sage.

Howley, Kevin. 2010c. 'Part 2: civil society and the public sphere'. In: Kevin Howley (ed.), *Understanding community media*. Los Angeles: Sage.

Iskandar, Gustaff Harriman. 2006. 'Rekomendasi kebijakan pengembangan praktik seni media di Indonesia' [Policy recommendations for the development of media art in Indonesia]. In: Direktorat Kesenian, *Apresiasi seni media baru* [Appreciation of new media art]. Jakarta: Direktorat Kesenian, Direktorat Jendral Nilai Budaya, Seni dan Film and Departemen Kebudayaan dan Pariwisata, pp. 103–130.

Jagongan Media Rakyat. 2010a. 'Daftar peserta: pengisi acara' [List of participants: event contributors]. Available at: http://jagongan2010.combine.or.id/peserta/ (accessed 28 July 2010).

Jagongan Media Rakyat. 2010b. 'Program kegiatan' [Program of events]. Available at: http://jagongan2010.combine.or.id/peserta/ (accessed 28 July 2010).

Jagongan Media Rakyat. 2010c. 'Seminar nasional' [National seminar]. Available at: http://jmr2010.combine.or.id/seminar-nasional/ (accessed 14 August 2016).

Jurriëns, Edwin. 2009a. *From monologue to dialogue: radio and reform in Indonesia.* Leiden: KITLV Press.

Jurriëns, Edwin. 2009b. 'Frying the wires, freeing the waves: grassroots organizations in Indonesia are building communication media from the most basic of utensils'. *Inside Indonesia* 95 (January–March). Available at: www.insideindonesia.org/frying-the-wires-freeing-the-waves (accessed 14 August 2016).

Jurriëns, Edwin. 2009c. 'Hidupkan TV Anda! Sebuah perbandingan televisi komunitas di Australia Belanda Indonesia' [Turn on your TV! A comparison of community television in Australia, the Netherlands and Indonesia'. In: Muzayin Nazaruddin and Budhi Hermanto (eds), *Televisi komunitas: pemberdayaan dan media literasi* [Community television: empowerment and media literacy]. Jakarta: Ford Foundation, Combine Resource Institution, Program Studi Ilmu Komunikasi FPSB UII and Fakultas Film dan Televisi IKJ, pp. 90–99.

Jurriëns, Edwin. 2013. 'Social participation in Indonesian media and art: echoes from the past, visions for the future'. *Bijdragen tot de Taal-, Land- en Volkenkunde* 169(1): 7–36.

Kampung Halaman. 2010a. 'Dengar!: "sepintu pemali, sedulang timah" in Bangka' [Listen!: "at the door of Pemali, there is a pan of tin"]. Available at: www.kampunghalaman.org/index.php?option=com_content&view=article&id=103%3Adengar-sepintu-pemali-sedulang-timah-di-bangka&catid=38%3Adengar&Itemid=64&lang=en (accessed 9 August 2010).

Kampung Halaman. 2010b. 'Indonesian Youth Media Camp and Festival 2008'. Available at: www.kampunghalaman.org/index.php?option=com_content&view=article&id=56%3Aindonesian-youth-media-camp-a-festival-2008&catid=37%3Aberita&Itemid=61&lang=en (accessed 9 August 2010).

Kampung Halaman. 2010c. 'Kampung Halaman profile'. Available at: www.kampunghalaman.org/index.php?option=com_content&view=article&id=79%3Aprofil-kampung-halaman&catid=43%3Atentang-kampung-halaman&Itemid=62&lang=en (accessed 9 August 2010).

Kampung Halaman. 2010d. 'Opak house'. Available at: www.kampunghalaman.org/index.php?option=com_content&view=article&id=98%3Aomah-opak-&catid=37%3Aberita&Itemid=61&lang=en (accessed 9 August 2010).

Kampung Halaman. 2010e. 'Youth and disasters'. Available at: www.kampunghalaman.org/index.php?option=com_content&view=article&id=120%3Aremaja-peduli-bencana-&catid=37%3Aberita&Itemid=61&lang=en (accessed 9 August 2010).

Lowenthal, Andrew (ed.). 2009. *Videochronic: video activism and video distribution in Indonesia.* Research report by KUNCI Cultural Studies Center and EngageMedia. Collingwood: EngageMedia.

Miklouho-Maklai, Brita L. 1991. *Exposing society's wounds: some aspects of contemporary Indonesian art since 1966*. Adelaide: Flinders University.

Moelyono. 1997a. *Seni rupa penyadaran* [Conscientisation art]. Yogyakarta: Yayasan Bentang Budaya.

Moelyono. 1997b. 'Seni rupa kagunan: a process'. In: Jim Schiller and Barbara Martin-Schiller (eds), *Imagining Indonesia: cultural politics and political culture*. Monographs in International Studies, Southeast Asia Series 97. Athens, Ohio: Ohio University Press, pp. 121–136.

Moelyono. 2005. *Pak Moel: guru nggambar*. Yogyakarta: InsistPress.

Nazaruddin, Muzayin and Budhi Hermanto (eds). 2009. *Televisi komunitas: pemberdayaan dan media literasi* (Community television: empowerment and media literacy]. Jakarta: Ford Foundation, Combine Resource Institution and Program Studi Ilmu Komunikasi FPSB UII, Fakultas Film dan Televisi IKJ.

Shackford-Bradley, Julie. 2000. 'Mao's ghost in Golkar: 1960s artists struggled to create solidarity with the oppressed; one of their slogans survived in Golkar, but not their spirit'. *Inside Indonesia* 61 (January–March). Available at: www.insideindonesia.org/maos-ghost-in-golkar (accessed 14 August 2016).

Spanjaard, Helena Geertruida. 1998. *Het ideal van een modern Indonesische schilderkunst 1900–1995: de creatie van een nationale culturele identiteit* [The ideal of the art of modern Indonesian painting 1900–1995: the creation of a national cultural identity]. PhD dissertation, Rijksuniversiteit Leiden.

Sulistyowati, Fadjarini, Theodorus Wuryantono and Dian Astuti. 2005. 'Ruang publik desa: ruang partisipasi yang "kosong" ' [Village public space: an 'empty' participation space]. In: Fadjarini Sulistyowati, Yuli Setyowati and Theodorus Wuryantono (eds), *Komunikasi pemberdayaan* [Empowerment communication]. Yogyakarta: Program Studi Ilmu Komunikasi STPMD 'APMD' and APMD Press, pp. 163–203.

Supangkat, Jim. 1979. 'Seni Rupa Baru Indonesia 75' [Indonesian New Art Movement 75]. In: Jim Supangkat (ed.), *Gerakan Seni Rupa Baru Indonesia: kumpulan karangan* [The Indonesian New Art Movement: a collection of writings]. Jakarta: Gramedia, pp. 99–103.

Uttu. 2006. 'Distro: independent fashion moves from margins to mainstream'. *Inside Indonesia* 85 (January–March). Available at: www.insideindonesia.org/distro (accessed 14 August 2016).

Williams, Raymond.1980. *Problems in materialism and culture: selected essays*. London: Verso.

Wright, Astri. 1994. *Soul, spirit, and mountain: preoccupations of contemporary Indonesian painters*. Kuala Lumpur: Oxford University Press.

Youth Program Awards. 2011. 'Indonesia youth community media project'. Available at: www.nahyp.org/awardees/2011-awardees/international-spotlight-award-indonesia-youth-community-media-project (accessed 9 November 2011).

8 Video communities

One contemporary manifestation of the decapitalisation, deprofessionalisation and deinstitutionalisation aspects of community art and media in Indonesia is young adults establishing their own creative spaces and communities. These spaces and communities demonstrate that projects 'from, by and for the people' cannot reach their full emancipatory potential through collaborative art and media works only, but should also facilitate audience participation in the broader context of art or media ownership and management (Jurriëns 2015). This chapter discusses Indonesian new media art groups that have created relatively inclusive and interdisciplinary art works, communities, festivals and networks as alternatives to the more exclusive and monodisciplinary ideas and practices of established commercial or state-run galleries and academies.

Apart from Krisna Murti, various other artists such as Heri Dono (b. 1960), Arahmaiani (b. 1961) and Teguh Ostenrik (b. 1950) contributed to the early development of new media art in Indonesia in the late 1980s and early 1990s. These pioneering artists, all with a formal education in the arts, used television sets, film screens and video recordings among various other media such as painting, sculpture and found objects for creating art installations. Gotot Prakosa (1955–2015), who created animations consisting of drawings on celluloid and photographed drawings in the mid-1970s, could count as an even earlier pioneer of new media art. However, Prakosa is commonly and rather arbitrarily described as an experimental short film maker rather than a new media artist.

In the late 1990s and early 2000s, a younger generation of Indonesian new media artists emerged who have creatively engaged with video as well as various other, sometimes unconventional, media, such as digital technology, robotics and microbiology. Unlike the video art pioneers, the second generation does not always integrate video technology into art installations, but rather presents so-called 'single channel' videos on television or cinema screens as art objects in themselves (Hujatnikajennong 2006b: 25). Another difference is that many members of the younger generation, instead of undergoing formal education in the arts, take a multi-disciplinary approach, with ideas derived from such diverse disciplines as art history, media studies, anthropology, sociology, science and engineering (Hujatnikajennong 2006b: 26; Murti 2006: 60–61).

According to publisher and art critic Ronny Agustinus (2003: 115), the new generation of video artists grew up in a time of repression by the New Order regime and searched for alternatives in computer technology, alternative music videos on early MTV, and experimental films such as those directed by Quentin Tarantino. At the same time, they were also influenced by mainstream Hollywood films, western pop music and commercial television series. In some cases, they have been criticised by senior artists and critics for a lack of social engagement and insufficient critical reflection on, and distance from, the popular media genres by which they are influenced.

This chapter and Chapter 9 discuss and seek to balance some of the local and international interpretations and critiques of new media art, by examining to what extent Indonesian new media art communities can be considered avant-garde. The two chapters are intended to contribute to extending the analysis of innovative art ideas and practices beyond the West, and to other, to a certain extent newly authoritative, creative hubs in the world, including Indonesia. Rather than identifying a new canon of Indonesian artists, I seek to highlight important, but long overlooked, aesthetic and socio-political aspects of Indonesian new media art. While academics have rightfully drawn attention to the contribution of popular culture in post-New Order democratic reform (e.g. Heryanto 2008), it is important not to lose sight of other creative expressions, such as new media art. Though less impressive in terms of scale and audience size than popular culture, new media art has provided innovative models for socio-political change (Jurriëns 2013).

The theoretical focus is on Hutjanikajennong's (2005 and 2006a) idea of the 'post-avant-garde' (*pasca avant-garde*), based on Peter Bürger's (1984) standard work on the historical avant-garde.[1] To counter some of the criticism of contemporary new media art, and to argue that certain manifestations of this art form can be considered avant-garde in their own right, I focus on various Indonesian new media art communities, particularly HONF, as historically and socially specific interpretations of four key avant-garde principles: to break with the autonomy of art; to engage with the praxis of life; to provide utopian visions; and to present aesthetic innovation.[2]

In this chapter, I analyse how new media art communities collaborate with international and local universities, schools, NGOs and social groups in their efforts to re-engage with the praxis of life and break with the modernist ideal of the autonomy of art as promoted in Indonesia's major art academies. I argue that these communities build on the creative experiments conducted by the GSRB in the 1970s and 1980s, which explicitly referred to some of the techniques and strategies of the historical and neo-avant-garde. Chapter 9 demonstrates that initiatives such as HonFab Lab also expand and go beyond the GSRB projects, in their role as laboratories for exploring and providing micro-utopian alternatives to the realities of today's information and communication society. It also shows that the contemporary art communities have brought aesthetic innovation by exploring the field of presentation rather than representation.

Avant-garde or post-avant-garde?

To what extent is Indonesian new media art the product of contemporary consumer culture, and to what extent is it able to take critical distance from and provide creative alternatives to such culture? This key issue has been addressed by Indonesian artists, curators and critics such as Murti (2006: 60–61), Asikin Hasan (2003: 156) and Ronny Agustinus (2005: 17). Hasan (2003: 156) wondered why 'we never hear, for instance, that they proclaim this manifesto or that manifesto as the older generation did. It is as if they are not fighting anyone and anything, but instead, are occupied with their own celebrations'. With the 'older generation' he seemed to refer to the GSRB artists, and perhaps also the international avant-garde.

The most comprehensive discussion of the issue can be found in two thought-provoking essays by Hujatnikajennong (2005, 2006a).[3] The essays compare the Indonesian new media art of the 1990s and 2000s with the international avant-garde art of the 1910s and 1920s (the so-called historical avant-garde) and the 1950s and 1960s (the neo-avant-garde).

Hujatnikajennong's analysis of the early twentieth century avant-garde is primarily based on Bürger's *Theory of the avant-garde* (1984). It follows Bürger's argument that the historical avant-garde developed in reaction against the modernist principle of the autonomy of art. While traditional forms of creativity formed an integral part of social life and fulfilled practical purposes, modernist art was created in isolation of society and functioned to develop the aesthetic and philosophical potential of art itself ('art for art's sake'). Ironically, the modernist ideal of artistic autonomy did not lead to the liberation of creative work, but to the institutionalisation of its production, distribution and consumption in the workshops, museums, art galleries and auction houses that were managed by the wealthy and educated bourgeois elite. Avant-garde movements such as Dada developed in reaction to these trends, and attempted to de-institutionalise art and re-integrate it with 'the praxis of life' (Bürger 1984: 22; Hujatnikajennong 2005: 34, 2006a: 178–179).

Hal Foster (1994: 11) has criticised Bürger (particularly Bürger 1984: 57–63) for treating the historical avant-garde 'as an *absolute origin* [emphasis in original] whose aesthetic transformations are fully significant and historically effective in the first instance' and the postwar avant-garde 'as merely *neo* [emphasis in original], as so much repetition in bad faith that cancels the prewar critique of the institution of art'. According to Foster (1994: 16), the neo-avant-garde has extended or 'comprehended' rather than inverted or cancelled the project of the historical avant-garde. He argues that the neo-avant-garde developed the historical avant-garde critique of the conventions of traditional art media to a more specific and deconstructive – rather than abstract or anarchistic – analysis of the institution of art.

Unlike Bürger, Hujatnikajennong (2006a: 180–182) acknowledges the avant-garde character of movements such as Fluxus (active from the 1950s to the early 1970s), which attempted to resist the autonomy of art and reconnect it with daily life by organising art events in public spaces, amongst others. At the same time, he points out the irony that both the early and the late avant-garde eventually underwent commercialisation and were incorporated into the bourgeois institutions of the museum and the gallery.

According to Hujatnikajennong (2006a: 180–182), in the current era of advanced capitalism, artistic resistance and renewal seem even more futile. Art would no longer be a vanguard attack and subversion of hegemonic power and knowledge structures. Video art, for instance, would have become part of the spectacle culture of television and international art exhibitions supported by global capitalism, and no longer exercise the same type of subversion that was conducted by the Fluxus movement in general and the Korean video art pioneer Nam June Paik in particular (Hujatnikajennong 2005: 41–46).

Nevertheless, Hujatnikajennong (2005: 48–49, 2006a: 182–183) believes that another form of resistance, 'sub-version' or 'sub/version' is still an option. Artists who create sub-version are not the avant-garde, but the 'troupes of the second layer or echelon' (*pasukan lapisan/eselon kedua*), which come to the 'battlefield' (*medan perang*) 'to clear the remnants of the battle' (*membersihkan sisa-sisa pertempuran*). This means that their art is not offering something entirely new, but develops from existing power structures and forms of creative production. According to Hujatnikajennong (2006a: 183), sub-version does not necessarily imply 'sub-ordination' (*sub-ordinasi*), but functions as a strategy to avoid the mistakes and failure (*kekalahan*) of the earlier avant-gardes. Rather than oppose the system of advanced capitalism and technological globalisation, the 'second echelon' would deliberately try to change and undermine it from within. An example was ruangrupa's 2005 Ok.Video festival, co-curated by Hujatnikajennong and aptly titled 'Sub-version', in which artists offered 'hacker' strategies of 'citing, recording, and re-engineering' hegemonic socio-cultural practices and popular culture genres such as advertisements, television news, reality shows and internet sites (Hujatnikajennong 2005: 46).

Hujatnikajennong's observations are symptomatic of a new generation of artists and art curators who are open to technological and artistic experimentation and have a clear and relatively modest idea about their own position in the world. Steve Dixon (2007: 64) explains that new media artists in general appear to be less visible and vocal in public life as, unlike the earlier avant-garde movements, their main territory is not the material world, but virtual space. I believe another reason why it has become harder for their artistic and social messages to be heard or even recognised is that life in general has become much busier with mediated sounds and images. Perhaps due to this 'ecstasy of communication' (Baudrillard 1983) and the lack of explicitly political manifestos, it has gone unnoticed that the current generation of Indonesian new media artists may not only include post-avant-garde (*pasca avant-garde*) artists producing postmodern works, as Hujatnikajennong (2005: 34) argues, but also avant-garde groups creating 'post-postmodern' art.

Foster (1994: 26), in his critique of Bürger (1984), believes that 'the avant-garde continues' in contemporary art practices through 'subtle displacements' and 'strategic collaborations with different groups'. In a more polemic way, Bourriaud (2002: 45) argues that

> whatever these fundamentalists clinging to yesterday's *good taste* may say and think, present-day art is roundly taking on and taking up the legacy of the 20th century avant-gardes, while at the same time challenging their dogmatism and their teleological doctrines.

To this I would add that avant-garde concerns have not only continued over time but also dispersed over space. They are certainly no longer restricted to 'a loose grouping of North American and Western European artists' (Foster 1994: 5), if they ever were,[4] but have also been re-addressed, in very specific and often highly creative ways elsewhere in the world, including Southeast Asia. While GSRB was inspired by both the historical and neo-avant-gardes, and contributed to the questioning of art media and institutions in the specific context of Indonesia in the mid-1970s, members of the current generation of Indonesian new media artists can be seen as a *central* part of the avant-garde of the digital age.

Indonesian new media art breaks with the modernist ideal of the autonomy of art as promoted by Indonesia's formal institutions of art education and exhibition in various ways. For instance, by establishing multidisciplinary communities as an alternative way of organisation; creating collaborative art works as an alternative mode of production; organising joint exhibitions and festivals as an alternative form of display; and utilising public spaces as an alternative venue for exhibitions, meetings and discussions. The Indonesian new media art practitioners show a concern with the praxis of life through collaborative projects with local communities, and demonstrate an orientation towards the future through their experimentation with new technologies and simulations of, or scenarios for, a better society. They also provide artistic newness through the aesthetic exploration of post-postmodern modes of presentation such as pastiche, interactivity and virtual reality. This chapter focuses on the first two avant-garde characteristics, while Chapter 9 focuses on the last two.

Breaking with the autonomy of art: alternative art spaces

The first two avant-garde principles are illustrated by the emergence of new media art spaces and communities in Indonesia since the late 1990s. These phenomena illustrate the wish of young Indonesians with very diverse and not necessarily artistic backgrounds to communicate and engage in creative projects with each other in a way that is not facilitated by the established venues of art exhibition and education. Such venues include the government-run National Gallery in Jakarta, the various commercial art galleries in the main cities of Java and Bali, and the three best-known Indonesian academies for formal tertiary art education; ISI Yogyakarta, ITB and Institut Kesenian Jakarta (Jakarta Institute of the Arts, IKJ). At the same time, the trends in Indonesian contemporary art are a reflection of an international youth culture of networking, interactivity, conviviality, recycling and DIY, which dramatically accelerated with the introduction of the Internet and advances in computer and mobile technologies in the early 1990s.

One of the most compelling reasons for young Indonesian video artists to join together and establish new media art communities has been dissatisfaction with the government and business-supported Indonesian modern art establishment. This establishment heavily relied on the modernist ideas of the artist as a single and unique source of creativity, and the museum or art gallery as the standard venue for the display of works. Some video artists, especially the older generation, still follow these conventions, as they prefer to work individually and produce art that invites a relatively select audience to contemplate, rather than directly interact with, the artist and the work of art. Many young artists see the new medium of video as an opportunity to establish art communities as a different way of organisation, collaborative art works as a different mode of production, joint exhibitions and festivals as a different form of presentation, and public art spaces as a different venue for exhibitions, meetings and discussions.

This focus on community, collaboration, joint activities and publicness is not only a reaction against the modern art establishment, but also serves as a strategy to undermine some of the dominant principles of contemporary capitalist society such as individualism and the commoditisation of culture and space. The rise of new media art can be partly seen as a reaction against the increased commercialisation of Indonesian painting, which in the wake of the boom of Chinese contemporary art has become highly profitable (Hutjanikajennong 2009: 145). For instance, works of the Balinese painter I Nyoman Masriadi (b. 1973) have sold at auction houses for record prices of several hundred thousand US dollars each, putting him ahead of most of his Asian contemporaries.

New media art, particularly video art, is not insensitive to the market and is increasingly drawing the attention of private collectors. In general, however, site-specific video installations with multiple and sometimes anonymous creators, who often derive elements from existing works of art or popular culture, are less likely to end up in a system of commercial commodity exchange. This type of counter-strategy has inspired and is supported by many Indonesian video artists and was one of the central themes of the 2005 OK.Video 'Sub/version' festival. In addition to the spirit of creative collaboration and networking, another aspect of this strategy has been Indonesian video artists' embrace of piracy and Common Source hardware and software for their artistic production (Agustinus 2005).

Bourriaud (2002) uses the idea of 'relational aesthetics' as a way to understand some of the key developments in contemporary art, which also underlie the communities and activities of Indonesian new media art. While every form of art is relational with regard to the social setting of its reception, in relational aesthetics inter-subjectivity and interactivity form the very basis of creative concepts and production practices (Bourriaud 2002: 22). This type of aesthetics is not merely mimicking the dynamics of contemporary information and community society, but is meant to facilitate 'relational space-time elements', 'inter-human experiences trying to rid themselves of the straitjacket of the ideology of mass communications' and 'places where alternative forms of sociability, critical models and moments of constructed conviviality are worked out' (Bourriaud 2002: 44). The focus is on 'the dynamic relationship enjoyed by an artistic proposition with other formations, artistic or otherwise' rather than on a form or object 'closed in on itself by the intervention of a style and a signature' as in modernist art (Bourriaud 2002: 21). In Indonesian new media art, this relational aesthetics is reflected in a strong interest in creative processes through, or in the form of, the organisation of communities, festivals, performances, discussions and laboratory-like experiments rather than a concern with the creation of tangible art works as such.

Some of the dominant trends in global information and communication society, particularly the cultures of networking, interactivity, conviviality, recycling and DIY (Bourriaud 2002: 14, 26), are prevalent not only in new media art, but also in the contemporary music and design scenes of cities such as Bandung and Yogyakarta (Luvaas 2008, 2009). In general, there is a strong circulation of actors, ideas and practices among the various scenes. Gustaff Hariman Iskandar (b. 1974), co-founder of Common Room, argues that new media art in Bandung, including video art, SMS art and internet art, was influenced by earlier alternative communication experiments such as amateur radio and amateur internet. Examples are Amatir Radio Club (Amateur Radio Club, ARC), based at ITB since 1986, and PaguyubanNet (1992–1994), an internet network based on the infrastructure of amateur radio (Iskandar 2006: 109).

Another important incentive for the exploration of alternative art and media in Bandung was the 1994 ban on the current affairs magazines *Tempo*, *Editor* and *DeTik*. In reaction to the bans, stencilled, photocopied and on-line magazines appeared, such as *Submissive*, *Tigabelas* ('Thirteen') and *Brainwash* (Iskandar 2006: 114). From 2000 to 2002, Iskandar himself produced *Trolley*, a youth magazine about the latest trends in music, arts, design and fashion. *Trolley* is characteristic of the alternative art scene in Bandung, where strong links exist between different types of art and art communities. In popular and widespread alternative shops or *distro*,[5] young people sell their own retail clothing, zines, cassettes, Compact Discs (CDs), VCDs and DVDs.

One of the first independent contemporary art spaces in Indonesia was Cemeti Art House, established by Mella Jaarsma and Nindityo Adipurnomo in Yogyakarta in 1988 (Clark 2005). Cemeti Art House has built a solid reputation and is a highly successful model for the organisation of alternative art events in Indonesia (Harsono 2003: 21–22; Wardani 2003: 26–27). Former GSRB member Harsono (2003: 23–24) argues that art houses like Cemeti, unlike other Indonesian modern art establishments such as the National Gallery in Jakarta, were not created for government or business purposes. The alternative art houses have promoted a greater diversity of artistic media and events, including performance art, video art, digital art and music concerts, and have offered more opportunities for artists and other members of society to meet, engage in dialogue, and build a sense of community (Harsono 2003: 23). According to Harsono (2003: 25), the contemporary Indonesian art communities, spaces and events could be signs of a return to democracy and creative freedom after the fall of Suharto, and/or the result of developments in the international art world. He is not convinced, however, that the recent artistic initiatives are able to present strong local alternatives to globalisation, as they would lack clear ideological and aesthetic direction.

According to cultural critic and co-founder of independent Kunci Cultural Studies Center, Nuraini Juliastuti (2007a: 107), the explosion of alternative art spaces in Indonesia also tends to cause the concept of the 'alternative' to lose some of its vigour:

> [Talking about alternative art spaces] has become boring, because everyone seems to know already about the complex issues of these alternative spaces, the problems they are facing, and the possible solutions, as if there is nothing left to be discussed.

At the same time, she rightly acknowledges some of the accomplishments of the alternative art scene. These include the reinvigoration of cultural movements, social empowerment activities, and other contributions to the democratisation of Indonesian society, which were unlikely to be achieved by the official art and media institutions (Juliastuti 2007a: 115–117).

New media art communities and festivals

Some of the new media art communities that have emerged in the post-New Order period are, with varying degrees of activity and continuity: ruangrupa (Jakarta), Forum Lenteng (Jakarta), Common Room (Bandung), Tromarama (Bandung), Video Lab (Bandung), Ruang Mes 56 (Yogyakarta), HONF (Yogyakarta), Jatiwangi Art Factory (Jatiwangi), WAFT (Surabaya) and Klinik Seni Taxu (Denpasar).[6] These groups can be considered 'communities', as they consist of artists working collaboratively and sharing similar artistic and social interests. The various communities derive a sense of identity predominantly from the way in which they situate themselves in relation to the institutional forms, discourses and activities shaping other socio-cultural environments, including the worlds of contemporary art, popular culture, rural and urban development, education and health care. Each in their own way, the art communities adopt and react to aspects of one or more of these pillars of Indonesian and global contemporary life.

The constituents of many Indonesian new media art communities adhere to a dynamic concept of community, which is not based on preconfigured notions of structure and longevity, but on the principles of freedom, responsibility, social awareness and collaboration. This is illustrated by the following statement of the members of HONF (2010):

> The concept of this community is not to become a permanent group with a static membership and a leader, but rather to focus on an awareness of integrity in doing anything which is meaningful to them and their surroundings. The only commitment is to work together.

In one of her articles, Juliastuti (2007a) explores the history of one of Yogyakarta's longest running new media art communities, Ruang Mes 56. Ruang Mes 56 derived its name from the first space where it was based, which was the dormitory and the mess of the Indonesian Air Force. In 1993, the dormitory began to accept university students and developed into a meeting place for photography students of ISI Yogyakarta. The space was also used by a rich variety of other people, including retired Air Force members, performers of popular *dangdut* music, karaoke club singers, gamblers and hawkers. In 2002, it became home to a more formally organised independent art community, which adopted the name Ruang Mes 56, and started a programme of exhibitions, workshops and artist residencies (Juliastuti 2007a: 108–112).

Ruang Mes 56 attempts to keep its activities running by giving each of its members the responsibility for a specific art programme. The members are also required to donate a percentage of their private income to the Ruang Mes 56 community (Juliastuti 2007a: 113–114). The community's current focus is on photography and video art. It has produced the highly successful 'Video Battle' series consisting of 11 compilations of Indonesian video art and short films. Copies of the compilations are limited, several hundred of each series, and are available at galleries and *distro*. Prices are around Rp.50,000 (approximately US$5), similar to those of regular Indonesian VCDs and DVDs. The main producers, Woto Wibowo (better known as Wok the Rock) and Wimo Ambala Bayang, prefer to be directly involved in the sales, so they can choose customers who truly appreciate Ruang Mes 56's work (Juliastuti 2007c: 138).

The duration of the short videos is typically between 30 seconds and 5 minutes. Some of the videos consist of visual and conceptual explorations of space, objects and/or bodies, while others are predominantly for telling personal stories, for instance, to express feelings of love, anger, friendship, loneliness and/or concern about politics and society, including issues related to war, religion and class. The makers usually perform aesthetic experiments by manipulating the camera angle, recording speed and editing tools of hand-held cameras. Many of the videos can be seen as alternative video clips, as the visual experimentation is often accompanied by existing or self-composed music. Some of the videos make use of materials from mainstream television and popular culture, including MTV video clips, Indonesian soap operas and Hollywood movies from the silent film era. Other videos are self-made animations using everyday objects, clay figures, drawings and/or texts.

One of the most active and consistent Indonesian new media art communities is ruangrupa (Clark 2005; Crosby 2008; Berghuis 2011). It has made important contributions to the practice of and discourse on video art in Indonesia through its large-scale international festivals, comprehensive festival publications, critical print and online art magazine *Karbon*, and intensive collaborations with other art communities and educational institutions. Initially, ruangrupa could not afford a physical space for its community, because of the high costs of accommodation in Jakarta. The community worked on the basis of three or four-month projects that were funded by the sale of art works (Darmawan 2006a: 122).

Ruangrupa also received funding for its art festivals, publications and other activities from international NGOs such as HIVOS. According to one of its founders, Ade Darmawan (2006b: 98), it has not been easy for his and other alternative art communities to maintain continuity in their activities, because of financial problems, changing membership and management issues.

In 2003, ruangrupa held the first in its series of 'OK.Video' biennial video art festivals, one of the most important forums for exploring the idea and practice of video art in Indonesia. The festival was organised in collaboration with the Montevideo Netherlands Media Art Institute (The Netherlands), International Media Art Award (Germany), Potluck Video Festival (Denmark) and The Danish Video Art Databank (Denmark). Following the example of the international Bandung Video, Film and New Media Art Forum (bavf-NAF) organised by Murti in Bandung in 2002, it consisted of exhibitions, workshops, special presentations, music video screenings, seminars and artist talks. It was held at the National Gallery in Jakarta, which underwent 'the biggest temporary makeover it has experienced in its lifetime' (Streak 2003: 29). The organisers installed 13 video projection screens, 17 flat screen monitors and 30 DVD players to show 92 works of video art by 56 artists from 19 different countries (Streak 2003: 30). The special presentations included PULSE (South Africa), Videoart Center Tokyo (Japan) and Videotage (Hong Kong; Hujatnikajennong 2003: 86). The workshops, moderated by the German artist Oliver Zwink (2003: 34), included discussions and collaborative works on the theme of urban space.

In an article in the 2003 OK.Video festival catalogue, Agustinus (2003: 23) criticised the fact that the festival was organised at Indonesia's most authoritative centre of conventional modern art practice, the National Gallery. He explained that the institutionalisation of art in spaces such as museums and galleries had been problematic throughout the history of modern art. He wondered why video art had to be 'exhibited' at all, and believed a more efficient strategy of display was the broadcasting of video art on television. By using television broadcasts to reach a mass audience, video art would be able to undermine the conventions of mass communication (Agustinus 2003: 123).

Agustinus's comments illustrate that video art is not just a medium through which youth can talk and express their thoughts. It also makes youth talk, by directing their thoughts to topics that are inspired by the techno-cultural features of the medium. Indeed, what is most interesting about Indonesian video art, apart for some of the art itself, is the discourse it incorporates and with which it is surrounded. One of the participants in the 2003 international 'OK Video' festival in Jakarta argued that:

> if there are no video works, there is no discourse to begin with, but the reverse is the same. If there is no dialogue on the works created, those works will never have an existence in the scene and remain on the artist's shelf.
>
> (Hattori 2003: 27–28)

This discourse or dialogue is growing with the increase in the number of works created, communities established and festivals and exhibitions organised. It is also relatively well-documented, with references and cross-references in essays, newspaper articles, exhibition catalogues and video community statements. It is certainly better documented than much of the video work as such, which often disappears into oblivion after limited public appearance, and is at best recorded and stored by the individual artists themselves.

Perhaps partially in response to Agustinus' critical remarks, the theme of the second OK.Video festival in 2005 was 'Sub/version'. Organiser Darmawan (2005: 12) explained that video art 'no longer pretends to be "strange", nor does it perform acrobatics to receive attention … It exists within a media system in order to play, question, steal, inspire, influence, even destroy …'. Hujatnikajennong (2005: 48) agreed with Darmawan that (Indonesian) video art did not have to invent new territory. Instead, it had to demonstrate knowledge of, and have a critical attitude to, existing social and artistic practices and discourses, in order to create 'subversion' and correct 'failures from the past'.

Since 2004, ruangrupa has also organised the bi-annual art festival 'Jakarta 32 derajat Celsius' (Jakarta 32 degrees Celsius). The festival, specifically designed for university students from the Jakarta region, is intended to artistically document and stimulate the interaction between youth and their urban environment (Achmad 2006: 4). Apart from photography and video art, it includes graphic design, fashion, painting, drawing, sculpture and architecture. In 2006, during the second running of the festival, more than 250 works of art were presented over a period of three months. The Presentasi Khusus (Special Presentations) section showed the works of five independent groups of students – Project_Or, Sakit Kuning ('Jaundice'), Artcoholic, Propagraphic, and Forum Lenteng – who were challenged to work collaboratively and thrive as a collective (Shandra and Darmawan 2006: 11).

The festival also included workshops on the theme of *Bermain di ruang tunggu publik* ('Playing in public waiting rooms'). For two weeks, three times a week, the participants in these workshops had discussions with each other and the workshop moderators about how to approach the central theme (Yunanto and Pringgotono 2006: 24). The participants came up with creations that normally would not be displayed in public spaces because of their playful, personal or decontextualised character. The art works were installed at bus stops in Jakarta and included a sand sack for boxing exercises, the recorded sounds of a flight terminal, a horoscope prediction machine, comics and a map of *ojek* (motorcycle for public transport) stops along one of Jakarta's main roads (Yunanto and Pringgotono 2006: 24). The organisers refused to ask permission from the local authorities for these installations, as they felt the public was not notified about the installation of the many commercial billboards in their city (Yunanto and Pringgotono 2006: 25).

Yogyakarta-based HONF is one of the other prolific new media art communities in Indonesia. The name of the collective refers to organic interconnectivities of art, technology, science and society. The community was founded in

1999 by Director Vincensius Christiawan ('Venzha'), who is a graduate in Interior Design from ISI Yogyakarta and a self-professed technology and UFO maniac; Cultural Research Director Irene Agrivina ('Ira'), who is a fashion designer and poet; Interactivity and Technical Director Tommy Surya ('Imot'), who is a video jockey; and Istasius ('Itaz'), a graphic designer and comic artist. In addition to the core group, there are approximately 10 to 15 other young members who regularly contribute to the HONF programme and projects (HONF 2010).

The HONF members see themselves as an avant-garde of 'forward thinking' individuals who contemplate the future of art and technology in a positive and creative way. They believe that the combination of art and technology, in the form of new media art, provides 'unlimited' opportunities, and that anything can be, or become, art, as long as it is in line with people's sense of reason and responsibility (HONF 2010; Christiawan 2009: 25).[7] According to Christiawan (2009: 26), the technological aspect of new media art will normally not lead to the 'dehumanisation' of art, as its main media are human agents who are able to decide on the direction and development of technology for achieving certain social and aesthetic goals.

HONF attempts to gain and transfer knowledge about art, technology, science and society through its so-called Education Focus Program (EFP). The programme adheres to the 'open community' method and uses new media art as a tool 'to introduce modern ideas about a technological future that is in accordance with the uses, needs and knowledge of people living in a developing country' (Cellsbutton 2010). One of its aims is to fill in the gaps in the infrastructure and curriculum of the formal Indonesian education system, particularly in the field of media studies (Christiawan 2009: 27; Surat 2007: 19–21).[8] HONF attempts to give shape to EFP by bringing local and international artists, academics, communities and social and cultural institutions together in interdisciplinary research and education (Murti 2009: 134–135). Its collaboration partners include Waag Society in Amsterdam and various organisations in Yogyakarta, such as the Microbiology Lab of UGM, the Informatics Lab of Duta Wacana University, the Akprind Institute of Science and Technology, the Yakkum rehabilitation centre, the Pusat Penyelematan Satwa Jogjakarta (Wild Animal Rescue Centre Yogyakarta, PPSJ) and various junior and senior high schools (EFP 2010).

Since its inception in 1999, EFP has had various focus points: from 1999 to 2001, obtaining and sharing knowledge about new media art; from 2002 to 2004, the mapping of and networking with national and international creative and scientific communities; from 2005 to 2006, developing educational 'open community' projects and the organisation of the first Yogyakarta International Videowork Festival (YIVF); in 2007, the organisation of the first Cellsbutton new media art festival; from 2008 to 2009, creative and ecological sustainability; and from 2010 to 2012, empowering local resources and environmental reform (EFP 2010). Since 2011, HONF has been developing its own creative laboratory, HonFab Lab. This overview shows the development of EFP from the study and teaching of new media art and the organisation of video and new media art festivals, to the efforts made to embed art and technology in a broader social context of local development and environmental sustainability.

Instrumental in implementing the EFP vision is HONF's annual Cellsbutton festival. In line with the idea of 'natural fiber', the festival name refers to organic matter, cells, which grow into a living organism through multiplication and combinations with other matter. Networking and encouraging collaboration between different 'cells' of artists, academics and social groups is the main purpose of the festival (Cellsbutton 2010). It comprises a diverse range of activities, including artist talks; multimedia presentations; workshops about new media art, computer technology and microbiology; drawing, drama, music, electronics, literacy and numeracy workshops for children (so-called Cells-KID); electronic music and Video Jockey (VJ) workshops and performances (so-called Breakcore_ LABS); and dance parties. The activities involve local, national and international artists and communities, and take place over several weeks at various locations, including the HONF studios, universities, schools, art galleries, nightclubs, social and cultural institutions, and outdoor sites. The other annual festival, YIVF, has a similar format but focuses on new media in the more narrow sense of experimental video, sound art, and social media, such as blogs, podcasts, wikis and computer games.

Some of these new media art activities have been negatively judged and misunderstood by art critics. For instance, Yuswantoro Adi, artist and talk show host of *Dialog seni kita* ('Our art dialogue') at the commercial radio station UNISI FM in Yogyakarta, described the HONF events in an 8 August 2003 broadcast as 'cool art', or art created by people who engage in popular leisure activities such as 'clubbing'. Yuswantoro questioned the significance of this type of art in the context of the development of Indonesian contemporary art. Another participant in the talk show pointed out that clubbing was closely related to the use of drugs for the stimulation of the senses. Christiawan, who was a guest on the show, did not agree with the idea that some forms of art were cool, and others not (Surat 2003: 23). Elsewhere, he also tried to avoid the impression that his creative work was trendy, 'glitz art' (Christiawan 2009: 26). He believed that the main criterion for artistic significance was audience interpretation and appreciation (Surat 2003: 23).

As mentioned before, other art critics have criticised young new media artists for adopting, rather than taking critical distance from, genres of popular culture. In the words of Agustinus (2005: 17):

> you paint a photo of Mao, and add a Coca-Cola logo: your work is done. You look for a photo of Inul, and make a print in Warhol style: your work is done. As humour, it is not tickling enough, and as a critique it is not biting enough.

Referring to the supposedly self-celebratory and narcissistic character of the 'generation of 2000', Hasan (2003: 156) remarked that 'we are even surprised by small things in their video works, as in scenes where they are hurting themselves or exploring various sensations and issues connected with the body'.

Contrary to Agustinus, Hasan and others, who present a clear dichotomy between the first and second generations of Indonesian new media artists, I believe a more fruitful approach is to explore the diverse and sometimes paradoxical discourses and practices across generations. Hasan's quote confirms that some of the younger artists are concerned with politics not in an overtly ideological sense, but in more subtle and varied ways, by critically addressing themes such as the body, gender, historiography and mediation.

Engaging with the praxis of life

An example of a young artist addressing the politics of the body and gender is Reza Afisina, one of the ruangrupa members. Afisina created the short video films 'What' (2001), in which he repeatedly slaps his own face while reciting Qur'an verses, and 'Victoria the Victorian' (2002), in which he cuts passages of text into his arms. Another example is Wulia's short video film 'Violence against fruits' (2000) about the violence against women of Chinese descent during the May 1998 riots (see Chapter 6). Nerfita Primadewi (2006: 31–32) created the video installation 'Broken ring' (2002) about 'women's awareness of the values created by patriarchal society in defining femininity'. The work was based on a scene from the popular *wayang* epic *Ramayana*, in which Sita has to stay in a protective magical circle while waiting for the return of her guardians Rama and Laksmana. In the original version, demon king Rahwana tempts Sita to move out of the circle. In Primadewi's short video, on the other hand, Sita breaks her oath to Rama and Laksmana of her own free will.

Several youth art communities have addressed the politics of the representation of historical events, particularly the traumatic aftermath of the mass killings and socio-political turmoil of the mid-1960s. Examples are Taring Padi's ('Fangs of the Rice Plant') poster art, Kedai Kebun Forum's ('Garden Café Forum') art exhibition 'September something' (2005) and Klinik Seni Taxu's *Memasak sejarah* ('Cooking history', 2004). For *Memasak sejarah*, Klinik Seni Taxu organised a performance in which yams were cooked from a garden that was used for the killings of PKI members and alleged communists. The organisers wanted to demonstrate that historical events that were literally buried below the surface were still part of daily reality and haunting people's lives (Juliastuti 2007b: 142). The organisers also seemed to suggest that Indonesian society could only heal its wounds and come to terms with the traumas of the past if it was prepared to address, or 'cook' and 'eat', the historical events.

To a certain extent, the contemporary art collectives can be seen as a modern interpretation of the *sanggar*, or the Indonesian art communities of the 1940s and 1950s, in which a senior artist lived and worked together with groups of aspiring artists, in a spirit of communality and in support of nationalist, socialist or communist ideology (see Chapter 7). According to Rath (2003: 4), some of the contemporary communities are similar to their 'historical cousin', as they are 'politically outspoken' and concerned with 'the alleged neo-colonising effects of global exchange', 'national identity' and 'national culture'. While the *sanggar* generation participated in the revolution and protested against colonialism, part of the younger generation has searched for alternatives to the New Order legacy of suppressive state policies.

Other contemporary art collectives have been less politically motivated and rather aim at increasing their participation in 'an international arena of appropriated and reconfigured artistic, cultural, and social practices and discourse' (Rath 2003: 5). This second group displays 'the tendency to recycle those areas of social and cultural practices that have until now been left un-mined by dominant art discourses or practices', including 'urban-living experiences, pop/TV culture, and sometimes gendered spaces' (Rath 2003: 5).

In general, the majority of contemporary Indonesian video art communities are inspired by a combination of artistic, social, political and commercial considerations. They build on GSRB's pioneering of new artistic forms in Indonesia such as installation and performance art. At the same time, they go beyond GSRB's relatively limited social participation by also developing collaborative art projects for and with society. For instance, every Saturday, HONF organises activities for disabled children at the Yakkum rehabilitation centre. These voluntary initiatives derive from a personal connection between Christiawan and the Yakkum director. One of the activities is a monthly multimedia performance, in which the children have the opportunity to be on stage and play with light, projections, animations and slides (Iskandar 2002: 16).

Similar to NGOs that encourage local communities to work with video and other media, some art collectives believe that the social and political empowerment of disadvantaged communities can be strengthened by giving people access to media content, management and ownership. A telling example was ruangrupa's third OK.Video festival of 2007. This festival went one step further than the previous editions of the OK.Video festival by choosing the theme of 'Militia' and explicitly aiming at social empowerment (Hafiz 2007: 13; Crosby 2008). As part of the festival, ruangrupa organised intensive 7-day video workshops for local communities at 15 locations in 12 different cities.

The workshops gave the communities information about the OK.Video festival, the history of video art, and the links between video art and social, political and cultural conditions (Afisina 2007: 34). The participants were also taught the different aspects of video film production, ranging from making notes, keeping a diary and drawing scenes to the actual shooting and editing process. According to the organisers (Afisina 2007: 35), the workshops were intended to give the local residents a new perspective on their daily lives by 'recording' the places where they lived and worked. They hoped that the creative process would make the participants knowledgeable, critical and active in dealing with and adapting to changes in their social and physical environments.

'Militia' used the National Gallery in Jakarta for an exhibition called 'Video In', consisting of submitted video art as well as work created in the various festival workshops. In the 'Video Out' part of the festival, art works were displayed outside the National Gallery, in public spaces such as office buildings, cafes, shopping malls and railway stations. Artists were asked to match their work of art with the character of the work's place of display. A team of curators guided the creative process by mediating between artists and local communities, and helping both groups of participants with retrieving information about the history and patterns of utilisation of the different localities that functioned as public exhibition spaces. The 'Video Out' projects, similar to the regional workshops, were meant to record local narratives and produce collaborative works of art that were different from mainstream art (Hafiz 2007: 14–15).

Hujatnikajennong (2007: 24) observed that the third OK.Video festival had a strong interdisciplinary character and attempted to break with elitist hierarchies in the art world. According to the art historian, the festival focused on 'video' rather than 'video art' by presenting works of not only aesthetic, but also socio-cultural, relevance. Apart from the various workshops, there were other demonstrations of video 'militancy' at the festival, such as Irwan Ahmett's project 'TV Milisi' (Militia TV). This project was carried out by an underground group that had special equipment to shut down, change and distort channels on television sets in both public and private spaces. In the 'Video In' exhibition, the group presented posters and photo and video documentation of their radical anti-television campaign (Ahmett 2007: 172).

In a similar vein, Primadewi (2006: 30) describes new media art, including her own work, as art that 'manipulates images to contradict the visual appearances or linear processes that we normally receive, and to create a counter-attack that turns upside down the belief system built by the medium of television'. Primadewi (2006: 34–36, 40–41) has stretched her new media art beyond video and into other technologies, such as mobile phones. In her project '(Not) 100% free artists', she collected text messages from hundreds of Indonesian and foreign mobile phone users. The work included people's favourite, electronically archived short messages; poetry created, sent and received by SMS; and pictures made of letters and punctuation marks. Her SMS art was meant as a form of 'instantaneous art', which could be created by ordinary people, was not restricted to a group of expert artists, and did not result in a finished work of art. Another aim was to bring mobile phone technology out of the commercial realm and to document how technology can stimulate people's creativity and mutual interaction.

While the young Indonesian new media artists are relatively modest about their place in the world, they are full of confidence about their art works, communities and festivals. Murti (2011: 85) noticed that 'they do not wait to be invited to become international; they invite artists from abroad to take part in international festivals here in Indonesia. This is the opposite of previous generations of visual artists'. Festivals such as ruangrupa's OK.Video and HONF's YIVF have become events in the Southeast Asian region and attract dozens of participants from all over the world, including Europe, Australia and the United States. The Indonesian art communities do not play marginal roles in international festivals organised by others either, as illustrated by HONF winning the transmediale.11 in Berlin (see Chapters 1 and 9). Ruangrupa's Darmawan famously stated that local artists have long moved 'beyond the Dutch', who introduced the idea of contemporary art into colonial society (Knol 2009: 23).[9] Financially, however, many new media art communities, including ruangrupa, still depend on funding from organisations in the old colonial centre, including HIVOS, to cover the costs of their communities and festivals (Darmawan 2006a: 122).

Conclusion

In the late 1990s and early 2000s, a young generation of Indonesian new media artists emerged who organised themselves in communities. These communities have flexible membership and are based on shared interests and ideas rather than fixed categories of gender, class, ethnicity or religion. They also have a multidisciplinary or interdisciplinary character, and are not restricted to members with a formal education in art history or art practice. They are meant as an alternative to the practices and policies of the government and business-supported tertiary art institutions and galleries, which tend to be organised along the lines of single discipline, single medium and single authorship.

Apart from providing an alternative to the art establishment, many new media art communities have also tried to re-engage with the praxis of social life. They have positioned and defined themselves in relation to various aspects of contemporary life, such as the media industry, popular culture, urban infrastructure, historiography and gender. They have established shared spaces for meetings, discussions and collaborative projects for addressing these issues. One of their activities have been video and other new media art festivals and events, including workshops for local communities to manage their own video content and produce stories that normally never reach the national print and broadcast media.

The communities share similarities with earlier socially engaged Indonesian art movements, such as the *sanggar* of the 1940 to the 1960s and the GSRB of the 1970s, as well as the international historical and neo-avant-garde groups of the early and mid-twentieth century. They do not have the strong ideological foundations of their predecessors, but tend to address the more subtle politics of gender, the body, popular culture and others aspects of everyday life. Partly because of the availability of new technologies, their art projects generally bear a stronger interactive and experiential character than the works of the historical art communities. These projects give shape to a relational aesthetics in which the creative process, networking, generating discourse and audience engagement are at least as meaningful as the production of tangible art works. They also often function as avant-garde laboratories for exploring aesthetics as well as micro-utopian scenarios for a better present and future of Indonesian society, as will be further explained in Chapter 9.

Notes

1 'Historical' refers to the avant-garde groups of the 1910s and 1920s, such as Dada. Bürger (1984: 57–63) distinguishes the historical avant-garde from the neo-avant-garde of the 1950s and 1960s, such as the Fluxus movement.
2 For a list including these and some other key features of avant-garde art, see Berghaus (2005: 20–21). I am interested in art that covers a combination of these aspects. Of course, there have been century-long traditions of creative expression at the grassroots level that allow audience participation and engagement with the praxis of life. However, these traditions do not have the self-reflexive dimension of contemporary art forms such as new media art.
3 Agung Hujatnikajennong (b. 1976) is based in Bandung. He has a background as Chief Curator at Selasar Sunaryo Art Space, one of the leading independent contemporary art spaces in Indonesia, owned by the sculptor and painter Sunaryo (b. 1943). Dr Hujatnikajennong is currently Lecturer at the Faculty of Art and Design at ITB.
4 The international pioneer of video art and one of the key players in Fluxus, Nam June Paik, was 'a refugee from the Korean War and had studied both art and music history at Tokyo University before travelling to West Germany in 1956 to continue his studies' (Nash 2011: 98). This in itself refutes any easy distinctions between western and 'other' ideas and practices of contemporary art.
5 Short for 'distribution outlet', derived from the terminology of zines (Iskandar 2006: 106–107; Luvaas 2008; Uttu 2006).
6 Taxu' is derived from the Balinese word *taksu,* which refers to something that has magical or sacred power. The art community is critical that the term *taksu* has been applied to almost every aspect of Balinese art and culture. They feel that it has become merely a strategy, 'taxu' rather than *taksu,* and that it has served diverse interests and no longer bears any specific meaning. As a 'clinic', the community wants to heal Bali's 'unhealthy' contemporary art and education system by providing an alternative to the hegemony of abstract impressionism as well as the sometimes coarse and vulgar resistance to this hegemony (Klinik Seni Taxu 2004). Jean Couteau (2011: 40) calls the group the first 'genuine challenge' to 'the ethnic approach' of the Balinese modern painting style promoted by the Yogyakarta-based Sanggar Dewata since the 1970s.
7 This statement resonates with the philosophy of German neo-avant-garde sculptor and performer Joseph Beuys (1921–1986), who believed that, in principle, everyone is an artist, capable of creating works of art (Berghaus 2005: 165). However, HONF is not as explicit in its political views as Beuys, who propagated art as 'the only evolutionary-revolutionary power' in society (Berghaus 2005: 164).
8 Christiawan experienced these gaps as a student at ISI Yogyakarta. As observed in previous chapters, the Cultural Studies project in Indonesia relies heavily on the initiatives of independent media institutions, NGOs and transnational communication and collaboration platforms with an interest in the politics of culture and everyday life, such as HONF and Kunci.
9 This statement became the title of a combined exhibition of Indonesian and Dutch contemporary art at the Centraal Museum in Utrecht from 16 October 2009 to 10 January 2010.

References

Achmad, Laila. 2006. 'Editorial'. In: Indra Ameng, Ardi Yunanto and Andang Kelana (eds), *Jakarta 32°*. Jakarta: ruangrupa, pp. 3–4.

Afisina, Reza. 2007. 'Workshop OK.Video Militia'. In: Ardi Yunanto, Mahardika Yudha and Rani Elsanti (eds), *OK.Video Militia: 3rd Jakarta International Video Festival, 10–27 July 2007*. Jakarta: ruangrupa, pp. 34–35.

Agustinus, Ronny. 2003. 'Video: not all correct'. In: Agung Hujatnikajennong, Ade Darmawan and Farah Wardani (eds), *OK Video: post event*. Jakarta: ruangrupa, Jakarta, pp. 54–83.

Agustinus, Ronny. 2005. 'Sebuah esai tanpa hak cipta: an essay with no copyright'. In: Ardi Yunanto, Che Kyongfa, Agung Hujatnikajennong and Ade Darmawan (eds), *OK Video: sub/version, Jakarta video festival 2005*. Jakarta: ruangrupa, pp. 16–26.

Ahmett, Irwan. 2007. 'TV Milisi' [Militia TV]. In: Ardi Yunanto, Mahardika Yudha and Rani Elsanti (eds), *OK.Video Militia: 3rd Jakarta International Video Festival, 10–27 July 2007*. Jakarta: ruangrupa, p. 172.

Baudrillard, Jean. 1983. 'The ecstasy of communication'. In: Hal Foster (ed.), *The anti-aesthetic: essays on postmodern culture*. Seattle, WA: Bay Press, pp. 126–133.

Berghaus, Günter. 2005. *Avant-garde performance: live events and electronic technologies*. Basingstoke: Palgrave Macmillan.

Berghuis, Thomas J. 2011. 'ruangrupa: what could be "art to come"'. *Third Text* 25(4): 395–407.

Bourriaud, Nicolas. 2002. *Relational aesthetics*, translated by Simon Pleasance and Fonza Woods, with the participation of Mathieu Copeland. Dijon: Les presses du réel.

Bürger, Peter. 1984. *Theory of the avant-garde*, translated by Michael Shaw. Minneapolis, MN: University of Minnesota Press.

Cellsbutton. 2010. 'About Cellsbutton'. Available at: www.natural-fiber.com/cellsbutton/index.php?option=com_content&view=article&id=45&Itemid=53 (accessed 10 August 2010).

Christiawan, Venzha. 2009. 'New media art, teknologi, dan edukasi' [New media art, technology, and education]. *Gong: Majalah Seni Budaya* 113(10): 25–27.

Clark, Christine. 2005. 'Distinctive voices: artist-initiated space and projects'. In: Caroline Turner (ed.), *Art and social change in Asia and the Pacific*. Canberra: Pandanus Books, pp. 554–568.

Couteau, Jean. 2011. 'Balinese painting'. *Now Bali* (November): 38–41.

Crosby, Alexandra. 2008. 'ruangrupa: mapping a collective biography'. In: Alexandra Crosby, Rebecca Conroy, Suzan Piper and Jan Cornall (eds), *Gang re: publik; Indonesia-Australia creative adventures*. Newtown: Gang Festival, pp. 129–134.

Darmawan, Ade. 2005. 'Are we connected?'. In: Ardi Yunanto, Che Kyongfa, Agung Hujatnikajennong and Ade Darmawan (eds), *OK Video: sub/version, Jakarta video festival 2005*. Jakarta: ruangrupa, pp. 11–12.

Darmawan, Ade. 2006a. 'Comments of the 3rd Asia-Europe Art Camp 2005 participants'. In: Marie Le Sourd, Septina Ferniati, Lioni Beatrik Tobing, Mirna Adzania and Tarlen Handayani (eds), *The 3rd Asia-Europe art camp 2005: artist initiative spaces and new media arts post-event publication*. Singapore and Bandung: Asia-Europe Foundation and Bandung Center for New Media Arts, p. 122.

Darmawan, Ade. 2006b. 'Infrastruktur seni media baru?' [A new media art infrastructure?]. In: Direktorat Kesenian, *Apresiasi seni media baru* [Appreciation of new media art]. Jakarta: Direktorat Kesenian, Direktorat Jendral Nilai Budaya, Seni dan Film and Departemen Kebudayaan dan Pariwisata, pp. 87–101.

Dixon, Steve. 2007. *Digital performance: a history of new media in theater, dance, performance art and installation*. Cambridge, MA: MIT Press.

EFP. 2010. Available at: www.natural-fiber.com/cellsbutton/index.php?option=com_content&view=article&id=47&Itemid=55 (accessed 17 August 2010).

Foster, Hal. 1994. 'What's neo about the neo-avant-garde?'. *October* 70: 5–32.

Hafiz. 2007. 'Militia! Saatnya bergerak!' [Militia! Time to make a move!]. In: Ardi

Yunanto, Mahardika Yudha and Rani Elsanti (eds.), *OK.Video Militia: 3rd Jakarta International Video Festival, 10–27 July 2007*. Jakarta: ruangrupa, pp. 13–15.

Harsono, F. X. 2003. 'Meraba peta komunitas seni rupa Indonesia: deciphering the map of Indonesian visual art communities'. *Karbon* 5(5): 16–25.

Hasan, Asikin. 2003. 'A few notes on new media'. In: Saut Situmorang, Elly Kent, Mella Jaarsma and Nindityo Adipurnomo (eds), *15 years Cemeti Art House: exploring vacuum*. Yogyakarta: Cemeti Art House, pp. 155–156.

Hattori, Katsuyuki. 2003. 'As room for discourse'. In: Agung Hujatnikajennong, Ade Darmawan and Farah Wardani (eds), *OK Video: post event*. Jakarta: ruangrupa, pp. 26–28.

Heryanto, Ariel. 2008. 'Pop culture and competing identities'. In: Ariel Heryanto (ed.), *Popular culture in Indonesia: fluid identities in post-authoritarian politics*. London and New York: Routledge, pp. 1–36.

HONF. 2010. 'The House of Natural Fiber, Yogyakarta new media art laboratory'. Available at: www.natural-fiber.com/index.php?option=com_content&view=article&id=57&Itemid=57 (accessed 22 January 2014).

Hujatnikajennong, Agung. 2003. 'Memorandum, prolegomena, criticism'. In: Agung Hujatnikajennong, Ade Darmawan and Farah Wardani (eds), *OK Video: post event*. Jakarta: ruangrupa, pp. 6–10.

Hujatnikajennong, Agung. 2005. 'Tentang sub/versi: situasi pasca-avant-garde dan kemenangan globalisasi teknologis' [About sub/version: the post-avant-garde situation and the victory of technological globalisation]. In: Ardi Yunanto, Che Kyongfa, Agung Hujatnikajennong and Ade Darmawan (eds), *OK Video: sub/version: Jakarta video festival 2005*. Jakarta: ruangrupa, pp. 34–49.

Hujatnikajennong, Agung. 2006a. 'Avant-gardeisme dalam seni: otonomi, resistensi, dan "sub-versi"' [Avant-gardism in art: autonomy, resistance, and 'sub-version']. In: Alfathri Adlin (ed.), *Resistensi gaya hidup: teori dan realitas* [Lifestyle resistance: theory and reality]. Yogyakarta: Jalasutra, pp. 175–183.

Hujatnikajennong, Agung. 2006b. 'Tentang seni media baru: catatan perkembangan' [About new media art: notes on its development]. In: Direktorat Kesenian, *Apresiasi seni media baru* [Appreciation of new media art]. Jakarta: Direktorat Kesenian, Direktorat Jendral Nilai Budaya, Seni dan Film and Departemen Kebudayaan dan Pariwisata, pp. 11–27.

Hujatnikajennong, Agung. 2007. 'Video sebagai piranti sosial' [Video as a social instrument]. In: Ardi Yunanto, Mahardika Yudha and Rani Elsanti (eds), *OK.Video Militia: 3rd Jakarta International Video Festival, 10–27 July 2007*. Jakarta: ruangrupa, pp. 20–24.

Hujatnikajennong, Agung. 2009. 'Kenteringen in de hedendaagse kunst: de Indonesische kunstwereld en de nasleep van de jaren tachtig' [Turning points in contemporary art: the Indonesian art world and the impact of the 1980s]. In: Meta Knol, Remco Raben and Kitty Zijlmans (eds), *Beyond the Dutch: Indonesië, Nederland en de beeldende kunsten van 1900 tot nu* [Beyond the Dutch: Indonesia, the Netherlands and the fine arts from 1900 until now]. Amsterdam: KIT Publisher and Centraal Museum, pp. 139–145.

Iskandar, Gustaff Harriman. 2002. 'Garden of the blind'. *Trolley* 9(2): 12–17.

Iskandar, Gustaff Harriman. 2006. 'Rekomendasi kebijakan pengembangan praktik seni media di Indonesia' [Policy recommendations for the development of media art practice in Indonesia]. In: Direktorat Kesenian, *Apresiasi seni media baru* [Appreciation of new media art]. Jakarta: Direktorat Kesenian, Direktorat Jendral Nilai Budaya, Seni dan Film and Departemen Kebudayaan dan Pariwisata, pp. 103–130.

Juliastuti, Nuraini. 2007a. 'Ruang alternatif, alternative spaces'. In: Nuraini Juliastuti and Yuli Andari Merdikaningtyas (eds), *Folders: 10 tahun dokumentasi Yayasan Seni Cemeti: 10 years of documentation work by Cemeti Art Foundation*. Yogyakarta: Indonesian Visual Art Archive, pp. 106–118.

Juliastuti, Nuraini. 2007b. 'Seniman dan persoalan kerakyatan, artists and society issues'. In: Nuraini Juliastuti and Yuli Andari Merdikaningtyas (eds), *Folders: 10 tahun dokumentasi Yayasan Seni Cemeti: 10 years of documentation work by Cemeti Art Foundation*. Yogyakarta: Indonesian Visual Art Archive, pp. 140–149.

Juliastuti, Nuraini. 2007c. 'Video sekarang, video now'. In: Nuraini Juliastuti and Yuli Andari Merdikaningtyas (eds), *Folders: 10 tahun dokumentasi Yayasan Seni Cemeti: 10 years of documentation work by Cemeti Art Foundation*. Yogyakarta: Indonesian Visual Art Archive, pp. 134–139.

Jurriëns, Edwin. 2013. 'Between utopia and the real world: Indonesia's avant-garde new media art'. *Indonesia and the Malay World* 41(119): 48–75.

Jurriëns, Edwin. 2015. 'Shaping spaces: video art communities in Indonesia'. In: Barbara Hatley with Brett Hough (eds), *Performing contemporary Indonesia: celebrating identity, constructing community*. Verhandeling van het Koninklijk Instituut voor Taal- Land- en Volkenkunde 297, Southeast Asia Mediated 6. Leiden and Boston: Brill, pp. 98–119.

Klinik Seni Taxu. 2004. 'Tentang Klinik Seni Taxu' [About Klinik Seni Taxu]. Available at: http://taxu.netfirms.com/profile_tetang.html (accessed 19 October 2010).

Knol, Meta. 2009. '*They are beyond the Dutch*: Indonesië, Nederland en de beeldende kunsten' [They are beyond the Dutch: Indonesia, the Netherlands and the fine arts]. In: Meta Knol, Remco Raben and Kitty Zijlmans (eds), *Beyond the Dutch: Indonesië, Nederland en de beeldende kunsten van 1900 tot nu* [Beyond the Dutch: Indonesia, the Netherlands and the fine arts from 1900 until now]. Amsterdam and Utrecht: KIT Publisher and Centraal Museum, pp. 11–23.

Luvaas, Brent. 2008. 'Global fashion, remixed'. *Inside Indonesia* 92 (April–June). Available at: www.insideindonesia.org/global-fashion-remixed-2 (accessed 14 August 2016).

Luvaas, Brent. 2009. 'The Indie takeover'. *Inside Indonesia* 95 (January–March). Available at: www.insideindonesia.org/the-indie-takeover (accessed 14 August 2016).

Murti, Krisna. 2006. 'Media baru: kultur gerilya hingga seni gadget' [New media: from guerrilla culture to gadget art]. In: Direktorat Kesenian, *Apresiasi seni Media Baru* [New media art appreciation]. Jakarta: Direktorat Kesenian, Direktorat Jendral Nilai Budaya, Seni dan Film and Departemen Kebudayaan dan Pariwisata, pp. 45–66.

Murti, Krisna. 2009. *Essays on video art and new media: Indonesia and beyond*. Yogyakarta: Indonesian Visual Art Archive.

Murti, Krisna. 2011. 'Indonesian video art and new media culture'. In: Ibrahim Tahir, James Lui and Lindsay Davis (eds), *Video, an art, a history 1965–2010: a selection from the Centre Pompidou and Singapore Art Museum collections*. Singapore: SAM Publisher, pp. 77–85.

Nash, Mark. 2011. 'Video ecologies: Asian and European dialogues in artists' moving-image work'. In: Ibrahim Tahir, James Lui and Lindsay Davis (eds), *Video, an art, a history 1965–2010: a selection from the Centre Pompidou and Singapore Art Museum collections*. Singapore: SAM Publisher, pp. 97–105.

Primadewi, Nerfita. 2006. 'Seni SMS = seni jempol (bukan isapan jempol)' [SMS art = thumb art (no lie)]. In: Direktorat Kesenian, *Apresiasi seni media baru* [Appreciation of new media art]. Jakarta: Direktorat Kesenian, Direktorat Jendral Nilai Budaya, Seni dan Film and Departemen Kebudayaan dan Pariwisata, pp. 29–43.

Rath, Amanda. 2003. 'Perihal seni alternatif dan ruang seni alternatif, altered-natives and altered-spaces: alternative art and alternative art spaces, altered-natives and altered-spaces'. *Karbon* 5(5): 4–15.

Shandra, Ary Buy and Ade Darmawan. 2006. '72 DPI'. In: Indra Ameng, Ardi Yunanto, Andang Kelana (eds), *Jakarta 32°*. Jakarta: ruangrupa, pp. 8–11.

Streak, Greg. 2003. 'It's more than OK'. In: Agung Hujatnikajennong, Ade Darmawan and Farah Wardani (eds), *OK Video: post event*. Jakarta: ruangrupa, pp. 29–31.

Surat. 2003. 'Tema: "seni rupa di kalangan anak muda, kayak apa?"' [Theme: 'what's fine art like among youth?']. *Surat* 17: 23.

Surat. 2007. 'Cellsbutton 1: Yogyakarta International Media Art Festival'. *Surat Yayasan Seni Cemeti* 30: 19–23.

Uttu. 2006. 'Distro: independent fashion moves from margins to mainstream'. *Inside Indonesia* 85. Available at: www.insideindonesia.org/distro (accessed 14 August 2016).

Wardani, Farah. 2003. 'Obrolan bersama, a conversation with: Mella Jaarsma'. *Karbon* 5(5): 26–32.

Yunanto, Ardi and M. G. Pringgotono. 2006. 'Menunggu untuk bermain' [Waiting to play]. In: Indra Ameng, Ardi Yunanto and Andang Kelana (eds), *Jakarta 32°*. Jakarta: ruangrupa, pp. 22–26.

Zwink, Oliver. 2003. 'OK urban space, OK urban life'. In: Agung Hujatnikajennong, Ade Darmawan and Farah Wardani (eds), *OK Video: post event*. Jakarta: ruangrupa, pp. 32–35.

9 Video simulations

Micro-utopian models for the present and the future

This chapter focuses on HONF and Indonesian contemporary art more broadly, as a historically and socially specific interpretation of the third and fourth key avant-garde principles: to provide utopian visions and present aesthetic innovation. A characteristic of HONF's creative projects is the exploration of the interaction between life, art, science and technology in both practical and aesthetic ways. The projects not only reflect on the tremendous impact of communication media and other technology on social and natural environments in Indonesia and worldwide, but they also provide scenarios for alternative ways of dealing with these environments. Aesthetically they are innovative in using and developing presentational modes such as pastiche, interactivity and virtual reality (Jurriëns 2013). The various projects are the result of global networking, but they also build on the pillars of Indonesian contemporary art and respond to the dynamics of local society. Consequently, they need to be interpreted in the framework of both international and domestic ideas and practices.

The art works, or rather art events, by the HONF community can be classified in three broad categories: performance art, VJ presentations and dance parties, and laboratory experiments and installations. All three categories contain visions of existing and/or preferred interactions between people and their social environments. Roughly, the first category analyses such interactions, the second recreates or simulates them, and the third offers possible alternatives. According to Richard Noble (2009: 14), it is the combination of such reflections on the present and the search for solutions that constitute the (political) character of utopian art:

> [It] proceeds from an awareness of the imperfections of our social and political conditions towards some sort of understanding of, and possible solution to, what the artist perceives these to be. It is art oriented beyond existing conditions, sometimes to the future, sometimes to the past; it is art that asks us difficult questions about the conditions we live with and the potential we have to change them.

The utopia presented in contemporary art such as HONF's has a different character than the utopia of the historical and neo-avant-gardes. Today's art is less concerned with grand, evolutionary and explicitly political visions of the future, but is more focused on 'learning to inhabit the world in a better way' (Bourriaud 2002: 13). According to Bourriaud (2002: 45), 'these days, utopia is being lived on a subjective, everyday basis, in the real time of concrete and intentionally fragmentary experiments'. He calls the contemporary forms of utopia 'hands-on utopias' or 'micro-utopias' in contrast to the earlier forms of 'radical and universalist utopia' (Bourriaud 2002: 9, 31, 70).

Performance and dance laboratories

An example of HONF-related performance art was Christiawan's collaborations with Kuswidananto in Garden of the Blind. The performances earned Christiawan and Kuswidananto and, indirectly, the HONF community, only small money, approximately two to three million rupiah per work (approximately US$250; Iskandar 2002: 17). As explained in Chapter 6, Garden of the Blind used modified guitars, cassette players, bicycles, oxygen masks and other 'found objects' to produce experimental sounds and visual effects. In a discussion on new media art at the Indonesian Visual Art Archive (IVAA) in Yogyakarta on 19 January 2012, some participants argued that this type of performance art did not sufficiently express local identity and was merely a laboratory for introducing and repeating western ideas and practices. This may have been inspired by the lack of direct references in the performances to quintessential, if not stereotypical, Javanese cultural philosophies and symbols such as *wayang*.

While the ideas and activities of HONF are well documented on the art collective's website, Christiawan was reluctant to elaborate on the meaning of his performance art, as he believed that it became less interesting if explained in detail (Iskandar 2002: 13). His attitude can be explained as an attempt to avoid being trapped in one of the dead-end artistic or socio-political categories of the late New Order or early *Reformasi* and to continue his creative, spiritual and ideological journey in relative freedom (Iskandar 2002: 15). I believe, however, there is a strong sense of localness in the way his performances use found objects and build on and contribute to rhizome-like networks. These creative strategies reflect the social strategies used by ordinary Yogyakarta people to 'handle existence' and overcome the juxtapositions and contradictions encountered in daily life.

Similar strategies have been applied in the pioneering new media art of Dono and Murti. For instance, Dono's 1997 'Gamelan of Non-communication' used found objects to juxtapose the everyday reality of the common people in Central Java with the pleasures of modern consumer life that are beyond the reach of many.[1] While the installation represented a certain level of creativity and technological knowledge of the commoners, it also demonstrated that the found objects could not live up to the communicative quality of professional musicians or the smooth sounds of more expensive and sophisticated media equipment. Murti[2] mentioned that even if he had the financial means to do so, he would not aspire to make his video art as technologically sophisticated as the work of Bill Viola or other influential international video artists. Similar to HONF and Dono, Murti's main considerations are the use of materials that can effectively express creative ideas and respond to social situations.

This does not mean that the Garden of the Blind performances are free from any socio-political engagement other than using found objects. In Chapter 6, I argued that many of the performances were both euphoric and critical about the possibilities of mediation, as reflected in titles such as 'Glorified' (2001) and 'Ultra-output' (2002). The performances seemed to suggest that mediation can only be successful if the participants in the process understand the character of the medium they are using and respect their interaction with other participants. It is this type of critical analysis of media environments that makes the Garden of the Blind performances highly relevant to contemporary information and communication society (Jurriëns 2009: 284–285).

The difference between Christiawan's performance and installation art and HONF's annual Cellsbutton festival is the higher degree of audience interaction in the latter. The VJ presentations and dance parties that are part of Cellsbutton encourage audiences not only to reflect on their media environments, but also to recreate such environments and immerse themselves in them. As shown by Wardhana (see Chapter 3), for the majority of young adults in contemporary information and communication society, including Indonesian urbanites, the mass media and other media environments have become their 'natural' habitat and importantly influence their ideas, actions and behaviour. The Cellsbutton events can be seen as simulations of, and possible testing grounds for, human interactions with these environments. The festival visitors are positioned not as mere observers but as agents who, by reacting with their bodies and senses to the videos, sounds and light effects of the VJ, can influence the ambience of the art space and the shape and progress of the art events.

The critical references to HONF's VJ presentations and dance parties as 'cool' and 'glitz' art (see Chapter 8) are not entirely out of place. However, to see these purely as events where wealthy urban young adults engage in hedonistic activities such as clubbing, dancing and drug use would ignore key aspects of the contexts in which they take place. The events are always integrated in special art activities and themes, such as the Cellsbutton festivals and the Breakcore_LABS workshops for experimental musicians, Disc Jockeys (DJs) and VJs. On the one hand, the dance parties can be interpreted as a sign that participants partly accept the realities of contemporary capitalist society and make use of the opportunity, or even see it as their 'right', to seek leisure and pleasure and to unwind from normal routine. On the other hand, they function as a testing ground for HONF and the invited artists and audiences to put audio-visual and bodily experiments into practice as alternative ways of communication. The dance parties constitute a natural evolution from Christiawan's early experiments with electronic music and performance art, and can be seen as a specific type of workshop or laboratory that shares similarities with HONF's other laboratory-type art works and activities.

Bricolage laboratories

Less ambiguous examples of art laboratories or workshops that have come out of the Cellsbutton festivals since 2007 are Indonesia Bricolabs and HonFab Lab. Indonesia Bricolabs is an interdisciplinary discussion forum in which artists, scientists and social institutions share information about the invention and improvement of technological applications that can stimulate local development. Indonesia Bricolabs was founded with help from Rob van Kranenburg, co-founder of the international Bricolabs network and member of Waag Society, a Dutch independent organisation for creative technology and social innovation. An example of an Indonesia Bricolabs seminar took place in August 2008 at Duta Wacana University in Yogyakarta. This seminar had presentations by Rob van Kranenburg about the very idea of Bricolabs; Ir. Irfan Dwidya Prijambada from UGM about the agricultural possibilities of the genetic reconstruction of plants; and Arifin Wicaksono from Bio Chemicals Indonesia about the advantages of non-toxic water-based paint and coating (Bricolabs 2010).

Bricolabs is derived from 'bricolage' or 'bricoleur', as conceptualised by Claude Lévi-Strauss (1968: 16–22) and further developed by Deleuze and Guattari (1977: 7). According to Lévi-Strauss (1968: 16–18), a 'bricoleur' is 'someone who works with his hands' and collects and uses 'whatever is at hand' or 'come[s] in handy'. Lévi-Strauss (1968: 19) uses the bricoleur as a figure of mythical thought, who 'by inclination or necessity always remains within … the constraints imposed by a particular state of civilization'. He contrasts the bricoleur with the engineer, who, as a figure of modern science, 'is always trying to make his way out of and go beyond [these] constraints'.

Lévi-Strauss's (1968: 22) argument that art 'lies half-way between scientific knowledge and mythical or magical thought', or between 'engineering' and 'bricoleur', is illustrated by activities such as Bricolabs. As 'bricoleurs', the HONF members attempt to give their works and projects an experiential, if not 'magical' or 'outerworldly', character. They also situate themselves within the social and economic constraints of Indonesia as a developing country. According to Christiawan,[3] HONF recognises and attempts to build on the often ingenious responses from society to problems that are not addressed by government or business. As 'engineers', on the other hand, they creatively explore the 'unlimited opportunities' provided by alliances between art, science and technology. This means they attempt to go beyond the boundaries of their, or Indonesia's, immediate situation, and to present small-scale utopian scenarios for an alternative present or future.

What is unusual about these and other forms of HONF bricolage is that they bring together different types of elements, and by doing so, also change the nature of these elements. The experiments can be seen as 'rhizomatic' in the sense of Deleuze and Guattari (1987: 21). The work of Deleuze and Guattari is likely to have reached the HONF members in one form or another through their active participation in numerous international festivals and networks.[4] It provides a framework for understanding the art community's special interest in combining machines and human bodies into cyborg-like installations, and using science and technology for producing prosthetics and manipulating the growth of plants. The HONF collective and events such as Cellsbutton could be translated as offshoots of lateral, rhizome-like movements of people, ideas and materials, including the international communities of bricolabs and fabrication labs, which although temporary and unfixed, react to and grow in accordance with the specificities of time and place.

The idea of the rhizome to describe HONF's community and activities is also productive in the context of the popularity of specific arborescent motifs in Indonesian contemporary art, such as the 'tree of life' (*pohon hajat*). This motif can be found in the work of modern painters including Ahmad Sadali (1924–1987), Nyoman Erawan (b. 1958), Bagong Kussudiardjo (1928–2004) and Tulus Warsito (b. 1953; Fischer 1990: 16; Wright 1994). In this work, trees and mountains are often stylised as *kayon* ('wood-like') or *gunungan* ('mountain-like'), both symbols from *wayang* theatre and Hindu-Buddhist philosophy denoting 'the universe in all its components of earth, fire, water, flora and fauna [...] the cosmic mountain where all life and nature is contained and, above all, where the gods dwell' (Fischer 1990: 14). Whereas the modern painters have used this motif to express spirituality, mysticism and aspects of Javanese or Balinese cosmology, the approach of new media artists such as the HONF is more down-to-earth, or indeed 'rhizomatic' and participatory, if not activist, in character. While HONF's engagement with nature does not exclude spiritualism and mysticism, it most importantly shows that nature and societal relations are not predetermined or untouchable in either a biological or political sense, but can be constructed, contested and modified in line with people's ideals and creativity.

The fact that most of HONF's activities are as much part of the worlds of nature, science and technology as the world of art as such is a clear divergence from the modernist emphasis on the originality and autonomy of the work of art. The work of art, as a singular form or product, has largely disappeared due to changes to its 'genes'. Contrary to the modernist emphasis on the creative genius, most of HONF's art does not have a single name attached to it, as it is the result of collaborative effort. This art should be described in terms of processes or events rather than works, since it unfolds in time and space and rarely reaches a finalised form. The creation of networks, experiences and discourses has become the 'real' art rather than, or in addition to, the creation of tangible products.

Fabrication laboratories

HONF's other lab, HonFab Lab, is meant as a workshop for the actual production of creative technology. It adheres to the 'Open Hardware' philosophy, which similar to the 'Open Source' and 'Open Content' principles promotes the exchange of products and ideas relatively unhampered by commercial or politico-administrative restrictions. HonFab Lab is part of a global fabrication laboratory network of standardised open hardware setups developed by Neil

Gershenfeld from the Massachusetts Institute of Technology (MIT). HONF developed its own fab lab with help from Waag Society, which created Fablab Amsterdam in The Netherlands (Fablab 2010). Since its official launch in July 2011, it has explored the social applications of a wide range of technology, from the use of robotics in health care to microbiology for the improvement of agriculture.

The HonFab Lab projects have a micro-utopian character, and are deliberately designed to redevelop social environments through technological, artistic and social innovation. They are the cultural equivalent of the development and testing of technological prototypes in scientific laboratories and the Research and Development divisions of industrial manufacturers. The trend of art and media laboratories is also reflected in the names of the new media art communities Video Lab (Bandung) and Klinik Seni Taxu (Denpasar), and the community media initiative Youth Media Community Lab of Kampung Halaman (Yogyakarta). This trend is linked to the aesthetic strategy of 'modelling ' in utopian art, or postulating 'other ways of being', 'possible worlds', 'what ifs' and 'the logical implications of current practices' (Noble 2009: 14). While the historical and neo-avant-garde art's main concern was 'to prepare and announce a future world', in the contemporary (Indonesian) examples there is a stronger focus on 'modelling possible universes' (Bourriaud 2002: 13).

In order to achieve its goals, HonFab Lab has a different way of engaging with the audience than the other two HONF art activities. Christiawan's performance art takes place in public and allows relatively restricted interactivity, while in HONF's dance parties, the performance artists and the singing and dancing crowd seem to merge almost completely. In HONF's collaboration with university labs, on the other hand, the participating artists and scholars take considerable distance from the general public in order to engage in elaborate and undisturbed research and reflection. Examples of HonFab Lab projects in progress are 'Under $50 Prosthetics', 'Condition: Public Transportation', 'Intelligent Bacteria', 'Condition: Food Improvements', 'P.A.D.I.' and 'S.A.T.U.'.

'Under $50 Prosthetics' has been a collaborative project with Fablab Amsterdam and Yakkum since early 2009. Its aim is to invent below-knee prosthetics that are under US$50, which would be much more affordable for Indonesian clients than the current alternatives. In line with HONF's aesthetic mission and requests by the patients themselves, the project partners attempt to give the prosthetics a natural look, so users are not embarrassed by them. In January 2010, HONF members were invited to The Netherlands in order to learn from Fablab Amsterdam on using the equipment and developing collaboration strategies. The two art communities experimented with the use of three-dimensional scanners and cheap Indonesian materials such as bamboo for the production of prosthetics. The HONF members were also on a study tour to Kamer Orthopedie in Amsterdam, a company specialising in manufacturing prosthetics (HONF Prosthetics 2010).

The project 'Condition: Public Transportation' is meant to invent or improve facilities that give mobility to disabled people. One of the tools that HONF is trying to develop is a portable ramp that makes it easier for people in a wheelchair or with a walking stick to get onto a bus when it arrives at a bus stop. Another tool is a wheelchair horn with a sensor that alerts people nearby to make way for the person in the wheelchair (Public Transportation 2010). With these small-scale projects, HONF tries to relate to the daily problems faced by disabled people that are often neglected or considered social taboos by the government and general public.

'Intelligent Bacteria' is a project in collaboration with the Microbiology Department of UGM. Its main idea is to find new methods of producing cheap and safe alcoholic drinks, to reduce health problems caused by unsafe homebrew. According to HONF, these problems intensified after the Indonesian excise duty on alcohol was increased in March 2010, and those from the lower and middle social income groups created or bought cheap home brew with high levels of methanol due to unhygienic fermentation in the production process. HONF has experimented with various types of fruit as fermentation materials such as *salak* and sweetcorn to create wines in various colours and tastes.[5] The art collective presented their own wine factory as installation art at Festival Kesenian Yogyakarta (Yogyakarta Art Festival, FKY) in July 2010. The installation derived its aesthetic and performative qualities not only from the colourful materials and mechanical devices, but also from the use of gases during the fermentation process for the generation of experimental sounds. In February 2011, it was this installation that was crowned winner of the Berlin transmediale.11.

The background to the 'Condition: Food Improvements' project was the New Order government programme on agriculture that focused on the short-term increase of agricultural production. Paradoxically, these actions often led to the long-term degradation of soils, as local conditions were not considered. One of the key problems was a lack of communication between the various parties involved. The government officials often did not have the scientific knowledge to inform local farmers, whereas the scientists did not communicate their findings adequately to other parties. The 'Food Improvement' project is intended to improve Indonesian agriculture by facilitating better communication between the government, farmers and scientists. The project will allow farmers without internet access to receive text messages on their mobile phones from a database of agricultural information. In compiling scientific information about issues such as soils, fertilisers and the genetically modified seeds, HONF receives help from UGM's microbiology department. Pilot projects have been taking place in villages in Yogyakarta's Bantul region (Food Improvements 2010).

Since 2010, HONF has tried to develop other projects for and with farmers and rural communities as part of its so-called 'P.A.D.I.' ('rice' in Indonesian, but also an acronym for Paradigm of Antidotes to Deconstruct the Infrastructures) programme. The programme addresses the irony that Indonesia, as a predominantly agricultural society with some of the most fertile soils in the world, is also one of the world's largest importers of rice. HONF tries to give the Indonesian public a more positive image of agriculture through new media art and educational projects at schools and universities (P.A.D.I. 2010).

An example of how HONF uses new media art to direct public attention on agricultural issues is the art installation 'S.A.T.U.' ('one' in Indonesian, and also an acronym for 'Saturn Analogy of Trans Urgency'). This installation was presented at the Next Wave Festival in Melbourne from 13 to 30 May 2010. The name of the installation refers to the reflection of hexagonal shapes from the planet Saturn. The installation imitates some of the experiments done by scientists to explain the appearance of such shapes, which also occur in various natural phenomena and are represented in symbols of ancient civilisations around the globe (Next Wave 2010).

The installation consists of three rotating hexagonal aluminium structures in a dark room. While rotating, the structures transmit so-called ultra-sound (above 20 kHz) or infra-sound (below 20 Hz) that cannot be heard by human beings, and near-ultrasonic, audible sounds that are meant to give the audience a sense of presence in the space. The use of sound in the installation represents 'the basic form of energy created by the vibration of matters' (Next Wave 2010). The installation is meant to test the effects of this type of proto-energy within the proto-structure of the hexagon on life forms such as plants as well as non-life forms such as water. The HONF community believes that spectacular experiments such as 'S.A.T.U.', in which the energy derived from sounds, shapes and movements may help plants grow in the dark, can renew people's interest in agricultural growth processes and, in a broader and more philosophical sense, give shape to utopian ambitions such as the creation of 'an alignment between art and science, individual and community, energy and space' (Next Wave 2010). 'Grow kitchen: 5 kingdoms of life' (2014) is one of HONF's more recent multimedia installations, combining elements of both 'S.A.T.U.' and 'Intelligent bacteria', which reflects on the mutual relationship between bacteria, protista, fungi, plants and animals, or the 'five kingdoms of life' (Figure 9.1).

The end of representation

The HONF art works and events have an avant-garde character because of the issues they address as well as the aesthetics used. The art projects derive their artistic 'newness' from their exploration of the possibilities of presentation rather than representation, which in itself is an expression of the dynamics of today's 'society of the spectacle' (Debord 1994). Both in Indonesia and globally, information and communication technology such as television, computers and mobile phones have become an integral part of daily life. The dramatic increase and impact of these technologies has not meant the end of representation, but has certainly encouraged modes and values of social engagement with a high 'presentational' character such as interactivity and virtual reality.

HONF's presentational aesthetics are reflected in its interactive projects and laboratory experiments, and build on some aspects of the Indonesian performance art of the 1980s and 1990s, and the installation and other art of GSRB in the 1970s and 1980s. While Indonesian and international modern art has been struggling with issues of representation for centuries (Morse 1998: 160), the

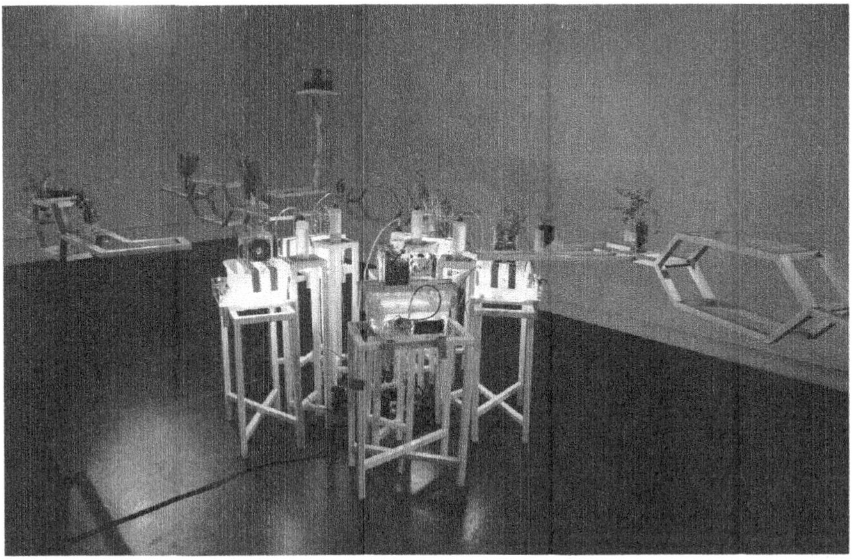

Figure 9.1 'Grow kitchen: 5 kingdoms of life' (The House of Natural Fiber; HONF), multimedia installation, 2014.

Source: photo courtesy of Tommy Surya Rahadyanto.

exploration of the field of presentation is relatively recent, and can only be expected to further develop in the future.

Roughly, in representational art, the focus is on worlds beyond the time, space and material conditions in which the encounter between a work of art and an audience takes place. According to Margaret Morse (1998: 160), representation 'invokes things apart from us, using language as a window on another world'. Representational art thus functions literally as 're-presentation', or standing in for an absence, by evoking the various circumstances of a distant world. This type of art creates physical distance and encourages the audience to take a mental leap to absent worlds through stimulating their imagination and intellect (Morse 1998: 160–161).

The 'arts of presentation', on the other hand, focus on the 'act of enunciation', the 'here-and-now', 'the body' (rather than 'the mind') and 'experience' (rather than 'transcendence') (Morse 1998: 159–163). In other words, they turn the encounter between, or the world shared by, work of art and audience into their main focus. They have a highly experiential character and establish a relatively physical relationship with their recipients by stimulating and/or literally touching their senses and bodies. In this type of art, the audience is encouraged to undergo the temporal, spatial and physical appearance of art and thus explore the world they share with it, instead of, or in addition to, imagining or reflecting on the worlds that may be represented by it.

In some cases, the experiential and physical character of presentational art is confirmed and heightened by forms of interactivity, which allow the audience to alter the various dimensions of the work it is in contact with (Morse 1998: 163). Another form of presentational art, virtual reality, provides a simulated environment with its own temporal, spatial and material dimensions. The audience can immerse itself completely in this environment and test scenarios for an alternative future of the 'real' world (Morse 1998: 17).

Normally representation is not absent in presentational art, but plays a relatively minor role in the way audiences derive meaning from it. Similarly, representational art is partly able to evoke other worlds by triggering the viewers' imagination through presentation or the aesthetic dimensions of its relatively less dominant materiality in time and space. In general, the encounter with the work of art and the worlds evoked by it are both meaningful for audiences, but in presentational art the emphasis is on the former and in representational art on the latter.

The first signals of a change of emphasis from representation to presentation in Indonesian contemporary art came from GSRB artists experimenting with the medium of installation, including Jim Supangkat (b. 1948), F. X. Harsono (b. 1949) and Bonyong Munni Ardhi (b. 1946). According to another pioneer of Indonesian installation art, the Balinese artist Nyoman Erawan (b. 1957/1958), installation art 'responds to space' (*merespon ruang*), is 'interactive' (*interaktif*), 'can be felt' (*bisa dirasakan*) and is 'conceptual in a direct and wide-ranging way' (*konsepnya luas dan langsung*; Erawan 2009: 24). Moelyono (b. 1957, see Chapter 7), basing himself on the works and concepts of early twentieth century avant-garde artists such as Kurt Schwitters (1887–1948) and Marcel Duchamp (1887–1968), also refers to the conceptual and spatial dimensions of installation art: 'The essence of installation art is its conceptual basis. Furthermore, installation art usually becomes real when the creator attempts to redefine the exhibition space that s/he will occupy' (Moelyono 1997a: 24–26).

The work of Dede Eri Supria (b. 1956), who had his first solo exhibition in Jakarta in 1979 (Miklouho-Maklai 1991: 71), demonstrated the versatility and diversity of styles of the GSRB artists. In his work, Supria uses near photographic techniques in so-called 'hyperrealism'. He creates 'harsh beauty' and expresses the displacement, confusion and alienation of ordinary city dwellers by placing 'real' people in semi-abstract, labyrinth-like urban environments (Harsono 2009: 106–108; Miklouho-Maklai 1991: 84–85; Moelyono 1997b: 1–6; Wright 1994: 229–231). His hyperrealism can be seen as a postmodernist mode of expression that stretches representation to its limit. Supria seems to suggest that regardless of the degree of photographic detail used in his work, the gap between the viewer and the poverty of the people depicted remains unbridgeable.

A problem with the work of Supria and other Indonesian artists is that it represents urban poverty in an aesthetically sophisticated manner in the highly commoditised and market-driven medium of painting. This problem has been raised, among others, by Moelyono (1997b: 4; see also Miklouho-Maklai 1991: 75, 82): 'What is arising is not a feeling of emotion or caring for the fate of construction builders, but an artistic visual impression that stops with providing a mesmerizing view, and does not yet give a reflection on their fate'. Ironically, Supria himself has become very wealthy from his paintings about poverty. To a certain extent, examples such as this may have stimulated a younger generation of artists to move away from realism and other modes of representation, and to start experimenting with more tactile and interpersonal as well as less commoditised art works that incorporate modes of presentation such as interactivity and virtual reality.

Parody, another mode of expression used by the GSRB artists, can also be interpreted as a postmodernist strategy to signal the end of representation. Postmodernist parody has the ability to recontextualise and deconstruct cultural and artistic manifestations and illuminate the ideological structures behind their production and interpretation. It can demonstrate that the meaning of these manifestations is not universal, but ideologically grounded in specific socio-historical settings (Hutcheon 1989: 8, 17). In Indonesia, parodic forms such as *plesetan* or word puns were important cultural weapons in undermining the monological discourse of the New Order regime (see Chapter 4).

Supangkat's controversial installation 'Ken Dedes' (1975) was an example of GSRB art that used parody to address the politics of representation. In this work, a replica of a classical statue of the Hindu queen Ken Dedes was placed on a pillar with a comic or 'fashion model' style drawing of a scantily clad, 'modern' woman. The work juxtaposed and thus critically questioned the aesthetic and socio-political conventions behind two completely different art traditions (Miklouho-Maklai 1991: 30, 63–65).

Some art and cultural observers have interpreted postmodernism as the end of creative production (Danto 1987), by referring to parodic and hyperrealist strategies as forms of endless repetition and decontextualisation. By providing critical insights into discourse and representation practices, postmodernism may indeed have signalled the limitations of representation. However, to conclude that postmodernism has prevented the development of new forms of creative expression is to ignore the field of presentation. Indonesian art curator and critic Farah Wardani (2002: 7) seems to refer to the possibilities of presentation by explaining that one of performance art's main contributions is precisely in providing 'resistance against this hype of "The end of everything", where everything is just merely reiteration or citation, and life then, including art, becomes boring'. Performance art, including forms of new media art, would be able to provide an alternative by 'exploring possibilities' and 'creating a new sign/ language, to the world that is suffocated by reiterated signs' (Wardani 2002: 6–7).

Another example of GSRB's presentational art, in addition to its installations, was Priyanto Sunarto's (b. 1947) 'concrete poetry' (*puisi konkret*). Concrete poetry foregrounds and experiments with the material rather than referential aspects of sounds (in oral performance) and images (in print). Sunarto (1979: 81–85), a lecturer at the Faculty of Art and Design at ITB, derived his understanding of the genre from Dadaism and specialised in the graphic aspect of poetry as a two-dimensional visual medium.

The influential Indonesian art critic Sanento Yuliman (1979: 98) observed that the 'newness' of GSRB was precisely in the way in which the artists used the 'concreteness' (*kekongkretan*) of their media and styles to establish 'concrete' links with the audience and its immediate social environment. Yuliman's observation succinctly describes a transition point in Indonesian contemporary art history from a focus on representation to the creative exploration of presentation. Nevertheless, GSRB artists seemed to be more occupied with exploring, commenting on or protesting against the politics of representation than experimenting with the full range of possibilities of presentation itself. One could say that the GSRB installation art ignored representation by using found objects for what they were; Supria's hyperrealism made representation seemingly disappear by making it transparent to perfection; and Sunarto's concrete poetry covered or disturbed representation through its extreme opaqueness.

The creative exploration of presentation

A more comprehensive creative engagement with the field of presentation in its own right took off with the new media art of the 1990s and 2000s. For instance, ruangrupa's Darmawan explains that Christiawan and other contemporary Indonesian performance artists use their bodies as tools of presentation, not of representation, to create an experience in which both the performer and the audience take part (Karbon 2002: 60).

To others, new media art is merely a field of spectacle, detached from reality. Even Christiawan himself downplayed some of his early 'sound explorations' (*eksplorasi bunyi*) as 'entertainment' (*hiburan*; Karbon 2002: 56–57) and 'meaningless' (*tak bermakna*; Karbon 2002: 58). He may have made these statements for pragmatic purposes, in order to avoid being trapped and restricted by the history of ideologically charged debates on the preferred direction of Indonesian art. At the same time, his mention of 'entertainment' could also be read as 'creating an experience' for recipient-participants, while 'meaningless' could imply 'non-representational'. Christiawan himself acknowledged that 'what is meaningless can become meaningful' through the dynamics of aesthetic presentation (Karbon 2002: 58).

Similar to the critics of Indonesian new media art, the US scholar Fredric Jameson (1991: 19) has negatively characterised aspects of contemporary art and media culture as pastiche, or a degenerated form of parody:

> Pastiche is, like parody, the imitation of a peculiar or unique, idiosyncratic style, the wearing of a linguistic mask, speech in a dead language; [b]ut it is a neutral practice of such mimicry, without any of parody's ulterior motives, amputated of the satiric impulse, devoid of laughter and of any conviction that alongside the abnormal tongue you have momentarily borrowed, some healthy linguistic normality still exists.

However, this is based on Jameson's interpretation of pastiche as a mode of representation rather than presentation. I argue that pastiche as a mode of presentation is not necessarily meaningless 'simulacra' (Jameson 1991: 19), but establishes relations with reality in a different way than representation.

The three types of HONF art activities are all forms of pastiche, which address important social issues such as the role of modern information and communication technology through their temporal, spatial and material aspects rather than their explicit content. They create physical and thus 'worldly' and meaningful connections with people's senses and bodies by immersing them in a performance art, dance party or laboratory setting. They can be seen as 'social experiments' that provide a positive answer to what Bourriaud (2002: 9) calls 'the most burning issue' in today's 'society of the spectacle': 'Is it still possible to generate relationships with the world, in a practical field art-history traditionally earmarked for their "representation"?'

The fact that the HONF projects are, to a certain extent, relieved of the 'burden of representation' (Tagg 1993) gives them more freedom and opportunity to build simulations of alternative realities. These simulations are connected to reality less through a vertical, meta-physical relationship of representation than a horizontal, presentational relationship of temporal, spatial and material proximity (Morse 1998: 11). Simulation can thus be conceptualised as a layer or membrane (Morse 1998: 98) that covers or takes over the 'real' world, without necessarily being detached from it.

More specifically, the Garden of the Blind events are combinations of performance and installation art that provide an aesthetic experience through their emergence in and interference with the conditions of the world of their viewers. The HONF DJ presentations and dance parties are forms of virtual reality, which enable the participants to submerge themselves in the temporal, spatial and material circumstances of the performances. The HonFab Lab projects can be seen as simulations that are relatively separate from, but also parallel to and providing scenarios or blueprints for, 'reality', or the wider world of the anticipated users of the laboratory output. The three categories allow for or anticipate various degrees of interactivity, in which their recipient-participants can modify the time, space and materiality of the art works or art events.

Elsewhere I have shown how simulations of an alternative present or future can also be found in Indonesian popular culture. For instance, the commercial radio serial *Dongpless* projects an alternative vision of Sundanese culture by inventing the new performing arts genre of *dongeng plesetan* ('tales of punning'; Jurriëns 2004: 147–166). Another example is *Newsdotcom*, which presents the imaginary Republic of Dreams as a mirror of and testing ground for the real Indonesian nation-state (see Chapter 4). Due to its limited access to channels of mass distribution, it is less likely that new media art will have the same reach and number of recipients as popular culture. At the same time, it has the potential to develop more radical and in-depth solutions for the present or future than popular culture as it is ideally less constrained by commercial interests and institutional structures.

Conclusion

The use of the idea of the avant-garde facilitates a comprehensive interpretation of Indonesian new media art, beyond characterisations of this form of art as a strategy to undermine capitalism from within at best, and just another form of entertainment at worst. It demonstrates that the art encompasses a complexity of spatial and temporal dimensions, social discourses, interpersonal and inter-worldly connections, interdisciplinary collaborations, aesthetics explorations, and alternative, and ultimately also political, visions. The example of HONF resonates with a multitude of texts and contexts of international, national and/or local scope, including issues of art history, social interaction, technology, education, the mass media, the environment and health care.

Being earmarked as avant-garde does not mean that HONF and other Indonesian new media artists and groups simply imitate or reiterate the social and aesthetic experiments of the historical and neo-avant-garde. Instead, they temporally and spatially expand some aspects of the earlier avant-garde in directions that respond to specific domestic concerns, as well as more universal problems of the digital age. One striking aspect of HONF's art is its focus on building communities, networks, laboratories, festivals and projects rather than the production of individual, tangible and finished creative works. The community explores and is the product of rhizome-like connections between people, nature, science and technology. This decentred artistic approach can be seen as a specific, space- and time-bound translation of the avant-garde principles of undermining the autonomy of art and re-engaging art with everyday life.

The art community is also avant-garde in its use of performances, festivals, events and laboratories for reflecting on and testing alternatives for contemporary social and environmental conditions. HONF, similar to the majority of new media art communities in Indonesia and elsewhere, and unlike the historical and neo-avant-garde and GSRB, has not proclaimed grand visions about the future, but is concerned with micro-utopian criticism on, and interventions in, daily reality. Examining and modifying the impact of the mediation of human and natural life has been one of the major concerns in projects such as Christiawan's cyborg performances and HONF's audio-visual manipulation of the growth of plants.

The various art projects also show an avant-garde concern with aesthetic innovation by using and developing modes of presentation rather than representation. The application of these modes of presentation is part of a relational aesthetics that turns interconnections between people, objects and environments into the main focus of art production, distribution and reception. Christiawan's performance art and the HONF festivals, events and laboratories are all forms of pastiche with various degrees of audience interactivity and immersion. Being less restricted by the conventions of representation has increased opportunities for HonFab Lab-type simulation or scenarios for a different and better present or future. The artistic laboratories confirm that the links between Indonesian new media art and 'real worlds' and politics are there, but expressed in different, perhaps more immediate, ways than in purely representational art.

Notes

1 This work consists of second-hand electronic goods such as tape recorders, fans and water pumps that put a traditional gamelan orchestra in motion automatically (Hujatnikajennong 2006: 23).
2 Personal communication, Jakarta, 15 April 2008.
3 Personal communication, Yogyakarta, 29 June 2010.
4 For instance, Rhizome is also the name of a New York-based Non-Profit Organisation (NPO), which in line with HONF's work, 'is dedicated to the creation, presentation, preservation, and critique of emerging artistic practices that engage technology' (Rhizome 2012). On its website, the work of HONF has been publicised several times.
5 Christiawan, personal communication, Yogyakarta, 29 June 2010.

References

Bourriaud, Nicolas. 2002. *Relational aesthetics*, translated by Simon Pleasance and Fonza Woods, with the participation of Mathieu Copeland. Dijon: Les presses du réel.

Bricolabs. 2010. 'Indonesia Bricolabs!'. Available at: www.natural-fiber.com/index.php?option=com_content&view=category&layout=blog&id=92&Itemid=97 (accessed 10 August 2010).

Danto, Arthur. 1987. *The state of the art*. New York: Prentice Hall.

Debord, Guy. 1994. *The society of the spectacle*, translated by Donald Nicholson-Smith. New York: Zone Books.

Deleuze, Gilles and Felix Guattari. 1977. *Anti-Oedipus: capitalism and schizophrenia*, translated by Robert Hurley, Mark Seem and Helen R. Lane. New York: Viking Press.

Deleuze, Gilles and Felix Guattari. 1987. *A thousand plateaus: capitalism and schizophrenia*, translated by Brian Massumi. Minneapolis, MN: University of Minnesota Press.

Erawan, Nyoman. 2009. 'Instalasi: isme yang mendobrak' [Installation: a breakthrough-ism]. *Gong: Majalah Seni Budaya* 113(10): 24.

Fablab. 2010. 'Fab Lab Amsterdam'. Available at: www.natural-fiber.com/index.php?option=com_content&view=article&id=163&catid=83 (accessed 22 January 2014).

Fischer, Joseph. 1990. 'The traditional sources of modern Indonesian art'. In: Joseph Fischer (ed.), *Modern Indonesian art: three generations of tradition and change 1945–1990*. New York and Jakarta: Panitia Pameran KIAS and Festival of Indonesia, pp. 14–41.

Food Improvements. 2010. 'Condition: food improvements'. Available at: www.natural-fiber.com/index.php?option=com_content&view=article&id=169:condition-food-improvements&catid=87:conditions&Itemid=89 (accessed 17 August 2010).

Harsono, F. X. 2009. 'Tema kerakyatan dalam seni lukis Indonesia: perbandingan masa Persagi dan Orde Baru' [The theme of the people in Indonesian painting: a comparison between the Persagi period and the New Order]. In: F. X. Harsono, *Seni rupa, perubahan, politik* [The fine arts, change, politics]. Magelang: Langgeng Gallery, pp. 96–114.

HONF Prosthetics. 2010. 'HONF prosthetics workshop II'. Available at: www.natural-fiber.com/index.php?option=com_content&view=article&id=220:honf-prosthetics-workshop-ii&catid=89:workshop&Itemid=90 (accessed 22 January 2014).

Hujatnikajennong, Agung. 2006. 'Tentang seni media baru: catatan perkembangan' [About new media art: notes on its development]. In: Direktorat Kesenian, *Apresiasi seni media baru* [Appreciation of new media art]. Jakarta: Direktorat Kesenian, Direktorat Jendral Nilai Budaya, Seni dan Film and Departemen Kebudayaan dan Pariwisata, pp. 11–27.

Hutcheon, Linda. 1989. *The politics of postmodernism*. London: Routledge.

Iskandar, Gustaff Harriman. 2002. 'Garden of the blind'. *Trolley* 9(2): 12–17.

Jameson, Fredric. 1991. *Postmodernism, or the cultural logic of capitalism*. London: Verso.

Jurriëns, Edwin. 2004. *Cultural travel and migrancy: the artistic representation of globalization in the electronic media of West Java*. Leiden: KITLV Press.

Jurriëns, Edwin. 2009. 'Motion and distortion: the media in the art of Jompet and Tintin'. *Indonesia and the Malay World* 37(109): 277–297.

Jurriëns, Edwin. 2013. 'Between utopia and the real world: Indonesia's avant-garde new media art'. *Indonesia and the Malay World* 41(119): 48–75.

Karbon. 2002. 'Performance art, spekulasi soal latar, bentuk, dan juga publik; performance art, speculating the background, the form and the public'. *Karbon* 4: 19–86.

Lévi-Strauss, Claude. 1968. *The savage mind*, translated by John Weightman and Doreen Weightman. Chicago, IL: University of Chicago Press.

Miklouho-Maklai, Brita L. 1991. *Exposing society's wounds: some aspects of contemporary Indonesian art since 1966*. Adelaide: Flinders University.

Moelyono. 1997a. *Seni rupa penyadaran* [Conscientisation art]. Yogyakarta: Yayasan Bentang Budaya.

Moelyono. 1997b. 'Seni rupa kagunan: a process'. In: Jim Schiller and Barbara Martin-Schiller (eds), *Imagining Indonesia: cultural politics and political culture*. Monographs in International Studies, Southeast Asia Series 97. Athens, OH: Ohio University Press, pp. 121–136.

Morse, Margaret. 1998. *Virtualities: television, media art, and cyberculture*. Bloomington and Indianapolis, IN: Indiana University Press.

Next Wave. 2010. 'HONF in Next Wave 2010'. Available at: www.natural-fiber.com/index.php?option=com_content&view=article&id=236:honf-in-next-wave-2010&catid=1:latest-news&Itemid=50 (accessed 22 January 2014).

Noble, Richard. 2009. 'Introduction: the utopian impulse in contemporary art'. In: Richard Noble (ed.), *Utopias: documents of contemporary art*. London and Cambridge, MA: Whitechapel Gallery and The MIT Press, pp. 12–19.

P.A.D.I. 2010. 'P.A.D.I.'. Available at: www.natural-fiber.com/index.php?option=com_content&view=article&id=208:padi&catid=100:project-collaboration&Itemid=102 (accessed 22 January 2014).

Public Transportation. 2010. 'Condition: Public Transportation'. Available at: www.natural-fiber.com/index.php?option=com_content&view=article&id=167:condition-public-transportation&catid=87:conditions&Itemid=89 (accessed 17 August 2010).

Rhizome. 2012. 'Rhizome'. Available at: http://rhizome.org (accessed 3 September 2012).

Sunarto, Priyanto. 1979. 'Puisi kongkret = seni rupa = seni bunyi' [Concrete poetry = fine art = sound art]. In: Jim Supangkat (ed.), *Gerakan Seni Rupa Baru Indonesia: kumpulan karangan* [The Indonesian New Art Movement: a collection of writings]. Jakarta: Gramedia, pp. 81–85.

Tagg, John. 1993. *The burden of representation: essays on photographies and histories*. Minneapolis, MN: University of Minnesota Press.

Wardani, Farah. 2002. 'Performance art, thy will be done: some notes on performativity and performance'. *Karbon* 4: 4–7.

Wright, Astri. 1994. *Soul, spirit, and mountain: preoccupations of contemporary Indonesian painters*. Kuala Lumpur: Oxford University Press.

Yuliman, Sanento. 1979. 'Perspektif baru' [A new perspective]. In: Jim Supangkat (ed.), *Gerakan Seni Rupa Baru Indonesia: kumpulan karangan* [The Indonesian New Art Movement: a collection of writings]. Jakarta: Gramedia, pp. 96–98.

Part IV

Media ecologies

10 Sustainable media

This chapter examines Indonesian new media art communities with a special interest in urban life and infrastructure. The main focus is on collectives from Jakarta and Bandung, which use works of art, exhibitions, festivals and other activities to involve a diverse group of people and institutions, including artists, governments, businesses, NGOs and ordinary citizens, in rethinking, reimagining and, where possible, redesigning urban space (Jurriëns 2014). I demonstrate how their specific engagement with urban space can be seen as an aspect of a 'back to the city' movement in reaction to the socially disengaged elite urban development projects from the mid-1970s to the late 1990s.

After analysing the various ways in which Jakarta-based communities represent the social life and material infrastructure in their city, I shift attention to Bandung-based communities who use new media art to reimagine urban space. The Bandung communities have created their own art laboratories to develop utopian visions of communication and connectivity between people and their virtual and material environments. These communities can be seen as the latest exponents of a long tradition of laboratory-like creative experimentation in the city of Bandung.

The main focus of this chapter is on the Bandung-based new media art collective Common Room, which has been a pioneer in introducing and developing the idea of the creative industry in Indonesia. Common Room's status as an independent art community has enabled it to simultaneously promote and take critical distance from creative industry projects and discourses, and explore these in the more comprehensive context of urban ecology. I discuss its annual Nu-Substance festival for new media art and urban ecology, which has been able to support imaginative projects and engage a multitude of voices beyond those of politics and business. This and other Common Room initiatives demonstrate the added value of certain aspects of the creative industry such as local economic development. At the same time, they confirm the necessity of continuing art activities outside the realm of commerce and government policies.

'Back to the city' in new media art

The end of the totalitarian New Order and Indonesia's path to renewed democracy with increased civil liberties has been reflected in a 'back to the city' movement in urban space and architecture. 'Back to city', as coined by Abidin Kusno (2010: 72), refers to the efforts of and strong competition between a multitude of actors, including the state, business groups and citizens from various economic classes, to reclaim urban space after decades of state control over urban development and other aspects of public life. It can also be seen as part of a process to reverse the long-term effects of the 1997–1998 economic crisis, and to heal the trauma of the human loss and material damage from the upheaval in various Indonesian cities before and after the fall of Suharto in May 1998 (Kusno 2010: 80–84; Van Leeuwen 2011: 163–167).

On the one hand, this 'back to the city' movement has manifested itself in a growing 'unruliness' in Jakarta and other metropolitan areas in Indonesia, in contrast to the Suharto regime's obsession with order and centrally controlled economic development or *Pembangunan*.[1] On the other hand, there has been a growing awareness among administrators, urban planners, architects, real estate developers, artists and ordinary citizens about the necessity of new and more sustainable ways of shaping and using urban space, and taking into account issues such as social context, the environment and cultural heritage. To a certain extent, the new paradigm of architectural and urban design is 'contextuality', as the design tries to resonate and create dialogue with its social and natural surroundings (Kusno 2010: 73). One example is 'independent brand' (*label indie*) architecture for the urban middle class, inspired by the design and life-style of urban lower-class community settlements or *kampung*, and promoting low-energy consumption and the use of non-industrial local materials (Kusno 2010: 75–76).

Indonesian contemporary artists with an interest in urban life and design have given expression to the 'back to the city' idea in various ways. In some cases, they engage in practices of 'unruliness' and 'guerrilla art' by appropriating and re-designing existing architecture and infrastructure. Examples are the murals by the graffiti artist Darbotz in Jakarta and the Apotik Komik ('The Comics Chemist') collective in Yogyakarta, or some of the subversive elements in the public performances and festivals of ruangrupa. Other new media art communities, such as Common Room, seek a different application of the contextual paradigm by promoting and reflecting on the creative industry and urban ecology.

Ruangrupa's engagement with (urban) space is expressed by its very name, 'space of shapes' (Crosby 2008: 129–134). In December 2010, the community celebrated its tenth anniversary with the exhibition 'Expanding the Space and Public' at the National Gallery in Jakarta. In his exhibition catalogue essay, aptly titled 'For those who are (so much) in love with the city (of Jakarta)', Hujatnikajennong (2010: 11–13) explained some of the reasons why the founders of ruangrupa decided to establish an independent art community in Jakarta. These included their desire to avoid the high level of bureaucracy in government-run galleries and the limited opportunities for creative experimentation in commercial galleries. They also wanted to contribute to Jakarta's struggle to step out of the shadow of the two Indonesian cities most noted for their arts and creativity, Yogyakarta and Bandung (Hujatnikajennong 2010: 12).

Ruangrupa has expressed its bond with Jakarta by establishing and maintaining its own art space in Tebet, one of the southern suburbs of the city. This has required strong commitment from its members, considering Jakarta's lack of a contemporary art infrastructure and ambience, and the many problems related to the city's design, including pollution, traffic jams and the high costs and low quality of housing. Ruangrupa relocated three times to more affordable and suitable accommodation within the first ten years of its existence, but it never considered moving from Tebet, the place where it was first established. An essential part of the community's identity is its interactions with its social surroundings, including dumpling sellers and motorcyle-taxi drivers (Hujatnikajennong 2010: 12; Moetidjo 2010: 190–197). The city of Jakarta has been a theme and/or location for most of ruangrupa's art initiatives, including its biennial art festivals 'OK.Video' and 'Jakarta 32 Degrees Celsius' (see Chapter 8).

Another Jakarta-based new media art community with a strong commitment to the themes of urban space and social life is Forum Lenteng. Forum Lenteng was established in Lenteng Agung, South Jakarta, in July 2003, by ruangrupa's Hafiz and several students of Institut Ilmu Sosial dan Ilmu Politik (Institute of Social and Political Sciences, IISIP) Jakarta. Forum Lenteng promotes social engagement in media and art through its video art and short documentaries, participatory video projects, public video screenings and discussions, and media research and publications. The community's research publications include *Footage*, an on-line video and film journal and *Videobase*, a collection of essays on the social history of video in Indonesia (Hafiz 2009).

'Akumassa' ('I'm the mass') is its programme of participatory video workshops with local communities (Crosby and Thajib 2010: 97). Since 2008, workshops have been organised in ten different urban and semi-urban areas in Java, Sumatra and Lombok. After receiving basic video training, the participants are encouraged to record aspects of their daily lives that normally do not reach the mass media. The videos are usually embedded in a blog explaining the background of the filmed story and posted on the *Akumassa* website.

Videos by Forum Lenteng's members have been published by the independent Indonesian DVD label and distributor The MarshallPlan. The videos appeared on a DVD tellingly titled 'Repelita 1: Urbanisasi' (2008). The title is a play on the official five-year economic development plans of the New Order government or Repelita, an acronym for Rencana Pembangunan Lima Tahun (Five-Year Development Plan). Each of the official development plans had its own focus, for instance agriculture, industrialisation or transportation. The video label playfully picked its own theme of urbanisation.

There have been hundreds of other short videos at the ruangrupa festivals and other new media art events that in their style and content represent various aspects of urban culture, lifestyle and identity in Indonesia. One of the best Indonesian examples of this 'urban video generation' (*generasi video perkotaan*) is the Video Battle series distributed by Ruang Mes 56 (see Chapter 8). According to Murti (2009: 101–104), 'after watching "Video Battle", we realised that these works had been too narrowly interpreted in the perspective of video art. Watching these pieces ... was like watching contemporary urban society as it is'.

Bandung art laboratories for urban utopia

In addition to establishing their own communities, providing video training to other groups, installing art and organising screenings in public spaces, and creating fictional and documentary-like films about urban life, Indonesian independent art and media communities have also attempted to rethink urban life and space by presenting themselves as creative laboratories (see Chapter 9). The art communities with the strongest commitment to the critical analysis and imaginative re-design of urban space and architecture are based in Bandung. These communities, including Video Lab, Biosampler and Common Room, follow in the footsteps of a long tradition of creative innovation in the city. This tradition has been addressed in Helena Spanjaard's (1990) essay 'Bandung: the laboratory of the West?'. This essay takes a critical stand against the ideas of Indonesian artists and art critics in the mid-1950s and western art critics and curators in the late 1980s, who, each on their own grounds, rejected western-oriented Indonesian contemporary art practice.

In the early years after its inception in 1950, the art academy in Bandung, which would later become part of ITB (formally established in 1959), stood out by its creation of art with abstract subject matter, inspired by its founding Dutch drawing and painting teachers. In terms of style, however, the art academies of Yogyakarta (also established in 1950) and Jakarta (established in 1968) were just as westernised. Spanjaard (1990: 65) argues that, 'the supposed East-West antagonism, much discussed in Yogyakarta and Jakarta, did not exist to the same extent in Bandung which had been a very westernised Dutch colonial city'. She also rightly wonders why western collectors and curators, who praise the efforts by artists such as Gauguin, Picasso and Matisse to creatively explore other cultures, consider the 'western' orientation of some Indonesian contemporary art as 'inauthentic' and 'derivative' (Spanjaard 1990: 75).

While discussions about issues such as authenticity are important for the deconstruction of colonial and neo-colonial art ideas and practices, they also run the risk of putting too much weight on the 'West versus East' question, and narrowing or even excluding the less controversial but versatile idea of the Bandung art communities as social and creative laboratories in their own right. Spanjaard (1990: 61) explains that there has always been 'a close relation between the Free Art and Design departments and a close bond with the Architecture department' at ITB, which may explain why ideas about the creative industry and urban ecology emerged and developed in Bandung ahead of other Indonesian cities. The founders of Video Lab and Common Room have all been graduates of ITB. Since 2006, ITB has also been the organiser of the biennial Arte-Polis, a pioneering Bandung-based conference on research and policies related to urban space and the creative industry in Indonesia (Voragen 2012: 38–39).

An example of a profound intervention in and refunctioning of urban space was Video Lab's 2004 'Beyond Panopticon' project. The 'panopticon' in the project's title referred to Indonesia's first Palapa satellite, launched in 1976 during Suharto's New Order. According to Video Lab, Palapa contributed to 'the construction of the identity of a nation through a 'virtual' control system' (Siregar 2004). The satellite, similar to the panopticon prison system, could exercise surveillance without being noticed by the people under observation. Control was also exercised through the propaganda of Indonesia's state broadcaster TVRI, which, by means of Palapa, was able to cover most of the archipelago (Siregar 2004).

Video Lab attempted to undermine these types of control, and go 'beyond panopticon', by using television screens in one of Bandung's busy shopping malls to display their own short videos in public. Shopping malls stand out as the most imposing and recognisable symbols of New Order developmentalism and the lifestyle aspirations of Indonesia's growing middle class. They have been the grounds for displaying and training the 'imagined and formalised standards, norms and formulas' of 'middleclassness' (Van Leeuwen 2011: 169). Because of their connotations of wealth and consumerism, they were the target of anger, severe violence and looting during the mass riots preceding the fall of President Suharto in May 1998 (Van Leeuwen 2011: 163).

On the one hand, malls maintain a connection with the outside world through the continuous flow of shoppers as well as their usually large tinted surfaces of glass. In 'Beyond Panopticon', this connection with society was strengthened by the opportunity for the mall visitors to interact with the video art works and participate in creative workshops, although the project did not provide the same level of audience participation as ruangrupa's and Forum Lenteng's participatory video production and screening sessions.

On the other hand, the mall provided a certain distance from the outside world necessary for creative imagination. Malls are also associated with 'non-space', or 'utopian realms', in which 'communications as a flow of values between and among two and three dimensions and between virtuality and actuality … can "take place"' (Morse 1998: 102, 106). The status of the shopping mall as a semi-porous, simultaneously opaque and transparent, entity was cleverly utilised by Video Lab, which transformed the local mall into a gigantic lab for exploring alternative ways of using public space and producing and consuming television.

Biosampler, another Bandung-based new media art group, in which Common Room's art director and co-founder Iskandar is closely involved, also focuses on micro-utopian imaginations of alternative interactions between people and their virtual and material environments. Using the slogan 'every space is a stage, and everyone is a performer', Biosampler has used and reused a wide range of urban spaces for their performances, from dance clubs, art galleries, theatres and libraries to warehouses and tunnels. They have performed at domestic and international art exhibitions, rave parties, music, dance and theatre shows and other events (Insomnia 2004).

One of Biosampler's international performances was at the 'Insomnia 48' event of the 'SENI: Singapore 2004, Art and The Contemporary' festival, organised in Singapore from 1 October to 28 November 2004 (Iskandar 2004). Its performance, titled 'no_placia', consisted of sound samples and video and image projections. The title was derived from Thomas More's (1478–1535) novel *Utopia* (1516), which itself is a combination of the Greek expressions for 'no place' and 'good place'. Considering the location and context of the performance, it may have been an ironic comment on the image of Singapore as an internationalised, clinical place that lacks creative ambience and spontaneity. Alternatively, it could have referred to the performance itself, as an experimental site of unbridled social and artistic freedom. The organisers of 'Insomnia 48' deliberately tried to present a different image of Singapore as a city not merely focusing on the economy, but also appreciating and supporting local creativity and social life.

The use of space, sound and light was partially derived from the entertainment industry, and partially meant to satisfy people's desire for pleasure and individual expression. However, the highly experiential rather than representational character of the performance did not imply a complete detachment from reality or a capitulation to capitalism, hedonism or individualism. The performance also functioned as a testing-ground for examining and modifying the impact of space, music, light and other media on people's emotional, bodily and social behaviour. Contextually and aesthetically, it was related to some of the laboratory-like experiments of HONF (see Chapter 9), Video Lab's 'Beyond Panopticon' and Common Room's Nu-Substance festivals. These are all new media art strategies to celebrate, study and create awareness about the dynamics of social life in a globalised information and communication society, and to test and invent small-scale, micro-utopian models or scenarios for the improvement of people's virtual, material and natural environments.

Common Room and the creative industry

Common Room is arguably the Indonesian new media art community with the most consistent and comprehensive focus on urban matters. It is known for promoting the idea of the 'creative industry' by linking art and culture to local economic development. After years of struggle by Common Room and various other groups and individuals, this idea is now generally accepted and is high on the agenda of the Indonesian national and regional governments. Common Room's concepts and activities are not restricted to the creative industry in a narrow sense, however, but cover a broader area of urban ecology, including environmental issues.

Common Room was established in 2003 as a joint initiative of the new media art community Bandung Center for New Media Arts (BCfNMA)[2] and the independent bookshop Tobucil.[3] Common Room was initially meant as an open space for community-based activities and the promotion of literacy and creative development (BCfNMA 2005). Its venue comprised a small library, guest room, computer workshop, studio and exhibition space. It widened its scope and changed its name and status to Common Room Networks Foundation in 2006, after merging with BCfNMA and registering as an NPO with the Ministry of Law and Human Rights. Similar to its predecessor BCfNMA, Common Room generates income from book sales, profits made on art projects, and funding from international NGOs such as the Dutch HIVOS.

On its website, Common Room presents itself as an open platform for the study and development of art, culture and ICT (Common Room 2016). Its name confirms that the interests of the community go beyond the field of art as such, and also cover issues such as urban space, civil society and social networking. Similar to other Indonesian new media art communities and, in line with trends in the international contemporary art world, Common Room focuses on collaborative art projects and events rather than tangible art works. The projects and events are a way to connect people and groups and create discourse and knowledge on art, culture and society. They include cultural festivals, exhibitions, screenings, concerts, public lectures, workshops and discussions, and cover media as diverse as film, video, music, digital art, architecture, design, fashion and literature (Le Sourd 2006).

One of Common Room's early projects to explore and promote the idea of the creative industry was the 2005 project 'Urban Cartography'. This project was meant to map DIY communities in Bandung since the mid-1990s, including punks, skateboarders and independent fashion, book and music businesses. These communities have been using a diversity of media and techniques, ranging from assembled computers, pirated software, photocopies and silk-screen to radio, internet and SMS, for producing various types of creative output, such as music, fashion, websites, journals, zines, posters, video clips, stickers and badges. For many of these communities, the economic crisis that hit Indonesia and the rest of Southeast Asia in 1997–1998 was an important incentive to find alternatives to expensive imported consumer goods. The Urban Cartography project covered 23 creative communities in Bandung, which were presented in a collective exhibition 'Bandung Creative Communities 1995–2005' at the CP Biennale in Jakarta from 5 September to 5 October 2005 (Ambyo 2005: 224–225).

To further develop the creative industry in Bandung, Common Room's Iskandar co-initiated the Bandung Creative City Forum (BCCF), sometimes also referred to as the Creative Community Club of the City of Bandung, on 21 December 2008 (Sihombing 2008). BCCF's first chair was M. Ridwan 'Emil' Kamil (b. 1971), who is also founder of the Urbane architect office and winner of the 2006 British Council Award for International Young Creative Entrepreneur of the Year (IYCEY) in the field of Design (BCCF 2012). Iskandar won the same IYCEY award in 2007 (IYCEY 2007). Kamil was even elected mayor of Bandung in 2013, predominantly because of the electorate's high hopes about his vision for city development.

Among BCCF's first initiatives were the 2008 and 2009 Helar festivals.[4] These festivals were intended to promote Bandung as a creative city and explore the commercial viability of various types of local creativity such as traditional handicraft, film, music, architecture and design (Sihombing 2008). In 2010, BCCF organised another festival, Semarak Bandung ('Festive Bandung'), which included light projections on landmark buildings and an event to celebrate and restore the glory of the old colonial shopping street Braga in the heart of Bandung. Another BCCF activity was the 2011 International Children and Youth Conference on the Environment, jointly organised with the United Nations Environment Programme (UNEP) and the Indonesian Ministry of Environment. An important outcome of the conference was having one of Bandung's public parks, Babakan Siliwangi, declared a protected World City Forest (BCCF 2012).

BCCF has also been involved in the creation of a Bandung branch of the British Council-supported Creative Entrepreneur Network (CEN). This network consists of creative cities around the globe, including Glasgow, Bristol, London, Cebu, Bangkok, Taipei, Auckland, Kuala Lumpur, Hanoi and Yokohama. The British Council argued that Bandung's potential as a creative city was rooted in its long history of creative businesses, its relatively young population (60 per cent of the population is aged 40 or younger), its large number of public and private universities, and its strategic location close to the economic and political centre of Indonesia, Jakarta, and mid-way between the industrial areas of West and East Java (British Council 2009). The Bandung CEN branch was officially launched on 24 May 2009, and is intended to facilitate creative entrepreneurship, community networks, skills and knowledge development and links with international partner organisations (BCCF 2012).

Inspired by initiatives such as BCCF, Indonesia's former president Susilo Bambang Yudhoyono put the creative industry high on the national political agenda. On 18 October 2011, after a cabinet reshuffle, he created the new Ministry for Tourism and Creative Economy, which was led by former Trade Minister Mari Elka Pangestu (Indonesia Travel 2011). This department divided the Indonesian creative industry into 14 different subcategories: advertising; architecture; art and antique marts; handicrafts; design; fashion; film; video and photography; interactive games; music; performing arts; publishing and printing; computer services and software; and radio, television, research and development (Jumena 2011).

In spite of their support of the various government, business and independent initiatives, Iskandar and other members of Common Room and BCCF have remained critical of the development of the creative industry in Bandung and the rest of Indonesia. They have noted, for instance, that policies tend to support the owners of financial capital rather than the creative workers themselves, whose wages are usually below the minimum. Governments and banks are rarely prepared to fund community initiatives, and most creative projects are order- rather than idea-based (Jumena 2011). A lack of legal re-enforcement has led to unbridled piracy and has taken revenue away from local creative entrepreneurs. It is costly and time-consuming for these entrepreneurs to arrange copyright certificates, while the spread of piracy itself is thought indicative of a deficient Indonesian consumer market (Tempo 2008).

According to Iskandar (2008), official policies have focused on the material infrastructure of cities rather than the more urgent issue of creating human capital through increasing people's access to education and information. In Bandung and other cities, there is a shortage of public spaces where communities can meet and exchange ideas and information. In addition, there have been legal restrictions on the freedom of information and communication. For instance, the 2008 UU ITE allows the government to restrict access to the Internet and criminalise its users. Most importantly, the creative industry has been insufficiently supported, or even restricted, by the formal education system. Instead, it has developed predominantly in the local young people's extra-curricular activities, and friendship and community networks.

The Nu-Substance festival for urban ecology

Nevertheless, Common Room's relatively independent status has enabled the collective to critically examine the role of the creative industry in Indonesia from an alternative, contemporary art perspective. The notion of art is often left untouched or rather distorted in projects, debates and studies with a strong focus on, and some enthusiasm for, the political and economic dimensions and potential of the creative industry. An example is the otherwise useful and comprehensive volume of essays edited by John Hartley (2005a). In his introductory chapter, Hartley (2005b: 19), an enthusiastic proponent of the convergence between art and business, describes how the creative industry has changed the role of the artist:

> The 'creative industries' idea brought creativity from the back door of government, where it had sat for decades holding out the tin cup for arts subsidy – miserable, self-loathing and critical (especially of the hand that fed it), but unwilling to change – around to the front door, where it was introduced to the wealth-creating portfolios, the emergent industry departments, and the enterprise support programs. Win, win!

This, presumably deliberately provocative, statement is problematic for a number of reasons. First, capitalism is a concept conspicuous by its absence in Hartley's introduction and the edited volume as a whole, with the exception of Terry Flew (2005) and Angela McRobbie's (2005) chapters. McRobbie's (2005: 382–383) observation that many of the so-called 'independents' in the creative industry 'are, in effect, dependent sub-contracted suppliers' to the large corporations, with little opportunity 'to concentrate on their "own work"' resonates with the findings of the Indonesian practitioners about their order rather than idea-based work.

Second, Hartley's statement is a gross simplification of centuries of fine art tradition, disregarding diversity in style, genre, school and temporal, spatial and social context. In the Indonesian context, the idea of government subsidy has been alien to the great majority of local contemporary artists. The commitment and productivity of these artists is remarkable considering the limitations in formal art infrastructure and economic support. They have relied on DIY, networking and recycling strategies long before these became global trends with the rise of ICT.

Ironically, one of the ways in which Common Room has been able to promote and develop the idea of the creative industry in Indonesia has been through subsidy by foreign NPOs. Although this funding may have been partly steered by the interests of these organisations, in general these arrangements are more transparent and less intrusive than deals with international or local businesses. It has enabled Common Room to experiment with a broad range of media and genres, set up collaborative art works and festivals, and freely explore urban scenarios with a sometimes highly utopian character. It is doubtful whether the community would have been able to organise activities with the same critical and imaginative content if it had stronger ties to commerce and government politics.

Common Room's most important event is the Nu-Substance festival for new media art and urban ecology, organised annually since 2007. Over the years, the festival has developed and gradually shifted focus from creating, exhibiting and discussing new media art as a relatively new phenomenon on the Indonesian art scene, to using this form of art to reflect on the impact of urbanisation on people's social, material and natural environments.

The 2009 Nu-Substance, titled 'Resonance; Festival for Open Culture, Technology and Urban Ecology', introduced the issues of cultural diversity, the use of Open Source technology and environmental sustainability as Common Room's three focus points in its analysis of Bandung's urban development. The community believes that Open Source media technology is an effective means to create awareness about the problems caused by the worldwide increase in urbanisation such as intergroup conflicts, the degradation of living conditions and the decrease in natural resources. They also want to explore the extent to which art and technology can involve ordinary citizens in finding solutions or alternatives to some of these problems (Nu-Substance 2009).

In addition to the festival's routine events, such as art exhibitions, music concerts, and video and computer workshops, the 2009 Nu-Substance included public seminars about hacking, Open Source software, and alternative intellectual property and copyright arrangements such as Creative Commons. It also had presentations of the Babakan Asih Project and the Bandung Oral History (BOH) study club, two ongoing projects that address the intersections between new media art and urban ecology.

Babakan Asih is the name of a densely populated suburban area of Bandung, which is often hit by floods due to erosion of the soil. Since 2008, the Bandung-based architect company Urbane has assisted the local community in this area with constructing absorption wells for rainwater containment and other forms of ecosystem preservation and management. Common Room has provided documentation, research, social events and art exhibitions about the environmental issues covered by this project (Nu-Substance 2009).

The BOH study club, established in 2008, is a community organisation involved in research, discussions, exhibitions and film screenings on various aspects of Bandung's oral history. Amongst other experiments, BOH has mixed Sundanese oral literature with punk and electronic music. In the 2009 Nu-Substance, the musical experiments were led by the classical Sundanese music expert Iman Jimbot, and included traditional musicians such as Mang Ayi Ruhimat and Abah Olot as well as the Bandung-based contemporary music ensembles Trah, Karinding Attack!!!, Tcukimay and Ganjoles (Nu-Substance 2009). Their presentations showed Common Room's awareness that sustainable urbanism not only relies on urban design and architecture, but should also take into account the diverse heritage and cultural practices of the local population. These aspects are easily ignored by Indonesian and foreign governments and businesses, whose plans for the development of the creative industry more often than not lead to a gentrified form of urban renewal (Boontharm 2012: 73; Keane 2011: 56).

The Open Source software, Babakan Asih and experimental music projects were all continued during the 2010 Nu-Substance (Nu-Substance 2010). The 2010 edition of the festival also introduced the so-called 'Expert Meeting', which consisted of group and panel discussions, presentations, site visits and informal meetings with media and art practitioners, theorists and activists from Asia and Europe. The meetings were meant to contribute to formal policies in three different but interconnected fields: new media, civil society and environmental sustainability (Expert Meeting 2010). The participants in the meeting went on a field trip guided by the Kelompok Riset Cekungan Bandung (Bandung Basin Research Group, KRCB) to examine various social and ecological crises in and around Bandung, such as: the deplorable working conditions of the workers in local chalk mines; the floods and lack of clean water in various suburbs due to the construction of villas and housing complexes; and the environmental and social impact of the rapid privatisation and commercialisation of the previously protected forest around Bandung's famous Tangkuban Perahu volcano.

The Nu-Substance festivals demonstrate Common Room's comprehensive and imaginative approach to urban ecology. Common Room continues Bandung's tradition of art laboratories by facilitating a public space and a wide variety of creative media for people with diverse backgrounds to meet, discuss, research, be creative and fantasise about the past, present and future of their city. While supportive of the local creative industry, the art community is also concerned about the impact of this and other types of economic activity on the various social, material and natural aspects of people's urban environment. The artists seem to support the discourse of 'creative reuse urbanism' or 'an urbanism which is culturally rooted, locally related and deeply contextualised' (Boontharm 2012: 73), by taking seriously the cultural traditions and creative practices, social background, material conditions and daily life experiences of the groups that are most dramatically affected by Bandung's rapid urbanisation.

Conclusion

Indonesian new media art communities have been involved in a 'Back to the city' in post-totalitarian Indonesia, which has tried to promote a more open and democratic civic engagement with urban space and architecture. The results of this movement have ranged from new forms of 'unruliness' to efforts to involve many different voices, including artists, governments, businesses, NPOs and civil society, in critical and imaginative debates and projects about urban development.

The contributions of independent, multi-disciplinary art collectives in Jakarta, Bandung and other Indonesian cities comprise the establishment of urban art spaces, the organisation of exhibitions, festivals and events about urban space and life, and the representation of urban themes in a large variety of creative media such as paintings, sculptures, murals, cartoons, fashion, graphic design, installations, photographs, performances and video art. Arguably, the most far-reaching creative experiments have been the reimagining and redesign of urban space and life in the art laboratories of Bandung-based groups such as Video Lab, Biosampler and Common Room.

Common Room has used its own laboratory-like art space and events to critically and artistically explore the connections between the virtual, material and natural environments that constitute Bandung's cityscape. While supportive of using creativity to promote local economic development, the artists have remained critical of the impact of the creative industry and other aspects of the urban economy on social life, culture and nature. Their innovative projects and events demonstrate that the creative industry can only be sustainable when steered, monitored and, where necessary, resisted by creative thinkers and practitioners that keep a safe distance from the pragmatic, and often opportunistic, worlds of politics and business.

Notes

1 For more detail about *Pembangunan* and its impact on urban development in Jakarta, see Abeyasekere 1989: 217–221. Regarding the post-1998 urban 'unruliness', Kusno (2010: 34) observes that the Jakarta city administration, the middle class and the urban poor have all been 'performing different forms of illegality'.

2 BCfNMA was established in 2001 by Iskandar with the visual artist R. E. Hartanto and the architect T. Reza Ismail. Iskandar's wife, the graphic designer Reina Wulansari, joined BCfNMA as its Director. One of BCfNMA's main activities was hosting the international Asia-Europe Foundation 2005 Art Camp for talented young media artists (Le Sourd 2006: 314–318).

3 Its name is derived from *toko buku kecil*, or 'small bookshop'. In 2007, Tobucil moved to a new location and continued as an independent organisation focusing on book sales, literacy campaigns and courses for the general public on creative writing, crafts, journalism, feminism, philosophy and other subjects (Voragen 2008: 163–183).

4 *Helar* is derived from the Sundanese verb *ngahelar*, which refers to organising activities that are able to draw people's attention, such as art festivals.

References

Abeyasekere, Susan. 1989. *Jakarta: a history*. Singapore: Oxford University Press.

Ambyo, Rani. 2005. 'Urban cartography 1: Bandung creative community 1995–2005'. In: Rani Ambyo (ed.) *CP Biennale 2005: Urban/culture*. Jakarta: CP Foundation and KPG.

BCCF. 2012. 'About BCCF'. Available at: http://bandungcreativecityforum.wordpress.com/about (accessed 4 April 2012).

BCfNMA. 2005. 'About'. Available at: http://bcfnma.commonroom.info/about-2/ (accessed 11 August 2010).

Boontharm, Davisi. 2012. 'The idea of creative reuse urbanism: the roles of local creativities in culturally sustainable place-making: Tokyo, Bangkok, Singapore'. In: Limin Hee with Davisi Boontharm and Erwin Viray (eds), *Future Asian space: projecting the urban space of New East Asia*. Singapore: NUS Press, pp. 73–87.

British Council. 2009. 'Bandung: the creative city'. Available at: www.britishcouncil.org/indonesia-creativity-creative-cities-bandung.htm (accessed 2 May 2012).

Common Room. 2016. 'Profil' [Profile]. Available at: http://commonroom.info/about/ (accessed 14 June 2016).

Crosby, Alexandra. 2008. 'Ruangrupa: mapping a collective biography'. In: Alexandra Crosby, Rebecca Conroy, Suzan Piper and Jan Cornall (eds), *Gang re: publik; Indonesia-Australia creative adventures*. Newtown: Gang Festival, pp. 129–134.

Crosby, Alexandra and Ferdiansyah Thajib. 2010. 'Can open mean *terbuka*? Negotiating licenses for Indonesian video activism'. *Platform: Journal of Media and Communication*. A Creative Commons Special Edition (December): 94–105.

Expert Meeting. 2010. 'Expert meeting for new media, civil society and environmental sustainability'. Available at: http://nusubstance.commonroom.info/?paged=2 (accessed 11 August 2010).

Flew, Terry. 2005. 'Creative economy'. In: John Hartley (ed.), *Creative industries*. Malden, Oxford and Carlton: Blackwell Publishing, pp. 344–360.

Hafiz. 2009. 'Video base: melihat sejarah kita' [Video base: seeing our history]. In: Mirza Jaka Suryana (ed.), *Video base: video, sosial, historia* [Video base: video, social, history]. Jakarta: Pusat Informasi Data Penelitian dan Pengembangan Forum Lenteng, pp. 11–14.

Hartley, John (ed.). 2005a. *Creative industries*. Malden, Oxford and Carlton: Blackwell Publishing.

Hartley, John. 2005b. 'Creative industries'. In: John Hartley (ed.), *Creative industries*. Malden, Oxford and Carlton: Blackwell Publishing, pp. 1–40.

Hujatnikajennong, Agung. 2010. 'For those who are (so much) in love with the city (of Jakarta)'. In: Afra Suci Ramadhan and Ibnu Rizal (eds), *Decompression 10*. Jakarta: ruangrupa, pp. 11–13.

Indonesia Travel. 2011. 'Minister Mari Elka Pangestu leads Ministry for Tourism and Creative Economy'. Available at: www.indonesia.travel/en/news/detail/517/minister-mari-elka-pangestu-leads-ministry-for-tourism-and-creative-economy (accessed 2 May 2012).

Insomnia. 2004. 'Insomnia48'. Available at: www.theatreworks.org.sg/international/insomnia48/biographies.htm (accessed 24 April 2012).

Iskandar, Gustaff H. 2004. 'Insomnia 48: begadang 48 jam di Singapura' [Insomnia 48: staying up for 48 hours in Singapore]. Available at: http://bcfnma.commonroom.info/2004/biosample-no_placia (accessed 24 April 2012).

Iskandar, Gustaff H. 2008. 'Paradoks perkembangan ekonomi kreatif di kota Bandung'

[The paradox of the development of the creative industry in the city of Bandung], *Project Heterologia*, 19 May. Available at: http://bandungcreativecityblog.wordpress.com/2008/05/19/paradoks-perkembangan-ekonomi-kreatif-di-kota-bandung (accessed 4 April 2012).

IYCEY. 2007. 'IYCEY Design and Film Award 2007 Winners'. Available at: www.britishcouncil.org/indonesia-arts-iycey-winners.htm (accessed 2 May 2012).

Jumena, Erlangga. 2011. 'Era ekonomi kreatif' [The creative economy era]. *Kompas.com*, 3 November. Available at: http://bisniskeuangan.kompas.com/read/2011/11/03/06582548/Era.Ekonomi.Kreatif (accessed 2 May 2012).

Jurriëns, Edwin. 2014. 'Mediating the metropolis: new media art as a laboratory for urban ecology in Indonesia'. In: Larissa Hjorth, Natalie King and Mami Kataoka (eds), *Art in the Asia-Pacific: intimate publics*. London and New York: Routledge, pp. 173–190.

Keane, Michael. 2011. 'Harmonising creativity'. In: Michael Keane, *Redesigning China's creative space*. London and New York: Routledge, pp. 37–56.

Kusno, Abidin. 2010. *The appearances of memory: mnemonic practices of architecture and urban form in Indonesia*. Durham, NC and London: Duke University Press.

Le Sourd, Marie. 2006. 'Bandung Center for New Media Art: local commitment and international collaboration'. In: Marie Le Sourd, Septina Ferniati, Lioni Beatrik Tobing, Mirna Adzania and Tarlen Handayani (eds), *The 3rd Asia-Europe art camp 2005: artist initiative spaces and new media arts post-event publication*. Singapore and Bandung: Asia-Europe Foundation and Bandung Center for New Media Arts, pp. 59–63.

McRobbie, Angela. 2005. 'Clubs to companies'. In: John Hartley (ed.), *Creative industries*. Malden, Oxford and Carlton: Blackwell Publishing, pp. 375–390.

Moetidjo, Ugeng T. 2010. 'Archives on space, people, and idea in the process'. In: Afra Suci Ramadhan and Ibnu Rizal (eds), *Decompression 10*. Jakarta: ruangrupa, pp. 190–197.

Morse, Margaret. 1998. *Virtualities: television, media art, and cyberculture*. Bloomington and Indianapolis, IN: Indiana University Press.

Murti, Krisna. 2009. 'The urban video generation'. In: Krisna Murti, *Essays on video art and new media art: Indonesia and beyond*. Yogyakarta: IVAA, pp. 101–104.

Nu-Substance. 2009. 'Nu-Substance festival 2009: Resonance/Bandung, 19 Oktober s/d 8 November 2009' [Nu-Substance festival 2009: Resonance/Bandung, 19 October until 8 November 2009]. Available at: http://commonroom.info/2009/nu-substance-festival-2009-bandung-19-oktober-sd-8-november-2009/ (accessed 10 November 2013).

Nu-Substance. 2010. 'Nu-Substance festival 2010: Floating Horizon/Bandung, 9 Juli – 1 Agustus 2010' [Nu-Substance festival 2010: Floating Horizon/Bandung, 9 July – 1 August 2010]. Available at: http://commonroom.info/2010/nu-substance-festival-2010-floating-horizon-9-july-1-august-2010/ (accessed 20 November 2013).

Sihombing, Salomo. 2008. 'Perkumpulan BCCF resmi dideklarasikan' [The BCCF Club has been officially declared]. *DetikBandung*, 22 December. Available at: http://us.bandung.detik.com/read/2008/12/22/100257/1057484/492/salomosihombing.blogdetik.com (accessed 20 April 2012).

Siregar, Aminudin T. H. 2004. 'Melampaui kontrol pikiran lalu tubuh' [Exceeding control over thought, then the body]. In: Heru Hikayat and Herra Pahlasari (eds), *Beyond panopticon*. Bandung: Video Lab.

Spanjaard, Helena. 1990. 'Bandung, the laboratory of the West?'. In: Joseph Fisher (ed.), *Modern Indonesian art: three generations of tradition and change*. New York and Jakarta: Panitia Pameran KIAS and Festival of Indonesia, pp. 54–77.

Tempo. 2008. 'Bandung Creative City Forum: kami capek mendengar janji pemerintah' [Bandung Creative City Forum: we are tired hearing the promises of the government]. *Tempo Online*, 11August. Available at: http://majalah.tempointeraktif.com/id/arsip/2008/08/11/WAW/mbm.20080811.WAW127900.id.html (accessed 20 April 2012).

Van Leeuwen, Lizzy. 2011. *Lost in mall: an ethnography of middle-class Jakarta in the 1990s*. Leiden: KITLV Press.

Voragen, Roy. 2008. 'The city as autobiography: the self and the city as reflexive projects'. *Melintas* 24(2): 163–183.

Voragen, Roy. 2012. 'Creating places and connections: a review of Arte-Polis 4'. *The Newsletter – IIAS* 61 (Autumn): 38–39.

11 Disaster media

The role of art and media in disaster relief

This penultimate chapter focuses on the role of visual and other media in rethinking urban and semi-rural life and infrastructure before, during and after the dramatic circumstances of disaster. In no other circumstances are the connections between material and virtual environments, and mental, social and natural ecologies, tighter and more important. The chapter specifically deals with the role of community-based art and media – including community radio, popular theatre, performance art and community video – in disaster relief and community resilience in the aftermath of the May 2006 earthquake in Yogyakarta Province. In community art and media, different types of information and values 'are produced by the same people whose concerns they represent, from a position of engagement and direct participation' (Atton 2002: 16–17; Traber 1985; see also Chapter 7). These art and media forms not only complement the material reconstruction efforts of disaster-hit communities, but also relate to an informational and spiritual domain that has been insufficiently covered by domestic and international public and commercial media (Jurriëns 2014).

I first discuss how mainstream forms of *jurnalisme bencana* or 'disaster journalism' have been lacking in practical and respectful approaches to disaster victims, and largely failed to provide a constructive contribution to disaster relief and community resilience. I demonstrate how, in contrast, alternative forms of art and media have succeeded in meeting the standards of good practice as formulated by Indonesian critics of mainstream disaster journalism. The contributions of alternative art and media relate to various aspects of disaster management, such as providing an early warning system, assisting with trauma healing and rebuilding social cohesion and cultural identity. I argue that the mainstream media can learn from these alternative forms and practices, not only with regard to their coverage of dramatic events such as natural disasters, but also for their culture and communication-related practices in everyday life.

Disaster journalism

Journalists in contemporary Indonesia have been struggling, with greater or lesser success, with the challenge of redefining or providing alternatives to the

New Order-endorsed version of 'development journalism'.[1] Development journalism was meant as a tool for developing countries to fight western media imperialism, promote national economic development, pursue cultural and informational autonomy and establish solidarity ties with other developing countries (Kitley 2000: 178). However, the national governments of many of these countries, including Indonesia, abused the developmental and anti-imperialist aspects of this type of journalism in order to control the media and silence the opposition (Tobing 1991: 35, 47).

Some journalists and other media practitioners have used the increased freedom of expression since the era of democratic reform to experiment with and further develop alternative ideas and practices of news production, including virtual interactivity, interactive journalism, meta-journalism and community media (Jurriëns 2009). A remarkable trend across these genres have been the attempts to renew and strengthen the idea of a democratic Indonesian public sphere by addressing, representing and involving ordinary members of society in a direct manner: for instance, by representing the ambience of the site of a news event in virtual interactivity, interviewing ordinary people, publishing their letters or giving them phone-in opportunities in interactive journalism; discussing the conditions, quality and impact of journalism with media consumers in meta-journalism; and giving audiences access to news production and media management and ownership in various types of community media. These attempts at creating open and respectful public dialogue are especially important when the media deals with the most vulnerable groups in society such as communities that have been hit by a natural disaster. This type of dialogue is not easy to achieve considering some of the social and commercial pressures on the media.

Partially successful in resisting such pressures, disaster journalism has been one of the most remarkable dialogical genres of the post-Suharto era. Scholars from the Communications Studies programme at Universitas Islam Indonesia (Islamic University of Indonesia, UII) in Yogyakarta, including Masduki, Muzayin Nazaruddin, Anang Hermawan, Iwan Awaluddin Yusuf and Zaki Habibi, have made important contributions to the analysis and promotion of this genre. These scholars felt that Indonesian journalists were in need of self-reflection, and also of guidelines about how to report on natural disasters in the wake of the 26 December 2004 tsunami that hit Aceh and other areas around the Indian Ocean.

The main topic of their analysis has been the various news reports on another natural disaster that affected Indonesia not long after the tsunami, the Yogyakarta earthquake of 27 May 2006, in which more than 5,000 people lost their lives. While they had hoped that journalists had learned from the 2004 tsunami news reporting, they still found many flaws in the journalism of the 2006 earthquake and decided to further explore and conceptualise disaster journalism.

Some of the UII's and other scholars' main criticisms on the journalistic response to natural disasters concern the approach to and portrayal of victims, the depth and accuracy of news reporting and the involvement of media organisations in humanitarian aid programmes. Indonesian media analysts have particularly criticised the way in which the mainstream media has described and interacted with disaster victims. Many analysts feel that the way public and commercial print and broadcasting media cover natural disasters is similar to the way in which they deal with criminal cases. This means that the main media focus is on dramatic and graphic materials such as the sounds and images of panic, blood and dead bodies (Masduki 2008a: 226).[2] A horrific example in the coverage of the Yogyakarta earthquake was when a commercial television station filmed and interviewed an elderly woman, who was in pain while her broken finger was being treated (Masduki 2008a: 225).

According to Masduki (2008b: 215), this dramatisation of events draws attention away from the more fundamental aspects of people's lives before and after a natural disaster, such as conditions of poverty. He argues that the media should focus on the broader sociopolitical factors causing people's poverty, rather than assuming a direct correlation between natural disasters and poor economic conditions (Masduki 2008b: 217). People are often more likely to live in less developed or less protected disaster-prone areas because of their lack of resources, while they often remain in poverty after a disaster because of political unwillingness or incompetence in dealing with material and social redevelopment. This has been illustrated by the corruption and malpractice in the management of recovery funds in the aftermath of the Yogyakarta earthquake (Masduki 2008b: 213–214, 2008c: 243). Another negative aspect of the dramatisation of events is the lack of empathy with the victims. The victims are often pitied and portrayed as beggars who cannot improve their own situation but by asking for financial contributions from generous outsiders (Masduki 2008a: 227; Nazaruddin 2007: 171, 2008a: 234).

This has been a problem of not only the Indonesian press, but also international journalism. Silva (2010) has commented on the problematic nature of 'human interest' stories from Sri Lanka in the wake of the 2004 tsunami, broadcast at Cable News Network (CNN). The majority of these stories contained details about the lives and experiences of western tourists in the disaster-hit area. The local residents remained largely anonymous and the disaster was decontextualised from relevant socio-political circumstances such as Sri Lanka's long-term civil war (Silva 2010: 141–143). According to Silva (2010: 141), CNN's style of reportage 'evoked and reiterated First World expectations of the Other'. CNN applied the same decontextualised type of journalism in the wake of the August 2005 Hurricane Katrina by presenting New Orleans as the 'Third World at home' (Silva 2010: 143, see also Vis 2009: 65). Based on his study of the 7 February 2009 bushfires in Victoria, Australia, Muller (2011: 112–113) rightly argues that 'proximity' in both a geographical and a cultural or socio-political sense influences the styles of disaster reporting.

Some of the Indonesian news reporting on natural disasters has suffered from not only a lack of depth, but also a lack of accuracy. An example is an announcement made by a Yogyakarta commercial radio station that the Yogyakarta earthquake had triggered a tsunami that was threatening Central Java's south coast.

This announcement, based on inaccurate information, caused additional and unnecessary panic for the people who had not yet recovered from the initial shock of the earthquake (Nazaruddin 2007: 170–171). The media often fails to provide follow-up information or an overview of the development of events, and tends to focus on seemingly disparate, topical and fast-selling issues. According to Nazaruddin (2007: 169), 'there is no continuity in the reporting on disasters; the news that is available is fragmented, incomplete, lacking deep understanding and absurd. Those disaster reports do not have a vision and orientation towards rehabilitation'. Some of the 'absurdities' that happened after the Yogyakarta earthquake included commercial television stations continuing their broadcasts of World Cup soccer matches as if nothing had happened, and one station organising a live broadcast of a television quiz with exceptional prize money from one of the disaster sites (Yusuf 2006: 46).

Janet Steele (2011) comes to similar conclusions in her close reading of *The Jakarta Post*, *Kompas*, *Tempo* and *Surya* newspaper articles on the toxic mud flow in Sidoarjo, East Java, caused by the drilling activities of the Lapindo Brantas oil company. According to Steele (2011: 90; also see Chapter 3), most of these newspaper articles are 'episodic' rather than 'thematic':

> [T]he frames for the story include the suffering of the dislocated victims, the damage to the area economy and the question of who is responsible for fixing the problem. Left unasked are broader questions of accountability: how did the company get permission to drill in this area in the first place? How are political and military interests involved in the process of drilling exploratory wells? How many other wells have been built under similar circumstances? None of these questions are likely to be answered – or even raised – by episodic coverage of the news.

Disasters usually all but disappear from news coverage once other issues start dominating the interests of media producers and consumers. Although this practice is not uncommon in the national and international news media, some observers believe that the local press has a duty to continue reporting on the event for as long as it is impacting on local people's lives (Hermawan 2008: 219–220). According to Hermawan (2008: 221), one of the tasks of the local press, whether public, commercial or community oriented, is to function as a monitor or watchdog of the government-supported recovery programmes. He believes the media should promote debate and dialogue between the public and the government. It should allow the public to express its concerns and, if necessary, criticise aspects of the recovery programmes. Instead, the local press tends to focus on sensational or glamorous news that requires a minimum of resources (Hermawan 2008: 221).

Indonesian media organisations have also been directly involved in disaster-relief efforts. After the 2004 tsunami, commercial television stations organised events such as *RCTI Peduli* ('RCTI Cares'), *Pundi Amal SCTV* ('SCTV's Charity Piggy-bank'), *Peduli Kasih Indosiar* ('Indosiar's Loving Care'), *Dompet*

Amal ANTV ('ANTV's Charity Wallet') and *Indonesia Menangis – Metro TV* ('Indonesia is Crying – Metro TV') (Nazaruddin 2007: 168; Rohman 2008: 248; Fuad *et al.* 2006: 16). After the Yogyakarta earthquake:

> not only local Yogyakarta or Central Javanese local media, but also national media were competing to establish various control posts (*pos komando*, or *posko*) in various earthquake areas, of course with the logo or label of the company put up large on every control post or form of aid that was given.
>
> (Nazaruddin 2007: 168–169)

According to Nazaruddin (2007: 169), such direct media involvement in relief efforts raises the question of whether the media really wants, and is able, to help local communities, or merely takes the opportunity to improve their corporate image. This direct involvement also complicates the role of the media in giving a professional and impartial assessment of the distribution of aid.

A specialised study on media philanthropy in the wake of the 2004 tsunami mentions that by 10 August 2005, more than 150 Indonesian media companies had been involved in fundraising, with 35 of these companies accounting for US$36.7 million (Fuad *et al.* 2006: 9–10). The majority of the companies managed the funds themselves, even if they did not have the official permit for doing this (Fuad *et al.* 2006: 20). Fuad *et al.* (2006: 21) observed crucial flaws in the management of these funds such as the absence of daily fund records, the use of personal names for bank accounts and the lack of differentiation between multiple fundraising activities using the same bank account. The media usually made their own decisions about the allocation of the funds, without involving the donors or beneficiaries (Fuad *et al.* 2006: 22). According to Fuad *et al.* (2006: 27), '[T]he media is at its best, in terms of philanthropy, when it plays a role as fundraiser and leaves the management and distribution of funds to specialist organisations.'

Only a few media organisations have followed this strategy, including the *Tempo* daily in partnership with the Indonesian Red Cross, the Bali Post Group in partnership with the Provincial Government of Bali and the *Nusa Tenggara* daily in partnership with the Coordinating Ministry for Social Welfare (Fuad *et al.* 2006: 18). An alternative solution has been provided by the daily *Republika*, which established an autonomous organisation for managing donations, the so-called Republika Dompet Dhuafa Foundation, in 1993. Fuad *et al.* (2006: 23) praise Dompet Dhuafa's professional management of, and innovation in, fundraising. However, as the foundation still uses 'Republika' in its name, and links between the two organisations have remained strong (Sakai 2008: 270), further study is needed to establish the degree of independence in *Republika*'s coverage of Dompet Dhuafa activities.

Based on the shortcomings of some of the news reports on the Yogyakarta earthquake and other natural disasters, the UII scholars formulated criteria to which disaster journalism should respond. These criteria include the responsibility of the media to: provide accurate information; take a humane approach; be an advocate of the victims; support the rehabilitation of victims; and monitor the distribution of aid. The criteria imply that the media checks and rechecks information about how, when, where and to whom the disaster happened; gives a voice to the victims while respecting their privacy and the rules of the places or institutions where they are located (such as hospitals); provides practical information and moral support to people in disaster or disaster-prone areas; and critically evaluates the role of the government and other organisations in the relief efforts (Nazaruddin 2008b: 237–238; Hermawan 2008: 222–224; Masduki 2008a: 228).

The UII research team argues that different types of information are needed for each of the different post-disaster periods, which can be roughly divided into the emergency (*darurat*), recovery (*recovery*) and rehabilitation (*rehabilitasi*) stages (Nazaruddin 2008b: 239; Masduki 2008a: 228). Disaster journalism should also aim to increase the preparedness and resilience of people in disaster-prone areas by providing, and updating, relevant information on a continuous basis. This type of information includes campaigns aiming to reduce the risks of anthropogenic disasters by promoting environmental awareness and alternative, less consumption-oriented lifestyles. When a disaster takes place, or is about to take place, the media should be part of an early warning system that provides fast and reliable emergency information (Nazaruddin 2007: 173, 2008b: 238).

Another suggestion for the improvement of the news reporting on disasters includes partnerships between media organisations, research centres and other relevant institutions. These partnerships can be used to build databases with detailed information about disasters and disaster management. Media organisations can also create special media centres for the exchange of relevant knowledge among themselves. The central and regional governments are encouraged to regularly issue community service advertisements in the mass media, in order to provide the public with practical information about emergency situations (Yusuf 2006: 48). Hermawan (2008: 223–224) and Yusuf (2006: 48) rightly argue that journalists should have knowledge about local culture and context, so they can convey practical information and moral support in a language and style easily understood by the affected community members.

This is not to ignore that covering disasters is a very complex and challenging task for journalists, regardless of their level of professionalism. For instance, it is not uncommon for journalists and other disaster workers to be affected by Post-Traumatic Stress Disorder (PTSD; Hollings 2010: 234). Referring to media reporting on the 7 February 2009 bushfires in Victoria, Australia, Muller (2011: 64) identified four main sources of pressure on journalists, 'in addition to the emotional impact of being in the midst of large-scale horror, devastation and human misery'. These are the demands of editors, the competition from rivals in the media, the requirements and impediments imposed by the authorities, and the reactions of the people affected by the disaster. Similar challenges are faced by Indonesian journalists covering disasters for the international, national, and local, print and broadcast media.

Early warning system

In their research on news reporting about the Yogyakarta earthquake and other natural disasters, the UII researchers analysed the mainstream print and broadcast media. Other academics and activists have examined or participated in alternative art and media. These alternative platforms have addressed some of the key principles of the ideal of *jurnalisme bencana* such as providing early warning signals, giving a voice and practical and moral support to victims, monitoring aid distribution and analysing broader disaster-related social, cultural and political processes.

For instance, the first priority of the AirPutih ('WhiteWater') NGO in the wake of the 2004 tsunami was to restore community communication by establishing the Aceh Media Center for radio broadcasts, satellite telephone, wireless internet connections and various other media (Nugroho 2009; Arif 2010: 157). Another example of community media functioning as an early warning and monitoring system are the community radio stations on the slopes of the Merapi volcano, north of the city of Yogyakarta. These radio stations include Lintas Merapi (Sidorejo village, district of Klaten), Radio K FM (Ketunggeng village, district of Magelang) and Radio Merapi-Merbabu (Samiran village, district of Boyolali). The stations, with the support of several NGOs, developed an information system called Jaringan Informasi Lingkar Merapi (Merapi Circle Information Network, Jalin Merapi). This system enables local communities to quickly exchange emergency information from three different sides of the volcano (Nasir 2007: 143–144; Hermanto 2011: 21–26; Dewi 2010: 61–62).

This system was developed as an alternative to the volcano-monitoring system of the government, called Balai Penyelidikan dan Pengembangan Teknologi Kegunungapian (Research and Technology Development Agency for Vulcanology, BPPTK). According to Nasir (2007: 143), the communication services provided by the local community stations are faster than the governmental information system, which is burdened by a high level of bureaucracy. For instance, during the 22 November 1994 Mount Merapi eruption, information about the movement of lava and hot ash reached the vulnerable Hargobinangun village only after hours of stepped communication between a local observation post, BPPTK and the district, sub-district and village authorities. Partially as a result of the slow information, evacuation plans failed and 43 villagers died.

Each community radio station is equipped with a radio and transmitter. Information from the volcanic sites is transmitted via Handy Talkie or mobile phone text message to the radio stations, which in turn broadcast the information to local citizens. The radio stations receive the information from various sources, including Jalin Merapi volunteers, search and rescue officers, Red Cross workers and members of Organisasi Amatir Radio Indonesia (Indonesian Amateur Radio Organisation, ORARI) and Radio Antar Penduduk Indonesia (Indonesian Inter-Population Radio, RAPI). Jalin Merapi also posts the information on its own website, which was facilitated by the Yogyakarta-based NGO CRI (Hermanto 2011: 22). This website provides various other services, including interactive message boards and discussion forums, maps and databases. These services assist with the fast provision of aid that accommodates specific needs in specific circumstances such as gas masks in case of volcanic ash rain, or freshwater supplies in case water sources are blocked by volcanic material. Akhmad Nasir (2007: 144–145), former head of CRI and initiator of the Angkringan community media (see Chapter 7), believes that a combination of various types of technology and communication media will provide better outcomes than relief efforts based on one type of information provision only.

The community radio stations are funded by donations from individuals and local organisations. As they are non-commercial in orientation, they only accept advertisers who promote small-scale local enterprises. To maintain transparency, the media budgets are displayed in public, on the walls of the radio studios (Birowo 2010: 20). While many of the radio stations were initially designed purely for early warning purposes, local citizens started to also use the communication infrastructure for other types of broadcasts such as programmes with information about agriculture or home industry, or programmes with popular music or traditional art. In this way, community radio has also contributed to building a sense of social cohesion and shared cultural identity. By functioning as a source of knowledge about local communities and creating trust between citizens, it can smooth the execution of disaster management procedures (Birowo 2010: 21).

Radio plays a pre-eminent role in disaster communication internationally. Hughes and White (2006: 216) and Muller (2011: 100) refer to the swiftness of radio in covering bushfires in Australia. The coverage of other recent disasters also demonstrates a strong increase in convergences between different media technologies and genres. Vis (2009: 68) analyses the role of Wikinews at the 'crossroads' of collaborative, citizen and mainstream journalism in the reporting on the August 2005 Hurricane Katrina in the United States, while Nip (2009) addresses the role of citizen's blogs in the journalism on the 12 May 2008 Wenchuan earthquake in China. The Wenchuan case meant 'a rare moment of openness' for the Chinese media, in which 'citizen journalists shed light on the tragic events by being the first to report the earthquake and, more importantly, to question the government's culpability' (Nip 2009: 95).

This is not to suggest that community media is not without its own limitations. As local communities often lack media equipment and skills, they have to rely on the assistance of outside media facilitators. These media facilitators, often national and international NGOs, bring their own ideological interests, which are not necessarily in accordance with the interests of the local communities. As discussed at length in Chapter 7, such (potential) clashes of conflict have been noted in Indonesia in genres ranging from community theatre (Bodden 2010: 239–242, 256–258) and visual art (Aditjondro 2005: 85, 89, 91, 94, 98–100, 104) to community print and broadcast media (Sulistyowati *et al.* 2005: 196–200). Community media is only able to achieve its goal of communication 'from, by and for the people' when it involves a complex process of ongoing, open and respectful dialogue between all interested parties.

Moreover, the ideal of citizenship or people's active participation in public life can also be promoted by media forms other than alternative media. Both participatory and citizens' media defy any rigid distinctions between the commercial, the public and the alternative (see Rodriguez 2001). The distinction between mainstream and alternative media is also becoming increasingly fluid: 'citizen journalism(s) now assert their presence *outside*, *through*, and *within* today's mainstream news media' (Cottle 2009: xi; see also Allan and Thorsen 2009: 12). Elsewhere (Jurriëns 2009), I have shown how ideals of the public sphere and civil society have been expressed in Indonesian commercial, public and community radio. During the late New Order, commercial radio in particular provided a refreshing alternative to the propaganda of state radio and television.

Storytelling and social, cultural and spiritual renewal

Community media has also been able to contribute to disaster management in ways other than broadcasting early warning signals. Of special importance has been their contribution to trauma healing by enabling their audiences to hear the voices of victims, and addressing or reformulating the cultural roots and social values of the affected communities. In the aftermath of the 2006 Yogyakarta earthquake, visual genres such as popular theatre, performance art and community video played a special role in rebuilding social cohesion and cultural identity. The artistic performances were not community media in a strict sense, as they were conducted by professional artists. It should be noted, however, the performances were staged in disaster-struck areas and organised in close collaboration with local communities.

The Bantul district, south of the city of Yogyakarta, is home to many performing artists, including *wayang kulit* (shadow play) puppeteers and the scriptwriters, directors, actors and musicians of popular theatre forms such as *ketoprak*. Although many artists lost their homes and ran out of paid work after the earthquake, they continued their performances in order 'to sustain the spirits of the victims and keep local culture alive' (Hatley 2008: 282). One of the main initiators of post-disaster performances was the *ketoprak* director Bondan Nusantara (Hatley 2008: 282–283).

Barbara Hatley (2008: 283) observed that the performances were organised with minimal funds and facilities, while themes and formats were chosen in accordance with the post-disaster conditions. For instance, one of the performances had the theme of *Ken Warsih*, the story of a strong woman who is resilient to the many problems she is facing in life, including abusive males and natural disasters. The audience members were encouraged to express their own opinions and interact with the actors seated in front of them. By facilitating a children's gamelan concert and a children's music group from Solo, the artists enabled one of the most vulnerable groups in their communities, the younger generation, to reflect on and cope with their changed life circumstances (Hatley 2008: 283).

Some of the performances also contained socio-political criticism, including references to the way in which national and regional governments managed the distribution of aid. Nusantara scripted and directed a performance combining *ketoprak* with modern dance based on the story of Saidjah and Adinda from Multatuli's anti-colonial novel *Max Havelaar*. The majority of actors were real earthquake victims representing fictional earthquake victims who, similar to the victims of Dutch colonialism, suffered from the corruption and greed of local regents and other officials (Hatley 2008: 285–286).

The performance initiatives of artists from the Bantul district and elsewhere after the 2006 earthquake can be situated in a longer syncretic Javanese tradition of *ruwatan*, or 'cleansing the earth', on the eve or in the wake of major natural or socio-political disasters. In ancient Javanese kingdoms, courtly writers and performers would be sent to the villages in order to 'purify' the kingdom and save it from a serious threat (Clark 1998). A more recent example was the *Ruwatan Bumi* or 'Earth Exorcism' manifestations preceding the fall of President Suharto in May 1998. Hundreds of artists in the major cities of Java took part in these manifestations to signal the nearing of the end of the authoritarian New Order regime and to pave the way for a fresh start of democratic reform (Clark 1998).

Explicit references to the *ruwatan* tradition were made in a performance-art festival called 'Pembaharuan Spiritual/Spiritual Renewal', organised in Bantul from 25 to 29 April 2007, almost one year after the region was hit by the devastating earthquake. The festival was the third in a series of annual performance-art events called Perfurbance (Performance Art Urban Festival), initiated and organised since 2005 by the Performance Klub collective of Yogyakarta-based artist Iwan Wijono (b. 1971). While the first two Perfurbance festivals dealt with themes such as industrialisation, global capitalism and social injustice in the context of Indonesian urbanisation, the Spiritual Renewal festival was about various aspects of disaster relief in rural settings (Wen 2007: 28–29).

While *ketoprak*, *wayang* and *gamelan* are popular Javanese performing-art genres, performance art is an international contemporary art genre, which derives elements from various visual and performing-art traditions and is usually staged by academically trained, cosmopolitan artists. One of the challenges for the organisers was to bring performance art out of its urban context and into the traditional village environment of Gemblangan in Bantul. The Spiritual Renewal festival drew the participation of both local and foreign artists from around the globe. In addition to performance art, the festival also offered ancient religious art traditions and workshops and seminars about social, religious and environmental issues. According to Wijono (2007: 5), the activities were meant to make people rethink some of the local problems that were 'unearthed' by the natural disaster, including the complicated relationships between government and society, between local and central governments, between Indonesian and foreign governments, between fellow citizens and between family members. The festival successfully won the support of people and groups with very diverse backgrounds, including local and foreign artists, local citizens, district and village government officials and religious leaders (Arahmaiani 2007: 21).

The festival workshops and forums covered themes such as traditional, religious and spiritual values, alternative education, alternative medicine, herbal health cures and organic farming, and pollution and other environmental problems (Wen 2007: 29). Some of the traditional genres that were performed included *jatilan* (trance horse dance), *gejog lesung* (rhythmical pounding of rice), *sholawatan* (Islamic prayer songs) and *zikir* (chanted phrases in praise of God) (Arahmaiani 2007: 21–22). The contemporary art events included performances by renowned Indonesian artists such as Arahmaiani and Wijono himself. These performances were integrated with village life through their selection of themes and sites. They were not held on a conventional theatre stage, but in such unusual locations as people's homes, crossroads, rice fields, bushes, cow stalls and even grave sites (Arahmaiani 2007: 22).

In the *ketoprak* and performance-art events in the aftermath of the Yogyakarta earthquake, professional actors presented stories on behalf of, and in close collaboration with, local communities. In community media in a more strict sense, stories are told by the community members themselves, often with the assistance of local or international NGOs (Jurriëns 2013). Kampung Halaman (see Chapter 7) is an example of an NGO that has been involved in providing video equipment and training to local young people, including the young victims of natural disasters.

In various projects, Kampung Halaman has paid special attention to the impact of natural disasters on children and young adults. For instance, for young victims of the 2 September 2009 earthquake in Tasikmalaya, West Java, the NGO set up a media education programme consisting of community video, photography and writing workshops. The videos that were produced during the workshops were shown in several areas that were struck by the earthquake. For many local young people, it was novel that media such as video were not only for entertainment, but could also be used for the representation of social issues of more immediate urgency (Kampung Halaman 2010). The NGO also helped establish the community media centre Opak House in Bantul in 2007, when the region was still recovering from the severe impact of the 2006 earthquake.

An example of a community video from Opak House is *My Lovely Flowers* (2006). This nine-and-a-half-minute video was created by a group of village girls aged between approximately four and nine years old. The video shows the girls wandering through the streets of their severely damaged village, in search of people who can be interviewed about the reconstruction efforts. They are particularly interested in unravelling the reasons behind the decision to rename some of the destroyed roads and alleys with flower names. The people they interview include a group of student volunteers repainting street signs, the village head and housewives. The video is a telling example of the broader aesthetics used in many community media: relatively short narratives about local events in a local language, presented from a personal point of view, with unfixed camera recording positions and deriving from a variety of fictional and documentary genres.[3] From a production perspective, this is a very simple documentary, but it enabled the young girls to readdress the impact of the earthquake with each other, as well as with people outside their own circle, including local decision-makers and other adults.

A changing media approach to disaster reduction?

On 26 October 2010, Yogyakarta was hit by another natural disaster, the Mount Merapi volcanic eruption. In the context of this chapter, three aspects of this event are relevant for further analysis: the UII campus was directly affected by the eruption; the UII scholars and students became directly involved in disaster journalism and other relief efforts; and public radio collaborated with community media and media scholars and played a prominent role in information provision and related support activities. The media coverage of the eruption confirmed some of the lessons learned from the previous reporting on disasters, the growing importance of media convergence and the increased confidence and slowly changing direction of Indonesia's public media.

UII's main campus on the slopes of Mount Merapi was declared a disaster zone on 5 November 2010. Staff and students were forced to evacuate to another UII campus, in Yogyakarta City, until the end of November. The city campus became a place for hosting evacuees as well as UII's own impromptu editorial board for disaster journalism (Alwajih 2011: 42–44). The board consisted of Communications Studies students led by their lecturers, including Nazaruddin and Habibi. Their tasks included transcribing phone conversations, transferring SMS messages to Twitter and writing features for the Jalin Merapi website (Sebastian and Nanda 2011: 76–77). The UII students even received an official, temporary press card in order to assist the public radio station RRI in covering the disaster. Collaboration between UII and RRI was established by Masduki, Head of UII Communications Studies, who had recently been elected Director of RRI Programs and Production for the period 2010–2015 (Ambarwati and Handoko 2011: 111–113).

Thanks to the input of its reform-oriented leadership, including Masduki, RRI tried to contribute to various relief efforts in accordance with its official status as a public media organisation. Its activities included Merapi-related broadcasts on RRI's regular channels, 24-hour emergency broadcasts, broadcasts from a mini-studio at Yogyakarta's Maguwoharjo sports stadium, which hosted more than 30,000 evacuees, the production of online news reports in collaboration with Jalin Merapi, the organisation of entertainment and psychological assistance for evacuees and the management of donations in a special RRI charity programme (Masduki 2011: 32).

RRI's 24-hour emergency service was based at Badan Nasional Penanggulangan Bencana (Media Center of the National Agency for Disaster Management, BNPB) in Yogyakarta. It began broadcasting on the FM 100.2 MHz emergency frequency on 6 November 2010, after being granted a special broadcasting licence from the Department of Communications and Informatics in the record time of 30 minutes. In addition to RRI's own programmes, it included three government press releases per day, live press conferences from the BNPB Media

Center, information from community radio stations, summaries of Twitter, Facebook and other web site messages, and music (Urfan and Mardhani 2011: 92–93).

The theme of RRI's mini-studio at the Maguwoharjo stadium was 'One person, one piece of information'. The programmes, which were broadcast daily from 8.15 a.m. until 5 p.m. on RRI Yogyakarta's regular Pro 2 channel, consisted of 5 to 15-minute on-the-spot interviews with evacuees, volunteers, donors, government officials, military personnel, psychologists and others. The broadcasts, which took place from 6 to 16 November 2010, also included urgent evacuation information (Andiyansari and Damayanti 2011: 97–101).

Another key activity of RRI, in collaboration with Jalin Merapi and UII, was providing entertainment 'to soothe the distress' of the evacuees at the Maguwoharjo stadium. This entertainment consisted of *wayang* performances, film screenings and music (Hermawan 2011: 125–130). The performances were organised in the same spirit as community theatre activities, and illustrated the importance of communication and cultural expression for stress relief and trauma healing. In general, the RRI activities confirmed that connectivity and collaboration between various agencies, including media organisations, government institutions, NGOs and universities, are substantial improvements to the effectiveness of relief efforts.

Conclusion

My examples of Indonesian community radio, popular theatre, performance art and community video illustrate the positive contribution that information and communication media of either a journalistic or an artistic character can make to disaster relief and community resilience. The potential of these media is rooted in their sensitive understanding of and close interaction with people and communities directly affected by disasters or disaster threats. These media not only provide practical information such as early warning signals and evacuation and rebuilding plans, but also play a role in representing the personal stories of victims, questioning and rebuilding communal ties, social structures and cultural identities, and monitoring the aid efforts of governmental and non-governmental organisations. These crucial pillars of disaster relief and community resilience have been insufficiently supported, and are sometimes even undermined by the mainstream public and commercial print and broadcast media, as demonstrated by the sensationalist and inaccurate reporting in failed forms of *jurnalisme bencana*.

As reflected in the arguments of the UII and other media scholars, disaster journalism should not be restricted to reporting about a disastrous event, but also include the broader contexts of how people live their lives and interpret and interact with their social and natural environments. Unfortunately, the Indonesian print and broadcast media are hampered in providing important information and education on these matters by the narrow commercial and political interests of their owners and management. Rather than covering ecological issues on a regular basis, they tend to present stories and advertisements promoting potentially harmful production and consumption behaviour.

This situation urges more ecology in the media as well as a re-evaluation of the ecology of the media itself. The analysis of various forms of disaster journalism can help to unearth the principles on which media institutions and news reporting are based and to test whether these principles are in accordance with the needs and values of local societies. If the mainstream media does not meet these needs and values in matters of life and death such as natural and human-made disasters, they are unlikely to meet the same basic social demands in their reporting on day-to-day affairs. Nevertheless, if the 2010 Mount Merapi eruption journalism and relief efforts by Indonesia's public radio station RRI are something to go by, signs of improvement are slowly emerging.

Notes

1 The concept of development journalism was first explored in UNESCO meetings during the 1970s and 1980s. During the meetings representatives from developing countries expressed their concern about imbalances in the global distribution of information sources (McPhail 1987: 73–76; Ansah 1986: 65).

2 Other, non-UII-related observers, have come to similar conclusions, for instance Arif (2010: 140) and Fuad *et al.* (2006: 15).

3 This refutes Henk Schulte Nordholt and Fridus Steijlen's (2007: 9) observation that community videos predominantly imitate soap opera and other popular styles from mainstream television.

References

Aditjondro, George. 2005. 'Membongkar Moel guru nggambar' [Uncovering Moel the drawing teacher]. In: Moelyono (ed.), *Pak Moel: guru nggambar* [Mr Moel: the drawing teacher]. Yogyakarta: InsistPress, pp. 81–104.

Allan, Stuart and Einar Thorsen. 2009. 'Introduction'. In: Stuart Allan and Einar Thorsen (eds), *Citizen journalism: global perspectives*. New York: Peter Lang, pp. 1–14.

Alwajih, Ahmad. 2011. 'Dari balik meja redaksi: kami hanya punya akses, itu saja!' [From behind the editors' desk: we only have access, that's all!]. In: Muzayin Nazaruddin and Zaki Habibi (eds), *Jurnalisme warga, radio publik dan pemberitaan bencana* [Citizen journalism, public radio and disaster reporting]. Yogyakarta: Penerbit Komunikasi UII, pp. 39–49.

Ambarwati, Mimin and Aan Mei Handoko. 2011. 'Mengudara: kapanpun, dimanapun' [Broadcasting: whenever, where ever]. In: Muzayin Nazaruddin and Zaki Habibi (eds), *Jurnalisme warga, radio publik dan pemberitaan bencana* [Citizen journalism, public radio and disaster reporting]. Yogyakarta: Penerbit Komunikasi UII, pp. 111–116.

Andiyansari, Popi and Anindita Damayanti. 2011. In: Muzayin Nazaruddin and Zaki Habibi (eds), *Jurnalisme warga, radio publik dan pemberitaan bencana* [Citizen journalism, public radio and disaster reporting]. Yogyakarta: Penerbit Komunikasi UII, pp. 97–102.

Ansah, Paul A. V. 1986. 'The struggle for rights and values in communication'. In: Michael Traber (ed.), *The myth of the information revolution*. SAGE communications in society series. London: SAGE Publications, pp. 64–83.

Arahmaiani. 2007. 'Seni lumpur dan kuburan' [Grave and mud art]. In: Performance Klub, *Perfurbance 3 pembaharuan spiritual, spiritual renewal: performance art urban festival 25–29 April 2007 Gembalangan Bantul Jogjakarta Indonesia*. Yogyakarta: Performance Klub, pp. 21–23.

Arif, Ahmad. 2010. *Jurnalisme bencana bencana journalism: kesaksian dari tanah bencana* [Disaster journalism is a journalism disaster: testimony from a disaster area]. Jakarta: KPG.

Atton, Chris. 2002. *Alternative media*. London: Sage.

Birowo, Mario Antonius. 2010. 'The use of community radio in managing natural disaster in Indonesia'. *Bulletin of the American Society for Information Science and Technology* (June-July): 18–21.

Bodden, Michael. 2010. *Resistance on the national stage: modern theatre and politics in late New Order Indonesia*. Ohio University Research in International Studies, Southeast Asia Series 123. Athens, OH: Ohio University Press.

Clark, Marshall. 1998. 'Cleansing the earth: in the weeks leading up to 21 May, Indonesia experienced a cultural explosion of new life'. *Inside Indonesia* 56 (October-December). Available online at: www.insideindonesia.org/cleansing-the-earth-2 (accessed 16 August 2016).

Cottle, Simon. 2009. 'Series editor's preface'. In: Stuart Allan and Einar Thorsen (eds), *Citizen journalism: global perspectives*. New York: Peter Lang, pp. ix–xii.

Dewi, Ambar Sari. 2010. 'Menolong lewat kicauan: kisah relawan admin Jalin Merapi' [Helping through twitter: the stories of the admin volunteers of Jalin Merapi]. In: Muzayin Nazaruddin, Sulistiyawati, Ahmad Alwajih, Noveri Faikar Urfan, Anggi Septa Sebastian, Zaki Habibi and Budhi Hermanto (eds), *Relawan berbagi* [Volunteers are sharing]. Seri Merapi memberi, warga berbagi 1 [The Merapi gives, the citizens share series 1]. Yogyakarta: Jalin Merapi, pp. 59–68.

Fuad, Muhammad, Hamid Abidin and Yuni Kusumastuti. 2006. *Donation for tsunami and a tsunami of donation: how the media mobilized and utilized donation for disaster (a case study of the 2004 tsunami in Aceh and Nias)*. Depok: Piramedia.

Hatley, Barbara. 2008. *Javanese performances on an Indonesian stage: contesting culture, embracing change*. Singapore: Asian Studies Association of Australia in association with NUS Press.

Hermanto, Budhi. 2011. 'Jalin Merapi: system informasi untuk penanganan bencana Merapi' [Jalin Merapi: an information system to handle Merapi disasters]. In: Muzayin Nazaruddin and Zaki Habibi (eds), *Jurnalisme warga, radio publik dan pemberitaan bencana* [Citizen journalism, public radio and disaster reporting]. Yogyakarta: Penerbit Komunikasi UII, pp. 21–26.

Hermawan, Anang. 2008. 'Media dan advokasi, agenda jurnalisme bencana' [Media and advocacy, the disaster journalism agenda]. In: Masduki and Muzayin Nazaruddin (eds), *Media, jurnalisme, dan budaya populer* [Media, journalism, and popular culture]. Yogyakarta: Program Studi Ilmu Komunikasi Universitas Islam Indonesia and UII Press, pp. 218–222.

Hermawan, Anang. 2011. 'Sepekan melipur duka pengungsi' [A week of consoling refugees]. In: Muzayin Nazaruddin and Zaki Habibi (eds), *Jurnalisme warga, radio publik dan pemberitaan bencana* [Citizen journalism, public radio and disaster reporting]. Yogyakarta: Penerbit Komunikasi UII.

Hollings, James. 2010. 'Reporting the 2004 tsunami: media, ethics, and the aftermath of a disaster'. In: Linda K. Fuller (ed.), *Tsunami communication: (inter)personal/intercultural, media, technical, ethical, philanthropic, development, and personal responses*. Cresskil: Hampton Press, pp. 223–239.

Hughes, Peter W. and Peter B. White. 2006. 'The media, bushfires and community resilience'. In: Douglas Paton and David Johnston (eds), *Disaster resilience: an integrated approach*. Springfield: Charles C. Thomas, pp. 213–225.

Jurriëns, Edwin. 2009. *From monologue to dialogue: radio and reform in Indonesia*. Leiden: KITLV Press.

Jurriëns, Edwin. 2013. 'Social participation in Indonesian media and art: echoes from the past, visions for the future'. *Bijdragen tot de Taal-, Land- en Volkenkunde* 169(1): 7–36.

Jurriëns, Edwin. 2014. 'From early warning system to trauma healing: alternative media and disaster relief in Central Java'. In: Minako Sakai, Edwin Jurriëns, Jian Zhang and Alec Thornton (eds), *Disaster relief in the Asia Pacific: agency and resilience*. London and New York: Routledge, pp. 147–168.

Kampung Halaman. 2010. 'Youth and disasters'. Available at: www.kampunghalaman.org/index.php?option=com_content&view=article&id=120%3Aremaja-peduli-bencana-&catid=37%3Aberita&Itemid=61&lang=en (accessed 9 August 2010).

Kitley, Philip. 2000. *Television, nation, and culture in Indonesia*. Research in International Studies: Southeast Asia Series 104. Athens, OH: Ohio University Center for International Studies.

Masduki. 2008a. 'Jurnalisme bencana alam di Indonesia' [Natural disaster journalism in Indonesia]. In: Masduki and Muzayin Nazaruddin (eds), *Media, jurnalisme, dan budaya populer* [Media, journalism, and popular culture]. Yogyakarta: Program Studi Ilmu Komunikasi Universitas Islam Indonesia and UII Press, pp. 225–229.

Masduki. 2008b. 'Media, bencana dan kemiskinan struktural' [Media, disaster and structural poverty]. In: Masduki and Muzayin Nazaruddin (eds), *Media, jurnalisme, dan budaya populer* [Media, journalism, and popular culture]. Yogyakarta: Program Studi Ilmu Komunikasi Universitas Islam Indonesia and UII Press, pp. 213–217.

Masduki. 2008c. 'Setahun berita gempa: perjuangan melawan lupa' [A year of quake news: a struggle against forgetting]. In: Masduki and Muzayin Nazaruddin (eds), *Media, jurnalisme, dan budaya populer* [Media, journalism, and popular culture]. Yogyakarta: Program Studi Ilmu Komunikasi Universitas Islam Indonesia and UII Press, pp. 240–244.

Masduki. 2011. 'Radio publik meliput Merapi' [Public radio covering Merapi]. In: Muzayin Nazaruddin and Zaki Habibi (eds), *Jurnalisme warga, radio publik dan pemberitaan bencana* [Citizen journalism, public radio and disaster reporting]. Yogyakarta: Penerbit Komunikasi UII, pp. 27–33.

McPhail, Thomas L. 1987. *Electronic colonialism: the future of international broadcasting and communication*. SAGE library of social research 126. Newbury Park: SAGE Publications.

Muller, Dennis. 2011. *Media ethics and disasters: lessons from the Black Saturday bushfires*. Carlton: Melbourne University Press.

Nasir, Akhmad. 2007. 'Pemantauan aktivitas Gunung Merapi' [The monitoring of Merapi Mountain activity]. In: Akhmad Nasir, Ade Tanesia, Imam Prakoso and Mulya Amri (eds), *Media rakyat: mengorganisasi diri melalui informasi* [People's media: organising oneself through information]. Yogyakarta: Combine Resource Institution with The Ford Foundation, pp. 140–145.

Nazaruddin, Muzayin. 2007. 'Jurnalisme bencana: sebuah tinjauan etis' [Disaster journalism: an ethical consideration]. *Jurnal Komunikasi* 1(2): 163–177.

Nazaruddin, Muzayin. 2008a. 'Kritik jurnalisme bencana' [Disaster journalism criticism]. In: Masduki and Muzayin Nazaruddin (eds), *Media, jurnalisme, dan budaya populer*

[Media, journalism, and popular culture]. Yogyakarta: Program Studi Ilmu Komunikasi Universitas Islam Indonesia and UII Press, pp. 230–234.

Nazaruddin, Muzayin. 2008b. 'Menuju jurnalisme bencana' [Toward disaster journalism]. In: Masduki and Muzayin Nazaruddin (eds), *Media, jurnalisme, dan budaya populer* [Media, journalism, and popular culture]. Yogyakarta: Program Studi Ilmu Komunikasi Universitas Islam Indonesia and UII Press, pp. 235–239.

Nip, Yoyce Y. M. 2009. 'Citizen journalism in China: the case of the Wenchuan earthquake'. In: Stuart Allan and Einar Thorsen (eds), *Citizen journalism: global perspectives*. New York: Peter Lang, pp. 95–105.

Nugroho, Yanuar. 2009. 'Hubs and wires: internet use in Indonesian NGOs is strengthening society'. *Inside Indonesia 95* (January–March). Available online at: www.insideindonesia.org/hubs-and-wires (accessed 9 March 2012).

Rodriguez, Clemencia. 2001. *Fissures in the mediascape: an international study of citizens' media*. Cresskill, NJ: Hampton Press.

Rohman, Abdul. 2008. 'Praktik CSR dan media massa' [CSR practice and the mass media]. In: Masduki and Muzayin Nazaruddin (eds), *Media, jurnalisme, dan budaya populer* [Media, journalism, and popular culture]. Yogyakarta: Program Studi Ilmu Komunikasi Universitas Islam Indonesia and UII Press, pp. 248–250.

Sakai, Minako. 2008. 'Community development through Islamic microfinance: serving the financial needs of the poor in a viable way'. In: Greg Fealy and Sally White (eds), *Expressing Islam: religious life and politics in Indonesia*. Singapore: ISEAS Publishing, pp. 267–285.

Schulte Nordholt, Henk and Fridus Steijlen. 2007. 'Don't forget to remember me: an audio-visual archive of everyday life in Indonesia in the 21st century'. Indonesian Studies Working Papers 1. Sydney: University of Sydney.

Sebastian, Anggi Septa and Dendy H. Nanda. 2011. 'Menulis berita: tak mau kalah melawan lelah' [Writing news: not wanting to lose the struggle against fatigue]. In: Muzayin Nazaruddin and Zaki Habibi (eds), *Jurnalisme warga, radio publik dan pemberitaan bencana* [Citizen journalism, public radio and disaster reporting]. Yogyakarta: Penerbit Komunikasi UII, pp. 73–81.

Silva, Kumarini. 2010. 'Race, nation, and ideology: CNN in Sri Lanka for Tsunami 2004'. In: Linda K. Fuller (ed.), *Tsunami communication: (inter)personal/intercultural, media, technical, ethical, philanthropic, development, and personal responses*. Cresskil: Hampton Press, pp. 133–146.

Steele, Janet. 2011. 'Indonesian journalism post-Suharto: changing ideals and professional practices'. In: Krishna Sen and David .T. Hill (eds), *Politics and the media in twenty-first century Indonesia: decade of democracy*. London and New York: Routledge, pp. 85–103.

Sulistyowati, Fadjarini, Theodorus Wuryantono and Dian Astuti. 2005. 'Ruang publik desa: ruang partisipasi yang "kosong"' [Village public space: an 'empty' participation space]. In: Fadjarini Sulistyowati, Yuli Setyowati and Theodorus Wuryantono (eds), *Komunikasi pemberdayaan* [Empowerment communication]. Yogyakarta: Program Studi Ilmu Komunikasi STPMD 'APMD' and APMD Press, pp. 163–203.

Tobing, Sumita. 1991. *Development journalism in Indonesia: content analysis of government television news*. PhD thesis, Ohio University, Athens, OH.

Traber, Michael. 1985. *Alternative journalism, alternative media*. Communication Resource 7. London: World Association for Christian Communication.

Urfan, Noveri Faikar and Erny Mardhani. 2011. 'Siaran tanggap darurat: dari dan untuk publik' [Disaster responding broadcasts: from and for the public]. In: Muzayin

Nazaruddin and Zaki Habibi (eds), *Jurnalisme warga, radio publik dan pemberitaan bencana* [Citizen journalism, public radio and disaster reporting]. Yogyakarta: Penerbit Komunikasi UII, pp. 91–95.

Vis, Farida. 2009. 'Wikinews reporting of Hurricane Katrina'. In: Stuart Allan and Einar Thorsen (eds), *Citizen journalism: global perspectives*. New York: Peter Lang, pp. 65–74.

Wen, Lee. 2007. 'Kita melakukan "perfurbing" di sini' [We are conducting 'perfurbing' here]. In: Performance Klub, *Perfurbance 3 pembaharuan spiritual, spiritual renewal: performance art urban festival 25–29 April 2007 Gembalangan Bantul Jogjakarta Indonesia*. Yogyakarta: Performance Klub, pp. 26–31.

Wijono, Iwan. 2007. 'Kata pengantar' [Introduction]. In: Performance Klub, *Perfurbance 3 pembaharuan spiritual, spiritual renewal: performance art urban festival 25–29 April 2007 Gembalangan Bantul Jogjakarta Indonesia*. Yogyakarta: Performance Klub, p. 5.

Yusuf, Iwan Awaluddin. 2006. ' "Ada kuis di tengah gempa": membangun epistemology liputan bencana di media' ['There is a quiz amidst the quake': to build an epistemology of disaster reporting in the media]. *Jurnal Komunikasi* 1(1): 41–51.

12 Conclusion

Media ecological interventions

We are in the digital age, with life highly affected by the unprecedented abundance and speed of visual and other media. The contemporary mass and social media have shaped and influenced mental, social and environmental ecologies, including the interconnections of political systems, urban infrastructure and nature. The multidimensional ecological impact of these media is hard to measure and map, let alone to understand or remedy. The media is an integral part of IWC, which simply seems too overwhelming, effective, attractive and addictive to resist.

On the one hand, there have been increased opportunities for access to information, interpersonal connectivity, networking and creative expression through consumer technology. On the other hand, the record turnover rate of cameras, computers and mobile phones has led to immense e-waste problems. Audiences worldwide have also been confronted with the monopolisation of media ownership, homogenisation of media content and surveillance and commercial exploitation of private information. The lines between journalism and political advertising are often hard to draw, and sensationalist reporting has affected the most vulnerable people in the most vulnerable of circumstances, such as natural disasters.

Considering the characteristics of IWC, technological and technocratic solutions alone are not sufficient to cope with the multiple and interconnected types of environmental destruction caused by it. As argued by Guattari, Postman and various proponents of eco-aesthetics, the multisided environmental issues urgently call for the more complex and comprehensive ideas of courageous and independent-minded creative actors, who are able to think beyond existing socio-cultural structures, institutions and lifestyles. Examples are the authors, media professionals, visual artists, community media practitioners and new media art collectives discussed in this book. Each in their own way, they have shown the interrelatedness of contemporary environments, by creatively engaging with, criticising and changing aspects of the media, particularly television culture, responsible for various types of ecological disasters.

Wardhana used televisual devices for his essays and literary work to provide media literacy, and critically analyse and parody the contemporary Indonesian cultural condition of 'TV or not TV'. The creators of *Newsdotcom* provided media literacy in both critical and humorous ways by directly interfering in the television industry itself. They analysed connections between media and political environments, and gave scenarios for the improvement of both, by presenting hyperreal simulations of Indonesian society. New media artists like Murti, Kuswidananto and Wulia also use televisual devices, particularly video, to address media-related issues. Deliberately working outside the institutional constraints of the media industry, they provide alternative media content and aesthetics by engaging audiences in an experiential manner. Their projects range from alternative health treatments and mobile community television to interactive games about issues such as media ethics, historiography and global geopolitics.

Community media facilitators and new media art collectives position audiences not merely as media consumers, but as collaborators and prosumers. In community video, such as the events organised by Kampung Halaman, ruangrupa and Forum Lenteng, ordinary viewers become the co-producers, managers and owners of media programmes and facilities. They cover topics normally excluded from the mainstream media such as youth, urbanisation and local cultural traditions. HONF attempts to bridge art, science and technology and developed its EFP and art laboratories to provide alternative media studies and solutions for health and agricultural problems. Common Room tries to analyse, recreate and possibly improve the interconnections between virtual culture, material infrastructure and natural environments by promoting urban ecology as a sustainable alternative to the creative industry. Visual artists and community media practitioners have also contributed to community resilience and trauma healing by rethinking and reshaping local culture, social structures and the built environment in anticipation of, during and after natural and anthropogenic disasters.

The creative individuals and collectives have their own manifestations, contexts, backgrounds and histories and provide their own specific answers to pressing contemporary issues. Wardhana originates in the worlds of journalism and entertainment, the creators of *Newsdotcom* come from academia and theatre, and the media and community artists and facilitators make statements that are not only about the media and other social issues, but also respond to and deviate from histories and traditions of art education and activism. At the same time, the various initiatives should be seen as parts of a continuum that include the same or similar actors, media and areas of concern. Some of the shared approaches and key words include accessibility, DIY, participation, collaboration, interactivity, connectivity, relational aesthetics and bodily experience.

Responding to eco-aesthetic scepticism

Acknowledging that ecological issues, including those of the natural environment, need multiple strategies and focus-points, this research focused on creative interventions, which analyse, critique and seek to alter the interactions between the mass media, particularly television, and surrounding social-political and natural environments. The media constitutes one of the most relevant subjects in the field, considering the ways in which this key force of IWC is shaping the fabric of people's mental and social worlds, especially their consumer behaviour, on a continuous, daily basis and in intensive, if not aggressive, ways. What has been relatively limited and western-focused is not only the study of the media as an environment interacting with other social, cultural and natural worlds, however, but also the academic analysis of the cultural counter-strategy of creative interventions.

One of the most thought-provoking eco-aesthetic scepticism has been provided by art historian Claire Bishop (2004, 2006). Bishop's critique concerns not ecological issues as such, but some of the contemporary art strategies that I have identified as key to eco-aesthetics. She is particularly sceptical about relational aesthetics and creative collaborations between artists and audiences, like the Indonesian new media art and community art and media discussed in this book. She has criticised this type of creative practice for prioritising notions of collaboration over notions of aesthetics as such.

According to Bishop (2006: 180), the so-called 'social turn' in contemporary art has led to an 'ethical turn' in art criticism, in which 'dynamic and sustained relationships provide markers of success, not aesthetics'. As a result, 'any art that might offend or trouble its audience – most notably the historical avant-garde' would be seen as inferior to dialogical and consensual projects aimed at conviviality and micro-utopias (Bishop 2006: 181). This critique of collaborative creativity is useful, but biased towards a specific, western approach to art.

For instance, Bishop (2004: 55, 57) argues that relational art 'privileges use over contemplation'. Many of my Indonesian examples refute such a strict distinction, however, by enabling audiences to contemplate a variety of issues and possibly change their lives and environments *through* use, that is, through their active participation in the creative process. Bishop's preferred examples of agonistic contemporary art, including the work of Santiago Sierra (b. 1966) and Thomas Hirschhorn (b. 1957), were preconceived by individual artists and executed by outsiders who were paid for their contributions. In the way they privilege the autonomy of the art and the authenticity of the artist, these works are not substantially different from modernist types of art, even if they take a different shape. At the same time, relational art aiming at a better society is not necessarily without conflict: it is because this art identifies certain frictions in the present that micro-utopian ideas can arise for the future (Noble 2009: 14).

Grant Kester (2011: 28) observes that collaborative art is meant 'to frame exchange (spatially, institutionally, procedurally), setting it sufficiently apart from quotidian social interaction to encourage a degree of self-reflection, and calling attention to the exchange itself as creative praxis'. He traces Bishop's scepticism about collaborative art to western concepts that are erroneously presented as universal principles of contemporary art and art criticism: for instance, the idea that artists would be corrupted and lose their independence and critical power by engaging directly with audiences and society at large. Rooted in a tradition of poststructuralist thought, this idea positions artists as sovereign thinkers who, through creative shock and disruption, are able to deconstruct social structures and discourses, and make the audience reconsider their own background, attitudes and behaviour (Kester 2011: 53–65).

Kester (2011: 76) himself believes that the renunciation of authorship by the creative actor and the immersion of the audience in the process of conceptualising and/or creating art facilitates 'reciprocal' instead of 'scripted' forms of agency, which are not 'simply symbolic', but 'generative' and 'improvisationally responsive' to specific sites and situations, including their natural environments. While Kester (2011: 37), in line with my own findings, asserts that 'some of the most challenging new collaborative art projects are located on a continuum with forms of cultural activism', both Bourriaud's and Bishop's examples of relational art are limited to the works of artists who predominantly work in the domain of established international art galleries and festivals. Kester (2011: 58) even identifies a 'circular relationship' between art practice and critical theory, in which artists 'read, recite, and invoke the same theoretical sources as their critics'.

Part of the problem is that most curatorial and academic attention is paid to the 'contemporaneous current' of national and global superstar artists (Smith 2013: 189), at the cost of artists working on a relatively smaller scale but with sometimes more comprehensive forms of creative collaboration. In his own research, Kester (2011) pays attention to the relational aesthetics of the collaborative community art projects of Park Fiction in Hamburg, Networking and Initiatives for Culture and the Arts in Myanmar, Ala Plastica in Argentina, Huit Facettes in Senegal and Dialogue in India. In terms of scale and approach, these projects are similar to the projects of the Indonesian independent or community-based artists and art collectives, spaces, festivals, works and networks.

The Indonesian video and other new media art and activism provide aesthetic innovation and have social relevance not only because they facilitate various degrees of audience participation and interactivity. They also present or are shaped in the form of laboratories for the simulation of alternative, more sustainable mental, social and natural ecologies. These multidisciplinary laboratories are not closed off from the outside world, but are strongly contextualised. They feed back into everyday life, including the ideas and practices of media organisations and governments. It is telling that the current Mayor of Bandung, one of the largest cities in Southeast Asia, comes from circles with a strong interest in the connections between new media art, urban infrastructure and the natural environment. It is also a positive sign that public media such as RRI have been adopting the people and strategies of community media and art in dealing with various forms of disaster preparedness and relief. Some academics and artists, like *Newsdotcom*'s Gazali, have even been able to present alternative approaches to the media and politics on national commercial television.

For a comprehensive and sustainable approach to the complex environmental issues of contemporary consumer society, the imaginative ideas of creative actors need to be embraced. These actors create ecological awareness and solutions beyond the discourses and policies of Green Politics, and confirm that in the age of IWC micro-utopian efforts may be more realistic and effective than grand political schemes, ideological manifestos or mass protests. In that sense, the alternative art and media practices from Indonesia deserve our attention not as mere examples, but as innovative *models* for urgent mental, social and environmental reform.

References

Bishop, Claire. 2004. 'Antagonism and relational aesthetics'. *October* 110 (Fall): 51–79.

Bishop, Claire. 2006. 'The social turn: collaboration and its discontents'. *Artforum* 44(6): 179–185.

Kester, Grant. 2011. *The one and the many: contemporary collaborative art in a global context*. Durham, NC: Duke University Press.

Noble, Richard. 2009. 'Introduction: the utopian impulse in contemporary art'. In: Richard Noble (ed.), *Utopias: documents of contemporary art*. London and Cambridge, MA: Whitechapel Gallery and The MIT Press, pp. 12–19.

Smith, Terry. 2013. 'Contemporary art: world currents in transition beyond globalization'. In: Hans Belting, Andrea Buddensieg and Peter Weibel (eds), *The global contemporary and the rise of the new art worlds*. Cambridge, MA: MIT Press, pp. 186–192.

Index

Page numbers in **bold** denote figures.